D1069218

Under the editorship of

LUCIUS GARVIN

Macalester College

The

The process, I said, is not the turning over of an oyster-shell, but the turning round of a soul passing from a day which is little better than night to the true day of being, that is, the ascent from below, which we affirm to be true philososphy?

Quite so.

PLATO, *The Republic*

Ascent from Below

TO PHILOSOPHICAL INQUIRY

WILLIAM L. REESE · *University of Delaware*

HOUGHTON MIFFLIN COMPANY · BOSTON

Also by the author

PHILOSOPHERS SPEAK OF GOD
(*with Charles Hartshorne*)

To my three girls —
Louise, the sine qua non,
Claudia, and Patricia —
who, alternately and to some extent respectively,
have helped and hindered in the production
of this manuscript

Contents

Introduction

"It is not all books that are as dull as their readers." Nor is it, adding an equal truth to the acid pleasantry of Thoreau, all readers who are as dull as their books. But the book before you fits not at all this dull-book-reader equation. As it turns out my book (properly, it is "ours") will be neither more nor less dull than its reader; it will be precisely as dull, and for that matter, exactly as interesting, as the one who reads it. Such, at least, is my contention. And since you are, quite obviously, the reader of this book, we have come upon a sticky point. Let me hasten to explain.

This is an open book in the sense that most of its conclusions cannot be reached until your insights have been added. Even if we have never met this is a book about your philosophy. Of course, it is also a book about my philosophy, and about the philosophies which are our heritage, having energized the lives of those who form our Western ancestry. A book about philosophy in the middle of the twentieth century, the age of automation, the age of nuclear fission and fusion? If this is one, I am sure it is not the only, instance of cultural lag within our century. But I shall defend the book on somewhat different grounds. Philosophy, I shall insist, is the essential ingredient missing from our modern lives. Its impractical discipline contains exactly what is needed to provide depth to our practical concerns. Since it is not widely known that this is to be — must be, or at least should be — an age of philosophy, I must first discuss the unusual claim which I have made.

Ours would seem to be the age in which man — with greater determination than ever before — is emerging from long servitude. The venerable masters of authority and tradition are no longer sufficient to serve as his guide in any field — even with respect to his religious and political affiliations. Now if man will not, or cannot longer, be ruled by another, then he must discover an inner discipline, capable of furnishing a means of rule for his life. And if man cannot, or will not, learn to rule himself, he must act at random, lashing out blindly at the world; or he must bind himself to some new master, and often to a more fearful master than the sometimes gentle authority and tradition he has escaped; or, finally, he will be reduced to inaction, feeling homeless and alone within himself. In our time one can find each of these reactions to the conditions under which human life continues. Clearly, we have not yet completed, even if we have begun, the task of achieving an inner discipline. Everyone admits our failure. Technology, as everyone remarks, has outrun our humanity. The world — so the remark continues — is highly fragmented, and lacking in direction. But, of course, this is a comment not about the world, but about ourselves. It is quite possible for men to live in this modern world, and to find within themselves, at last, a sense of disappointment with life itself. It is possible for modern men to feel their lives to be nothing more than half-a-life. The experience is not unique to our time, but it adds to the human problem, to our problem. I am not saying that human life was ever really better than it is at present — better for a few perhaps, and for this reason much worse for many others. At the moment I am insisting on nothing more than this: When we compare our present feelings about life in general with the anticipation we once directed toward it, we must admit our lives to be not at all what we once thought life might be — so busy and so empty, so hemmed by opaque rules and purposes, uncertainties and confusions, so lacking in deep happiness that we sometimes feel ourselves to be nothing more than a catalogue of rules, a cross-hatch of thumbworn purposes, a nest of fears and nameless anxieties. And if in this description we recognize nothing of ourselves, still most will find it relevant to the lives of those about them. But should anyone be satisfied with the general aspects of his life, finding my description of the human condition entirely inappropriate, possibly this book is not for him after all. The experience of inner turmoil which, quite as much as "wonder," requires one to philosophize has simply not begun within his life. This may not be a tragic flaw; in some lesser sense one may be better off without it. But, whatever your condition, it is not an isolated matter but a widespread fact — this inner sense of emptiness, this feeling of frustration and lack of deeper purpose, this experience of the nothingness of life. And, indeed, we are nothing — a cipher, a naught — unless, with all the outside world unravelled, there remains a core to one's being, an essence which is oneself. Now it is perfectly incredible that, compared to our expectations, we should be an unhappy people; and yet the evidence is all about us, and is in us. Because this is too largely so, there is reason for me to argue that it need not be the case.

The problem may be further complicated by an additional and obvious fact. Taken together we constitute a people. If, as persons, we find life too often disappointing, it is also all too likely that we shall be a disappointing people. And this might be the case, even if the whole world once looked upon us as the beginning of a new era in human history.

The additional and obvious fact requires me to expand my statement concerning the proper audience for these essays. Finally, as I have said, this book — at least this particular copy — is addressed to one person only; it is addressed to the particular, individual, and exceptional person which is yourself. And in a more general sense this book is, quite clearly, addressed to Americans, and to no other people speaking our language or another. In the most general sense the range of its interest could not possibly extend beyond the somewhat indefinite boundaries of Western culture. And we face, so I insist, a problem which requires us to philosophize in earnest. In fact, it is a double problem. The first side, and the deepest problem for each of us, is that man has a certain amount of force, or energy, to expend which for a number of decades remains fairly constant. *How can man order his life so that this energy will be expended with the happiest, and most satisfying, results?* The second half of our problem can be stated even more crisply: *How are we to achieve our social promise?* The two parts of our problem cannot be kept apart. We must learn to find ourselves both as persons and as a people. What we can become as persons depends profoundly upon what we are as a people. And the character of a people depends upon the persons who comprise that people. Here, then, is one statement of the problem which I claim to be important, and unavoidably yours as well as mine.

You might well grant the truth of my statement, and yet wonder how a mere book could offer any insight into such a problem. It may be true that one seldom finds an essence for his own self, a core to his being, through reading. No doubt, we read mostly half asleep. It is probably true that most who find a center, a point of reference which allows them to burst their bonds in real growth, find it in some interpersonal experience. Because of this the value of spilling out ink on paper is limited if what one wishes is for people to find themselves. Yet what other course is one to take? It is no particular enemy which must be struck down; one can act against a particular enemy. It is not a particular concrete condition which is it to be changed; one can legislate, assign work to be done, appoint a committee, or act in common against a particular condition. It is a widespread condition of our lives but nothing concrete; it is simply our emptiness, our pettiness, and our willingness to be in bonds. And yet there must be words addressed to our condition. It is my object to find these words. Thoreau follows his comment about the dullness of some readers with this passage:

> There are probably words addressed to our condition exactly, which, if we could really hear and understand, would be more salutary than the morning or the spring to our lives, and possibly put a new aspect on the face of things for us.

How splendid it would be to find such a book! Mind you, I do not claim this to be the splendid and indispensable book mentioned by Thoreau. But even if this is not the book, some of the essential words may be contained within its pages. And if our book does not contain, it may point the way to, those words which will speak to your condition. In the attempt to solve our basic problem we shall turn to the great philosophers of the past; there, if anywhere, these essential words are likely to be found.

But how, not knowing you, could I have written a book about your philosophy? It was possible (I speak as though the success of our venture were assured) because each of us must face the same basic questions, and each of us will choose from something like the same list of possible answers. Thoreau continues:

> These same questions that disturb and puzzle and confound us have in their turn occurred to all the wise men; not one has been omitted; and each has answered them, according to his ability, by his words and his life.[1]

[1] Henry David Thoreau, *Walden* (New York: New American Library, 1949). All three of the quotations are from the essay on "Reading," p. 77.

We shall work with these disturbing questions. I think I have discovered eight such questions, the answers to which, if found, will
enable us to come to terms with both aspects of the problem which
concerns our personal happiness and our social promise. These
eight questions are among the basic, and unavoidable, issues which
must intrude upon the consciousness of any thinking man: What
is the kind and quality of my freedom? What should I value? How
can I relate myself to truth? What importance, if any, has the experience of beauty for my life? How am I to distinguish right from
wrong? On what principles should society be founded? How do I
relate to the whole expanse of Western culture? Where can I
reasonably stand with respect to the questions of God and immortality?

In order that we might work together on these questions, I have
made a division, somewhere near the center of each discussion.
In the first part I try to understand the problem, distinguishing
its essential features. In the second part I try to work my way
toward a possible solution. In each case I present some kind of
answer; my philosophy is, then, open to you, but only as a sample
against which you may take your measure. I do not expect your
answer to be the same as mine. And I urge you to find the one
solution which is proper for yourself. To be sure, I am not un-
interested in the kind of answers you may reach. It is possible
for one to believe his life to be completely shaped by the outer
world, to look upon the instruments of life as representing the
only proper values, to identify truth and one's own opinion, to
scorn the beautiful, and to think the "right" completely individual,
or even meaningless; to think all social forms arbitrary; and history
a meaningless flux of events; it is possible to hold a point of view
which would permit one, were a magic button available, the pushing of which would destroy every vestige of organized religion,
to calmly push the button. There are currents, sweeping along
each of these opinions, and surely there must be a point where all
of them converge. At the point of their convergence exists (I do
not say "lives") a man whom I shall oppose point by point. In one
sense, so far as my philosophy is present in these pages, my book
is directed toward this man; unhappily, he will never be aware of
the fact since, among many other splendid qualities, his interests
in reading are somewhat limited.

We shall circle the two halves of our general, and double, problem with some care, moving from its first half — the unavoidable questions which concern you alone — through the second half — directing our attention to questions involving others. Finally, we shall try to fix our attitude toward cosmic matters. In a sense this will complete the circle, returning us to questions of intimate, personal decision. In another sense our progress will involve a continuous expansion of the horizon of concern, beginning with the problems which impinge upon the vital center which is ourselves, and successively enlarging the boundary of our attention to encompass problems which concern the lives of other men, the whole of our society, our position within the vast expanse of Western culture; at last, as we consider our relation to the universe, the area of our concern will have become cosmic in its dimensions.

But you may grant the importance of our problem, while denying that philosophy is the proper instrument for its solution. Certainly, the new sciences of human life offer an appraisal of the human situation. And those who are expert in such disciplines have offered us their corrective insights more than once. There exist also new forms of therapy, related to some of the new disciplines, and offering a remedy for our human condition. Should not the answers to our human problems be left to these new disciplines? The insights which they offer must be carefully considered; and their advice with respect to the very young, and the abnormal, must be taken into any honest account of human nature. But those who have successfully passed many of the stages of immaturity, and who are for the most part normal — sometimes, depressingly so — will find no clear directive for their lives in such descriptions. Indeed, these studies, because descriptive, are ill-equipped for telling us what we ought to do and be. In the rush pell-mell toward adjustment and "togetherness" a venerable and important form of therapy available to any man, called "philosophy," has too often been overlooked. Assuming ourselves to be neither infantile, nor abnormal, philosophizing may be exactly the therapy indicated for our lives.

But, you may ask, "Does philosophy any longer concern itself with the unavoidable personal issues of human life?" I understand the reason for your question. Philosophers, today, speak so much to each other — who can overhear? Philosophers communicate with each other in a highly specialized language, having at least the appearance of great profundity — who can understand? And philosophers are so careful, properly, to qualify their truths, that those who overhear may not quite catch the drift of what is true within these primly qualifying phrases. And perhaps philosophers, themselves, often do not have the time or energy to grasp the drift of truth within the qualifying phrases of their colleagues.

It is not wrong for some philosophers to talk all their lives among themselves. All of us must learn to respect the need for pure theory. But one excuse for theory is that practice may be bettered. Certainly, it is "dead wrong" for all philosophers to talk all their lives among themselves. There is a way of speaking "thinly" with each term honed razor sharp; this is the manner in which philosophers speak to each other. Terms are used with an edge so fine that they no longer fit common speech. Now what can be said thinly can also be said "thickly" — not to the experts who must shudder at the bungling way this common speech glides across distinctions which they can so adroitly make — but to the people who make experts possible. Indeed, nothing more is likely to be said in complicated speech; possibly, something less is being said, since the depth of common speech is missing. It is my object to speak with immense thickness about important matters.

But, remaining on the level of ordinary speech, to some extent separated from the experts, can my thickness of speech encourage a venture into genuine philosophy? The philosophic outcome can be genuine enough, but it will be personal, rather than technical, philosophy. A good deal of our time is spent in turning over oyster shells; but I shall call your attention in what follows to "the ascent from below, which we affirm to be true philosophy." [2] Plato comes upon this phrase while discussing the means of producing a philosopher-king. In fact, many of the usual descriptions of philosophy will fit into the context of this ascent. Philosophy is the desire for, and love of, wisdom; and wisdom is not merely knowledge, but the proper use of knowledge. The absence of this quality is an important part of our modern problem. Philosophy is the attempt to see the world clearly, and to see it whole. Philosophy is the attempt to make clear to oneself the meanings by which one lives, and the values which make this living worthwhile. Philosophy is man's attempt to see his place in the universe. Philosophy is the attempt to discern the significant unity of all our human knowledge.

[2] Plato, *Republic*, Bk. VII, Par. 521, from *The Dialogues of Plato*, Vol. I, tr. B. Jowett (New York: Random House, 1937), p. 780.

Philosophy is the effort of systematic doubt to find what cannot be doubted. For our purposes philosophy might best be said to be the whole set of general beliefs, principles, and attitudes, in terms of which we make decisions in every moment of our lives. In this sense not one of us can avoid having a philosophy. And yet for most of us this philosophy, this standing ground — or standpoint — upon the world, has not been very carefully worked out. Its elements have been picked up, here and there, along the path of our experience. This is to say nothing against such beliefs. What other initial source has any man? But philosophy is also the activity which reworks this material; and perhaps we can best gain clarity for the direction of our lives simply through bringing the total set of our important beliefs out of the recesses of our minds, stating them clearly, exploring them for their consequences, and refining and strengthening their content.

What other origin could be suggested, even for the systems of philosophy, than beliefs, held somewhere by someone, which have gained in clarity through the application of human thought, until at last they have lost the appearance of personal philosophies, and stand within our culture as candidates for the meanings by which men can shape their own beliefs? And what origin, apart from this, could one suggest for any portion of philosophy, however technical and forbidding its present aspect?

In any case our concern is wholly with our personal philosophies, their discovery, formation, and refinement. It is our object to find where we stand and why. Our goal is self-knowledge. And yet something further must be said about the difference between our approach, and the packaged systems of philosophy belonging to the great names of the past, to men like Plato, Aristotle, Thomas Aquinas, Descartes, Spinoza, Leibniz, Locke, Berkeley, Hume, Kant, Hegel, Nietzsche, William James, and Alfred North Whitehead. The works of these, and other, philosophers are often presented by the writers of the history of philosophy as opposed types. And, indeed, honest disagreement is the rule in philosophy. Some are scandalized by the disagreements among philosophers. It is a scandal, unless every philosophy is at last, somehow, a personal philosophy, having self-knowledge as its goal. In this case honest disagreement may be the means by which we increase our understanding. And if we drop our gaze ever so little from the rigid framework into which the writers of the history of philosophy tend to fix our great philosophical minds, exhibiting them as opposed types in a kind of philosophical zoo; if we drop our gaze from the framework of systems to their individual affirmations, we shall be rewarded by a wealth of ideas with considerable common content.

As you will discover, in these essays I am not interested in systems, or in lack of system; but in the discovery of appropriate answers to common human problems. This work takes its place at the outer fringe of mental activity where, in fact, each of us begins. Starting from the material of our present thought, I have been content to move through obvious objections to formulations of somewhat greater strength. I offer no more than a place, a time, and a framework to initiate your thinking. I am convinced that philosophy among us must be again reborn, and in some of us, have its birth for the first time. I am convinced that this inner movement is important; and that it needs to happen soon.

If philosophy is, as I think — agreeing with Plato — "the ascent from below," participation in its activity should not leave one unchanged. A considerable number of the great philosophers would agree with this judgment. There is, I contend, an arduous climb "upward" which is the successful working of philosophy. Philosophy involves an ascent to the spot where one can view himself, and his time, under some perspective, so that at last he can know his own destiny and that of his people, and where both fit. This kind of philosophy has never been content to say merely: Man is thus, the good is thus, and beauty so. It has discerned levels, stages, stairsteps, and has demanded of each man that he begin his own ascent. It involves a movement from the unexamined to the examined life, from a life of naïve to refined appreciations, from superficial to profound goodness, from society as a display of force to society guided by principle. When philosophy is understood in this manner, where else could we look for the insights missing from our lives than to venerable and patient philosophy?

Surely we must learn to be something other than blindly partisan in the purposes of our lives. Every man and every race begins a mere partisan everywhere in life; and from this point growth is needed. We must begin so; it is the condition of childhood where the world is shrouded in half-light, where feeling runs deeply, and knowledge is slight. Out of this half-light have come our myths and superstitions — of religion, race, family, state, and many more. No major element of life can be discarded; but every element of life must be refined. To be a partisan all one's life and never rise above it, to be a "clinger" all one's life and never stand erect; to hold to this creed or that presupposition with all one's vigor, full of feeling and devoid of thought, is to be less a man than one has a philosophic right to be. To be a partisan is to depend not upon one's self but upon anything but one's self. To be a partisan is to need something to which to cling. Not certain he can stand alone, the partisan wobbles until he finds a specific cause — for balance. Not having an inner balance, he veers wildly back and forth to find support. Rousseau somewhere remarks that partisans are not good material for democracy. The need is for citizens. And the difference between the partisan and the citizen is this: The citizen is more than his cause. The citizen can be himself; it is possible for citizens, because they are more than partisans, to have a common will. To gain qualities denied the merely partisan may be one consequence of engaging in philosophy.

Over and over in the great philosophers there occurs the demand that man grow — from the surface, the plain, on which he has been born — into his own excellence. We must learn that every man needs to find his own philosophy, a final summing up of wisdom for his life, and that he cannot allow any other man or institution to perform this personal duty in his place. Surely the time has come in this desperate age, when we must stop being careful about everything else, while exhibiting complete indifference with respect to the nature of ourselves. Every life needs to rise from stage to stage toward excellence; this does not happen at random, or by chance. The cultivation of one's nature may be called by many names. Its proper name is philosophy.

On occasion, making much — sometimes, possibly, much too much — of the common idiom, I have been impertinent and even impudent in my comments, I discover to my shame. Sometimes, I have overstated insights which, expressed more carefully, might turn out to be the truth. Even this I do not at the moment consider shocking. After all, if anything is to happen through these pages, you must do more than merely read. You must argue with me, complain, even rage against my mistaken notions, all the while probing deeply into your own life, and engaging in the search for reasons to support the point of view, which you discover to be your own. One final word of mingled warning and encouragement!

More than once, despite my firm intention of remaining on the level of ordinary speech, the complexity of one discussion or another seemed to increase alarmingly toward its end, as distinctions began to multiply. The situation is saved to some extent by the fact that each problem begins anew on the level of our ordinary experience. But should anyone find his progress interrupted toward the close of some discussion by the prolix nature of my thought, the simple expedient of flipping the six or ten remaining pages will return this reader to sense from the regions of my nonsense. Should this happen, I ask only that a return be made at a later time to the missing pages in order to determine if the nonsense of these pages may not have turned, through increased perspective and by a kind of inner alchemy, into a sensible account. And now, having done with these preliminary statements, I am ready, if you are willing, to begin.

Chapter One

Personal Freedom

I. The Problem of Freedom

With commendable energy you have worked your way through, or around, the title page, the table of contents, the introduction, and we are ready to begin our work. We shall *do* philosophy. But how is it done? Never mind! This question may answer itself as we proceed. Where shall we begin? For this question an answer must be provided. Whatever problem we select should provide a key, a wedge, a lever, to help us with the rest. Whatever our problem, it should center around an issue neither of us can hope to avoid — if we are to live with some awareness; if, that is, we are to do philosophy.

As you sit, thoughtful and reflective, following these words, the light falling on the page before you, you are aware of the room, the building around the room, the block around the building, its boundary streets leading out into the community, and joining that community to a wide and turbulent world full of so many problems, making our existence problematic — almost forcing us to self-examination, virtually requiring us to begin to do philosophy. And in this context I ask myself: What one problem, perhaps about ourselves, needs settling before we can address ourselves to any other?

The question suggests an answer, an answer which is a question, and which may turn out to be our problem. Must we not settle first of all the question of our power to settle questions? Possibly our first unavoidable issue concerns the question of our freedom.

This question is by no means the same as that expressed by the words: Have Americans still their ancient freedoms? The latter question is most important; but it is not the first, the unavoidable, question. In 1778 Turgot, writing about our people, our land, was gracious enough to say:

> This people is the hope of the human race. It may become the model. It ought to show the world by facts, that men can be free and yet peaceful, and may dispense with the chains in which tyrants and knaves of every color have presumed to bind them, under the pretext of the public good.[1]

I do not ask if you, today, feel yourself the hope of the human race, the model. Nor do I ask if Europeans still write of us in Turgot's manner. Turgot with his talk of chains has as the object of his thought human liberty, and the right to freedom. Mine is a prior question. Many others have been concerned about the chains which bind our human kind. Rousseau begins his Social Contract: "Man is born free; yet he is everywhere in chains." He means: "Man is born with a natural right to freedom; yet, alas, observe these chains!" Rousseau, perhaps, is closer to our question; but at last he too is occupied with the problem of man's right to freedom. And our question, I have claimed, is prior.

Then what is this prior question, and why is it prior? Let me explain. It is true that in our land one finds a love of freedom. Not only does a lawbreaker, when advised to mend his ways, insist: "This is a free country!" Not only do we hear about free merchandise, free coupons, free enterprise, and once upon a time free lunch. We hear also of freedom of speech, freedom of assembly, freedom of petition, freedom from arbitrary seizure, freedom of the press, and freedom of religion. Judging from the frequency of its expression we might seem to fit the description by Plato of a state where "everything is ready to burst with freedom." These freedoms date from the time of our first concern. And it was our first concern with the right to freedom which drew from Turgot the words set down above. But it is one thing to be told we have the right to freedom,

---

[1] See Turgot's "Letter to Dr. Price," *Works of Turgot* (Paris: Delance, 1810), Vol. IX, pp. 388–389.

it is one thing to have such rights printed in our laws and documents; it is quite another to exercise that right within our lives.

Our question asks about the possibility of freedom in human life. It asks if men can be free, and if so how that quality can be gained. It leads to searching questions, and perhaps to personal struggle. One is approaching our problem when he poses questions such as these:

Has my life the feel of a long series of choices making up my person? Or has it the feel of a web which, once begun and with circumstances what they were at every step, had to result in the pattern which describes me and my situation at present? As I spend my energies in a daily routine which has become fixed, which I enjoy or don't enjoy, in my social round, the amenities and responsibilities of my marriage, do I do these things freely, or as a result of some outer web of circumstances, and some inner web of needs, desires for prestige and security common to men as such, an inner and outer web in which I am caught so that I could not in fact change any of my life just now? And (*sotto voce*) what important facets have I ever changed?

There is a web, more or less closely drawn, about us all; sometimes certainly the world is very like a web. Every life has its limiting conditions, its circumstances. But in addition to the web, do we not feel some independence in our lives? Should we say that so far as we are controlled by the web we are not free?

We can imagine a man for whom this web around is all-controlling, a man who is merely a reflection of the forces which play upon him. He goes through life doing nothing more than transmitting feelings, thoughts, ideas, earlier transmitted to him by others. His voice is the voice of the outer world. His dress is the mode of the times. His opinions are syndicated and stamped with a partisan political label. His personal emotions are celluloid. His joy is physiological. His responses are typical. His desire is to be normal, average, unnoticeable, and so unnoticed. And he is. Because this is his desire, we shall call him Mr. Mass Man. Perhaps there is no such man, and yet certainly it is possible that the conversation should never lag, the furious pace never slacken, with man thinking only syndicated thoughts, and feeling only wide-screen, celluloid or 36-inch picture tube feelings. The headline is black and huge, of course, each morning if he wishes to speak the report language, to be a headline for his friends. The editorial page is at hand if he wishes

his abstractions done in copyright. The television set is ready —
always too much ready — if he wishes feelings to reflect to others.
And having described our Mass Man, it is clear that we would not
believe him free even should he have the right to freedom.

But should we say that so far as we are independent, we are free?
We can imagine a man in whom independence is fiercely manifest.
Indeed, the man has already been supposed: Cyrano in *Cyrano de
Bergerac*. Here are the pointed words in which Cyrano savors free-
dom:

> What would you have me do?
> Seek for the patronage of some great man,
> And like a creeping vine on a tall tree
> Crawl upward, where I cannot stand alone?
> No, thank you! Dedicate, as others do,
> Poems to pawnbrokers? Be a buffoon
> In the vile hope of teasing out a smile
> On some cold face? No, thank you! Eat a toad
> For breakfast every morning? Make my knees
> Callous, and cultivate a supple spine, —
> Wear out my belly grovelling in the dust?
> No, thank you! Scratch the back of any swine
> That roots up gold for me? Tickle the horns
> Of Mammon with my left hand, while my right
> Too proud to know his partner's business,
> Takes in the fee? No, thank you! Use the fire
> God gave me to burn incense all day long
> Under the nose of wood and stone? No, thank you!
> Shall I go leaping into ladies' laps
> And licking fingers? — or —to change the form —
> Navigating with madrigals for oars,
> My sails full of the sighs of dowagers?
> No thank you! Publish verses at my own
> Expense? No, thank you! Be the patron saint
> Of a small group of literary souls
> Who dine together every Tuesday? No
> I thank you! Shall I labor night and day
> To build a reputation on one song,
> And never write another? Shall I find
> True genius only among Geniuses,
> Palpitate over little paragraphs,
> And struggle to insinuate my name
> Into the columns of the *Mercury*?

No, thank you! Calculate, scheme, be afraid,
Love more to make a visit than a poem,
Seek introductions, favors, influences? —
No, thank you! No, I thank you! And again,
I thank you! — But . . .
                    To sing, to laugh, to dream,
To walk in my own way and be alone,
Free, with an eye to see things as they are,
A voice that means manhood — to cock my hat
Where I choose — at a word, a *Yes*, a *No*,
To fight — or write. To travel any road
Under the sun, under the stars, nor doubt
If fame or fortune lie beyond the bourne —
Never to make a line I have not heard
In my own heart; yet, with all modesty
To say: "My soul, be satisfied with flowers,
With fruit, with weeds even; but gather them
In the one garden you may call your own."
So, when I win some triumph, by some chance,
Render no share to Caesar — in a word,
I am too proud to be a parasite,
And if my nature wants the germ that grows
Towering to heaven like the mountain pine,
Or like the oak, sheltering multitudes —
I stand, not high it may be — but alone! [2]

We would probably agree that, compared to Mass Man, Cyrano
has achieved some degree of freedom. Certainly he declares his
independence from the compromising world. Is freedom, then, to
mean simply independence? When Cyrano picks out Mass Man as
his particular aversion, finding the absence of freedom in men who
bow and scrape before the world, who seek light goals in petty
ways, whose struggle is only to reach the top of a given social pyramid, who have learned the priceless art of walking on their knees,
should we simply agree that Cyrano stands for freedom, and our
Mass Man for the lack of freedom?

The case is not so simple. In fact, when we examine closely what
Cyrano is telling us, three meanings of human freedom are to be
found within the passage. Freedom means to him doing as he
wishes no matter what — no matter what the mass men who, in his

[2] From *Cyrano de Bergerac* by Edmond Rostand, and translated by Brian
Hooker. Act II, Scene 8. Copyright, 1923, by Henry Holt and Company, Inc.
Copyright, 1951, by Doris C. Hooker. Used by permission of the publishers.

opinion, make up society may wish, for example. This meaning gives us the sense of his desire for independence from the world. But it is equally clear that Cyrano believes in choice; he could always have done other than he has in fact done; at a given moment he can "fight — or write." Finally, he is possessed by the belief that freedom means being authentic: "Never to make a line I have not heard in my own heart."

These three meanings may provide us with the means for an advance. It would not be surprising should freedom have several meanings. And there is a good chance that these three meanings have real importance. As I think now about Western philosophy all three of these meanings are to be found within its history.

In one sense freedom means simply: *doing what you want to do.*

In a second sense freedom means: *being able in a moment of decision to accept any one of two or more alternatives.*

In a third sense freedom means: *acting in accord with the unique nature of one's own self.*

If you want to travel to the moon, and are able to do so, you are free in the first sense. If you cannot do it, you are not free in that sense. If having gone home by way of Divinity Avenue you could equally well have gone home by way of Oxford Street, if having done one thing you could equally well have done the other, you were free in our second sense. Otherwise, not free. If you have the ability to paint murals of Kansas City, and do paint murals of Kansas City, you are free in our third sense. The first sense supposes power to gain what is desired; the second meaning presupposes power to do otherwise; the third supposes a capacity in life, which is unmistakably "you," an authentic part of your nature.

We have a triple question: (1) Since its meaning is not single, what should we mean by freedom? (2) Given our meaning, is man free; or is it possible for man to gain this freedom? (3) If freedom can be achieved, how are we to act in order to gain or to increase the freedom of our lives?

What Should Be Meant by Freedom?

Having found three meanings for the word, each of these must be examined with some care.

To be free is to do what you want to do. On this view all acts are free except when we are restrained by walls, laws, strait jackets, or a mother's wishes. At first it seems eminently sane to think of freedom simply as doing what we wish. The view has had wide, hard usage. It seems radiant with common sense, clear, and simple. We know what we want to do; and sometimes we can do it; when we succeed in doing what we wish to do, freedom is ours. Could anything be more simple? It is simple enough, to be sure, but it is far from being clear.

David Hume, who held this view, asks in effect: Who would ever want to do what he did not wish to do? No one, of course! Then who could ever want more freedom than is provided here? One feels inclined to say, again, No one! But let me caution you against this answer, for problems lie near at hand. Hume says, in effect (once again), and all who hold this view consent: Liberty and necessity are not opposed; all things can be necessary, without depriving man of freedom, for the opposite of freedom is not necessity, but constraint. As we had said: One knows what he wants to do; even if he also knows these wishes have been molded by the world in which he lives.

Voltaire agrees with Hume. In *The Ignorant Philosopher* Voltaire, likewise using "liberty" where we use "freedom," writes:

> My liberty consists in doing what I choose; but I must *necessarily* choose what I will; otherwise it would be without reason, without cause, which is impossible. My liberty consists in walking when I have a mind to walk, and I have not the gout.
>
> My liberty consists in not doing a bad action when my mind necessarily represents it as a bad action. . . . It is strange that men should not be content with this measure of liberty, that is to say, the power which they have received from nature of doing what they choose; the planets have it not; we possess it, and our pride makes us sometimes believe that we possess still more. We figure to ourselves that we have the incomprehensible and absurd gift of election without reason, without any other motive than that of free will.[3]

---

[3] Voltaire, *The Ignorant Philosopher*, Chap. 13, from *The Best Known Works of Voltaire* (New York: Blue Ribbon Books, 1927), p. 439. Italics mine. Through the course of his writings Voltaire occupied a number of positions on this question. In the *Traité* he defends our second meaning for freedom. His more usual position is that given here. And in the "Franc Arbitre" he comes directly to the position we have stated: "Freedom, therefore, is not and cannot be anything other than the power to do what one wishes," while recognizing that what one wishes is determined by forces beyond one's control. See the discussion of Voltaire in George Boas, *Dominant Themes of Modern Philosophy* (New York: The Ronald Press Co., 1957), pp. 339–341.

The view is stated more boldly in the work of Thomas Hobbes:

> *Liberty* and *necessity* are consistent: as in the water, that hath not only *liberty*, but a *necessity* of descending by the channel; so likewise in the actions which men voluntarily do: which, because they proceed from their will, proceed from *liberty*; and yet, because every act of man's will, and every desire, and inclination proceedeth from some cause, and that from another cause, in a continual chain, whose first link is in the hand of God the first of all causes, proceed from *necessity*.[4]

It could not be more clearly said. And in the same chapter we are told, "Liberty, or freedom, signifieth, properly, the absence of opposition. . . ."

Not only can one find philosophers who hold this view of freedom. One finds theologians in this group as well; indeed, belief in a God who controls the world and knows the total future disposes one toward belief in a world where things happen as they must, and where freedom holds our present meaning. Jonathan Edwards, John Calvin, Augustine belong, in whole or part, to this present grouping.

But the view must face some questions. If freedom means doing what we wish to do, and if we could not have done otherwise, are our wishes really ours, or are they wishes of the community, of the forces which have shaped us? When I reflect upon this meaning, it seems to me unstable, tending to change itself into some other meaning. If we are really doing as we want to do, will not what we are doing have to reflect us uniquely, and not just the outer world? If we are really doing what we want to do, does not this mean we are doing something we have chosen? And if the choice is truly ours, do we not need the power of doing something else instead?

At least for me, our present sense for freedom involves the other meanings, raising the issues which they raise. Even if this is not the case for you, we need not yet part company — for this reason. Suppose that we cannot do otherwise, and that we have no unique nature; still the simple meaning can be held; we can do what we find our determined selves wanting to do. This shows us that our first meaning is weaker than the other two; it demands less of the world. The weaker meaning would not be necessary could a

---

[4] Thomas Hobbes, *The Leviathan* (Oxford: Basil Blackwell, 1955), pp. 137–138.

stronger meaning be maintained. The deceptively simple meaning, then, can be held as a last resort while we inspect the other two.

To be free is to be able in a moment of decision to accept any one of two or more alternatives. Could you have done otherwise, the situation remaining the same; or does the whole world, along with your total past, conspire toward your choosing A instead of B? If this meaning for freedom is to be held, it must be true that you could have done otherwise; it would have to be the case that as you choose today you could have chosen something else in just that situation. This meaning for freedom threads its way through the history of philosophy. It is the meaning, qualified perhaps by "fate," which Plato and Aristotle have in view. In the Middle Ages, the Renaissance, and today, some philosophers of weight have always held this view of freedom. It is no wonder that this is so; it seems to me the meaning implicit in language and common speech. One of the clearer statements is found in the works of Locke. By "liberty" one means "the power a man has to do or forbear doing any particular action." "Liberty, it is plain, consists in a power to do, or not to do; to do, or forbear doing, as we will. . . ." How does this freedom work? We are "at liberty in respect of willing, and that is the choosing of a remote good as an end to be pursued." [5] For Locke there exists an area in life where we are free to do otherwise.

To be free is to act in accord with the unique nature of one's self. This meaning also has a basic question in it. Is there any unmistakable "you"; or is it the case that you, having no unique nature, simply *are* the influences of your culture, your friends, your teachers, and the circumstances of your life? If this meaning is to be held it must be true that not all of your choices are a reflection of the outer world; it must be true that you do have or can have a unique nature; it is true only if you are or can be something more than a transmission belt for the forces which play upon you. Something like this meaning is necessary for Spinoza near the end of his *Ethics* (although earlier he had denied it); Spinoza's expression precedes the time of the great flowering of this view. In fact, there is a hint of this meaning among the Greeks, and in the Middle Ages; but the view becomes more prominent in the nineteenth century. It is

[5] John Locke, *An Essay Concerning Human Understanding* (Oxford: Clarendon Press, 1894), Vol. I, Bk. II, Chap. XXI, Sec. 57.

expressed by Hegel; later we shall quote Nietzsche's employment of this meaning. We have here, then, a romantic meaning for freedom; it is freedom as unique self-fulfillment.

Freedom means doing what we ought to do. We have found three meanings for freedom. In fact, one more at least calls for some attention. We can allow Montesquieu to phrase this meaning for us. Freedom "can consist only in the power of doing what we ought to will, and in not being constrained to do what we ought not to will." [6] One is disappointed in probing further into Montesquieu; he does not develop the meaning as he might have done. And yet here, too, one finds a meaning having had wide use. I would suggest the Middle Ages as its point of origin, and "perfect freedom is the inability to sin" as its illustration. This view combines the question of the right, of what one "ought" to do, with that of freedom. Or it transfers the problem of our freedom into the sphere of right and wrong. We shall not explore this meaning in our immediate discussion, for the reason that one must come to terms with freedom in one of our three meanings before the question of what one "ought to do" can even be raised. The question would seem to be a later one as to whether the "right" and the "free" do finally combine.

The meanings we must examine with the greatest care are our second and our third. Our problem is to find whether or not we are free in one or more of these meanings, and what that discovery has to do with us, or we with it.

And the question is: Can we be free in either one of these two meanings? The question requires us to take thought about our lives. But can we envision our lives clearly enough to think about the problem? It is much easier to keep a table clearly in mind than a human life; its edges are more definite. Does not your life tend to merge with the lives of those about you, and even with the place where it is lived, the souvenirs and possessions which are "yours"? Do you remember the books which at an earlier time insisted "You are what you eat," "You are what you think"? It is just as true, and not completely so, that we are what we possess, what we remember, what we hope for, what we appreciate.

Of course, there is a fading away of relevance in these items which

[6] Montesquieu, *Spirit of the Laws,* trans. Thomas Nugent, revised by J. V. Pritchard (London: G. Bell and Sons, Ltd., 1878), Book XI, 3.

make up our lives. We have already said that close to the center of our problem is choice, the making of decisions. What is involved in choice? Man is in the position of choice when he sees several ways he might go, although he always goes only one. We come to a fork in the road; the two paths of the fork are the alternatives; the way we have come, as we hesitate, is also an alternative. We narrow this multiplicity of alternatives to a single one. And it is said: he has made a choice. We may be choosing a life purpose, such as the vocation we shall follow; clearly, there are here alternative purposes. Or we may be choosing among alternatives which will satisfy a purpose, such as the best route to one's work. And this must be the material of our thought: alternative purposes, and alternatives which will satisfy a purpose.

Even if you have been spared the pleasure of eating in an automat, consider this inviting prospect. We enter with a purpose one hardly chooses: to eat. And we choose from the possibilities before us. These possibilities are the alternatives with which we hope to satisfy our purpose. Clearly there are many alternatives here, each couched in its own place, behind its pane of glass — a host of alternatives in a continuum of nickel plate. Our basic purpose, to eat, can be satisfied by innumerable combinations. Should it be our purpose to eat well, the alternatives are less numerous. We decide and the tray fills with articles of food. Later we shall be deciding in some sense which morsel goes upon the fork. Finally, our body takes over for us.

Every action of our lives begins with these alternatives, and out of them through choice a perfectly definite life is molded. The question still is: In gaining the perfectly definite items making up our lives, are we free in either of our basic meanings? Have we ever made a free choice in either sense? The issue must be faced squarely. Let us examine the most pervasive of our meanings. But note in passing that on either hand we have a critical decision before us. Either it is true that sometimes in the same situation we could have done otherwise; or it is true that in no case could we ever have done otherwise. Either it is true that sometimes we can act in accord with our own unique nature; or it is true that all our actions are a reflection of the world. These two pairs of sentences, these two sets of ideas, are so opposed that we must take one, we cannot take both, and if one is true the other in that pair is false. We cannot, then, avoid deciding.

The Second Meaning Examined

This meaning holds that we are free if we can take any one of two or more alternatives; we are free if we could have done otherwise. But could we have done otherwise in any decision of our lives?

The obvious reply is: Why not? What could have kept us from doing other than we have done? This is what we must explore. Looking back over our course, two factors were mentioned which must be considered here: the circumstances in which our lives have been set, and the influences of others. Thinking further over the conditions of our lives, there is habit; and possibly we must include an element of chance. Let us try to see what part these factors play.

In the decisions we have made, are there not items which are ours by *chance,* not real choices but elements in our lives by accident, elements for which there are no reasons?

We must consider whether *circumstances,* the physical conditions, the set of things, either occasionally, or most, or all of the time, block our following any other course than the one we have in fact followed.

We must consider whether *influences,* the opinions of those around us now and in the past, merely helped us to decide, or whether it is finally that whole powerful set of attitudes on which we did and do rely in making up our minds.

Since the habitual looms more and more through the years, since life tends to gain a weight of *habit,* since one is not choosing freely when he is merely allowing habit to rule his life, we must consider how far this factor goes toward reducing the alternatives before us to a single one.

We must consider then whether we have ever really made a choice which is more than just a blend of the factors named above. In considering the matter, unfortunately you know the conditions of your life, and I do not. Perhaps it is better so; the probing is yours to do. But this being the case, we shall have to think together along parallel lines, each of us fitting the decisions of our lives into a set of neutral examples. The examples can be trivial. They furnish only an outline sketch into which we can fit the really important decisions of our lives. Let me ask you, then, to review the basic decisions which are yours. Holding them in mind, ask in the light of what follows if you could ever have done otherwise in the decisions you have made.

Chance

Have we not many times seen the alternatives before us, and with no particular preference, we yet somehow ended with a decision on our hands? Something like choice happened without our having chosen. Perhaps we merely delayed until events had chosen for us. Or we did the thing at random. We would have to say of such occasions that this became part of our lives only by chance. The automat may furnish our example.

Suppose yourself in the creeping line of our automat. There is a sort of necessity in such a line; you are aware that any delay to choose with care will hold up that line, moving like a kind of fate behind you. And now you face the momentous decision: salad with Thousand Island or Roquefort dressing? Who cares? The appeal of each may be the same, the hold of either on us very slight, or even nonexistent. But the salad with the Roquefort dressing is within reach as the line inches along behind you; now, it is on your tray. Must we not say that it is there by chance, no reason being available? If you chose at all, your choice concerned not salad, but the holding up of a cafeteria line. Such situations have been called a "freedom of indifference." Buridan's ass, between two stacks of hay, could avoid starvation by exercising such freedom since any reasonably prepared hay is better than none at all. But this isn't freedom, really; it is rather chance. And how often in life do we claim to have chosen, when chance has really done the work? There are many elements which belong to our lives only by happenstance.

Circumstance

Such apparent decisions must be ruled out; they can furnish no help in discovering the status of our freedom. Then leaving all such occasions out of account, we must consider only those where we do something to gain one of the alternatives. This leaves still a great many of the choices of our lives. With some of these in mind can you recall a choice in which circumstances did not decide the course you followed? Very likely you can. However, we must recognize that when we can think of many paths that might be taken, often circumstances are blocking all but one. A simple sketch: We are to drive our car from its shelter. The vestigial gear-shift in a modern car still allows a choice: reverse or forward. Should we be so fortunate as to possess the more conventional and less expensive shift we have four alternatives (the happy trucksters, I am informed, have six) whenever the car is started. But the very circumstance of any sound garage with its forward wall excludes every possibility except reverse. Not always does circumstance treat you so unkindly. But life has made it clear that often — indeed, how very often! — circumstances unyielding as any forward wall close out all the possibilities except for one (and that, often, the least alluring). We know then that circumstances work to limit choice. We also remember situations where, so far as we could judge, more than one course remained open to us. Then, from all the choices of our lives we must rule out the decisions made by chance and those in which circumstances had reduced the alternatives to one. If freedom is to be found anywhere, it will be found in one of the decisions which still remain.

Influences

But even where alternatives are not reduced to one, consider our third factor. Do we not recognize the force of others' influences upon the choices which we make? A curious illustration: You have emerged from the drive with great skill; for the moment your car is stationed at the curb. Again, the two alternatives! But would you be willing to incur the displeasure of passing motorists by backing against their forward motion? Very likely, even if you wished to do it, your knowledge of their displeasure would cause you to choose as they have chosen, bravely forward and in conformity. The case is trivial, but can you recall having gone against what was clearly the preponderant influence of your life? I am not denying that this is possible; I wish only to learn how it is possible; and whether you find it in your life. And if you ever have, surely this is not the way with most of your decisions. That would be an intolerable burden for any man. And indeed what is one doing when, faced by a choice, he sets out to find what his friends think about the matter; what is he doing then but seeking the weight of influence among those around him? This is not to prohibit advice, but to suggest that if one's life is shaped in every situation by the often-sought and never-controverted advice of friends, that life has not the shape of freedom.

Must we not admit that our political party, our church, our vocation, our membership in organizations, were not so much simply decided upon by us; but that if they were not in fact inherited, still the influences and opinions of others led us to them? Perhaps this will not be true of all such decisions, but of how many! In all of these choices we might have taken many courses; yet were not very few of these anything like *possible* courses for our lives?

In addition to circumstance and chance, the influence of those around us adds its bit in reducing the alternatives for choice toward a single one. I am very much afraid that these three factors explain most "choices" of our lives without the slightest need to mention freedom.

Habit

Still we have not finished, for there is habit. Habit may or may not stand for choices once made and made forever. By habit is meant a pattern of activity which follows almost automatically when triggered in situations which look like those of choice. To gain our outline sketches (filled in, of course, by weightier matter from our personal lives) we seem to favor the worlds of food and motoring; and so to food once more. When it comes to drinking coffee, one has four alternatives at least — black, white, with or without sugar. And one of these has doubtless become habitual. Who would hold we "really" choose when we name our habit pattern to the waitress? Nor is it common to choose to form a habit. I am not saying we can't change this pattern; sometimes we rebel against a habit to show that we can break it; sometimes circumstance requires a change. It should be noticed that commonly we don't rebel. And when we do, the change can be traced, usually at least, to some weighty circumstance or influence.

And is it not true that as the years pass life seems more and more to descend into habit? A role is assumed; life has gained a set of personal customs; and often it appears that life is ticking out and the habitual is in control. The force of habit reaches far beyond its presence in the single habit pattern, pervading more and more of life.

We are looking for a case where we can say, with some reasonable hope of upholding the saying: Here we were free to do otherwise. I suppose the most fitting case would be one where with circumstances not controlling we go against the major influence of our lives, and not through chance or habit. Let us assume that you have found within your past decisions such a case. Perhaps you have not found a great number of such cases. One will be enough. And does this case show your freedom to do otherwise? The case has still an obstacle before it. It is a fifth factor; the obstacle concerns the nature of a set purpose.

Set Purpose

Again, I am forced, not knowing the details of the case you have in mind, to call forth an awkward image. Let me suppose rebellion on your part some pages back at my insistence that the influence of the motoring world required you to drive forward down the street. Let me suppose you answered: "I know I could have done otherwise; I could have chosen to back down the street; I could choose to smash through the forward wall of my garage; that I do not do so is not evidence that I could not do so. Indeed," you may go on, "predict for me what you think I shall do and it will please me to do the opposite." Surely, to be free should not require tearing up the world. And I think everyone would grant that you can do all of these things: back down the street, destroy the precious grillwork of your car against the wall of your garage; and do something other than most announced predictions about your life. But the question is: Under what conditions can these things be done?

Let me hold to my substitute example, backing against the traffic. One does act to achieve his purposes, and with some dispatch. The purpose of going to work, taken in practical terms and apart from any other consideration, requires forward motion. This is life, or traffic, and we did not arrange it so. Were you actually to back against the traffic, would you not expect us to ask your reason? And in giving us a reason you would state a purpose. You decided to back against the traffic in order, possibly, to demonstrate your freedom.

Then note how you shifted purposes before you shifted gears. Your new purpose closes the other alternative. You could not now choose forward motion — without shifting to still another purpose. You were determined to show your freedom; then, perhaps, determined by your very purpose. Could it be that one can do otherwise only when possessed by a different purpose?

What we do is, of course, controlled in large part by the purpose which we have. That we sometimes do and at other times refrain from doing a certain thing cannot show that we might have done otherwise, if both the doing and the decision not to do are controlled by purposes which differ in the nature of their demands (even as here by the difference between the purpose of "going to work" and the purpose of "showing that you are free"). It seems, then, one does not demonstrate his freedom by backing down the street, by rebelling against a command. No rebellion against the world, I now believe, can show our freedom. For the first time we may be suspicious of the freedom of Cyrano; is there in his independence a measure of rebellion?

If we suppose a man whose whole life is a rebellion against, a long series of expressions of hatred toward, another individual, we would not call such a man free. His is a lifelong expression of a determined motive. It is possible that Cyrano and the Mass Man are related; if we suppose a man whose life is shaped in every situation by the main chance, whose motivation is the break in circumstances rather than any inner growth, this man too is shaped by the circumstances in which he finds himself.

The point is simply that along with chance, circumstance, influence, and habit, the very purposes which we have require some alternatives and eliminate some others. We have not found a single clear case which demands, in addition to our now five factors, the additional factor, freedom as the ability to do otherwise.

But one possibility is left. Perhaps in the case we are considering, the case where circumstances, chance, habit, and influence, are not controlling, but where one's purposes require the doing of this rather than that, our purposes are freely chosen. Here we move "up" from thinking about choice among the alternatives which satisfy a purpose to thinking about choice among the purposes which control alternatives.

Can this case be maintained? Can one argue that his purposes are freely chosen, that purpose-wise he is self-determined? One's purposes grow, do they not? And even the most important among them contain much accident in their origin. Had your background not been this particular one, would your purposes, indeed, be what they now are? Probably not, if we are candid. One teaches Philosophy rather than practicing law because of a very definite chain of events which could be set down. Reflect upon the events which led you to your present set of purposes: the influence of a parent or friend, an inspiring teacher, a fellowship for graduate study which made a difference, an experience of out-and-out chicanery in a vocation you were considering. Had the parent or friend been otherwise; had you not elected that particular course on registration day (Did you not almost flip a coin?); had the fellowship not been granted; had the disgusting experience not occurred; had these facts not been as they were who would argue that his final purposes would today have been the same? The particular course of events one meets and chance have much to do with final purposes. And this infuses the same old factors, but especially circumstances, influence, and chance, into the substance of every final purpose.

Begin to understand your life from either end. Work backwards from this moment; the things you have done today, were not most of them done under some compulsion? Could you easily avoid them? And were not many of the rest done to fulfill your purposes? And did you *really* decide upon these purposes? And if there are still some items left in what you have done today, did not many of these, at least, just happen — unforeseen, unthought, almost unwilled? And working backward through the years were not all days like this day? How many chances, accidents, circumstances were involved at every step! Or taken the other way: You were born into a situation already made. Nothing much at first, you absorbed the outside world, accepted the attitudes around you, became a faithful reflection of your time and place — and where you have since rebelled, was it not through some more recent influence or circumstance? The very alternatives you saw, and the way you viewed them, came from this world into which you were born.

One final and infuriating circumstance is that one cannot simply *prove* once and for all either that he is free to do otherwise or else that he is not. At least the matter cannot be demonstrated for all to see because of the very nature of choice and of time. William James illustrates the point in a famous lecture calling up a choice of two streets, either of which will lead him home.

> . . . I ask you seriously to suppose that this ambiguity of my choice is real; and then to make the impossible hypothesis that the choice is made twice over, and each time falls on a different street. In other words, imagine that I first walk through Divinity Avenue, and then imagine that the powers governing the universe annihilate ten minutes of time with all that it contained, and set

me back at the door of this hall just as I was before the choice was made. Imagine then that, everything else being the same, I now make a different choice and traverse Oxford Street. You, as passive spectators, look on and see the two alternative universes, — one of them with me walking through Divinity Avenue in it, the other with the same me walking through Oxford Street.[7]

James points out how one who does not believe in freedom would say of either course, after the fact, that it had to be. Yet, could time be turned back, it might be found that the decision could have been otherwise; so the case against freedom isn't really proven. It just might be that, were time rolled back, James could have taken Oxford Street, and you could have chosen the great missed opportunity of your life. But the argument works both ways; even James admits the hypothesis is impossible; time cannot be rolled back. And this means neither James nor you can prove dramatically, once for all, that the might-have-been might really have been.

All of us say, "I might have done otherwise"; often we say, even, "I should have done otherwise." But no one can prove he *could* have done so, for the very meaning of choice is that we take one course and let the others go. And in a different time we never find conditions quite the same; no one makes a choice twice over.

If we cannot prove our freedom to choose, if no one can prove our lack of freedom, the problem seems hopeless. Usually a hopeless problem is dismissed as worth no more concern. But can we dismiss this problem when what should be dared in life may depend upon whether life can be free? At any rate, we have gained a conclusion of the greatest consequence: Much of what we may have considered our freedom is just a reflection of our time and place; and any man will reflect these in his being. The lack of freedom in the world is due at least to this, that every man must reflect his time and place. But whatever the limitations may be we have not yet lost the case for freedom.

Indeed, we have one item which positively supports the present meaning of freedom. We have the feeling which goes with us in most decisions that we could have done otherwise. This may turn out to be very important. Sometimes we feel unfree and sometimes free. Most will grant our lack of freedom when we feel unfree. But a similar courtesy is not extended to our positive feeling of being free.

[7] William James, "The Dilemma of Determinism," from *The Will to Believe and Other Essays* (New York: Longmans Green and Co., 1897), p. 155.

We are here being presented with the strange doctrine that all, or almost all, men are suffering from the same lifelong illusion that they can do otherwise. Other illusions we can dispel — by approaching the oasis in the desert, by withdrawing the bent stick from the water. Now we can be told we are under a lifelong illusion which cannot be dispelled, but it will be very hard to believe.

Two other items may be added to show how topsy-turvy is a world without freedom to do otherwise. If no one could have done otherwise the common notion of responsibility is out of phase with truth. Ordinarily we say a man could have exercised better judgment, could have made another decision than the one which destroyed these human values; if he could have done otherwise, then we may say he is responsible for what he did in fact do. If he could not have done otherwise, society takes on a strange coloration. Human responsibility disappears along with human freedom. Now it is part of our common belief, and certainly part of what we have discovered so far in this discussion, that sometimes men are the victims of circumstance, environment, and the like. But if no one is in fact responsible for what he does, we are given a second lifelong illusion which will be as hard to believe as was the first.

If no one could have done otherwise we are equally at the mercy of the factors which play upon us, although their play shapes us each in a different way. What then happens to the notion of objective truth? If because of the circumstances, influences, habits, and chances bearing upon his life (most of them certainly not "scientific") the scientist whom we revere comes to his conclusion and could not have done otherwise, his total life being what it was, why should we believe him? Everything he says will be a report on his biography. You may respond: "But he is better off than others. Accidentally, of course, his life has been lived in a kind of context where objectivity is stressed." Yet how can this be? His associates are also determined as were his teachers. If he could not have done otherwise why accept his word above our own? Both words are equally determined. But "truth" requires the granting of some freedom in accepting and rejecting, in handling ideas. He must be able to do otherwise. If he has no capacity to accept or reject on a level beyond the preponderant weight of influence, he is in no better case than we. Once more then, if we fail to establish freedom our judgments concerning truth and error are amiss, even though we could not do without these judgments.

Maybe everything does have this strange color of illusion. Certainly the three items taken together do not prove our freedom. But they do require us either to find a place for freedom, or else admit to this very strange topsy-turvy world in which man as such, not just this or that man, is continually mistaken in his most basic daily judgments. This means at the least that could we find an acceptable view of freedom, the view would be strengthened by these considerations.

The Third Meaning Examined

We have learned how false is the thoughtless presupposition of our radical freedom. And since our second meaning has not led to freedom, we had better look to the third: To be free is to act in accord with the unique nature of one's own self. With this meaning a man is free when his purposes are his own. But within the last few pages, forced in our discussion to move "up" from alternatives to the purposes which control them, we found accident, circumstance, and the force of influence also in our purposes. Is man, then, only a residue of the things about him? If so, he is not free even in our present meaning.

In some ways the third meaning seems more promising than our late lamented second. The bothersome issue of choice seems not likely to arise. Yet other problems are before us. If we can avoid the question of choice, yet we cannot now avoid asking about the nature of the "self." And this counter for our thought might constitute a separate problem. But let us see if we can come to terms with ourselves with some celerity. We use the words, "I," "me," and "mine." To what do we refer when we use this language of "I-me-mine"?

> . . . when I enter most intimately into what I call *myself*, I always stumble on some particular perception or other, of heat or cold, light or shade, love or hatred, pain or pleasure. I never catch *myself* at any time without a perception, and can never observe anything but the perception. . . . If anyone, upon serious and unprejudiced reflection, thinks he has a different notion of *himself*, I must confess I can reason no longer with him. All I can allow him is, that he may be in the right as well as I, and that we are essentially different in this particular. He may, perhaps, per-

ceive something simple and continued which he calls *himself;* though I am certain there is no such principle in me.[8]

For David Hume the self was a kind of theatre in which perceptions, ideas, feelings, purposes, would pass, succeed each other, fuse, and mingle. He was certain of its complex nature, and certain of change in the parts of this complexity. The issue is: What can we mean by the self? At this juncture men can disagree. Some may find a lifelong unity they call "themselves," while others will be impressed by the feature of constant change. But I suggest that each of us must allow much of this complexity so clear to David Hume; and if there is more to "self" than this, I see no reason why it would alter very much whatever is to follow. Must not all of us admit much of what he says? Do you not find this constant change within yourself? Your mental content — what you sense, think, feel, and purpose — is surely different at this moment from what it was one hour ago. The ideas in your mind yesterday at this time — what were they? Can you even recall their nature? One hears of lifelong purposes; but these grow and change; to some extent they change from day to day; at last they are exchanged, sometimes, for other purposes. Surely, part at least of what we mean by "self" is this complex, this compound of thought, purpose, feeling, and whatever else.

If we can mean this, at least, by "self" our question becomes a bit more pointed: Is there anything in this compound self, unique to me, and not to another? A man would be free in our third meaning if his purposes were uniquely his. But having found accident, circumstance, and the force of influence also within our purposes, we have found these factors in the basic elements of this compound self.

Let us now ask, not whether we could have chosen other purposes (this we could not discover); but let us ask if purposes uniquely ours can be achieved. Let it be granted that one's purposes can be fixed by the world; the question here is: Can one move to purposes primarily his own, to the point where (if this makes sense) he reflects himself?

But is it sensible to speak in this strange manner? Have we reason to believe in purposes which would be at last our own? The

---

[8] David Hume, *A Treatise of Human Nature,* Book I, Part IV, Sec. VI, from *The Philosophical Works of David Hume* (Boston: Little, Brown and Co., 1854), Vol. I, p. 312.

thought does not outrage our common sense. Remember the advice offered once when you were ill at ease: "Be natural," "Be yourself!" But no one has a self ready made. Exactly there lies the problem. How can one know what, if anything, is natural for him? How can he know what it would be to be himself? And let us recall the commonplace remark, applied to one who holds our confidence, when his performance has been disappointing: He has not yet found himself, we say. Or in other circumstances it might be said: However natural that kind of behavior may be for someone else, it is not natural for him. All such language suggests the point before us: No one has a self ready made, yet in some way he may have a self to find, natural to him, and not to another; and it would then become his task to find that self and to develop it.

However puzzling this may seem, the view has been maintained by more than one philosopher. And one of these, Nietzsche, expressed himself in these words:

> At this point I can no longer evade a direct answer to the question, *How one becomes what one is.* . . . The fact that one becomes what one is, presupposes that one has not the remotest suspicion of what one is. From this standpoint even the blunders of one's life have their own meaning and value, the temporary deviations and aberrations, the moments of hesitation and modesty, the earnestness wasted upon duties which lie outside the actual life-task. In these matters great wisdom, perhaps even the highest wisdom, comes into activity. . . . Meanwhile the organizing "idea" which is destined to become master, grows and continues to grow into the depths, — it begins to command, it leads you slowly back from your deviations and aberrations, it prepares individual qualities and capacities, which one day will make themselves felt as indispensable to the whole of your task, — step by step it cultivates all the serviceable faculties, before it ever whispers a word concerning the dominant task, the "goal," the "object," and the "meaning" of it all.[9]

About what in the world is he talking? He seems to find a difference between what one is, and what one *really* is, as though residing in us at some deeper level were an authentic self which is our own. Many allow their lives to be framed wholly by what appears on the

[9] Friedrich Nietzsche, *Ecce Homo,* trans. A. M. Ludovici (London: George Allen & Unwin Ltd., and New York: The Macmillan Company, 1930), pp. 48–51. Used by permission of the publishers.

surface of consciousness, seeking the main chance, calculating a role for every situation, hearing only the voice of the outer world. But Nietzsche claims "growth" can occur in human life; this growth has a natural direction which can be known if only we do not force our lives into a foreign mold; our purpose is something different from all the obvious rules, precepts, social goals, the circumstances, and influences which clutter the surface of consciousness and are so much in the focus of attention; the patience to wait and learn is the means by which our whole being can gain the pattern of a life task developing, but slowly, into the position of command. If this can happen, it would support, and make significant, our present view of freedom.

Many allow their lives to be formed wholly from what appears on the surface of consciousness, but can we so account for Beethoven or any other major artist? Search Beethoven's outer world and you do find many forces which played upon him and are reflected in his music. But do you find among them anything adequate to explain his Third Symphony? Can one really hold that Beethoven, he at least, is just a reflection of his time and place? It seems we must admit his music goes beyond this time and place; or it is to be found in only one time and place, that of Beethoven himself. Include Beethoven in the survey and you have explanation enough. But what is the Beethoven factor? Is it not obviously his genius, his capacity to take the influences of his time and produce a kind of music beyond the reach of his contemporaries, although the same forces had played upon their lives? In short, to speak sensibly of this matter do we not have to admit that Beethoven possessed a *potentiality* out of which, with these influences and circumstances, such music could be born?

But of course we can affirm so much! A man grows to maturity through experiencing, that is clear enough; and every man must reflect his time and place. But some men, while reflecting their own times and places, likewise transcend those times and places. This is the fact which must remain forever puzzling to anyone who does not grant a factor of potentiality in the life of man. We are saying only that man has a certain potential which, when made actual, is his own natural and true self. And this would be the fact which allows each age a different set, which provides the opportunity for each age to do more than just reshuffle the same old cards. Aristotle long ago added the notion of "potentiality" to philosophy; and, as elsewhere, he did apply it to the self. It is reassuring to find in Aristotle the idea which has emerged. Now this is the feature of man which the psychologists have been describing for decades when they have referred to an element of heredity as distinct from that of environment, when they have analyzed types of physical make-up, in their intensive study and restudy of the intelligence quotient of an individual, when they have spoken of native aptitudes. These aspects of personality, when brought together, are collectively what we can now understand as a person's potentiality. And whatever it is, it is not just nothing; nor does it lie on the surface of our consciousness; it may provide the deeper level we had sought.

Now if this meaning for freedom is to stand, we must be able to affirm our present luminous possibility in everyone. Can we, then, add to influence, circumstance, habit, chance, and set purpose, a factor of one's own potentiality? I can think of nothing which would deny the point; that my limits may stop short of yours is nothing to the point. Each of us has the factor of his own potential. And if our purposes reflect this factor we are free in our present meaning; we are then prepared to act in accord with our own unique nature. This uniqueness of our potential will lie at least in the discovery of a single and authentic center for our complex selves; and when developed our uniqueness may signify the presence in ourselves of elements which cannot be duplicated elsewhere in the world. In the first of these two senses, and possibly in both, each of us can point to unique qualities within his life. Many doubts can still arise; but that all men can act, at least some of the time, in a manner uniquely their own, and that some men *do* so act, may now be granted. In the light of this fact, experience can become as much the set of steps by which one moves toward his own unique nature, as a sheer environment shaping one into what he has to be. One *may* respond with something more than just the color of his past experiences. Something of his own potentiality may be in that response. One is making the best of sense, then, when he grants to man a certain potential which, when made actual, is his own natural and true self; something of one's own potential can enter the purposes, thoughts and feelings of this complex, changing self.

Can we now say: Let your potentiality become actual, and you have achieved a standing ground for choices which reflect no one but yourself; that is, you have gained the ability to act freely in our present meaning? Unhappily, we have not gotten quite so far. We have made progress, but there are questions still before us.

What is involved in the idea of development, in going from where one is to something more? What is involved in the development of what is essentially your own — your genius, *you?* If one can find his own potential and develop it, growth has occurred in that man's life. But how are we to understand growth, the growth of one's being, or the growth of Beethoven's Third Symphony?

Whatever the development of one's potential turns out to be, it should be the reason why Beethoven had to master the techniques of music before he could write it, the reason for the weary hours of practice, the strain, the building of a platform on which, later, to work at an advanced level. And it should be the reason why Beethoven had first to write in the common style, for his own had to develop through time. And it should be the reason why Benvenuto Cellini had to make settings for ladies' rings before he could cast his salt cellar, and both of these before he could be equal to the casting of his statue, Perseus. Through all the stages he was developing his own potentiality. And this is also why you began life with smaller tasks, and then replaced these with larger ones; this is why you may now be ready for a life-task — even though you may not know its nature even now. Everyone is pushed around more or less in life; but the man free in our present meaning will be preparing, all the while — no matter what happens — his own self.

In all these examples something merely possible comes to be an actual part of human life. Beethoven wrote his Third Symphony; when that was merely possible, it did not exist in Beethoven in the same way and with the same form it had once down on paper. Had this been so, he might have just set it down without struggle. He made it up, as we say, and the making was arduous. Arduous, indeed, since he was really adding the new quality of his Third Symphony to the universe! What was involved in the struggle, the arduousness, of the symphony? Was it not this: At every one of the almost innumerable steps contained in its writing Beethoven had to eliminate the countless possible paths this music might have taken in favor of the one possibility which really belonged? At every step he was gaining a perfectly definite work out of boundless possibilities, any other set of which if followed would have made a different work, many of which if followed would have made a work less worthy, or would have marred what he had achieved to that point. What an intense amount of concentration was needed to create a thing of actual beauty from the possibilities of musical art!

There is a mystery here. One can make a case for saying that a man can develop his own potential. But one cannot demonstrate that he might have done otherwise. Yet we cannot describe what happened in the writing of this symphony — the development of a Beethoven potential — without saying that Beethoven continually chose one possibility rather than another out of a vast continuum of possibilities. Alternatives, possibilities, very numerous were reduced time after time to a single one. Every advance involved a choice, and the separate advances were immense. He was not finished with the task of choosing among alternatives until the symphony itself was finished; at least it is natural to say he *chose* until the action of the symphony was complete.

Do we here lose all the ground which we have gained, or have we gained still more? It is one or the other. What we have discovered is this: Our two meanings for freedom belong together, and involve each other. And we have not avoided the problem of choice, as we had thought. We cannot talk about the development of a unique potential without using the language of choice. Must we now say that if you see and develop your potential you do this, too, as a result of circumstance and the rest, unfreely? One has a certain capacity, this is clear enough. One decides whether or not to develop his potential. And at every stage in its development situations of choice succeed each other. From the standpoint of choice three questions can be posed, probing this freedom of unique expression.

First, how did we happen to gain the capacity which is ours? What was its source? Certainly we did not choose it for ourselves. The adolescent, struggling to come to terms with his changing person, announces in rebellion, "I did not choose to be born." Indeed, not! Nor did you choose your parents, or your parents' parents. And so you did not choose the capacities and limitations which characterize your life. Go through the matter at your leisure, think positively or negatively, think in sociological, physiological, or genetic terms, circumstance and chance determined your potential.

Second, once the basic framework of a life is fixed does not one

choose either to develop his potential, or to go on reflecting the
world about him? And do not circumstance and influence play
about one as he decides to make, or not to make, the effort? Might
not the choice to develop one's potential be determined by the
world?

Third, suppose we have decided to turn toward our capacities,
develop them, and add their burden to the factors making up our
lives. We shall then be plotting, in whatever field, something like
a symphony; that is, we shall face over and over the problem of reducing the possible choices to a single one. And since we cannot
defend our second meaning, since we have not shown we might
have chosen otherwise, then may not chance, circumstance, influence, and fixed purpose, shape the burgeoning potential which
seemed so full of promise not many pages back?

Then when, if ever, has man freedom? The question is really a
cry of anguish; for the picture we have found is one which forever
to a thoughtful man must wipe the smugness from his self-an-
nounced freedom to control his life: the number of circumstances,
of influences, of chance happenings, the growth of his purposes
and habits out of whatever cluster of circumstances may happen to
surround him, the possible dependence of his capacities upon the
circumstances of his birth, and the influence which turned him
toward himself.

Are these objections weighty? They are not cavalier. Do they,
entangling our third meaning with the second, rob this meaning of
its promise? You will have to be the judge. My elation over our
apparent progress with this meaning may prevent me from confronting these objections with the appropriate gravity of mind.
But should these, or other, objections be decisive, clearly we would
be directed back to the first, and simple, view of freedom: Do
what you want to do, for you can do no other. And this, in turn,
would force us to accept the causal network, determining every
aspect of the world, not excluding human life.

You may now hold both of these convictions. For my part I shall
try to answer the most recent objections which have been raised.
The discussion has reached a critical state; we can gain much or
lose all. It is not a small thing to determine the kind and quality of
human freedom. And in any case the problem is yours as well as
mine. We have explored the problem of our freedom. How do you
make out its answer?

II. *Toward Personal Freedom*

Back to the fray! We return to the point. Our two meanings belong together, and the stakes are high. Rescue the third meaning, and the second is likewise gained. The claims against this meaning were as follows: (1) Capacity, one's potential, derives from circumstance and chance. (2) Circumstance and influence determine whether or not one turns to his potential. (3) As one chooses, shaping some potential into an actual work, at every step chance, circumstance, habit, influence, and former set purpose control the final product. What of these claims?

The *first* is to be granted. One does not choose the initial framework of his life; it is, indeed, a result of circumstance and chance. Yet the fact does not perturb me. I did not expect to choose it. Indeed, expectancy is just not possible until that initial grant, some measure of potential, has begun the adventure of one's life. Our discussion centers on the freedom of the self, once formed. If I am this inherited framework, how it came to be is a matter of indifference. The question is: How free, once formed, can this self be?

The *second* claim, I think, can be denied. It has some force, of course, but does not say the final word. Most evidence from the histories of those who turn toward their capacities is that they do so, often, against great difficulties, against the circumstances and against the major thrust of influence on their lives. It is always simpler merely to reflect one's surroundings than to separate one's self, and begin to develop from inner sources. The claim simply lacks the power to exclude freedom as reflection of one's inner nature.

The *third* claim is more serious. Can it be also met? And the case before us is Beethoven's once again. One difference between the development of a unique Beethoven potential and the examples which earlier failed to reveal our freedom is very clear. When one develops his potential, he is not choosing among actual things, but among mere possibilities. Perhaps one is never choosing freely when he selects among actual things, weighted as they are by the outer world. But just as one cannot hold Beethoven to be merely a reflection of his time and place when he has gone beyond that time and place, so one cannot hold that the conditions of his life determine him to choose each musical alternative for he has gone beyond the actual conditions into those further possibilities which are not yet subject to the pressures of the actual world.

How could one argue that the five disheartening factors of our first discussion will control the musical conclusions to which Beethoven may come? This development cannot be thought a result of chance, because it is nothing random but, instead, full of purpose. It cannot have been merely a result of circumstance and influence, for it does not merely reflect the circumstances and influences of his life but goes beyond them. It cannot have been a result of habit, for it is something new. It cannot have been just the reflection of a controlling purpose, since it is precisely a new purpose which is here emerging. Now if it was not a result of chance; if it was not a result of habit; if it was not the result of a set controlling purpose, then must we not have come upon an element of genuine choice where Beethoven could have selected, indeed, any one of many possible alternatives?

We have reached the critical point of our discussion. As you can see, I am about to affirm that we can be free in both our basic meanings. I shall do this because it seems to me we have found the point in life where only freedom has the power to explain that life. And the more I review all of these considerations the more compelling does the argument become. At this point determinism reveals to me its broken back. But I may be wrong. From the point at which I took the initiative, your mind has been closed to me. I could not hear your murmured protests; perhaps you noted the place where my argument went astray. But again you may agree. Do not go with me unless convinced the case is made. Until you confront me with your counterarguments I must assume the case is made. Assuming this, our three supporting items — the feeling of freedom, moral responsibility, and truth — can be of further use, strengthening the view that freedom is possible in human life.

A Conception of Freedom Based on the Two Meanings

We had come upon the element of genuine choice where Beethoven could have selected any one of many possible alternatives. Then why did he choose precisely as he did? In a sense even this can be answered: because he was defining his own nature. And this answer begins to pull the two meanings for free, dom into each other.

Indeed, it seems that this was the object of the French philoso- pher, Henri Bergson: to describe how an act can be both a reflec- tion of one's nature and a result of choice. Bergson arrived at his point by urging that nature, through all the course of evolution, had been trying to reach freedom; and nature did so, finally, in man. Nature achieved in man a being of such complexity that freedom was possible. Where in another creature the patterned act follows its stimulus almost automatically, in man a stimulus occurs and this releases not one but many possible acts which confront the actual self. So man must stop; his indecision is a sign that he can be free. Between this moment of indecision and the act Bergson pictures the self wavering among the possibilities, undecided and deciding, moving in a narrowing arc, becoming a self which re- flects *this* possibility as part of its nature. What is at one moment just a possibility confronting the self — envisioned, entertained — is at a later moment part of its very being. Once the first decision has been made, other possibilities of various kinds arise for the developing act; and again the self must grow and incorporate some one or more into its being; and on and on, the self defining itself as the arc narrows, until what was at first merely possible has now be- come quite actual, and the act falls from the self. Bergson says "the act falls from the self as the ripe fruit falls from the tree." And in the figure one includes the long period of maturation until a per- fectly definite apple falls in a perfectly definite way from a per- fectly definite tree. Bergson here seems perfectly right. This does explain how our two meanings fit together, and also how the nature of an act may be a novel possibility which was not even among the original possibilities envisaged.

And the Anglo-Saxon philosopher, Alfred North Whitehead, can help us to see how an act can be both free and yet contain all the factors of chance, circumstance, influence, habit, and earlier set purpose which help to constitute our human life.[10] It is his emi- nently sane suggestion that an act divides into two stages. In the first the act is being externally determined; it is open to outer in- fluences; the world is having its way; one is gathering material; one *is* the gathering of the material; the elements of the complex are

[10] A. N. Whitehead, *Process and Reality* (New York: The Macmillan Com- pany, 1929), pp. 41–42, 74–75.

forming. In the second stage the elements of the complex have been gained. Some standing ground, some standpoint, has now been reached; the outer world has less effect; the complex begins to gain its own impetus moving toward definitude. The act has begun to be insensitive toward the outer world; it becomes an influence in itself, and helps you to stand against opposed influences of other kinds. In this stage the act defines itself from among the relevant possibilities. This description, supplementing Bergson's, allows us to insist upon the presence of circumstance, chance, habit, influence of all sorts playing through our lives and yet claim the possibility of freedom. But the freedom of our act depends upon what is done with these conditions, whether their further possibilities and your potential together find a way into some new result so that the act finally becomes your own.

This then is our hard-won result: The two meanings for freedom do finally blend. To act freely is to act in such a manner as to reflect uniquely your own self; but this reflection of a self in action is (where freedom has been gained) the reflection of a self which has grown into its unique nature, which has chosen among alternatives, and in the choosing has become the kind of self which reflects this act as part of its authentic being. One is free in our first sense when deciding among alternatives which go beyond the world. One is never free in our first sense (at least we have not found reason for saying that he ever is) when deciding among alternatives already fixed and settled by that world; our examples of food, motoring, and walking home after lectures were all beside the point although they led us to the point. One is free in our second sense when his purposes are native to himself; the freedom to be authentic *might* be reflected in examples of food, motoring, and walking home. But one must also become authentic; this means that here, too, one must go beyond the world to the discovery of himself.

Freedom, then, is possible for you in both senses, but only if (1) you are willing to grow and change and alter with each possibility for choice; (2) you attend to your potential and reflect it in your life; (3) you command your force to stand as often as necessary against the world; (4) your decisions take you beyond that cluster of ideas, opinions, purposes, circumstances handed you by the world in order to create your own ideas, opinions, purposes, and to become a circumstance oneself.

Freedom is possible, even if we tend merely to reflect the world about us.

4x

What is the Free Man Like?

Now we know more certainly that a man is not free when he is merely a reflection of his surroundings; and he is not free when his loyalty is a blind adherence to any cause whatever; and one is not free when he is complacent about and content with what he is; and man is not free when he acts in a spirit of sheer calculation; and man is not free when his work is for the return from the working rather than because this work fits his energies, needs, drives, and abilities; and man is not free when he binds his life to things; and man is not free ever when the quality of his act is shaped by the world outside; man is free only when his act reflects himself.

If we are to consider what the free man is like, we can defer no longer probing our disquietude concerning Cyrano de Bergerac. Cyrano closed his praise of freedom with the words:

"I stand, not high it may be — but alone!"

His friend, Le Bret, answered:

"Alone, yes! — But why stand against the world?
What devil has possessed you now, to go
Everywhere making yourself enemies?"

And Cyrano once more:

"Watching you other people making friends
Everywhere — as a dog makes friends! I mark
The manner of these canine courtesies
And think: 'My friends are of a cleaner breed;
Here comes — thank God! — another enemy!' " [11]

It does not trouble me that Cyrano knew he had to stand alone. There is something about the nature of freedom which requires that any man learn to stand sometimes alone. Nor does it trouble me that Cyrano is willing to stand against the world. Any free man should be willing to stand, when need be, against the world. What troubles me is this: I recognize in the fierceness of his spirit, exulting in his list of enemies, something beyond the words, an attitude deeply grounded in the spirit of the West, rising now and

[11] *Cyrano de Bergerac, op. cit.*

again to the surface, infused with both greatness and destruction. I am caught by its grandeur and troubled by its capacity to destroy.

Even through disquietude we can fill the doctrine in. Let us then produce for Cyrano, and in his spirit, the outline of an essay on freedom. Since this is a lyrical spirit, the description will itself be lyrical.

Outline of an Essay on Freedom

— by any Cyrano

I. The Proclamation — To stand erect and breathe the air in sovereign manner, to act and know one acts because the act is his; to leave the grovelling, calculating means–end ratio and be one's self, to live in such a manner that one knows the only friends remaining to him are true friends — not friends by convenience or utility, to lead one's life in an utterly authentic manner; this it is to be free.

II. Man, the Social Animal — In this highly patterned social web the free man must be viewed as somewhat suspect. He is not weak enough; he does not cringe enough. For this reason a free man is not likely to rule a state, find his way to the top of any enterprise where he has to deal with other men and where the weapons are covert slander, the "unintended" blunder which allows one to assassinate character without feeling himself a character assassin, and the friends one makes by walking on his knees.

III. Freedom and Power — The free man may smile tenderly, a little sadly and ironically, a trifle contemptuously, where others offer their deep respects to consecrated power in order to preserve their positions, purchase their homes, retain the self-respect they never had, and sacrifice whatever slight integrity of spirit might still remain to them. The free man will exchange all this for breathing room. Not ruling others, or wishing this, he alone will be the ruler of himself; his supreme disavowal of the "petty game" allows such a man to become his own property, a status purer than that of his less fortunate, slavish, and much propertied acquaintances. The only power for which he aims is that leading to a society organized laterally, not vertically, where every man can stand his ground and stand erect, where every man can have his elbow-room, where no man will make himself ignoble.

IV. A Suspicion Concerning Property — Much power, much property, is highly suspect. It is an evidence — not a proof, perhaps, but an evidence — that someone has made his goal not the increase of his being, but only the increase of his means, and has climbed the backs of others, or has bribed someone to lift him up that he might gain such power. The possessing is not a proof. But one's achievements require attention; and one tends one's values. The possessing is hence an evidence of the paltriness, perhaps of the lack of principle or vice within, or the clinging grasping nature of, someone's decisions as to value.

V. The Free Man Unbound — The one who would be free will allow no other man or group or institution to retard his growth. Nor will he finally use anything whatever as the crutch to keep his life upright; he will know his life must stand alone. Hence, there is the requirement that he regard all his associations as voluntary associations which he reaffirms by daily choice. To gain the needed unity, he must retain his basic choices. But as a free man they are his choices, and in affirming them he is aware he can negate them. As a free man he is absolutely bound by nothing. He binds himself anew in every moment of decision.

VI. The End of Freedom — The man who keeps his life free must live with concentration; his total force, that is, his total self, must be gathered up and thrown into the acts before him; he must live with energy. And if one can find this spirit, so full will be his life, so rich its broad dimension with everything given to it and nothing held back, that he does not need — indeed, must smile at those who think they need, having lived so little here — another place and time and set of circumstances, to add the eternity to life which ought to be experienced here.

VII. And Anarchy — Freedom is suspect in the eyes of very many, is thought to be a wild, anarchic thing tending away from established order. For this reason lovers of order absolute do not welcome such a principle. And freedom *is* anarchic — regrettably, blessedly so. When life becomes too much pressed down, let the old order be broken, let freedom rise. For freedom is of the nature of life, and extreme order is of the nature of death. Then man must be free to be himself. This is the medicine which can save us. If the sense of life is missing from your being, what you very likely miss is your proper sense of freedom.

VIII. And God — (A quote from an interesting conversation to be pondered): [12]
    Zeus: Orestes knows that he is free.

[12] The following lines are from Jean Paul Sartre, *The Flies*, trans. Stuart Gilbert (New York. Alfred A. Knopf, 1947), Act II, Scene II, pp. 135–136.

Aegisthus *(eagerly):* He knows he's free? Then, to lay hands on him, to put in irons, is not enough. A free man in a city acts like a plague-spot. He will infect my whole kingdom and bring my work to nothing. Almighty Zeus, why stay your hand? Why not fell him with a thunderbolt?

Zeus *(slowly):* Fell him with a thunderbolt? *(A pause. Then, in a muffled voice)* Aegisthus, the gods have another secret.

Aegisthus: Yes?

Zeus: Once freedom lights its beacon in a man's heart, the gods are powerless against him. It's a matter between man and man, and it is for other men, and for them only, to let him go his gait, or to throttle him.

To some this outline form will seem but jumbled words. To others it will appear that something final about life has here been stated. Of course the words filled in may not really represent Cyrano. We know his defiance may have stemmed in part not from his view of freedom, but from the mere refusal of a lady. Le Bret suspects that this is so, and says: "Tell this to all the world; but say to me, 'She loves you not.'" But Le Bret is partly wrong. The lady provides the occasion, but every Cyrano savors in this doctrine a freedom which scores many times over. Do we not recognize the "manner of these canine courtesies"? To prize freedom as independence from a compromising world; is there not something ultimate in this? To wish a kind of social life where men no longer have to bow and scrape; is that not desirable? To seize the moment in its fullness, and find life there, has not this a claim upon us? And as for the cry of freedom against the tyranny of any given social order — that cry has long been sounding in the west as though it were part of our very nature.

Then why draw back? I recognize and admire this tremendous indictment of human kind. Indeed, while one is riding the crest of seemingly boundless energy this view of freedom, where everything is given to life and nothing held back, seems the final word. Then it has the ring of truth. But the prospect is exhausting, and what when the energy recedes, when indeed one needs a thing to which to cling? Le Bret is partly right. This energetic freedom does contain rebellion against the world. And we have seen that simply to rebel is not the heart of freedom. And yet this mere rebellion is presented as an absolute. Indeed, the rebellious man is placed so high it would be difficult to imagine anything above him.

Our Cyrano senses this and perhaps begins to play the part. The stance of freedom becomes a bit like playing God; the free man, like God, is alone, superior, pure, and immune. Again, this may be but the case is not made by proclamation. But finally, I think, one may properly draw back because this free man, who feels himself alone, is at last bound by nothing. There is no sense here of an obligation made once and forever. Freedom has here overridden every other philosophic insight. The issue can be raised again when principle in life becomes our theme. Taken as given, this freedom has a hollow ring.

We must say then: Standing over against all the rest is perhaps a moment in freedom, a preparation, perhaps never more than the essential first step. Still, one side of this idea is very saving: One must have strength to stand alone when need be. No happening in the sphere of one's relations, personal or social, should be allowed the power to sweep one from his feet, to make of one an abject creature, to wreck the onward movement of his life. This idea of freedom rightly demands an inner power to withstand, if need be, the breakdown of his most cherished relations. There is then truth in what we have given Cyrano to say, and in this truth lies mixed the falsehood that life can be lightly given.

And yet these sentences have been an interlude; at best, no more than a warning. The problem for most of us is not too much freedom, but too little, not a freedom which goes beyond its bounds, but which does not command us to dare in the slightest. Still for us, the arresting phrase of Nietzsche, "How one becomes what one is," forms the central problem. I assert that we know even now in part what we feel and want and are; we feel within ourselves the power to exercise choice far more radically than we ever have; I assert that we can stand even against the modern world when need be to become what we most deeply desire — the self which is really ours. Mere timidity, mere cowardice, mere inertia, these alone, stand in the way of our choosing freely — hindering us, haltering us, keeping us from reflecting a uniqueness of our own in life. These alone cause us to stand still when we might be always becoming more nearly what we even now most deeply are.

All that has been said implies a certain kind of life, a certain bent of character; I should rather say, a certain lack of bent in character. But if for long one does not know what individual he is; if he does not know what is natural for him; if he does not know what it would be to be himself, how does he ever find out? One begins where he is, of course. Now, what is given for any man, what is given for you? An elaborate set of relationships already fixed, most of which you could not give up, most of which indeed you should not give up. But the number of fixed relationships is simply amazing: social, vocational, political, religious, and whatever else. All together these furnish the framework within which you act; all together these conspire to form your nature. Would you wish, sometimes, to act in a spirit of utter spontaneity, and in disregard of this complex? That is impossible. Can you find spontaneity even in the cluster of relations which constitutes your life? This is more nearly possible. Out of the movement of your inner life you must become what will satisfy all your energies. What that is must come from you, but a number of suggestions can be made.

How, Since It Is Possible, Can Freedom Be Gained?

My *first* suggestion is very simple: Let one not spend all his time living the life of the world. Let man retire from external pressures and learn how to feel his own feelings and to think his own authentic thoughts. Knowing what the world wishes of you, what can you willingly and freely grant?

Second, learn patience. Learn to wait. Unexceptional people make this their hallmark. It does have power. And if you would be your own individual you must wait; refuse to cast yourself into the first mold which comes along or that one most convenient. We have seen some truth in Nietzsche's comment; and we must learn to wait so that within ourselves, out of the material of our being, our lifetask, your life-task, can begin to form. If only you do not compress yourself too soon into some stunted form! Meanwhile, any job, any place, will do — to add the needed time.

Third, even though we cannot find a sign to give concerning what is truly yours, the matter is so personal, yet there are many signs concerning what is false for you. When you begin your work and have to force yourself to do it, this means that the work is not really yours, perhaps was never yours, but is properly another's. Then leave it for that other. How can you be yourself doing work which

is not your own? The first sign of strangeness, then, the first remoteness, the first sense of emptiness and futility in what you have
assigned yourself, is a warning: This may not belong to you. Let us
underline the futility of picking out a personal goal for any other
reason than that it wells up out of one's very nature. Should one
try to cramp his life into a foreign mold, he will experience not life
but an unnatural strange existence. The feeling of remoteness, of
futility, of waste of your being, is your warning: This way lies
bondage. The punishment is lifelong if one does not seek the one
thing which is his own.

Fourth, learn to read the smaller print of life; seek the exceptional, the subtle. I cannot say here just what this means. It is the
burden of our later chapters on truth, beauty, and principle in life.
But it involves making of yourself a more sensitive instrument that
you can become at length more than just an instrument.

Fifth, reflect upon the choices already made which now constitute your being. Most of these will be conventional, obvious,
general choices as we have seen. But are there not some which
contain a mystery; a content which is unique, subtle, personal,
particular? It is in these that one would be most likely to discern
the dim reflection of himself. Can you read the mystery?

Sixth, however long one waits, someday he must begin to find
the choices which will lead him to himself. A direction can be seen
before one sees the goal. How does one find the direction he must
go? Suppose you have discerned within some past decision a quality which is particular, mysteriously attractive as you look upon it,
unlike the choices made by flipping up some mental coin. Take this
seriously! And now as you choose again, reflect: Supposing this is
really mine, which of the possibilities in my present choice is most
akin to that? Or even better, which of these alternatives can advance the quality of this past decision which seems so much my
own? I think this means one ought not absolutely to negate his
past choices in any present choosing; no unity of self lies in that
direction. Present choices ought at least to reaffirm the past
choices which seem to you significant. Or present choices should
employ the past to begin a splendid arc. Let that past choice serve
as the base of an arc for your life; now let this choice go beyond
and above the last. You have been molding the settings for ladies'
rings; are you ready to cast the salt cellar? Or have you been casting salt cellars; are you ready for the more difficult casting of

Perseus? Cellini's later choices completed those he made earlier until his life reached its apex.

Seventh, even where your past choices have been poor, there may be some quality around your act which can lead you toward yourself. Apparently, one cannot affirm every past choice he has made, but one can nonetheless ofttimes affirm their spirit. Then in some past choice now seen to be misguided, you may yet find much in the quality of the act — the intent, the motive, the expected use, the spirit — which should be retained and which may furnish a clue to the meaning of one's self. If it is a spirit of adventure, how important to preserve that in later acts!

Eighth, in all of this we are holding out for a certain kind of goal. What kind of goal? In discussing a far different question do you remember Aristotle holding that a work of art has proper unity when it is so arranged that one cannot disturb any part without affecting the quality of the whole? One cannot remove this musical phrase or that, one cannot remove this character from the plot, or this scene from the act, without disturbing (should these have merit) the quality, the meaning, the coherence of the whole. If the musical phrase be omitted, the character or scene left out, without injury to the whole, these things should be done. If they can be omitted, they do not belong to the organic unity of the object. In the same way your life has gained its organic unity if all the parts — your desires, beliefs, ideas, purposes — contribute to the whole with nothing nonessential, nothing which could have been successfully omitted. What you must discover is a unity which will include all the themes of your life, a difficult unity.

To begin to understand what this may be, you must learn to accept even the discordant elements of your personal nature, even the conflicts. In a certain sense you must learn to avoid self-pity. You must learn to exult in the fact that your life up until now has not been otherwise. One can change the future; we have seen that no one can recall, hence no one can alter, the past. You must learn to accept every element of your past: the noble, the despicable, the open, the hidden. Once the past has formed no might-have-been can enter. Face resolutely away from that; wish nothing different within that past!

What I am now saying does not contradict the rest. Indeed, the more diverse, the more conflicting, the elements within your being, the more arresting is the problem of your personal unity; and the grander must be the conception which will allow you to become your own individual. The greatest works of art are those which pose the greatest problems; an easy unity is not the most compelling. So it is also here.

Ninth, one cannot simply *decide* to settle for an easy unity of the themes which constitute his life. One can try to deny that claim, belief, idea, opinion, this segment of his settled past and so reduce himself to mediocrity, lacking the depth or richness which comes from contrast. To do so, however, is to enslave oneself to a part only of his life. And always one must then be on guard; for the rejected claim will rise again, and one's life will be an anxious censorship, and not a glad becoming.

Of course, if one has a natural and easy unity of self genuinely his own, so much the better, although it will promise a rather placid life. Even placidity might be the proper end of life for some. But if this is not the case with you, then know that as among drives even incompatible in appearance, one does not gain his own unique nature, his genuine being, through sacrificing any one. Let him wait and learn, treasuring his difficult incompatibilities for a time. The world has a way of altering; or, since one's world is no more vast than his appreciations, as one's understanding grows his world will likewise grow, and in a vaster world he may even see how these incompatibilities are to lead him to his place, the place of his more richly complex self. Then let him wait with his conflicts for the turn of the world.

Tenth, how well we know the individual, Hamlet, or perhaps — to be more realistic — the hero of some detective novel. We study to learn his motives, what may be expected of him, how he will act. How much less we know about ourselves! The final adventure is not to escape one's self by living within another's nature, any more than to escape one's self by living only within the realm of things; the final adventure is to unfold the nature which is one's own. What source material is proper to the human quest? This idea, book, musical phrase, that person (especially, that person) — these make up the human material out of which one may begin to know his deepest nature. We must seek, of course, only the genuine in idea, book, musical phrase, and person; such persons do not exactly crowd the human scene, but whenever found their gaze can help our vision. We must pay much attention to, we must give the greatest attention to, the "merely" human side of life.

The man who keeps his life free must live with concentration; his total force, that is his total self, must be gathered up and thrown into the acts before him; he must live with energy. The man who keeps his life free must be continually turning up elements of growth within himself; he must foster new genuine aspects of his developing nature; he will know that to arrest his growth is to lose his freedom. If one is free, every association to which he binds himself must allow areas of spontaneity in which he may develop his own being.

The man who is free will allow nothing false within his life, for this twists and binds; he will be genuine and at least semitransparent. Since every situation in life is somehow new, the man who keeps freedom in his life cannot allow his important set of choices to become habitual. The free man is his own standing ground, and has shaped this standing ground under pressure from the materials of his world.

And if a man lives freely he will pour out his abilities, whereever he is, whatever they are, making life thick and rich, not thin and paltry. In doing so he is apt to engage in creation, in making actual some possibility which lies before the world and which no one else, most men living as they do for some reshuffling of the objects already envisioned and created, had yet managed to envision or bring to life. To live freely in the fullest sense, one must go beyond his age.

One's task, at whatever stage of life he fully grasps the problem of his freedom, is to retain that essential complex of past decisions, the total datum which is at once the matrix of his free becoming and the limitation within which his life is cast, and let the complex work freely to become what it can. But, being free, should not one negate his past decisions, alter — since he can — the basic conditions of his life? In some cases, of course one should. Yet it must be remembered that since what one is rests upon and rises from his settled past, to destroy one's basic decisions is to destroy substantial portions of one's self. But cannot one rebuild? Again, of course one can; but the sundered self remains vestigial and still part of one, one's scars. And any self will have its limitations; and any set of conditions will bind, once chosen. And most important life, like time, is irreversible. To exercise one's freedom bluntly, devastatingly, is not to start over (this is impossible); but to start at a later point with less time. It means a loss of time, irretrievably and utterly. The building of a self is a task not of the ages, of course, but surely a task of the decades. And we have seen that freedom has a double sense. Then let one not destroy, by chance or impulse, the pattern already fixed; but keeping to our double meaning, let one as a rule follow his partial fabric out to the "possible" which lies beyond the world by now achieved and finished; and find his freedom there.

Chapter Two

Value

I. The Problem of Value

What is the set of values you would preserve if it took your total fortune? Such a question might cut deeply into the alleged uncertainty about our values. But one can scarcely keep this question separate from another which might be raised: What in your opinion, separating yourself from every other person for the moment, are the "true" values for the living of your life? What, after deep consideration, do you take to be the proper ends for life, and the proper means for reaching them? The question, asked so many ways, has two parts. It asks what in fact you value; and then, are these the things you ought to value?

This, then, is our question. Anyone can pose the question; but only one person can find its total answer. No one can tell you what it is you value; no one else could do the searching which might conduct you to those values which are precisely yours. Some would try to tell us what it is we ought to value. Whether this is or is not possible will become a later question. Possibly we will not find an "ought to be" for human values. Or possibly we shall find an "ought to be," but no one else can do the searching which would lead to values precisely what, since they are yours, they ought to be. In any case you know the ways of acting, the values, of your group; are you so certain that you approve them? You know the values of your early years. Are you so certain that they satisfy you now? You know the values practiced by the world. Which of them are truly yours? If we could come to know the real and proper values of our lives, how confidently we might move with a direction of our own. It is possible to lack this information. And if we do not know the real and proper values of our lives that is regrettable, but not — I hear — unusual. It merely means we have not yet discovered — at this point in our arching lives — what we are in our own right. It might mean we are still what man is first of all, a reflection of his time and place. Should this be true of us, it may mean further that, not having values of our own, we shall have to follow the values of everybody else, even should this turn our lives completely upside down.

If a man suspends the activity of his brain, follows without questioning the values imposed upon him by any part of the world outside, he surely cannot claim to be his own man; he cannot claim to be self-directed in the course of life. He has robbed himself of his own force! That many of us do not know, that many of us have not tried to probe, our values may have something to do with the emptiness we are told exists in modern life. This emptiness, this uncertainty: what can be its source? Well, everyone says the values of the world are changing. One may be sure that this is true, for it has always been the case. The rate of change only has increased, and with this quickened tempo, what men ought to value seems less certain than it has for centuries.

It is time to consider our lives in terms of the values they sustain. Our first discussion had much to do with choice, deciding among alternatives. The decision reached, choice flows out into action. We act and the work of our mind becomes part of the public world. What we finally become emerges from our being in a seven-decade series of detailed acts, and each act contains its mark of value, of what was in fact preferred. At least I suggest that this is true: Every choice we make gives preference to one value over some other. If so, we had better learn clearly what it is we value for soon if not ourselves, at least the whole world besides, will be in a position to know.

How is it that my act contains a mark of value? It is a matter of exchanging one word for another. What we desire, what we prefer, that we value. And upon reflection the self-portraits of our first discussion seem not completely lifelike. At least we had begun by picturing our lives as though they had been shaped and formed by an outer world while we remained passive, yielding material to be formed. And yet we are centers of immense activity and commotion, full of restlessness, constantly making demands upon the world which we expect the world to satisfy. Our conscious lives are full of trembling hopes which may be disappointed, needs which must be satisfied, and desires which inwardly are as strong as needs. Life is one long affair of honor and we demand satisfaction! If our hopes are fulfilled, our needs satisfied, our desires calmed, we generate at once further hopes and new desires; needs stay satisfied only for the moment, and the pressing round begins again. For almost all of us life is essentially problematic, its solutions temporary, its satisfactions leaving much to be desired. Literally, in demanding satisfaction we demand to be made full; but the fullness is never complete, leaves still a void, recedes, and leads to new demands. Perhaps philosophy cannot change this situation; but the presence in the world of such a creature poses, as a real and serious question, the problem of human value.

What we desire, what we demand, that we value. Whatever else value may be it cannot be sundered from human preference. And every choice puts the mark of preference on what was chosen compared to what we might have chosen. But what, more exactly, is value? Let us first of all use the distinctions in describing value which emerge naturally as we talk about it. Proceeding in this manner, these, I think, are among the things which might be said:

Value is *an estimate of importance concerning what should be chosen.* The values of our lives consist of the objects we desire, both things and very un-thing-like objects, too. In the most general sense all that strikes a person as desirable belongs also to his range of values, including things, attitudes, types of conduct, principles, and ideals.

Most men, at least some of the time, value beefsteaks, automobiles, electrical appliances, houses, currency, endowment policies, and retirement programs.

Most people some of the time, and some people most of the time, value prestige, reputation, recognition, fame, positions of influence, and introductions to important people.

Some people, at least some of the time, value wisdom, courage, temperance, justice, beauty, truth, goodness, honesty, integrity, benevolence, faith, hope, and love.

Beefsteaks and acts of heroism both have value. Perhaps any desire translated into words is a value. Perhaps there are desires and fulfillments so transitory, so exceptional, that no words mark them; these, too, would have value. And one can be mistaken; he can desire something which at last he would find undesirable; some valued things, then, are false or only apparent values.

There is another division of which we must take account. Consider our three lists of value words. The first list, featuring "beefsteaks," consists of the kind of values traditionally called "instrumental." Some of the things, attitudes, types of conduct, and the rest, among our values are prized because they are instrumental in achieving something else.

The third list is made up of values which can be called end values; they are expected to be not the reason for anything further, but the end for which all that preceded is a reason. Traditionally, such values have been called "intrinsic."

The second list — made up of "prestige," "reputation," "recognition," and the like — is more confusing. These states of being are desired; they are sometimes used as instruments to gain, oddly enough, what we have called instrumental values; yet at the same time they are regarded by some, and often the same some, as the final end of their existence. And all the time these attitudes may be of the kind which are desired while being found — at last — to be among the false or only apparent values. The status and nature of these values is so equivocal that I propose we call them values of appearance; and try to understand them later.

Thus far we have stayed very close to things desired; the word "desirable" has been used in a modest sense, only slightly extending the meaning of "preference" or "desire." Can we take the further step, natural to our speech, and grant the existence of desirable things, which we do not desire? If we can, then some things we do not even desire likewise have value. This further step would bring us to the second part of our initial double question. We would then be confronting the "ought to be" of value.

Philosophers engage in heroic, gargantuan, and sometimes pointless, disputes over just this question. And some philosophers believe value to be merely an expression of desire; they believe a thing is desirable because we desire it. Others hold values to be at least as objective as the color of a flower; they believe we are led to desire some things because they are desirable. The dispute is honorable; the disputants are capable; and the disputation is endless. It would not be easy to employ the findings in this dispute; there has been more seeking than finding; the game is more like hide-and-seek than seek-and-find.

But the question is much like the one we faced when concerned with personal freedom. Even if it seems less poignant this question, too, is unavoidable. Are things good because we desire them, or do we desire them because they are good? We can make a case on either hand. The good is simply what we desire; consider the variety of things desired; in other times, other preferences; who would argue over taste? But on the other hand if we prize ignorance, injustice, falsehood, do these become as valuable as wisdom, justice, truth? Does it make sense to speak of something being desirable, which yet we do not desire? Certainly the whole history of dissatisfied people shows us how a man can desire something intensely, and upon gaining that thing discover it is not desirable. Just as certainly, every parent has daily evidence that his children do not uniformly desire what is desirable for them; the evidence is made up of an aversion to medicines, healthful foods, personal hygiene, and improving their little minds. And parents work daily at the age-old task of creating a desire for the "desirable"; in the present age we call this "providing motivation." How can this task be understood if the good is simply what men desire? In ordinary usage the desirable does not reduce to things desired. If we are to accept the difference here, if this distinction is not to be avoided, then what we desire may be desirable; what we desire may be undesirable; or very likely what we desire — that is, the values of our lives — would be a mixture of the two. But nothing as yet is settled. There may be nothing to the "ought to be" of value. Indeed, this tangled issue must be postponed for many pages.

More than once a double reference has occurred — to things desired, and things which ought to be desired. This double reference suggests we have a double problem. We must divide the question, and to begin where a beginning is possible let us ask first what it is we value. But we have learned that what we desire might likewise be desirable. It would not be surprising if our search for what we value led us to the question of what, if anything at all, we *ought* to value.

The Values of Our Lives

If we are not certain of our values, there is work to do which cannot wait for any other time or place or set of circumstances. And the first step is to probe our lives, this time to find its value. But is our acquaintance still so slight that I cannot ask you to consider your life with care in order to discover the set of values which that life supports? You might answer that the request is a simple, even a trivial, thing; you might say you are so busy acting, choosing, providing material about your values, that you have no time to reflect upon, arrange, and order this material. The reply recalls Tristram Shandy, who began to write his autobiography but had to give it up because the material was accumulating more rapidly than he could set it down, the first two years of his creative effort having covered only the first two days of his life. Happily, it is not an autobiography we need. The request is simple; and yet, far from trivial, it may be of the greatest moment.

Then let me urge you to accept my simple request. As we approach the problem it may seem much less simple. Indeed, perhaps the most essential quality will be the courage to look within our lives. We may have the sense of standing at the edge of an abyss. Action may have outrun thought; we may have contradictory values in our lives; we may become aware of reprehensible items. But I think it very unlikely that any real horror lies within; such reports have been very much exaggerated. There will be tangles in our set of purposes, a sensitive spot or two we are not ready to call our own, many instrumental values, some intrinsic, some false values.

How can we find out what it is we value? To start our thinking, let me suggest five ways. Each is obvious enough, and yet if we do not know where we stand on this important matter, some time and concentration may be needed in coming to know this aspect of our lives.

First, one can acquaint himself with value words. Many words in our language stand for attitudes, "states of being," principles, and ideals. Note that most of our words have to do with facts; yet often there are values standing by them. The courthouse is a fact; the value involved is justice. The billiard emporium with its flashing sign is a fact; the values are less certain — amusement, comradeship, prestige. The church building is a fact; it stands for many values, all the values of religion. Now suppose to find the values of our world we consult the dictionary in scientific singleness of heart. Open this reference work at random. We see "confession," "confessional," "confidant," "confidence," "confidential." And "confidence" is a value word. We shall try again: "gowk," "gowpen," "grab," "grabble," "grace," "grace cup," "graceless," "gracile," "gracious," "gradate." Here is an improvement! Even without "gracile" we have gained several value words. Once more: "simple," "simplicity," "simulant," "simulate," "simultaneous," "sin," "sinapine," "since," "sincere," "sincerity," "sincipital." Three good value words, and some which are related. But it amazes me that the value words are so much in the minority. The thickest concentration I discover, and not through opening the dictionary at random, surrounds "wisdom": "wiry," "wis," "wisdom," "wise," "wish," "wishbone," "wishy-washy," "wisp," "wistaria," "wistful," "wit." There is altogether too much "gowk," "gowpen," and "grabble" to make progress with value ideas by this means.

We can do better merely by introspection. Consider the institutions of your country and the values which they serve. Consider the plot of any play, and note that it contains a value conflict, somehow resolved. Refer to the all too brief lists of value words given at the beginning of our discussion. You could easily fill a sheet of the finest vellum with similar words, carefully inscribing the surplus on the back. It might be well to do so, merely to refresh your mind concerning the possible values which your purposes may require. In examining their variety you may know at sight some of those which have importance for your life.

Second, what were the values of your early years? The sense of distance between our present state and that early version of ourselves may help us here. And it would be very strange should one find within his present striving nothing carried over from those years. Then let us admit that just as man begins a pawn in life and has to work his way toward freedom, so it is with value. A set of values had been impressed upon our lives long before we could raise the question of their nature. Before our entry on the scene a general scheme of values existed in the lives of those ready to undertake our care. The gentle force of influence was busy from the first shaping our lives into the image of that particular frame to which we were born. For long, doubtless to this moment, involved in our

purposes, in what we desired, in what we thought desirable, were
and are all the factors rising from the past and helping to shape
each judgment. Even now we have an attitude toward the world;
we are conscious of certain ends for which to strive, and have a
sense for seeking them in a certain manner. And we have gained all
this with a certain blindness; for long there was no alternative.
Much of what we desire, and find desirable, came from this initial
shaping. What is the set of values you would preserve if it took
your total fortune? You may find many of them by looking toward
the most intimate and personal portions of your past.

Third, we have said that when man acts values always spring to
life. If we wish to know our values, let us examine the decisions we
have made. So far as it is possible, let the choices of your whole
life pass before your mind in panorama. What have you chosen,
compared to what you might have chosen? Through this reflection
we can begin to learn the values we have been supporting through
the years. Which attitudes give way, which tend to stand in times
of value conflict? By reflecting on the choices he has made, one
may not only discern his values, but learn their relative importance.

Fourth, following these suggestions should provide a great wealth
of value words, and the attitudes for which they stand, somehow
belonging to our lives. But so far they may exist in great confusion;
we had gained them pell-mell, as reflection brought to mind now
one and then another. And yet our third suggestion contained the
thought that some have more, some less, importance in the conduct
of our lives. Then let us more directly examine their variety, raising
the question of importance: Which seem more important to you
now? The question, entertained, will begin to sort these values,
will begin to shape a kind of value-profile. Let one ask: How can
this collection of values constitute a single life? It can, because our
values will be ordered, colored, shaped, by those which have the
most importance. In examining the whole collection I think you
will discover that some of these values are more final, while others
have importance only in making other values possible. And, of
course, this is our distinction between intrinsic and instrumental
value; if it reflects a difference which you find within your life we
shall assume it to be a real distinction. How then do the values of
your life shape up? Do the instrumental values support your final
values? Are the final values then in control of your instrumental

striving? This may be the shape one's value-profile ought to have.

But is it so for you? We are not yet interested in what ought to be; we wish to find the values which are ours. Certainly it is much easier to be aware of the things we desire — they are so tangible —than of the ends we expect these things to serve. And if we do have trouble setting out our values, this uncertainty will very likely center on the ends our actions serve. Now I think it can be shown that the instrumental choices we have made imply some final value. Let us imagine a person who expects from his concern with things only a comfortable old age. This supposes a life with little depth, so flat its passage that room is left for real finality only at its nether end. This man does not expect to stand erect until his final years; by then one is too weak to stand. But even this person wants his things for something other than a thing; he has a value of contentment or security. Now, contentment and security, what are these? In this case they lead to nothing more; they are final in the sense that he wants contentment only in order to be contented; he wants security only in order to feel secure. Even here are final values; but he might have had a depth of value in every day, finality in the heart of life, not restricted to its supposed, golden end.

The fourth suggestion is that we can find our final values by questioning ourselves with complete candor about all the things we have or wish to have until the answer repeats itself over. The repeated answer should be a value wanted for itself alone. In this wise: Why did I volunteer to serve on that committee? Because it put my name before the community. Why do I wish my name before the community? Because it adds to my prestige. Why do I wish prestige? Because I do. If the answer here is that I desire it because I do then, so far as one can learn his motives, he has come upon a final value, something desired for itself alone. Why do I put such intensive drive into my job? For the return, the money, and possible promotion, and more money. Why do I wish this? To be in a better position to purchase the goods of life. Why do I wish this? At last, to be secure. And why do I wish to be secure? Because I do. This brings me to an end, security as a final value. Why, really, do I want to attend this concert? Because all the best people will be there. Why do I want to be where they are? Because people will think more highly of me. Why do I want this? Because I value my reputation. And why this? Because I do. Now, I do not actually believe that all of my answers, or yours, would be

of this kind. We might well have found truth, beauty, and goodness among our final values.

The conservative approach was followed, probably because
there is a danger that in trying to find our values we shall substitute what we think we ought to value. Security, prestige, reputation — these are suspiciously like the list we have called values of
appearance. How can it be that these could serve anyone as the
end of life? What is the source of such values? Why do they
operate in the lives of men? The answers to these questions, too,
must be postponed for a time.

The point is that by questioning ourselves about the events of our
lives, our final values, those intrinsic or of appearance, can be
found with some precision.

Fifth, let us be completely honest in this attempt to find our
values. The way in which we spend our time should tell us something of our values. Then consider how your time is spent. During
the hours of your day certain values are being served; we can now
say that some of these are instrumental and some intrinsic. What
are these values? In all honesty, do we not find that much of this
expenditure fits neatly and without remainder into the listing we
have called "instrumental value"? Is not much of our time concerned with beefsteaks, automobiles, electrical appliances, houses,
currency, endowment policies, retirement programs, and the rest?
Have we not a great appetite for these, much greater than our
desire for what we termed "intrinsic values"?

At least this possibility is worth further reflection. So let one ask
himself: To what extent is my life a pursuit of instrumental values?
Admittedly, to catalogue one's time is a deceptive task; a very
clever person can sometimes demonstrate that even counting over-
time one works scarcely two weeks out of the year. Yet knowing
the answer may be overstated, the question can be put: *In an
average day, or during an average week, to what extent is your concern centered on instrumental values?* Consider the sixteen waking
hours. To begin, half your time is spent for instrumental worth —
the eight hours of your job, your daily work. These hours have
instrumental intent, whether they be to gain media of exchange, or
whether yours is the more direct task of keeping a house functioning that life may be lived there. Of course, if we work not for the
money (or to complete the task) but for the work itself, feeling
some finality in it (this supposes it has finality in it), then the work

is intrinsically our own. It would be well if it were not so done, but is not work done today largely for instrumental reasons and with instrumental intent? It ought not to be the case, but let us suppose that your work is wholly an instrument for the gaining of other things; then one-half your waking time is spent on instrumental worth. The hours spent in eating are instrumental when one eats to avoid the inevitable headache, or to have energy for one's work; perhaps at times eating may have intrinsic or final value; but for harried Americans, one would suspect, this is not the usual case. Three more instrumental hours; the total is eleven out of sixteen. The time is often more, but let us suppose one hour in going to and coming from one's work — an instrumental hour. The total is now twelve of the sixteen. It is the evening hours which remain. Surely these will concern final value, no longer instrumental. They should; but the hours spent huddled over bank statements, planning budgets, calculating how to purchase this large item or that, such hours are instrumental with possibly nothing final in them. The evening hours with friends may be intrinsic but not if one's friends are intended primarily for use. The evening hours at concerts may be intrinsic, but not if one expects his appearance there to serve some further end. The evening hours spent in ways to gain reputation and prestige in the community by serving on this committee or that are also instrumental when what one wishes is this further thing, the prestige, the reputation (and then these last are our values of appearance). But if one cannot find much intrinsic value within the week, there are the weekends! The hours spent in recreation, a small enough portion of the average weekend, if spent in an effort to relax so that one will be fit to work when work begins, or if spent to forget the tedium of work, or if spent on the golf course to break ninety and impress the other three in the foursome, are instrumental hours. Such hours can be spent to give intrinsic satisfaction; but then one could not concentrate so fully on the strokes, the par, the lie of the ball, or the lie on the score card. Even the hours spent in religious exercises may not be intrinsic in their value, as we shall see. The world is so arranged that one must spend all his time with instrumental values? Then perhaps the world is wrongly so arranged.

Clearly, something is wrong with the account suggested by our question; yet it is not so very wrong. Something is wrong because we laugh, and the value of laughter is (often) intrinsic. It is not a means to something more. The wrong lies in assuming falsely that one engaged with instruments must be devoid of final value. But is it not amazing how much of our time is taken up with instrumental value, with the preparation, the getting ready for — what? Our account is not so very wrong. As one devotes himself more and more to things of instrumental worth may not these things insensibly take the place of final values? Might they not become quite the final objects of our striving? And are we sure the instruments of life are not our final goal?

Should this be possible it deserves still further thought. If our desires do tend toward instrumental values, the fact may mark a tendency in the world. We might learn more about our values through considering one dominating aspect of our modern world. Wishing more knowledge of our values, let us suppose a type of man who cares for nothing more than instrumental value — an Instrumental Man. And placing such a man in our selected modern world, let us ask: What will be the shape of human values? The picture boldly drawn — in the manner of a political cartoon — the strength of our concern with instruments can perhaps be somewhat more precisely estimated, comparing that picture with our lives. The dangers of the tendency can perhaps be seen. And possibly along the way we can explain our second list of values — the values of appearance. In the comparison we shall doubtless find it is not instruments alone we value.

The sense that final values should control our instrumental striving has begun to color our reflections. And if need be I shall use this notion in the "cartoon" soon to be constructed even though its testing time still lies ahead. If when the question is raised we find no reason to support the view, it will be withdrawn with apology and in confusion.

The Mass Man of Chapter One now becomes the Instrumental Man of Chapter Two; and to find his values we must ask what everybody values; that is, what is this particular time and place in the life of Western man?

The answer will be suggested in:

A Mixture of True and False Opinion Purporting To Show How Modern Men Suffer From Inverted Values, Among Divers Other Defects

Many concerns are proper to this age. Ortega says this is the age in which everything is done in furious haste. But why the hurry? Considering the matter from a height, and comparing it to other times and places, we may say for one thing: This is the age in which man is manufacturing, processing, packaging, transporting, wholesaling, retailing, advertising, and in these ways earning money to buy, several thousands of varieties of aids to living which were unknown to the most exceptionally elite one century back. More than that, this is the particular time and place in which whole portions of the world have been raising the human level to a new height. The opportunity had only to be presented and man gladly labored to raise his human level. Is this not good? Of course it is. Splendid! And yet we shall show that in this splendid and exceptional age man's values have been turned completely upside down; for this is also the age in which man's life has tended to become just another instrument, another arm of the machines he builds.

This, then, is the age in which industry has made available to whole peoples the means to an existence in which machines are heating, toasting, stirring, washing, rinsing, drying, lighting, perking, cleansing, polishing, entertaining, conveying, and disposing — all for man's purposes, to satisfy this or that whim, desire, or need. Man's life has been altered, and the indications are that this will continue. Yet man seems no more richly endowed with wisdom, courage, temperance, justice, beauty, truth, goodness, happiness, benevolence than he was formerly. Indeed, man today is less richly endowed with these qualities than were those men a century, a millenium, three millenia earlier, who held the approximate position in life now held by modern industrial man. Not only is this the case; a nature lover named Rousseau, a New York *Tribune* correspondent named Marx, a landowner named Jefferson, living at the juncture of this happening, who saw it begin to happen were certain it had happened, would happen, must happen whenever man was separated from nature and surrounded (as we become constantly more surrounded) by the artifices of man alone.

Now what, exactly, has happened? We are surrounded by automatic furnaces, heaters, toasters, mixers, dishwashers, clothes washers, dish dryers, clothes dryers, electric fixtures, coffee percolators, vacuum cleaners, waxers, radios, television sets, record players, automobiles, and garbage grinders. Certainly one cannot say of these that they are in any sense wise, courageous, temperate, just, true, good, happy, benevolent, faithful, hopeful, or loving. They are merely complicated, and they function. They do something, and many of the things we had formerly to do laboriously and by hand. They are then instruments, all of them, the instruments of modern life. And each instrument has its separate function: to pop up toast, mix up batter, grind up waste, emit heat, or capture waves of some mysterious sort to shape into sounds and pictures.

Functions, instruments, tools! And what is their value? Obviously, the value of an implement, a utensil, an instrument — then instrumental value, "utensility," if you will.

To prize a thing for its use alone is to think of that thing in terms of *instrumental value*. Let us suppose, as some believe, that this is the only kind of value. Then here are the values of your life: the car, the set of golf clubs, the luggage, the clothes you purchase, the home you have purchased or are saving to purchase another day. And is not the job you hold primarily an instrument to make possible the gaining of these other instruments? Work yields currency, the instrument of instruments, which can be stored in banks, vaults, coffee cans, and under mattresses.

Man contrives and the result is a contrivance. Even a city with its streets, buildings, telephone wires, power plants, industries, plumbing, aqueducts leading in and out, is a set of instruments to make possible a satisfying life. Then why is life not satisfying?

The natural resources of the earth are most often viewed by man in terms of instrumental values, and used accordingly. The farmer seems so to view his fields; businessmen in oil, or lead, or zinc, or coal so view their lands. The same is true of anyone whose chief concern is to turn his earth into that instrument of instruments. Most, then, of what we can touch, taste, see, or use, can be treated as an instrument.

And if we have only instruments to value, then here is the gash in the heart of the country which is your city; its broken-paving streets, flanked by looping telephone wires and brown-scarred poles, its temporary three-or-four-decade white frame houses, horrid synthetic brick, thick tar-paper sidings. And here is your home; however fine an instrument this home may be it grows progressively worse; your labor and money are needed every year to bring it back to where it was. If there are only instruments to value how we are caught and bound in the effort to maintain, replace, repair, improve upon, our instruments.

But ought not so many instruments to free us? Of course, they ought to do so. But the fact is that life can be fettered by the instrumental values we pursue; and often our lives are so fettered. But having so many instruments, having learned to view all the world as a set of instruments, should not man's life be happy? On all sides the testimony is offered that it is not. Again, this may be because man's life is bound by his pursuit of instruments. We desire ever more things to pop up, stir, whirl, grind, clean, and roll; more houses, cars, currency, fields, mineral deposits, securities, and the like — instruments in exchange for instruments in a great circle. Much of this wild pursuit, which gives our life its treadmill pace, is childish.

Ironically, with so many instruments to free his life of tedium, man's life is most tedious — in some ways more tightly bound than ever — in gaining, repairing, and improving upon the instruments which were to free him. To this mad circle there need be no end; for many there is no end — except, of course, *the* end, a whole life properly misspent.

If there are only things to value then there is no point where man could have stopped and stood erect: one thing being done always for the sake of something else, instruments and instrumental values, yet where is the finality? The very meaning of "instrumental" alerts us to expect something else, less transitory, more terminal, something further, something for which these instruments are intended, something the instruments are *for*. And if this something does not appear, if man lives only among his instruments, if the means never reaches to its end, one would expect a sense of incompleteness, of lack of fulfillment. And this, despite our many aids to living we certainly do experience; here I think our poets are right, and they have been stressing it for decades — the undeniable absence of finality in modern life.

Do you not sense what a lift it would give our spirits to find some moment in which our task is no longer to bend our backs but to stand up straight in appreciation, something no longer just another means, but an end?

As a means is a means to some end, so an instrumental value is an instrument for some final goal. When the meaning of "instru‑ mental" alerts us to expect something further, some end, to what are we being alerted? Obviously, to another kind of value — an end value, a fulfillment value — not the reason for anything further but the end for which all that preceded is a reason. The idea is as old as the Greeks; and this is the kind of value we have called intrinsic. Instruments, we have said, are to serve life — and what is life? Life, then, would have to be itself the compound of intrinsic values, not to be used as a further instrument; but to be itself one's own develop‑ ment, flowering, or growth. The instruments are so many in modern life: the flood of the factories, the arable countryside, the resources of the earth, the whole of your city. No wonder instrumental man has been misled! And the intrinsic seems so neglible, so insubstan‑ tial. Indeed! Yet it may turn out that this insubstantial kind of value is the very ingredient missing from our lives.

Perhaps there is here an answer to the question: Why, having learned to view the whole world as a set of instruments, is man not happy? The answer is that if one has only instruments to value, they are not just instruments for something further; they become the ends of life. Why are we so completely bound? The answer is clear; we have made a fatal inversion and all facts bear this out. What is the nature of this inversion? Does not our concentration on things show that we have taken the merely instrumental to be the intrinsic portion, the final end, of existence? We have thus had no control over the things we seek; indeed, we have had only things to seek.

Enter, Mr. Instrumental Man.

Here is our Instrumental Man. Let us suppose that he has granted final worth to things; he has decided that things alone have any importance. To decide this is to believe that things — that is, the instruments of life — are satisfactory in themselves, intrinsic in their value with nothing beyond them. Suppose we expose him to situations in which he may gain wisdom, courage, temperance, justice, beauty, truth, goodness, integrity, benevolence, faith, hope, and love. Having considered the gaining of instruments to be the intrinsic portion of existence, what will he naturally do? He will naturally, inevitably, convert these intrinsic values into instruments to gain certain things the more. And he has! This is what one means by an acquisitive man and an acquisitive age. Everything is overturned and appears in the wrong perspective. Life is foreshortened, or life is crushed out. And we crawl about the earth.

Wisdom is surely a final value — a goal, an end, valuable in itself. What will the instrumental man do with wisdom? He will extract only enough to yield him "cunning." He will apply himself diligently but only in order to gain, and only insofar as it helps him to gain, an advantage over others in his quest for quantities of this and that.

Goodness is intrinsic in its most exalted sense. But this man's goodness will be the calculated attitude, the seeming and not being most likely to be helpful in his instrumental quest.

Beauty is intrinsic; but this man's beauty will be his feeling of pleasure in nothing more exalted than his success in acquiring and contemplating the most expensive and splendid of modern instruments.

We have said that intrinsic values are the development, the flowering of one's nature. Their locus then is precisely within man himself. This being so, the manner in which Instrumental Man treats other men should be instructive. Consider friendship: One's hours with friends should have intrinsic worth, shared views, a kind of intellectual beauty. The petty posturing gone, the attempt at show — the show of intellectual or social superiority, the calculated means-end sequence, the calculated effect — should drop away. One is willing even to be mimicked; good feeling rises and in laughter one feels his basic humanity and his identity with his friend. But how often do such friendships occur? How often does one pose before his friend? Or add to his prestige and reputation in the friendly circle? Or how often does one hope to profit by his friends? There are friendships of convenience and utility. How many? There are friendships of collusion — relations for private advantage, yielding contracts, profits, or some other needed thing. The man who has inverted values, at least, will have as friends those who can lead him to possess more goods. His friendships will be based on usefulness to himself, alliances for the doing of mutual favors.

One would expect religion to be its own value, a contemplation of final things, a perfect opening for intrinsic value. But the Instrumental Man will make even his religion an instrument of profit in this world or another: in this world through his friendships of utility, in the other through his assurance of another kind, an unearthly kind, of reward. Where one expects of religion *mainly* some assurance of a personal and private reward, religion has been turned — wrongly and basely — into a value no less instrumental than a pop-up toaster or a checking account.

So on through the list of final values; this man will make them all subservient to things. He will reach the final inversion: The instruments will be his ends; the ends of life will be his instruments. Such a man is neither wise, nor good — nor uncommon!

When instrumental values are judged to be intrinsic, then the proper intrinsic values become instrumental. And more than this, unable to remain themselves, they become values of appearance, hollow, stressing seeming and not being. But perhaps we have not been fair to our Instrumental Man. His values may not be completely upside down. Perhaps the final values stand in place with cunning in the place of wisdom, prestige for excellence, reputation for integrity. This would be to say that he has exchanged the real values of existence for values of appearance. He may just as much use his instruments to support an increase of cunning, expediency, prestige, and reputation in himself, as use these things to increase his supply of instruments. Very likely it works both ways in a rolling pyramid, the values of appearance and the instrumental values taking turns in being apex and base of the structure. But whatever the position, these values of appearance are still too thin.

And what is the joy, the happiness, of this pursuit? There is joy only in the novelty of acquisition, and enjoyment only until the novelty wears off. Then monotony sets in once more. This is too thin; this is not enough. At last man, too, becomes an instrument. Imagine: man an instrument to himself! Viewed by others as a tool to gain, sustain, and condition property and things, he at last comes to view himself in the same light. The people have gone away and only a world of instruments is left. No wonder man feels as he does. He lets himself become nothing, and then wonders that he does not feel himself a man.

How, then, can life be improved? We think it can be done by paving the streets, replacing frame houses with tidy brick, passing zoning ordinances against tar-paper siding and running the telephone lines underground. But this cannot be done in full and when, if ever, will it be done in your community? And to imagine that this will restore value to life is grossly false; for this is the pretense that life can become intrinsically satisfying if only we pay still more attention to the instruments. The repair of instruments can at best serve only as the platform upon which a man not bound to instruments might find himself.

What is really demanded, the more basic thing, is a change of perspective, a proper evaluating of what is the instrument and what the end, a re-inversion placing the value of man far above that of any commodity. To say it in other words: the need is for a greater depth of value.

For the heartening word is this: The whole set of conditions making up the ugliness of your community is properly subordinate to man; these are not the final conditions of our lives, but instruments intended for our use. In fact, any instrument which does its work is as good as any other. Has not the expected operation been performed — even by an older car on a broken-paving street? Then it's done. We have our instruments, our platform. Richness has never yet entered life through instrumental values, however modern. Keep instruments as instruments! Don't try to make them something more.

Such is our contention; it is plausible, offered — as we had agreed — without supporting proof. But how much of it is certain? Well, certainly the modern web is greatly tangled, an impossible confusion of values, both intrinsic and instrumental, with instruments very prominent in this confusion. And it is certain that we stand in danger, if it is a danger, of prizing instruments as the end of life. And a plausible explanation, somewhat less than certain, has emerged, explaining how and from what source the values of appearance take their rise. And we have seen the possibility of three arrangements of our values: the intrinsic values may be in control, or the instrumental values, or the values of appearance. And we shall find the value structures of our lives comparable to one of these.

The Further Look

The field of our discussion becomes more cluttered by the page, but not yet certain of our values, we must probe more deeply into our problem. In effect we have three problems: (1) we need to find our final values. (2)We need an answer to the question: Should we accept the time-honored, or at least timeworn, intrinsic values as the proper ends of life? (3) And if the answer is "Yes," then we would need to discover if any given final value is in some special way *the* end of human life. We can approach the answer to all of these disturbing questions, and all at once, by looking to the judgments made by others who have reflected on this value problem. Many contentions have been laid down; so many alternatives have been tried, representing all of the arrangements listed above. Many have argued for a final value. In looking toward these judgments, noting whatever reasons might be offered, we may find help in making a judgment of our own about the "ought to be" of value. We may claim a triple purpose for the new step we are taking.

Happiness

If asked to name the single final value of their lives some clear majority of almost any group would answer, "Happiness." This was Aristotle's answer. Aristotle was a man of common sense, who helped to shape our common sense. In addition, one gathers from the passage which follows, Aristotle's common sense was shaped by the common judgment of his time.

> . . . if there is only one final end, this will be what we are seeking, and if there are more than one, the most final of these will be what we are seeking. Now we call that which is in itself worthy of pursuit more final than that which is worthy of pursuit for the sake of something else, and that which is never desirable for the sake of something else more final than the things that are desirable both in themselves and for the sake of that other thing, and therefore we call final without qualification that which is always desirable in itself and never for the sake of something else.
>
> Now such a thing happiness, above all else, is held to be; for this we choose always for itself and never for the sake of something else, but honour, pleasure, reason, and every virtue we choose indeed for themselves (for if nothing resulted from them we should still choose each of them), but we choose them also for the sake of happiness, judging that by means of them we shall be happy. Happiness, on the other hand, no one chooses for the sake of these, nor, in general, for anything other than itself.[1]

Upon consideration you may find happiness to be your final

---

[1] Aristotle, *Nicomachean Ethics*, Bk. I, Chap. 7, 1097b, *The Basic Works of Aristotle*, ed. Richard McKeon (New York: Random House, 1941), p. 941. Used by permission of the Oxford University Press.

value. Should this be so, would it solve our problem? Not quite, I think. One must know what will constitute happiness within your scheme of values. Aristotle points out how, although all men seek happiness (as he thinks), they expect to find it along different paths. Some expect to compound it out of pleasures; others expect to find it in man's social life — in social attitudes and social relations; still others look for it among intellectual pursuits. Should happiness seem your final value, we still have work to do. If this is the apex of your value pyramid, we need the building blocks which constitute its total mass, especially those other final values which give your "happiness" its special shape. But do not fail to notice how Aristotle supports the difference we have found between intrinsic and instrumental values. He would seem to urge something like our repeated question; the desirable in itself is what is chosen for itself alone.

What other value does one find suggested as the end of life? Better, what value has not been thus suggested? We can find support for almost any value you might name. Perhaps somewhere a philosopher has argued for "fame" as life's final value. If so, I have not discovered it.

Fame

But I do recall one expression in which fame is named the final value. Prince Andrew soliloquizes before the start of the Battle of Austerlitz. The account has an authentic ring; and I suspect the value treated is someone's final value, perhaps yours or mine.

'. . . if I want this — want glory, want to be known to men, want to be loved by them, it is not my fault that I want it and want nothing but that and live only for that. Yes, for that alone! I shall never tell any one, but, oh God! what am I to do if I love nothing but fame and men's love? Death, wounds, the loss of family — I fear nothing. And precious and dear as many persons are to me — father, sister, wife — those dearest to me — yet dreadful and unnatural as it seems, I would give them all at once for a moment of glory, of triumph over men, of love from men I don't know and never shall know, for the love of these men here,' he thought, as he listened to voices in Kutúzov's courtyard. . . . 'I love and value nothing but triumph over them all, I value this mystic power and glory that is floating here above me in this mist!' [2]

[2] Leo Tolstoy, *War and Peace* (London: Macmillan and Co., Ltd., 1942), pp. 282–283. Used by permission of the Oxford University Press.

I have quoted from a novel, but these words have the air of a moment of genuine self-knowledge, and such knowledge has come in such a moment to more than young Prince Andrew. The Prince has discovered fame to be the final value of his life. We, too, might find this, or something like it, to be our final goal.

Riches

Nor have I found a philosopher willing to support wealth, the gathering of possessions, financial power, as the end of life. This is curious, since such goals seem to work among us, and philosophy sometimes reflects into theory the common practice of our lives. I do find men presenting the pursuit of wealth as man's personal goal because, they claim, by this pursuit society is improved.

The contrast between the palace of the millionaire and the cottage of the laborer with us to-day measures the change which has come with civilization.

This change, however, is not to be deplored, but welcomed as highly beneficial. It is well, nay, essential for the progress of the race that the houses of some should be homes for all that is highest and best in literature and the arts, and for all the refinements of civilization, rather than that none should be so. Much better this great irregularity than universal squalor. Without wealth there can be no Maecenas. The "good old times" were not good old times. Neither master nor servant was as well situated then as today. . . .

The price which society pays for the law of competition, like the price it pays for cheap comforts and luxuries, is also great; but the advantages of this law are also greater still than its cost — for it is to this law that we owe our wonderful material development, which brings improved conditions in its train. But, whether the law be benign or not, we must say of it, as we say of the change in the conditions of men to which we have referred: It is here; we cannot evade it; no substitutes for it have been found; and while the law may be sometimes hard for the individual, it is best for the race, because it insures the survival of the fittest in every department. We accept and welcome, therefore, as conditions to which we must accommodate ourselves, great inequality of environment; the concentration of business, industrial and commercial, in the hands of a few; and the law of competition between these, as being not only beneficial, but essential to the future progress of the race. . . . Nor is there any middle ground which such men can occupy, because the great manufacturing or commercial concern which does not earn at least interest upon its capital soon becomes bankrupt. It must either go forward or fall behind; to stand still is impossible. It is a condition essential to its successful operation that it should be thus far profitable, and even that, in addition to interest on capital, it should make profit. It is a law as certain as any of the others named that men possessed of this peculiar talent for affairs, under the free play of economic forces must, of necessity, soon be in receipt of more revenue than can be judiciously expended upon themselves; and this law is as beneficial for the race as the others. . . .

We might as well urge the destruction of the highest existing type of man because he failed to reach our ideal as to favor the destruction of Individualism, Private Property, the Law of Accumulation of Wealth, and the Law of Competition; for these are the highest result of human experience, the soil in which society, so far, has produced the best fruit. Unequally or unjustly, perhaps, as these laws sometimes operate, and imperfect as they appear to the Idealist, they are, nevertheless, like the highest type of man, the best and most valuable of all that humanity has yet accomplished. . . .

Poor and restricted are our opportunities in this life, narrow our horizon, our best work most imperfect; but rich men should be thankful for one inestimable boon. They have it in their power during their lives to busy themselves in organizing benefactions from which the masses of their fellows will derive lasting advantage, and thus dignify their own lives. The highest life is probably to be reached, not by such imitation of the life of Christ as Count Tolstoi gives us, but, while animated by Christ's spirit, by recognizing the changed conditions of this age, and adopting modes of expressing this spirit suitable to the changed conditions under which we live, still laboring for the good of our fellows, which was the essence of his life and teaching, but laboring in a different manner. . . .

Thus is the problem of rich and poor to be solved. The laws of accumulation will be left free, the laws of distribution free. Individualism will continue, but the millionaire will be but a trustee for the poor, intrusted for a season with a great part of the increased wealth of the community, but administering it for the community far better than it could or would have done itself. The best minds will thus have reached a stage in the development of the race in which it is clearly seen that there is no mode of disposing of surplus wealth creditable to thoughtful and earnest men into whose hands it flows, save by using it year by year for the general good. This day already dawns.[3]

The following, at least, is clear: The most valuable goal for personal living is the accumulation of wealth; the best men will naturally emerge in the position of commanding this wealth; the added benefit of rising to such position is in being able to do Christ's work "in a different manner," by administering one's wealth as a trustee of the community "far better than it could or would have done for itself." In this one can discern a value cluster, combining wealth with the values of the gospel, and forming a general attitude toward the world. Is this attitude part, perhaps, of our final motivation?

Pleasure

Or once again, we may look back to the Greek philosopher of life, Epicurus, for a still different judgment concerning final value.

Pleasure is our first and kindred good. It is the starting-point of every choice and of every aversion, and to it we come back, inasmuch as we make feeling the rule by which to judge of every good thing. And since pleasure is our first and native good, for that reason we do not choose every pleasure whatsoever, but ofttimes pass over many pleasures when a greater annoyance ensues from them. And ofttimes we consider pains superior to pleasures when submission to the pains for a long time brings us as a consequence a greater pleasure. While therefore all pleasure because it is naturally akin to us is good, not all pleasure is choiceworthy, just as all pain is an evil and yet not all pain is to be shunned. It is, however, by measuring one against another, and by looking at the conveniences and inconveniences, that all these matters must be judged. . . .

When we say, then, that pleasure is the end and aim, we do not mean the pleasures of the prodigal or the pleasures of sensuality, as we are understood to do by some through ignorance, prejudice, or wilful misrepresentation. By pleasure we mean the absence of pain in the body and of trouble in the soul. It is not an unbroken succession of drinking-bouts and of revelry, not sexual love, not the enjoyment of the fish and other delicacies of a luxurious table, which produce a pleasant life; it is sober reasoning, searching out the grounds of every choice and avoidance, and banishing those beliefs through which the greatest tumults take

[3] Andrew Carnegie, "The Gospel of Wealth," *North American Review*, Vol. 148, No. 391, June, 1889, pp. 653–664, *passim*.

possession of the soul. Of all this the beginning and the greatest good is prudence. Wherefore prudence is a more precious thing even than philosophy; from it spring all the other virtues, for it teaches that we cannot lead a life of pleasure which is not also a life of prudence, honour, and justice; nor lead a life of prudence, honour, and justice, which is not also a life of pleasure. For the virtues have grown into one with a pleasant life, and a pleasant life is inseparable from them.[4]

As you can see, here is a more self-conscious reflection on final values. Pleasure is the end of life; by measuring pains and pleasures, by seeking the greatest long-run balance of pleasure over pain, the life of value is achieved. And once again the final value colors all the rest, and yet requires the rest, since prudence, honor, justice, and other values are necessary to the life of pleasure. Still, the search for pleasure is truly final. Elsewhere Epicurus writes: "If every pleasure could be intensified so that it lasted and influenced the whole organism or the most essential parts of our nature, pleasures could never differ from one another." But pleasures differ in intensity, and in their relation to pain; so we must select with care the "proper" pleasures. And, further, Epicurus claims not only that pleasures ought to be our final goal; we have no alternative; we are so constituted that pleasure must be our final goal, our dominating motive. But when conscious of this fact, we can become more expert in our selection, and thus build a more satisfying — a more pleasant — total life. Is pleasure, then, your final value?

Wisdom

Fame, riches, pleasures of sense; each has been suggested as the end of life. Would it be of interest to come upon a man who denies each of these in turn as a proper final value? In fact, it would not be possible to avoid this man, once one has decided to do philosophy. Denying each of these, through personal struggle he discovered — at least for himself — the proper final value. The man was Spinoza; the value was "wisdom"; and because his reflections may be helpful to our thinking, because no man could be more strongly dedicated to the good than he, we must hear him out even though the passage reaches somewhat awesome length.

[4] Diogenes Laertius, *Lives of Eminent Philosophers*, in the Loeb Classical Library, trans. R. D. Hicks (Cambridge: Harvard University Press, 1925), Vol. II, pp. 655–657.

After experience had taught me that all the usual surroundings of social life are vain and futile; seeing that none of the objects of my fears contained in themselves anything either good or bad, except in so far as the mind is affected by them, I finally resolved to inquire whether there might be some real good having power to communicate itself, which would affect the mind singly to the exclusion of all else; whether, in fact, there might be anything of which the discovery and attainment would enable me to enjoy continuous, supreme, and unending happiness. I say, 'I finally resolved,' for at first sight it seemed unwise willingly to lose hold on what was sure for the sake of something then uncertain. I could see the benefits which are acquired through fame and riches, and that I should be obliged to abandon the quest of such objects, if I seriously devoted myself to the search for something different and new. I perceived that if true happiness chanced to be placed in the former I should necessarily miss it: while if, on the other hand, it were not so placed, and I gave them my whole attention, I should equally fail.

I therefore debated whether it would not be possible to arrive at the new principle, or at any rate at a certainty concerning its existence, without changing the conduct and usual plan of my life; with this end in view I made many efforts, but in vain. For the ordinary surroundings of life which are esteemed by men (as their actions testify) to be the highest good, may be classed under the three heads: Riches, Fame, and the Pleasures of Sense: with these three the mind is so absorbed that it has little power to reflect on any different good. By sensual pleasure the mind is enthralled to the extent of quiescence, as if the supreme good were actually attained, so that it is quite incapable of thinking of any other object; when such pleasure has been gratified it is followed by extreme melancholy, whereby the mind, though not enthralled, is disturbed and dulled.

The pursuit of honors and riches is likewise very absorbing, especially if such objects be sought simply for their own sake, inasmuch as they are then supposed to constitute the highest good. In the case of fame the mind is still more absorbed, for fame is conceived as always good for its own sake, and as the ultimate end, to which all actions are directed. Further, the attainment of riches and fame is not followed as in the case of sensual pleasures by repentance, but, the more we acquire, the greater is our delight, and, consequently, the more we are incited to increase both the one and the other; on the other hand, if our hopes happen to be frustrated we are plunged into the deepest sadness. Fame has the further drawback that it compels its votaries to order their lives according to the opinions of their fellow-men, shunning what they usually shun, and seeking what they usually seek.

When I saw that all these ordinary objects of desire would be obstacles in the way of a search for something different and new — nay, that they were so opposed thereto, that either they or it would have to be abandoned, I was forced to inquire which would prove the most useful to me: for, as I say, I seemed to be willingly losing hold on a sure good for the sake of something uncertain. However, after I had reflected on the matter, I came in the first place to the conclusion that by abandoning the ordinary objects of pursuit, and betaking myself to a new quest, I should be leaving a good, uncertain by reason of its own nature, as may be gathered from what has been said, for the sake of a good not uncertain in its nature (for I sought for a fixed good), but only in the possibility of its attainment.

Further reflection convinced me, that if I could really get to the root of the matter, I should be leaving certain evils for a certain good. I thus perceived that I was in a state of great peril, and I compelled myself to seek with all my strength for a remedy, however uncertain it might be; as a sick man struggling with a deadly disease, when he sees that death will surely be upon him unless a remedy be found, is compelled to seek such a remedy with all his strength, inasmuch as his whole hope lies therein. All the objects pursued by the multitude, not only bring no remedy that tends to preserve our being, but even act as hindrances, causing the death not seldom of those who possess them, and always of those who are possessed by them. There are many examples of men who have suffered persecution even to death for the sake of their riches, and of men who in pursuit of wealth have exposed themselves to so many dangers, that they have paid away their life as a penalty for their folly. Examples are no less numerous for men, who have endured the utmost wretchedness for the sake of gaining or preserving their reputation. Lastly, there are innumerable cases of men, who have hastened their death through over-indulgences in sensual pleasure. All these evils seem to have arisen from the fact, that happiness or unhappiness is made wholly to depend on the quality of the object which we love. When a thing is not loved, no quarrels will arise concerning it — no sadness will be felt if it perishes — no envy if it is possessed by another — no fear, no hatred, in short no disturbances of the mind. All these arise from the love of what is perishable, such as the objects already mentioned, but love toward a thing eternal and infinite feeds the mind wholly with joy, and is itself unmingled with any sadness, wherefore it is greatly to be desired and sought for with all our strength. Yet it was not at random that I used the words, 'If I could go to the root of the matter,' for, though what I have urged was perfectly clear to my mind, I could not forthwith lay aside all love of riches, sensual enjoyment, and fame. One thing was evident, namely, that while my mind was employed with these thoughts it turned away from its former objects of desire, and seriously considered the search for a new principle; this state of things was a great comfort to me, for I perceived that the evils were not such as to resist all remedies. Although these intervals were at first rare, and of very short duration, yet afterward, as the true good became more and more discernible to me, they became more frequent and more lasting; especially after I had recognized that the acquisition of wealth, sensual pleasure, or fame, is only a hindrance, so long as they are sought as ends not as means; if they be sought as means they will be under restraint, and, far from being hindrances, will further not a little the end for which they are sought, as I will show in due time.

I will here only briefly state what I mean by true good, and also what is the nature of the highest good. . . . Nothing regarded in its own nature can be called perfect or imperfect; especially when we are aware that all things which come to pass, come to pass according to the eternal order and fixed laws of nature. However, human weakness cannot attain to this order in its own thoughts, but meanwhile man conceives a human character much more stable than his own, and sees that there is no reason why he should not himself acquire such a character. [This character is] . . . knowledge of the union existing between the mind and the whole of nature. This, then, is the end for which I strive, to attain to such a character myself, and to endeavour that many should attain to it with me. In other words, it is part of my happiness to lend a helping hand, that many others may understand even as I do, so that their understanding and desire may entirely agree with my own. In order to bring this about, it is necessary to understand as much of nature as will enable us to attain to the aforesaid character, and also to form a social order such as is most conducive to the attainment of this character by the greatest number with the least difficulty and danger.[5]

Knowledge of the union existing between the mind of man and the

[5] Benedict Spinoza, "On the Improvement of the Understanding," from *Spinoza Selections*, ed. John Wild (New York: Charles Scribner's Sons, 1930), pp. 1–5.

whole of nature, understanding the details of our lives in universal terms; directing one's whole life toward growth in understanding; in short, the achievement of wisdom: this is Spinoza's choice for final value. Other values cluster around this central one: integrity, independence, simplicity, love of the eternal. And in addition, he presents an argument. The proper final value should be a fixed good, certain in its nature, somehow infinite, not subject to loss by chance, a value which does not rob one of independence. The three values we have mentioned will not do for our Spinoza. What is wrong with these? There is nothing certain in them. To speak only of fame and riches we cannot be certain of gaining them, or of retaining them, once gained. And to gain either we must commit our lives to their demands; we become slaves to the goals we ourselves had set. The man whose goal is fame must conduct his life according to the wish or whim of those adherents whose attention constitutes his fame. Here is the wealthy man, and there his wealth; here the famous person, and there the others whose attention is demanded. Let the money go; we no longer have a wealthy man. We have only an ordinary man when the people have become forgetful. What is Spinoza telling us? The final value must be something which cannot be taken away. Fame and wealth are possessions, but they are not ourselves. By contrast wisdom, once gained, cannot be taken from us. It becomes part of our character, part of one's self. Wisdom, then, can fulfill the demands of final value; throughout life one can increase his understanding, his store of knowledge. Is the argument convincing? Does wisdom now become your final value? And note, along the way, how Spinoza finds some values — wealth is one of these — fit to serve as means even though false when taken as the end of life. Here, once more, is our distinction between instrumental and intrinsic value; here, too, is support for our claim that the instrumental values should be controlled by those which are intrinsic.

Has Spinoza dislodged pleasure as the proper final value? We must be fair to Epicurus. Perhaps the argument of Spinoza — stressing the shifting, uncertain nature of our feelings — has shown "pleasures of sense" to be lacking in what is needed for the final value; but does his argument touch Epicurus' sense of pleasure? It does not, unless to become conscious of pleasure as one's final value is to change all satisfactions into "pleasures of sense," reducing life to pleasant feelings; should this be so — and it may well be the case — Spinoza's argument against the life of pleasant feeling reaches even Epicurus.

Arguments Appear Concerning the "Ought to Be" of Value

Still, we have not given his due to Epicurus. Pleasure occupies the final place, and not only because Epicurus found it so within his life. His argument is that men by nature must seek pleasure. If man must seek pleasure as his final end, then pleasure is man's final value, and there is the end of the matter. If this has to be, then it makes no sense to offer something else as the "ought to be" of human value. And suddenly we have come upon two ways of arguing for a final value. Here is one avenue to final value: Could we come to know man's nature, we would know his proper final value.

Spinoza walks a very different street! The proper final value is the fixed and certain good; fame, wealth, pleasure do not meet his test. Wisdom does, and so becomes what "ought to be" man's final value. Here is a second route leading to our goal: Could we discover the fixed and certain good, we might have found man's proper final value.

Which path should be taken? The different ways would seem to lead to different final values. But let us consider further. Can we be certain of man's nature? Do the judgments of men agree with Epicurus concerning human nature? They do not. Aristotle picked out reason as most basic to man's nature; with this judgment we could follow the argument of Epicurus and yet restore wisdom to the place of final value.

Power

But still other readings have been taken of man's nature. Some have considered man's essential drive to be a will to power.

> Here one must think profoundly to the very basis and resist all sentimental weakness: life itself is *essentially* appropriation, injury, conquest of the strange and weak, suppression, severity, obtrusion of peculiar forms, incorporation, and at the least, putting it mildest, exploitation; — but why should one forever use precisely these words on which for ages a disparaging purpose has

been stamped? Even the organisation within which, as was previously supposed, the individuals treat each other as equal — it takes place in every healthy aristocracy — must itself, if it be a living and not a dying organization, do all that towards other bodies, which the individuals within it refrain from doing to each other: it will have to be the incarnated Will to Power, it will endeavour to grow, to gain ground, attract to itself and acquire ascendency — not owing to any morality or immorality, but because it *lives*, and because life *is* precisely Will to Power. On no point, however, is the ordinary consciousness of Europeans more unwilling to be corrected than on this matter; people now rave everywhere, even under the guise of science, about coming conditions of society in which "the exploiting character" is to be absent: — that sounds to my ears as if they promised to invent a mode of life which should refrain from all organic functions. "Exploitation" does not belong to a depraved, or imperfect and primitive society: it belongs to the *nature* of the living being as a primary organic function; it is a consequence of the intrinsic Will to Power, which is precisely the Will to Life. — Granting that as a theory this is a novelty — as a reality it is the *fundamental fact* of all history: let us be so far honest towards ourselves! [6]

Which analysis of man should be accepted? Does man by nature seek pleasure or is it power? If he seeks power, and if fame and wealth are the means to power, then our rejected fame and wealth spring back as candidates for final value, as natural as any other. This doctrine, not held exclusively by Nietzsche, would tend to bring along self-interest or self-love as likewise basic to man's nature.

Love

And yet again, for contrast, remember how for countless numbers "love" has long stood as man's proper final value. Even if self-love is basic to man "in his natural condition," a different kind of love — an outgoing, selfless love — is sometimes presented as the "ought to be" of human life. In the passage which follows, this kind of love is called by its Greek name, Agape:

Self-love is man's natural condition, and also the reason for the perversity of his will. Everyone knows how by nature he loves

[6] Friedrich Nietzsche, *Beyond Good and Evil*, from *The Philosophy of Nietzsche* (New York: The Modern Library), pp. 577–578. Used by permission of George Allen & Unwin Ltd.

himself. So, says the commandment of love, thou shalt love thy neighbour. When love receives this new direction, when it is turned away from one's self and directed to one's neighbour, then the natural perversion of the will is overcome. So far is neighbourly love from including self-love that it actually excludes and overcomes it. . . . If love for one's neighbour is to be real Agape it must above all be spontaneous and unmotivated. But where does it show itself more spontaneous and unmotivated than when it is directed to enemies, whose behaviour would most reasonably and naturally provoke the precise opposite of love? It is at this point that it first becomes quite clear that neighbourly love is born of God's Agape and is an outflow from its creative life. . . .

Just because Agape means a completely reckless giving, it also demands unlimited devotion. As creative and productive of fellowship, it becomes also an annihilating judgment on the selfish life which will not let itself be re-created into a life of love and refuses the offered fellowship. It is in the presence of the Divine Agape that a man's destiny is ultimately decided. The question is whether he will let himself be won and re-created by God's love, or will resist it, and so encounter it only as a judgment on his life.

There is, consequently, no weakening of the idea of judgment when the spontaneity and groundlessness of Divine love are pressed to the uttermost. Nor does the idea of Agape suffer by being set in the light of judgment. On the contrary, these two ideas belong together, and each gains in depth and significance along with the other. Only that love which pronounces judgment on all that is not love is in the deepest sense a restoring and saving love. At the same time, no judgment pierces so deep as the judgment of love; and whatever refuses to be won by the reckless self-giving of love cannot be won at all.[7]

Nor does this man stand alone, contending for Agape — or selfless love — as the goal of human life. After many battles the no longer young Prince Andrew, dying from his wounds, reflects again upon our problem. And we find, looking in upon his mental life, a vastly different final value.

To love one's neighbours, to love one's enemies, to love everything, to love God in all His manifestations. It is possible to love someone dear to you with human love, but an enemy can only be

[7] Anders Nygren, *Agape and Eros*, trans. Philip S. Watson (Philadelphia: The Westminster Press, 1953), pp. 101–104, *passim*. Used by permission of The Westminster Press and of the Society for the Promotion of Christian Knowledge.

loved by divine love. . . . When loving with human love one may pass from love to hatred, but divine love cannot change. No, neither death nor anything else can destroy it. It is the very essence of the soul.[8]

As in the case of Spinoza's final value, this value becomes one's own through personal struggle; so Nygren claims. And Tolstoy shows us, step by step, the transformation in Prince Andrew's self. Unlike Spinoza's view both of these accounts suggest that help from an agent, not oneself, is needed to provoke the transformation. But even here our "ought to be" emerges from what in some extended sense is natural — or, even, supernatural — to man.

Bewildering as is this variety, the list could be lengthened until our patience had reached its end; and only the breaking point of patience would terminate our list. If you have neared the breaking point, then we have done enough — perhaps too much. Let us turn at once to the question: Can we move from statements about human nature to the "ought to be" of value? This was the question which had led us to extend our list of claims concerning final value. As the list grew I, at least, felt more and more inclined to answer "No," instead of "Yes." Did you not read these claims, reflect upon them, and find yourself saying, as did I: Yes, this is part of human nature, also that, and again the other? What was the meaning of this response? We seem to have been recognizing in man's nature most of all his ability to *be* so diverse, so many-faceted. In short the most obvious feature of man seemed to be his plasticity, his capacity to take so many shapes. And in this attitude I find an argument against moving from a doctrine about man to the "ought to be" of value. The danger lies at the point man shapes his doctrine explaining human nature. The danger is that the doctrine, once announced, will shape the man. If man is as sensitive as we think, this is not an idle fear. It is, after all, a man who will be deciding about man's nature. He will offer his description, his explanation, to himself and others. He will offer it for belief; he will believe in it; if he is persuasive, others will believe it, too. But no theory about man can be sheer analysis. In the nature of the case every theory acts also as an instrument of persuasion. And if the doctrine is persuasive, it may turn out to be self-confirming in the bargain. How can this be so?

Convince us as men that we must always seek pleasure; our thinking so may bring us to seek pleasure with a vengeance. Let it be

[8] Tolstoy, *op. cit.*, p. 1016.

"known" that sex is man's dominating motive, let this become the major premise of every dime novel (whatever its monthly book club price), let this notion be accepted widely within a culture, let the natural human drive be reinforced by theory, and it should not be surprising to observe our plastic humankind beginning to confirm the theory by conforming to it. Again, let self-interest be stressed; allow this theme to be reflected in countless subtle ways — in the structure of our social life and in our institutions; we should not then be surprised to observe ourselves becoming more strongly creatures of self-interest. And so with all theories of this kind about man's nature; they tend, when believed, to be self-confirming. At least, this is my contention.

"The plastic nature of man," not an altogether heroic theme, conveys the variety in man's nature, while suggesting a nature much like modeling clay. But grant man's freedom, and the meaning alters. If man can be free, he would not have a block and single nature; he would possess the power to shape himself. And should man have this power, one would hardly expect to find in a doctrine about man's nature any more than a partial reading of our humankind, including what its author believes about man's final value. And if all of this is true, we have lost one of our ways of moving toward the "ought to be" of value. But do not regard my claim as finally decisive; you may do better than I, and find at last man's proper human nature; but more conspicuous — you will agree — is this capacity of man to take upon himself many different forms.

If passage to the proper final value cannot be made by way of theories about our human nature, what of Spinoza's fixed and certain good? Wisdom, he says, is a fixed good, certain, somehow infinite, a quality of life which remains securely ours. But is "wisdom" unique in these respects? Courage, integrity, truth, the appreciation of beauty, ethical goodness; is not each intrinsic value a quality of life which, once gained, remains securely ours? And is not each of these "somehow infinite" in that one can progress in each quality, as with wisdom, without end? Why, then, should Spinoza single out "wisdom" from the rest? It may be his choice for final value, but must we not choose as well? And if other values will do as well as wisdom, Spinoza has not told us what we ought to value. Indeed, might he not have told us only of his personal choice? Do these remarks close off the other path toward proper final value?

The Summing Up

We have not found the "ought to be" of value. Still, these paragraphs may have struck within us some sparks of recognition of a value, one or more, final for us or among our final values. Has your final value yet been stated? If not you still have work to do; or Aristotle may be wrong; and your system of appreciations may not require a final value.

Again, we have explored our problem, and have not resolved it. Many suggestions have been made. As we sought a proper final value two kinds of argument were discerned in their support. But we could not fail to notice the many different candidates for final value. And we have found problems in the arguments supporting this or that value as the one men "ought" to hold. Here is where the matter stands. And where stand you?

II. Toward Increase in Value

Here is the arc of your life — birth, childhood, maturity, senility, death — the rise, decline, and fall of your personal empire. The early years, as another has said, are wasted on the young. They cannot then be used to found a life on proper value. The final years are too late to gain the proper foundation for one's life. The old man putters in his garden plot; the old woman lives in the letters to her children. The pattern of life has become fixed; the friends who have called already will call unto the end; the favored memories will be remembered; the privileged thoughts will be rethought. At a certain point — even with our claim of personal freedom — life can be virtually predicted to its end; it will change but little in its factual details, its attitudes, its values, its appreciations.

We have values before we think of them, and values after thought has run its course, the natural arc of life rising from a matrix to which it at last returns. Only toward the center of the arc, when we have come to consciousness about ourselves, can we rework and temper the values of those early years (shaded by now, perhaps, into appearance) into a scheme which will require and so release all our energies. It does not happen by necessity; if it did, there would be no hollow men. Indeed, this arc moves so steadily, almost frighteningly, toward completion that one might find his energies in decline without having shaped any real significance for his life.

For the middle years the values given to our being are not enough; and very likely we are on the rise. As we rise from the base of given value, the higher value has its chance. At least, this is what I wish to argue.

But since the issues, left in doubt as we explored the problem, cannot be settled by my personal fiat, in honesty I must face the tangled questions of the "ought to be" of value.

The "Ought to Be" of Value

Returning in a sense to the first part of our discussion, let me make a fantastic assumption about our lives. Let me assume that deep reflection had revealed our final values, and these values were: security, prestige, reputation, and the like. Would not this be a marvelous discovery? It would be the discovery that our Instrumental Man is real, and indeed, really ourselves. In this case further probing might complete the circle, revealing further that we want these values to better our chances in the game with instruments. We might find ourselves possessed of final values without the needed richness, final values which stress only the appearance of being a man, final values molding us — their possessors — into facsimile men, final values keeping us half-stooped with our eyes fixed on the instruments of life. But we could find all of this, only if intrinsic values are the proper end of life.

Your life, we are assuming, reflects the full inversion; and moreover, you are willing to defend it. Now, what arguments might be used to convince you that intrinsic values are the final end of life?

For one thing I could ask you to look still more closely. I could use an argument of the form: Are you really clear that this is what you want? One does count greatly on this, the hope that seeing something clearly will of itself produce a change. The argument would not be decisive; but if no one, having thought long and carefully about the matter, would want to be an instrumental man, there would be some point in asking you to take this second look.

And if, as we have insisted, life is fettered and empty when man confuses the instruments with the ends of life, the question might be put in such a way that the confusion can be readily discerned. This emptiness is long unnoticed by those who have the power to surround themselves with instruments; it is noticed from the start by those who do not emerge — by temperament or chance — as successful instrumental men. The question must make this emptiness, more noticeable in our later years, obvious from the start. The question, then, must be addressed to the long run, to the total span of life.

Let one imagine that he has arrived at the place where, to use Proust's figure, he is standing on great stilts of time, ready to topple, such a burden of time beneath him and within him, that all his energy is required merely to hold his physical frame together and somewhat erect; then, since this is a picture of every man, of the place at which he must one day arrive, let any man ask himself if he really believes the values of his present life capable of supporting the weight of these later years.

The question might be put in these words: *Have I values genuinely my own, and rich enough to support my life not only in its present circumstances, but through whatever weakness and pain I may yet face?* If I try to grasp the whole of my life in a single instant of vision — including its loss of energy, its physical breakdown, the playing out of its themes, the possible frustration of its goals, its unrealized hopes; in the light of all this, the end toward which we move in common — are my present values rich enough to make that total span desirable, to make the effort of living worth while, to make the game — as we used to say — worth the candle?

To repeat these themes in brief, the question of value in life finally becomes this: *How can my life be made significant in the face of pain, played out themes, unrealized hopes, and eventual frustration?* Of course, we may refuse to look so far; and if we do refuse, then all the more likely would seem the recognition one day of a final disappointment with one's own strand of living.

Whoever is not impressed by the question, despite our many ways of putting it, can be offered no argument which would decisively change his mind. One test of our values is whether they match the demands which the seriousness of life will put upon them. We are urging that it is the intrinsic values which can bear the seriousness of life.

There is no automatic guarantee that in sum the moments of happiness will outweigh the moments of unhappiness, the moments of inner serenity will outweigh the moments of anxiety, the moments of pleasure will outweigh the moments of pain, that our hopes will be realized or our purposes fulfilled. This is no counsel of despair but a claim that our final values must fit the problematic character of life.

Now each intrinsic value makes an infinite demand upon us, a demand we cannot meet; at the same time each such demand can be partly met no matter what may happen to us. The fact that we can never exhaust the requirements of such values allows them to introduce perspective to our lives. This is a positive gain. Against such an ideal our partial lives can gain a certain measure. Our not being able to exhaust these values (although they might exhaust us) gives to each of them the position Spinoza reserved for wisdom. They can lead us all our lives; in this sense each is truly final. Intrinsic values, I am arguing, comport with the seriousness of life.

Second, it can be argued that there is something objective about these values, and no alternative to them. How would this argument proceed? Finally, it would be said, wisdom is nothing more than man reasoning at his best, powerfully and sensitively, over the issues of life and the data of the universe. And courage is man acting wisely and with integrity to preserve values somewhere in this world. And goodness is man discerning how best to unify his complex life, or a complex situation in his world, without loss of value. And temperance is man discovering how to gain and keep some order in his life. And integrity is simply man asserting his intrinsic qualities with courage. And truth is the unity man thus far envisions, and the promise of further unity, in the knowledge he possesses. And beauty is man in his finest moments of creation — working out a unity from among the sheer possibilities of his material. These are of course just sample descriptions with nothing final in their statement. But in the sample, note that to describe one of these values we must refer to others. This may mean that in a way difficult to grasp there is a unity of all these value ideas which have grown through experience and reflection during the course of ages. And the unity may be such that we may say the final values have an objective nature. There is a unity of these ideas; but put along with the rest "duplicity," giving the term a fair meaning, and you will find the unity gone, and "duplicity" in conflict with the rest.

Third, if you grant the importance of unity in an individual life and in man's relations with his fellows, there is a third argument supporting intrinsic values as the proper end of life. There is this important difference between instrumental and intrinsic values. If you possess an instrument it cannot be possessed by me. It can serve you or it can serve me — but not both. So we must compete. But not so with intrinsic values. These may be shared. My wisdom does not decrease yours in the least but may, indeed, increase your store. If I experience beauty this does not forever eliminate you from such experience. Indeed, an experience of beauty may be shared, and be more beautiful for the sharing. Perhaps it must be shared; at least, artists try very hard to do so. Your gain in courage will not diminish mine; it may very well increase my courage. Your character and goodness will not rob me of mine. The same is true of your temperate nature. Through the whole realm of intrinsic value the struggle in which we are in conflict with each other is not needed; for such values are gained through sharing. Indeed, one prerequisite for gaining them is to diminish one's sense of struggle and slow one's pace that growth may occur in the intrinsic portion of one's nature.

Fourth, if culture is granted to have importance there is an added argument. The very idea of culture requires that man be intrinsic. It is the flowering of his nature. Let man prize only instruments and his culture becomes derivative and not intrinsic. Culture becomes falsified, becomes pseudo-culture. Having only the products of a past culture and not the spirit which produced those products is to have a quantity of received symphony, sonata, history, literature, philosophy which confront the eye, and ear, and mind as something foreign and external. Art, literature, perhaps even pure science, cannot be understood so long as man is viewed, and views himself, merely in instrumental terms. Let man concern himself with qualities, not mere quantities, and culture becomes intrinsic.

If these reasons do not make the case for final values, the case cannot be made by me. You may think my arguments inconclusive (If only I could know the reasons!); I am not myself certain of their force. Yet perhaps they contain enough to justify our holding the intrinsic as superior to instrumental values. Instrumental values ought to serve those which are intrinsic; and the intrinsic values have something objective in their nature; such is my claim.

Toward Growth in Value

It is time to withdraw my preposterous assumption which fixed you in the mold of Instrumental Man. And now the question can be fairly asked: How can my life be made significant? Or, less simply: How can I defeat the tendency toward inverted values? I shall set down but three suggestions.

The *first* suggestion is clear. If the modern world, like a tribe of children, is concentrating in deadly earnestness on the latest toys, as if these were of final worth, we at least must stop it. We have seen that to have the final values of Instrumental Man is to be possessed as well by the values of appearance, of seeming and not being. How can one straighten himself out, break the calculated posture toward life with its half crouch? The problem is answered as soon as one sees how fettered and empty is the life which concentrates on instruments as though they were the ends of life. One needs merely to take a more natural, a simpler, view of living. It is much less simple to introduce duplicity than to do without it. Instead of twisting everything into a semblance which is not real, let us decide to go straight. This advice applies more widely than to those engaged in the more obvious types of crime. Let one merely enter into his possible experience for the sake of that experience and feel its value depth. Then the germinal intrinsic values stand ready to spring into being as the end of life; for now we are taking them for what they are, instead of something false.

And the point is that only the intrinsic values offer any means for controlling one's instrumental striving. Without the intrinsic values, or with the intrinsic values warped beyond recognition, we have no control. But when the instrumental is kept in the service of the intrinsic, the binding power of instruments is broken. I think this means one will be founding his life not on any preconceived ends without which life would break down, but on the quality of the experience itself. And since each experience is in the present, it means he will be living more deeply, more completely, in the present. To find depth in the present moment, this is one suggestion for defeating the inversion of values which tends to bind us in modern life.

Second, all that can be said by another is that one's guiding final values must be gained through personal struggle. Clearly, no one can tell us what in fact we value; but many, as we have seen, would claim that they can tell us what we ought to value. I now deny that this is possible. Why is it not possible? Everyone remarks, as we have noticed, how the values of the world are changing. Now, when the values of the world are changing at a quickened tempo, this must be the rule: Each man is the measure of his values. Excellent, but then let man measure! If each man is the measure this is not to say there is no measure. It is to say rather that there is no alternative: each of us must decide the important values for himself. Since man must be self-evolved in the value fabric of his life, he must use a truer eye in judging, a more penetrating mind in shaping, the values which are to be his guide. Man is the measure; therefore, let no one force a set of values on your life. Or therefore, do not condemn another because his values are unlike your own. But not: Man is the measure; therefore, everything is proper. This widely advertised conclusion does not follow. It may arise from our emptiness; it does not follow from our rule.

In the growth of culture as man becomes more aware of the conditions of his life, as his reason becomes a finer instrument, as his consciousness become more astute, the range of values becomes sharper, more pointed, refined, crystallized. We can trace this in the literature. When this happens in the growth of a culture, values emerge so clearly that each can be examined and discussed with care and at great length. The values of life, reflected through the human consciousness, can become crystal clear; subtle and powerful values may separate themselves from man's vague feelings of desire and aversion; and from what is there emerges a compelling "ought to be," a world transfigured and not yet formed.

In the present age of change and tension, each man must do this for himself. What happens in the growth of a culture can happen in the growth of one's personal life. Then through an intense and searching experience articulate as clearly as you can the nature of your values until the "ought to be" begins to form.

All that need be said is: Pay attention to the final values. Whatever final values one begins to stress will very likely be appropriate to his nature and relevant to the age in which he lives. In a certain important sense only what is relevant can be appreciated; the very climate in which we live tells us what is appropriate, once one has arrived at the stage of final value. The most difficult task is to learn to lift our eyes from the instruments, and to shear away from life the false, hollow, sham values. From here on let one develop in his nature whatever cluster of final values seems natural to him. Some will have a bent toward the search for truth, others toward the esthetic side of life, still others toward that practical aspect of things which makes the moral values primary. And along one's own direction his potential is also apt to lie. Then develop yourself in final value as you may.

Third, assuming in yourself a sense of those germinal final values by means of which the instruments of life are now to be controlled, the tangled question may arise once more. Is there some single final value in terms of which the rest are shaped and understood? The answer is, simply: There may be — for you. Others have found such single final values.

Granting our total argument, you might still find happiness, pleasure, wisdom, or love to be your final value. Our argument would seem to have excluded wealth, because of its instrumental nature, and fame as a value of appearance. And because power, or the will-to-power, is so closely bound to the instrumental portion of our lives, our argument may have cancelled this as a candidate for final value. Again a value term such as satisfaction, peace of mind, or contentment may occur to you as quite the most final result of your value striving. These words one hears today, as though they marked a final goal.

But we must insist upon the fact of an essential vagueness in these topmost value terms. Happiness, satisfaction, peace of mind, contentment, pleaure: what one person means in using one of these some other person will mean by another. Such general terms are almost like an X to be given content by more specific value terms. What Aristotle says of happiness is true of all the most general value words. And yet the attempt to find a name for the general orientation of one's values is not without its point. There is certainly a difference between the life which picks out pleasures in order to gain their greatest sum, and the life which understands happiness in terms of achieving wisdom. There is certainly a difference between the values of *Mein Kampf* and those of the Sermon on the Mount.

And yet of any of these value terms only a gentle criticism can be appropriate. Peace of mind and contentment, one might remark, have a rather passive sound. As one might say of security, such values are not final but instrumental; one needs them to some extent, but only in order to build from this base more powerful values into human life. And satisfaction, as well as sounding passive, is a term completely neutral; it gives no hint of the decisions about value which may make it up. All three of these may miss the point that a life rich in value is not easily satisfied, not long contented at any point, or particularly peaceful. The ideas of development, growth, achievement seem to me more pertinent. But this is as may be, and for you it may not be.

For Aristotle, achievement held importance. By happiness he meant more than just a sum of pleasure; happiness meant achieving the form of a man, so that one could be happy (at least for a time) even with a balance of pain over pleasure in his life. And to gain the form of man a development of one's reason is required, and along with this a considerable range of values, including enough of the instrumental values to make possible this value achievement through the years. But happiness, even in Aristotle's sense, allows one to think of a time when the components have been achieved and life, its values gained, becomes placid.

This description calls to mind another term, self-realization, which has been used as the chief and final value. The term clearly means that the point of final value is to develop one's own being, that fostering this development is a lifelong matter, that there exists no point where one can stop and say "Enough!" And the term suggests, what we have found to be the case, that final values belong together, blend into each other, complete each other. In describing one value word we discovered a need to use other final values. Final values, this suggested, have a unity of their own. And this would seem to mean that in gaining one we should have to gain many more than one; to a certain extent there is reason to develop each basic final value. And all of this suggests that to develop in final value is to develop one's own nature.

But the value-profile is your own and you cannot put in it what is false for you. The important point, I think, is this: Life is good when it is rich in value. It is rich in value when man allows himself to develop in the specifically human ways we have briefly cited. The word "good" is also used as a synonym for "right"; good in the sense of what is right or wrong is the ethically good. This is to be discussed another time. But when a man rests back and sighs, "Ah, but life is good!" (This does happen, at least in the Middle West), he is saying that life for him is rich in value. I think our lives should be so rich in value that their very richness will amaze us. Since this richness comes (if it ever *does* come) from attention to a cluster of final values, it doesn't matter very much what one calls his absolutely final value. Indeed, it may be unnatural to look for such a name.

I do not insist upon the construction of a value pyramid. I would rather insist upon our understanding that there are values superior to those we have which we might begin to achieve, that it makes sense to speak of an increase in the quality of one's life. I would have us understand what some philosophers have seen: To begin to gain these forms of value is a matter of climbing, growing, striding — up stairsteps in our lives.

Spinoza has every man beginning life bound by the images of things around him; but through the development of his reason, he can rise to a higher level; the final stage is one in which through all experience man is able to sense eternity in time, the universal in all the particulars of existence. Whenever Plato raised the problem, his answer took this form. Every man begins, for example, with mere opinion; his eyes are clouded, his hands are fettered; and if he would gain the final value, truth, from this opinion, he must begin to free himself. He must rise stage after stage, criticizing his opinions, finding reasons for them, thinking deeply, until at a final stage he has gotten through appearance and begins to see the form of truth. Every man begins just with the things which please him, and the things which displease him, pleasure and pain; but this isn't the stage of real value or of the good. One must work upward until measure, limit, order begin to appear; finally, he will begin to sense the truly good. Every man begins, also, with the sights and sounds, the images and objects, which please him; but this is not the final value, beauty. Again, one must climb through a growing appreciation of forms of beauty everywhere, until he begins to sense true beauty "absolute, separate, simple, and everlasting, which without diminution and without increase, or any change, is imparted to the ever-growing and perishing beauties of all other things." However uncertain it may seem to our present power of vision, Plato believed that perfect forms of value, more real than the obvious facts of our experience, are finally discernible in the nature of things — perfect beauty, perfect truth, perfect goodness. And through the power of our minds we can begin to apprehend — can just begin, and never fully reach — the compelling "oughtness" of beauty, truth, goodness, and other forms of value.

We shall work through these three basic ideals of life in our next discussions, but their presence here leads me to suggest that the English Shakespeare did not begin to give the stages of a life. This was left for the philosophers. And the first, almost universal stage is this: bondage to the world in which one lives. The second is the possibility of freeing oneself. The third, fourth, fifth, and many more are the slow steps by which one climbs to worth. The final stage is this: a life the values of which are not external but internal, whose values are distinctly and explicitly human, whose values are truly final.

It may be wondered why I have so glibly identified working one's way toward freedom with working one's way toward final value. I have a reason. Such values are named by words; and while the meanings of these words can be given some precision, the meaning these "meanings" have for you will come from the total experience of your life. Your own meaning may be quite precise, but this meaning is an abstraction from your widening life as you lift your gaze from instruments to discover quality. And your application of these meanings will be your life poured out in action. Earlier in discussing value words we had said among other things that goodness is man discerning how best to unify his complex life, or a complex situation in his world, without loss of value. And truth is the unity man thus far envisions, with the promise of a further unity, in the knowledge he possesses. And beauty is man in his finest moments of creation — working out a unity among the sheer possibilities of his material. What is here true of man in general is also true of you. In the broadest sense, to turn one's attention to intrinsic values is to begin to develop not skills, or techniques, but merely one's own self. Thus it is that your growth toward final values is also the way toward personal freedom.

Chapter Three

Truth

I. The Problem of Truth

And now, I said, let me show in a figure how far our nature is enlightened or unenlightened: — Behold! human beings living in an underground den, which has a mouth open towards the light and reaching all along the den; here they have been from their childhood, and have their legs and necks chained so that they cannot move, and can only see before them, being prevented by the chains from turning round their heads. Above and behind them a fire is blazing at a distance, and between the fire and the prisoners there is a raised way; and you will see, if you look, a low wall built along the way, like the screen which marionette players have in front of them, over which they show the puppets.

I see.

And do you see, I said, men passing along the wall carrying all sorts of vessels, and statues and figures of animals made of wood and stone and various materials, which appear over the wall? Some of them are talking, others silent.

You have shown me a strange image, and they are strange prisoners.

Like ourselves, I replied; and they see only their own shadows, or the shadows of one another, which the fire throws on the opposite wall of the cave?

True, he said; how could they see anything but the shadows if they were never allowed to move their heads?

And of the objects which are being carried in like manner they would only see the shadows?

Yes, he said.

And if they were able to converse with one another, would they not suppose that they were naming what was actually before them?

Very true.

And suppose further that the prison had an echo which came from the other side, would they not be sure to fancy when one of the passers-by spoke that the voice which they heard came from the passing shadow?

No question, he replied.

To them, I said, the truth would be literally nothing but the shadows of the images.[1]

Twist and turn as we may, I think we will not be able to avoid Plato's belief that in our natural state truth is "literally nothing but the shadows of the images." If this is not correct, its falsity should become evident as we proceed. If it is correct, the following statements can be made:

Personal opinion is not truth; although an opinion, gained we know not where and held on grounds we know not what, might by accident be true.

What supports our most cherished values is not necessarily the truth; truth is not the crutch by which one supports his own irrationalities.

What we heard at our mother's knee is not necessarily the truth; this is maternal opinion.

What our church holds as dogma is not necessarily the truth; this is ecclesiastical opinion.

What tradition has enhaloed is not necessarily the truth; this is public opinion.

[1] Plato, *The Republic*, trans. B. Jowett, Vol. I (New York: Random House, 1937), Bk. VII, Par. 514–515.

That on which the experts agree is not necessarily the truth; this is merely expert opinion.

The decision of a court is, unhappily, not necessarily the truth; it is the pooled opinion of twelve housewives or a fraction thereof, brought up to full strength by the addition of business men, working under the guidance of an expert in judicial opinion.

What we read in our newspapers is not necessarily the truth; it is at best opinion, at middling best propaganda for someone's cherished values; at worst a perverted untruth.

What you read in this book is, strangely, not necessarily the truth; it is merely criticized opinion.

And yet always there may be, doubtless most often there are, truths to be found in the statements of mothers, churches, the general public, experts, court juries, newspaper reporters, and writers of books. One begins with this amazing welter of opinion, and the problem of truth in one sense concerns the treatment of this material; it is the problem of what to accept and what to reject. So difficult is the question of truth that it is best to begin by reflecting upon the nature of opinion considering not what truth is, but rather what truth is not.

What Truth Is Not

In our search for freedom and for value we came up against the fact that our lives are formed initially by the world outside. When discussing freedom we remarked that the number of fixed relationships is simply amazing. When discussing value it was necessary to remind ourselves how values were impressed upon our lives before we could begin to raise the question of their nature. And clearly, as soon as we had gained the power of speech — to some extent, one imagines, before we had mastered this complicated task (How do the little French children speak that difficult foreign tongue?) — the many beliefs which guide us through life had begun to form.

There is then surrounding each of us, in addition to the physical atmosphere, a mental atmosphere of scarcely organized beliefs, attitudes, customs, judgments, inherited from the past. It is drawn into our minds as readily as we draw the air into our lungs. It is the "culture" of the community almost in the laboratory sense of that term, the common prevailing point of view delivered to our being by the ages of common men, partly qualified by the opinions of exceptional men. It is a cloud of habit, idea, attitude, purpose, and emotion around us, within us. It is perhaps most like the atmosphere of London, as we are wont to imagine that imperial city, the density of its heavily charged fog rolling among us, sometimes giving way to brilliant sunlight, sometimes exhilarating, sometimes almost stifling. It is an ether permeating everywhere, initially shaping each of us. Or it is a gas in dispersion around us, and the emptiness of our early lives gains the form within which represents the kind of dispersion which obtained without our lives. Whatever figure is best, it exists around all our social intercourse. It is reflected in conversation, is infused in the ordinary premises of everyday arguments, is embedded in our institutions. It is that which the people believes, that for which it hopes, that by which it lives. It is not philosophy and not science, although the philosophy and science of the past have added to it continually. Without question the origin of most of the massive sum of our beliefs has some source other than our own reason. Some of these beliefs are the result of a prior reasoning. Thus, we advance. Indeed, many of the phrases we use, the most common ideas now, can be traced to some exceptional thinker. Yet this "given" is not all fit material for the intellect. For example, it contains much confusion; sometimes it is contradictory; its wisdom is expressed cryptically. It is charged with metaphors which can be understood in many ways. It contains vicious judgments which are as blandly and confidently asserted as are its profoundest truths. It is not the values of life alone which are in conflict, and float in rapid change. The beliefs of men show the same kind of conflict, and are likewise swept by the current of change. The many figures we have used describe the fact that we do not choose our initial mental atmosphere; we do not choose our initial mental life. This was long since given. The other term for all of these beliefs is opinion.

One begins then with opinion. And opinion is multiform; it includes the unorganized, the poorly organized, the polyglot, the half-understood, the almost inarticulate, the articulate but illy conceived, the full range of what can be believed with or without grounds. The world of opinion is the world as we find it including its false causes which manage so long to maintain themselves and command a following, the special pleaders, the façades for ulterior motives. It is reason operating without self-control; it is mind sporting freely and sometimes throwing out monstrosities.

If we could find anyone satisfied with mere opinion, we would find his mind to be only an accumulation. Belief would add to belief as in some historic city one layer of its life covers the earlier, but there would be no unity. There would be only clutter — the refuse of a thousand thousand indiscriminate minds. Even granting that in the refuse there lie also treasures, the one in question would have no way of knowing what is treasure and what is trash.

Some Questions Concerning Opinion

Do you think the matter overstated? Perhaps it is, and yet it can be put to a very simple test. Let one reflect on the question: *What are the important beliefs of my life?* These are not so easy to determine; it would take some time; perhaps in fairness to yourself you should take that time. Having isolated these, examine the list and ask: *What important belief do I hold which originated within myself, which is truly my own?* The difficulty of finding an original idea is simply amazing. It is not true that "there is nothing new under the sun." New ideas do appear; but not often, and apparently not often in us. This means that what we most deeply believe — one of the most important elements of our being, differentiating each from the other — is largely not our own but is derived from those about us. This would seem to mean that we ourselves in this respect are largely derivative from the group around us — a puzzling fact, indeed.

Now perhaps this is not bad; and perhaps, too, the case cannot be otherwise. But this is not the goal we had in view when we declared that we would think our way through life.

The fact of our being so much derived calls for a closer look at the source of these beliefs. If one asks of his list of important beliefs, *Where did I get these beliefs?* the answer, we have seen, is that they come from outside oneself. Then more pointedly, let us ask: *At what sources in the outer world do these beliefs take their rise?* The very question begins to crystallize the realm of opinion, causing its major parts to stand out before our eyes. Then we must consider these sources, moving from least to most important.

Naturally, our minds have not been infected by every part of the vast realm of opinion. It is not likely that the alleged consequences of the conjunction of Mars with Venus act powerfully upon us, although a kind of tabloid astrology continues to shape the minds of not a few. And we know the differences well enough between science and science fiction, although this new kind of phantasy fills the minds of some. Departing rapidly and finally from the knowledge that science has something to do with conquering nature, the reader is offered a rather ghastly wonderland of adventure in interplanetary space, concerning men who have obviously failed to conquer themselves. The word "fiction" is written too baldly on this enterprise to convince any but the least discerning. Another rather unimportant source of opinion within this royal realm are the opinions of notorious and famous people. Movie stars and athletes (I do not say, respectively) have opinions on the highest matters. What they believe seems to some degree to influence what others will believe, and the extent of the influence seems related to the extent of the notoriety, or fame, possessed by, or possessing, the person. This is a very curious fact, and completely unreasonable. But fortunately in recent times the published opinions of such people have tended to channel themselves into one standard kind of opinion; namely, that a certain razor, lipstick, beverage, cigarette, or face cream is the way to social prominence, financial success, and personal well-being. Helpfully, even if we wished to believe this standard opinion we should be prevented by the counteropinion of some other athlete or movie star completely taken with the qualities of a different and competing product. It is a nuisance to be confronted so constantly with this set-to-set salesmanship, knowing these to be not even honest — but rather, hired — opinions; yet we are not misled. Still remaining with the least important sources for opinion, we come to an area of unquestioned power in forming opinions of a certain kind — fashion design devoted to the dressing (one thinks of adding "undressing" or "redressing") of milady. Looking at this realm, as I must, from the far periphery, does not everyone yield to the dictates of the current fashion? Is not everyone convinced that the "stunning," the "becoming," the "divine" are to be found in this year's fashions rather than in last year's? And is not the decision as to the mode of the year contrived by the few for the many in some smoke-filled or at least cologne-filled back room? And is not the rebellious woman finally driven to the wall? And is there not a basic cycle in this succession of styles, so that the "divine" creations for the coming year bear a

strong resemblance to a style discarded as outmoded and unbe-
coming twenty years ago? We have seen time-pictures of the
blossoming of a flower. If the morphology of women's fashion
should ever become a science, the half-century time-picture of the
costume of Western woman would be more surprising (and illu-
minating) than the morphology of any flower. Consider it in short:
We would behold the hair lengthening and shortening, writhing
into coils, falling straight, creeping to the ear; sleeves leaping to
the wrist, falling halfway back, dropping off completely from the
shoulder, puffing up and lying flat; the hemline falling to the ankle,
leaping to the knee, hesitantly rising farther still only to fall back
as modesty and the mode coincide for a time; even the basic
geometry of the figure alternating between cylinder and hourglass,
or double conic section, in a kind of pulsing fluctuation. And all of
this without reason, or with reasons scarcely comprehensible to
men. This powerful source of opinion fortunately is not within
the area of important beliefs; also it is happily thus far nonpolitical.
But, though unimportant in itself, it is a sign of the power by which
the outer world can mold our inner decisions.

Coming to our important beliefs, some of these have their origin
in political thinking; others have their origin in religion; still others
we have gained through education.

Political beliefs reflect particularly well the variety in the realm
of opinion. We have remarked upon the extent to which our political beliefs are a result of inheritance. And we inherit one or another of several sets of beliefs; in our two-party nation, one of two
sets of beliefs. Politician A presents the opinion which he believes,
one must assume, to be the truth. If he has stayed within the general area of what is plausible to his party, this opinion will be seized
upon and believed true by half the nation. The other half will also
seize upon it, but as an example of anything but the truth — as an
example, say, of opportunism in politics, and perfidy to the state.
Politician B has an opinion oriented toward the other party, and
upon its announcement we are presented with the negative of the
above picture — with the white now black, the black now white.
Since there is disagreement we cannot believe that we are being
presented with the simple truth in the statements of A and B. In
fact, these are partial truths liberally sprinkled with a partial and
selective (yet withal, honest?) reading of recent history, interlarded
with charges of policy mistakes by the opposition. As events seem

to prove or disprove these charges, as people become dissatisfied with their personal economic or social conditions, or alarmed at the drift of happenings in the world, the massive opinion of the public — shifting slightly — heaves one party out of office ("Turn the rascals out!"), and sends the other in ("And I, if elected, shall conduct the most complete unsnarling operation Washington has ever seen.") It would be most incredible for us to equate our inherited political beliefs with final truth, to claim that the opinions we happen to hold are, because we hold them, therefore true. There was never a "war party," never a "depression party," among us; yet these phrases have had power in molding opinion. And some of our important beliefs, I am sure, come from this partial reading. And these partial readings are reinforced by the editorial sections of newspapers, and news commentators, with political alignment. The power is some multiple of the number of newspapers hurtling through the presses, bearing the picture inset, and the familiar caption; by the number of television and radio sets turned on at a given time.

For many of us, really I think for almost all of us, religion has had a powerful influence in shaping our beliefs. What we believe about final questions is very often what we have gained through the religion of our parents. Before we had the power of decision, we were in the context of a certain religion. Now religions are in disagreement, even the many American varieties, at least on minor points. They disagree at least enough to be unable to unite. And the disagreement has, at times, been violent. Since they disagree we cannot say that the one in which our lives happened to be cast, is as such the final truth of things. There may be in it final truths; but the accident of our birth could make of our religion *the* final truth only by the slightest chance.

In addition many of our beliefs are gained from the field of education. What do we include in this field? The informal and personal education in the home; the twelve years of public schooling, plus however many more; and the serious books we have read since leaving home — and school. Our object is to find some way of describing this area, of finding the sense in which it is something distinct in the realm of opinion. It has to include knowledge of every kind. How shall we describe it? I think we can say that a community of inquirers has been creating since ancient times a pattern of thought; the pattern has been developing through the ages.

Whether we will or not something of this developing pattern, this shifting, moving stream of thought, has become a part of our lives. In our common schooling we learn "formally" the language in which our thinking will take place, the language we had begun to learn at home. We learn something of the use of numbers; we are introduced to the many fields of knowledge and experience. The same areas confront the student in college and in graduate study; the examination of them (and of the student) is only the more intense. The pattern of developing thought to which one is introduced by the school, it may be argued, is something different from the flux of opinion. The suggestion has merit; and yet once those children fortunate enough to be in school were taught, presumably, that the earth is flat. Surely there is an effort here to work only with reliable opinion. Indeed, there is; we must note only that we have here not a pattern which is fixed, but a stream of thought, controlled and yet in constant change. This thought in its most impressive aspect is called science.

Whatever most of us have gained from this discipline of thought, it has not been enough to free us from the imposition of opinions. Indeed, there is a likelihood here, too, that partial readings will be made; that phrases will be detached from some science or other, each with the crispness and ambiguity of a headline. "Space is curved." "Everything is sex." "The universe is running down." "Everything is relative."

Most of our opinions have come from these sources: our political and religious affiliations, our education, and a miscellany of other less common radiating centers. And even if we cannot point to a truly original belief, if we admit the origin of our beliefs to be outside ourselves, the test of our beliefs can continue with the most important question of the lot. The important questions to ask of our beliefs are these: *On what grounds do they rest? Are they reliable? What is their proof?* The hour would be most interesting in which we inquired for the proof of our important beliefs. This hour would raise the question, to use a different set of words: *How should the flux of opinion be ordered?*

How Order the Flux of Opinion?

Somehow for the world to be "right" there must be a conformation between my feelings and the feelings of those around me. Men

are thus to be found in groups. Men have thus the desire to belong.
It is also true, as we have seen, that we absorbed our opinions about
the world from those to whom, or better with whom, we have belonged. This is inevitable, and the first stage in our growth to manhood.

Man generally, then, takes as his beliefs the beliefs of those
around him, a sphere within a sphere, opinion within and opinion
without. And opinion is the polyglot. A man cannot be entirely
comfortable within the polyglot. The more conflicts, the more contradictions, he encounters, the more does his mind begin to work
upon this material, yearning for some welcome order and certainty.
The "truth" is that in this matter all humanity, and every man apart
has to do, and does, and must, raise himself by his own bootstraps.

But suppose we come to the place where we begin to notice the
collision of opinion; suppose we decide that something must be
done with this untidy confusion of disagreeing beliefs. Suppose we
see how our lives can be shattered by the play of incompatible
ideas. Suppose we discover the forces molding opinion — church,
school, political party, ideology, common sense of the past, science
of the present, trembling portents of the future, which in the periods
when life was of a single piece, furnished props to hold us up, now
tending to prop us each in a different way adding its own twist, its
additional strain. Suppose we see that a man who has no protection
from the gales of opinion can gain no solid and consistent foundation for his life. What should we do? The question is personal
history; for every one of us has faced the problem, and each of us
has done something about it. But what exactly have we done?

Or let us suppose ourselves at the point where something can be
done; yet here we are with the same opinions encased within us.
And still we have the need to move within an atmosphere of good
feeling.

By Good Feeling?

And the great temptation is to continue to accept what we shall
believe, although this is no longer necessary, from the feeling of
approval in the group around us. When we give in to the temptation we are saying: I shall believe whatever keeps me in harmony
with my friends. And this is one way of ordering our beliefs. You
remark that the attitude verges on hypocrisy. But it does not fit
this ugly name so long as we are not aware of what we are doing.

And to be unaware of this one needs only to cultivate a kind of false humility which discounts from the start the stirring of his own thought within himself, and grasps eagerly instead at the opinions held by those around him. This attitude is hypocrisy when we claim to believe what we no longer believe. And sometimes, it is true, for economic or social reasons, what one is to believe is taken as the lightest possible matter, and all one seeks is the view which will be acceptable to others. Where this is the case the word "hypocrisy" is appropriate. For one who senses the problem hypocrisy is no solution, because our question really is: How does one *properly* order the flux of opinion?

By Authority?

Here then is the untidy realm of opinion; and here are our lives. The conflict of opinion has become uncomfortable. Even the child has some sense that not every one of a number of conflicting opinions can be true. "That's not so — is it, mother?" This is an appeal to *authority* from the conflict of opinion. One manner of adjusting to the strain of the opinions which would push us in different directions, is to do what the child does so naturally. Seek a trusted authority, and hold only the beliefs recognized by this authority; or the further opinions which are in harmony with these recognized beliefs. One can reduce the confusion of his life by dismissing opinions incompatible with any one cherished opinion.

One of the things we tend to do when facing the conflict of opinion is to resolve the conflict by authority. We tend to take a political, a religious, an educational authority, and order our opinions in terms of one of these, or two, or perhaps all three. The first grade teacher contains a depth and breadth of wisdom surpassing that of any parent. Ask any first grade child. "But Miss Potter said. . . ." In this age — that is, in the modern world — for some the authority is the church; for others, the authority is composed of "men of science."

For some the authority is an institution. The institution, possessing more length of life than any man, is allowed to determine what shall be believed. The decisions of an institution at least have in them the meeting of several minds, and the proposed beliefs have the advantage over random opinions that they have been adapted through time to changing needs and situations. For some the authority is composed of "men of science." And usually the person who so constitutes his life has decided to admit as appropriate for belief only scientific answers to scientific questions. If not himself a scientist, he will read the popularizations of science, and keep his thought in conformity with these. Where the scientists disagree, he will suspend judgment, or possibly begin to think out some problem for himself.

Both of these ways of ordering opinion are by authority — the authority of an institution or the authority of an expert. But how is this expert opinion known to be preferable to the disorderly march of opinion itself? Do not the experts change their minds, and alter their opinions? But we were looking for something firm. And if these opinions are also in flux, can we rely upon them?

No matter who or what the authority, the question is: *Can we properly escape the flux of opinion by authority?* Can we properly order our beliefs by selecting out of the realm of opinion some authority whose words we accept without question? Let us follow the point carefully; it would be fatal to be mistaken here.

If we have chosen an authority there is a question which we cannot escape. It is this: *Why select this man or institution as our authority rather than some other?* How do we know that this authority is worthy of our trust? Let us call our authority "A," and try to see how we can answer.

Can we say, "I take 'A' as my authority, because my parents took 'A' as their authority?" Really, this attempts to escape the question. It transfers the question to our parents without an answer from ourselves. Clearly, this won't do.

Can we say, "I take 'A' as my authority because, when I was impressionable, I was told that 'A' was *the* authority?" This won't do either; it is exactly an escape from mere impressions which we are seeking.

The only other statement I can think of which we could make is: *"I take 'A' as my authority because what 'A' says is true."* The answer advances us somewhat but only to another question.

How do I know that what "A" says is true? The point is very important. Of course, we can bring order properly into the flux of opinion, if we have an authority who has the truth. But how, not knowing the truth, shall we know that "A" has the truth? And now we cannot answer in terms of our parents, or of something we were told when very young. The question is strictly with us. How can I know that what "A" says is true?

In fact, I can give only two answers. One is this: *"I know that what 'A' says is true, because 'A' is an authority."* But this cannot now be said. Compare this statement with the preceding statement in italics. Comparing them we can see that to give this answer would be to make a circle, proving nothing. The dog in chasing his tail advances nowhere. The answer must take us somewhere.

By the Offering of Reasons

The only remaining answer is this: "I know that what 'A' says is true, because 'A' can offer conclusive reasons for what he says." Looking back over our course we discover the only proper authority to be the one who can offer reasons. This means that authority rests on reason. Clearly, if "A" is an authority because he has reasons, then his opinion is to be accepted not because of his name or fame, but because of the nature of his reasons.

Much is still uncertain. We do not know what is to be meant by "truth." Although the term has been mentioned with increasing frequency we have not yet considered what meaning "truth" should bear. Nor do we know what would be meant by a "conclusive reason." Since we shall need to refer to "truth" in discussing the ordering of opinion by reason, "truth" has prior claim. We do not even know if there is a connection between truth and the offering of conclusive reasons.

But we do know what it is to offer a reason for an opinion. Authority has given way to the offering of reasons. And we may now ask of any opinion: For what reason should we entertain this opinion? What reason is there for believing in this opinion? In taking seriously only those opinions for which reasons can be given, we are on the way to some control over the flux of opinion.

Of course, you may believe there is no truth, but only the fierce claim and counter claim of opinion; the point comes up as we consider the meaning of truth.

The Meaning of Truth

The many descriptions of truth divide fairly well into three basic meanings:

Truth is the way, or a statement of the way, things really are.

Truth is the set of beliefs which orders one's life successfully and is in harmony with all the facts one knows.

Truth is the set of ordered opinions ultimately fated to be agreed upon by all who pursue inquiry far enough.

The first meaning would allow us to regard truth as a discovery, and somehow objective. Aristotle's statement of this meaning might be given in this form: Truth is saying of what is that it is, and of what is not that it is not. And when Aquinas says: "Truth is the adequation of thought to thing" he is giving his approval to the first of our meanings. As Plato continues in the dialogue already quoted he is employing the same meaning:

> And now look again, and see what will naturally follow if the prisoners are released and disabused of their error. At first, when any of them is liberated and compelled suddenly to stand up and turn his neck round and walk and look towards the light, he will suffer sharp pains; the glare will distress him, and he will be unable to see the realities of which in his former state he had seen the shadows; and then conceive some one saying to him, that what he saw before was an illusion, but that now, when he is approaching nearer to being and his eye is turned towards more real existence, he has a clearer vision, — what will be his reply? . . . will he not be perplexed? Will he not fancy that the shadows which he formerly saw are truer than the objects which are now shown to him?

> Far truer.

> And if he is compelled to look straight at the light, will he not have a pain in his eyes which will make him turn away to take refuge in the objects of vision which he can see, and which he will conceive to be in reality clearer than the things which are now being shown to him?

> True, he said.

> And suppose once more, that he is reluctantly dragged up a steep and rugged ascent, and held fast until he is forced into the presence of the sun, is he not likely to be pained and irritated? When he approaches the light his eyes will be dazzled, and he will not be able to see anything at all of what are now called realities.

> Not all in a moment, he said.

> He will require to grow accustomed to the sight of the upper

world. And first he will see the shadows best, next the reflections of men and other objects in the water, and then the
objects themselves; then he will gaze upon the light of the moon
and the stars and the spangled heaven; and he will see the sky
and the stars by night better than the sun or the light of the sun
by day?

Certainly.

Last of all he will be able to see the sun, and not mere reflections of it in the water, but he will see it in its own proper place,
and not in another; and he will contemplate it as it is.[2]

Plato adds the twist that somehow the truth is more perfect than
the things; but this can be passed over for the moment. (It is only
one of the most momentous doctrines in the history of philosophy.)

In one or another of its statements this first meaning seems to me
the deepest nature of truth and the one to which we must finally
hold. But we must note immediately the presence of two versions
of this meaning. The statements of Aristotle and Aquinas suggest
that samples of reality are somehow open to us, and we can compare our statements with the world. This version of the first meaning would hold we have truth when our statements are seen to
correspond to, or agree with, reality — a correspondence theory,
then. And certainly we do try to check our statements. If I say,
"The table is brown," I have attached the adjective "brown" to the
noun "table"; and if in fact the quality, brown, is "attached" to the
object, table, then the statement and the reality might be said to
correspond. If, however, we reflect on Plato's figure of the cave,
one begins to suspect the presence of a slightly different theory
about the truth. As prisoners in the cave we can observe all we
wish, and we shall never see more than darkling shadows; at this
point we are checking our statements against "appearances," and
how can this lead us to the truth? It is not observation, but working with ideas, which allows the prisoner to slip his chains. The
other version of our present meaning would point to the radical,
and human, inability of getting outside ourselves by observation;
in the attempt to do so we find only the appearances of things;
instead of this direct checking of the truth, we must use an indirect
approach. For example, it might be pointed out (it was not by

[2] *Ibid.*, with slight modifications.

Plato, but the conflict of these two versions continues to the present day) how the "brown" of the table is evoked only when two conditions are satisfied: a source of light and a perceiving eye. It is just impossible to say whether or not the table has this quality when not an object of perception. It is never possible, it may be claimed, to check these alleged correspondences. Locked in with our own sensations and ideas all we can do is to examine our experience and build systems of ideas which have inner unity and are adequate to the experience which is ours. On this version, we have truth when the unities worked out of our experience are adequate and coherent; this, then, is a coherence theory of the truth. Clearly, those who find themselves upholding the coherence point of view, believing we do not have access to "samples" of reality — denying, that is, what is assumed in the first version — and yet believing the way things really are can be approached through building systems, must have an assumption of their own. The assumption is: "reality is a system, completely ordered and fully intelligible, with which thought in its advance is more and more identifying itself." [3] If this is so, then the more adequate, the more coherent, the system, the greater will be its degree of truth. Going beyond most of those who stressed coherence, Plato believed the "really" real to be an ideal world, at least in part open to our minds, a world of forms standing as exemplar to the half-real world available to our senses. Most advocates of coherence would not so sharply separate the real world from the appearances known to us.

In any of its forms the devotee of correspondence can make his own objection. For example, he might point to the many systems of ideas which have been constructed — with inner unity — and which yet have been judged to be false. He might refer to the many systems of geometry, different in nature by virtue of different initial assumptions, as evidence for believing mere unity, coherence, consistency, to be an insufficient test of the way things really are.

Now, of course, both of these things — correspondence to fact, and coherence in thought — are employed by us in our thinking. For simple statements we probably do try to gain a direct check of correspondence with the fact, or with reality, despite the objection which has been made. And for our more complex kinds of statement, our explanations and theories, we are more concerned with their relations, with the *system* of ideas making up these statements; and we are not able in any case to compare such statements with reality; but even here through intermediate steps we do try in most cases to gain evidence which would allow us to decide about the agreement between these statements and the reality which lies beyond them.

It is only a matter of emphasis which allowed us to relate Aristotle to the correspondence view, and Plato to the coherence version. In a general sense one can claim a stress on coherence for those philosophers emphasizing reason, men such as Descartes, Spinoza, Leibniz. And in a similar manner philosophers stressing observation, the empiricists, can be claimed for correspondence; men such as Locke, Berkeley in his way, and Hume. But these philosophers, and most others, would employ both emphases, and so do we. The case for keeping these as separate paths to truth is not altogether clear. But the objections raised by each against the other are important, and will plague us in the sequel.

On either version, or even granting both, our problem is not settled; we cannot be certain, it would seem, of any given correspondence; and the finally adequate and coherent system of thought is not available. There are difficulties standing in the way of this meaning, however it is taken.

It is all very well to think of truth as the way things really are. As a man it is my right to know; but how can I know this way? If I try to adjust myself always more closely to the opinions of experts, must I not know that these opinions will shift and be different in another day? In fact, the more deeply I consider the matter, must I not begin to distrust the experts as purveyors of final truth? I must. I will not be able to avoid seeing how beautiful theories, able to sustain themselves a thousand years, are at last swept away. Even age and venerability — perhaps, age and venerability, especially — are no guarantors of truth. And where will this leave me? If I am convinced that every matter has its final truth must I sift for myself the mountains of data on every topic? The modern embarrassment of riches here presents itself. The quest for truth which began several thousand years ago in the life of Western man has been so successful that no man and no single organized group of men can retain in their minds the knowledge which has been amassed. Even if one's local library is several cuts below the average in the number and variety of its books, one could not read his way through all of the books concerning knowledge on its shelves. If I try to sift for myself the mountains of data on any single topic, must I not know that the limitations of my energy, time, patience, and intelligence will make this impossible, even if I decide to become a professor, all my life sifting the ashes of the past?

And if I should some day meet a final truth, what label would it bear? How would I know it? How could I understand that at last I had broken through? I could know only this: The idea before me seems to work; I know of no objection to it; it seems cogent; it fits all the facts known to me; it is in harmony with other ideas which seem to qualify in these ways. But this has been the case with other so-called truths, cast off through the centuries.

These considerations account for the persuasiveness of our second meaning for truth.

Truth is the set of beliefs which orders one's life successfully, and is in harmony with all the facts one knows. The second meaning holds truth to be an adjustment to the world. Truth is what Associate Justice Holmes can't help thinking, even though his "can't helps" aren't necessarily cosmic. When William James said, "The true, to put it very briefly, *is only the expedient in the way of our thinking, just as the right is only the expedient in the way of our behaving,*" he was plumping for this second meaning. When anyone says "truth is what works" he is uttering an abbreviated, and perhaps dilute, version of this meaning.

And the view is very persuasive. Consider, again, the theories about the world, holding sway for so long, and then in a sudden reordering of ideas, being completely overthrown. If the view of Ptolemy could hold its position as the truth about our solar system for a thousand years, and then be reduced to utter discredit, how can we suppose that any theory, seeming so obviously true today, may not in a thousand years, or a day, be overturned?

If this may be so, why not just say baldly that truths will be replaced by other truths, that truth is only the way of holding together the facts as we see them, that truths are temporary and destined to be outworn, outrun, discarded, and replaced? Because of its simplicity and its neatness in cutting the knot of human uncertainty this view is highly tempting. And yet several considerations of weight stand in the way of our acceptance.

If the view should be accepted, the statement, "Truths are temporary," would be a truth not to be swept away. And this would seem to add to the "displaceable truths" some permanent truths about the nature of things.

Again, if truth is the set of beliefs harmonized internally and in harmony with the facts we know then two different people may have harmonized their beliefs in such a manner that these beliefs are exactly opposite to each other. It does not seem possible for truths to be in inner conflict, yet this view would allow such conflicts. If we accept this view of truth we should be able to admit a certain view of the world — for example, that it is flat — as true for large segments of society during the Middle Ages, while asserting today the truth that the earth is a sphere, flattened at the poles. But surely this cannot mean that the earth, like an inflating basketball, became a sphere. The touch of common sense, "It was one way all along," carries us back toward the first meaning of truth. The second meaning does not really explain error. All the errors of mankind on this view were, when announced and believed in, truths.

Once again, when we think of the overturn of theories able to stand a thousand years, the favorite example of this is Ptolemy. And it is not quite fair to rest so much on a single, even if persuasive, case. Behind Ptolemy stood the authority of Aristotle; and the massive structure of medieval thought, including its theology, provided considerable support for both. In a sense the Copernican revolution brought science back to a different set of principles which had also been suggested by the Greeks. The historical problem is very complicated. But it is fair to suggest, at least, the nontypical nature of this favorite case. Normally a scientific point of view, once established, remains valid; in the light of later discoveries the theory is merely specialized, adjusted to the new ideas, taking its place as a special case; or limitations are placed around its range of applicability. Even so, the possibility of overthrow is haunting; and the possible need for later adjustment requires us to hold that no achieved point of view can be regarded as a final truth.

Further, consider this meaning for truth in personal terms: Suppose that statements have been made about yourself with respect to a given matter in which you sincerely did a given thing. The statements are: "He was deceitful in this matter and a demagogue," and "He was sincere in what he did." Are these statements equally true if they equally harmonize the beliefs of those who hold them? If the statement made by one person, e.g., you are a demagogue, is such that it harmonizes his ideas of you workably, do you regard this judgment as true as any other? This would be the case on the view we are considering.

Finally, consider the last part of our present meaning. There is a problem in the statement that truth is *in harmony with all the facts one knows*. The problem is: What is the nature of a fact? Is it, too, a belief in harmony with our other beliefs? If it is, then the view is indeed disjoined from the world, and we have only beliefs within beliefs. But if the fact is, as is suggested, something other than the beliefs, something of which the beliefs must take account; if the facts are somehow samples of the way things really are, then our second meaning requires the first to some extent.

It is evident that this view, too, does not avoid all difficulties; its failure to stand up satisfactorily brings us to a third meaning for truth.

Truth is the set of ordered opinions ultimately fated to be agreed upon by all who pursue inquiry far enough. This view would have all thinking start with the material of opinion. At any particular time, it would insist, final truths cannot be distinguished from the opinions which must some day be discarded. At the same time, it would hold, the purpose of inquiry is to find the way things really are, and things really are some way or other. It would hold inquiry to be self-corrective, the errors of inquiry subject to correction by further inquiry, and it would hold that, given enough time and search, the way things really are can be found out, and men can agree upon their being that way and no other. This meaning for truth does not push all truth off into the future. For some questions, perhaps for things near at hand, the "far enough" of inquiry may not be very far; for some questions we may need only to open our eyes and look. For other questions generation upon generation of patient inquiry may be required.

This meaning, then, — the contribution of Charles Peirce, American philosopher — includes within it the positive content of the first two meanings; on this view we are committed to working our way through the shifting substance of opinion; and we are also committed to objective truth as our final goal. The two are related by the contention that the first leads, or at least can lead, to the second; the testing of opinion, then, has direction. And this contention seems to require an element of faith. In a certain sense there is faith in this point of view, and yet I think it can be shown that thought itself cannot but require final truth. Let one say "There is no truth," or "There is no truth available to man," and he has caught himself expressing what he takes to be the truth, one which he is helping to make available to man. Is truth ever gained? One should consider a long time before answering "No" to this question. If I say "Truth is never gained" I am committed to believing in the statement, and in defiance of the very statement I have gained what I believe to be a truth. To affirm anything, to deny anything, is to believe in some truth about one's affirmation and denial. Whenever, then, we insist upon passing judgment the question of truth arises; commitment to final truth, it would seem, is implicit in all our discourse. If this commitment is unavoidable, the faith that truth can be found by inquiry is not an extreme faith.

If the third meaning includes the strengths of the other two, while avoiding their difficulties, it is a meaning for truth which is more acceptable than its predecessors. I incline to accept this meaning.

Having committed myself, in modest fashion, it would be a great relief to be able to find a bald statement of some final truth, however this might strike against my prized, protected thoughts. Had I taken the second meaning then any set of workable beliefs religious, scientific, lightly held or deeply opinionated, could have been called true. But we have discovered grave problems within this second meaning. The problem of the third meaning is that truth, while the end of inquiry, remains highly problematic, inscrutable, to us. The question is: Can final truth be found through inquiry?

And the question requires us to consider what is involved in the offering of reasons for an opinion.

The Offering of Reasons

Let us take a very uncomplicated opinion: for example, "Mr. Jones is an honest man." If I have exhausted myself in uttering the simple opinion, the assertion lays no claim upon your person in the way of belief. But if I say, "My reasons for saying this are the following: (1) Mr. Jones found a $100 bill on the street last winter. He could have merely put it in his pocket, but he registered his find with the police; it was properly advertised; and only when no one claimed the bill was Mr. Jones willing to accept it. (2) Last spring when Mr. Jones received the refund from his income tax he discovered that the federal officials had misread the figures on his tax form and had sent him a check too large by $500. Mr. Jones immediately contacted the bureau and returned the sum which was in error. (3) Last summer when Mr. Jones bought his ticket for the firemen's picnic the treasurer gave him change for a ten dollar bill. Mr. Jones quickly pointed out that he had tendered only a one dollar bill, and received the correct change. (4) During the autumn floods when law and order broke down and many prominent citizens were engaged in looting the village stores, Mr. Jones almost single-handedly organized the citizens' group which patrolled the business district and stopped the looting; this he did even though he has no connection with any of the village stores. (5) Mr. Jones' name has often come up in conversation with other residents of the village. I have talked to all of them at some time or another. It is the opinion of everyone in the village that Mr. Jones is as honest as the year is long."

The example is absurdly simple. And the year-round honesty of Mr. Jones may be beyond the rest of us. The point is: Consider the tremendous claim laid upon us by these reasons, all converging toward belief in Mr. Jones' honesty! Could we bring ourselves on this evidence to believe in the dishonesty of Mr. Jones?

But suppose yourself to be already possessed of a belief in Mr. Jones' dishonesty. You cannot now establish this opinion merely by claiming, "Oh no, he isn't particularly honest." You must also face these reasons; if you cannot advance counterreasons supporting Mr. Jones' lack of honesty, your silence is an admission that you have no reason to withhold belief.

In short, to advance reasons, to expect them, to require them, makes an immediate change in the realm of opinion. The opinion stands not alone but with its reasons. The opinion cannot be simply denied; instead, before it can be denied the reasons must be demolished by counterreasons, or you must show the reasons to be inaccurate, or that these things could have happened and still it would not follow that Mr. Jones is honest.

By taking every asserted opinion as a conclusion and asking for the reasons which support this conclusion, we have a method for testing opinion. The method was first given a definite form, certainly it had its first dramatic embodiment, in the person and work of Socrates. The heart of the famed Socratic method might be put in these words: *Let all ideas be tested; begin anywhere with anyone from a slave boy or a Sophist to a poet or a politician. The weak ideas will not stand up; the strong will survive your most pointed objections.*

When man begins to require a reason, method appears in the realm of opinion. Some opinions will not stand this test. We shall find some expressed opinions with no reasons to support them; of these opinions we have the right to be very skeptical. We shall find the reasons given for some opinions not in fact supporting those opinions, but some other; we have the right, then, to modify these opinions into some other which the reasons will support. We shall find some opinions supported by reasons which, when examined, are found to be false; if they are reasons which may be tested by observation, then in observing we may discover that the world does not operate in this, but in some other way. The discovery will very likely require us to modify both the opinion and the reasons. If we are to dispose of a belief supported by a reason, we must first dispose of the reason, perhaps by a counterreason. The counterreason, if strong enough to dispose of the initial belief, will suggest a more adequate belief. It will be more adequate in the sense that a false reason has been demolished, and we have taken account of a counterreason. Repeated objections and reshaping can lead us to an opinion which will stand against objections. An opinion can be gained which meets the objections known to us and those around us. This criticized opinion, it is our claim, will be more reliable than the opinions discarded along the way. But, it must be admitted, we work from the inside, and never get outside.

This method, as simple as it is effective, can obviously help us in ordering and testing beliefs in the realm of opinion. However, it can do this for us only if we are willing to grant to the results of inquiry power in shaping what we shall believe. If we continue to believe only what it is our custom to believe, what those around us believe, what an unquestioned authority believes, then searching criticism is impossible, and taking thought an idle game. The method is helpful only if we recognize that we have a moral obligation to believe, all things considered, what survives our most pointed objections.

In the case of Mr. Jones it was possible to say earlier only that we had no reason to withhold belief in his honesty. Now we have seen more clearly what is involved, and can say: If in the case of Mr. Jones the reasons stand and no counterreasons can be offered, we are obliged to believe in his honesty. Only by taking the results of inquiry seriously have those results the chance of being molded more and more into the likeness of truth.

And yet what we must here *take to be* the truth cannot be known *to be* the final truth about Mr. Jones. Mr. Jones will probably live a good deal longer, and the future is not yet part of the evidence. We could date our opinion, and say it is true of Mr. Jones at this time, but this would not turn our argument into final truth. Without any intent to malign the village's most respected citizen, it is remotely possible that Mr. Jones' honesty is an appearance; he might be beaming atomic secrets to a foreign power through a powerful transmitter in his attic. And he might require a shining reputation to cover this dishonest work. The problem of the finality of our apparently true conclusions is still with us.

We must then admit that what survives our most pointed objections may not be the final truth of anything; but is it not on the way to truth? Has not the prisoner by now slipped his bonds? He has learned, at least, to do something with the untidy flux of opinion. He may not have reached the final truth; but will he not have something more substantial than a shadow?

We have gained a most odd result; we can be committed to believing something which we cannot know to be the final truth. How did this come about? It is really a statement of our current embarrassment, and it comes about in this way: (1) We are committed to a method of ordering opinion which gives us confidence that we can distinguish the more from the less reliable opinion. (2) We are committed to a view which includes the notion of final truth. Each commitment is sensible enough. But we have found no way of moving from the first commitment to the second, no way of equating an opinion, however reliable, with final truth.

We can think out a pattern of ideas allowing us to believe in the honesty of Mr. Jones. But final truth would have certainty within it; and the pattern of thought pertaining to Mr. Jones is not, as we have seen, completely certain. There is no difficulty in arriving at conclusions which are absolutely certain; but there is great difficulty in gaining absolutely certain conclusions about the way things really are. In the case of Mr. Jones we had put together from experience an informal kind of pattern leading to a conclusion about our subject. If we want our conclusions to be certain, we need merely construct a formal pattern out of our heads in such a way that we can get from one part of it to another.

Suppose we decided on a scheme such that when any two parts of the scheme were put together it would yield a third. A and B together yield C; B and C together yield D; D and E together yield F. We do not have this situation, but one something like it, in arithmetic; 1 and 2 together yield 3; 2 and 3 yield 5; 3 and 4 yield 7; we can make an unlimited number of inferences in this scheme where any two numbers yield a third. The result is completely certain because the scheme is formal, and so constructed that it will allow these conclusions. Keep to the rules, and you have conclusions which are certain! At the same time this scheme, like the other, is not about the world in any obvious way. Such absolutely certain conclusions are possible in any system of geometry, and in every part of the field of mathematics. But it would be very puzzling were someone to say that these conclusions are the final truth of things.

What we want is both information and certainty. And the difficulty with final truth lies in the fact that the formal scheme belongs to man while the world is not, in the same sense, his construction.

Where then can we look for final truth? Science, certainly, in the eyes of most of us is thought to have a way — obscure to the uninitiated — of revealing more and more of the basic nature of things. And just as certainly most people, if asked on what final truth their lives rest, would answer in religious terms. Even though the developing pattern of thought which becomes science is in constant change, and even though it is by chance that our lives are cast in this religion rather than another, is not our most promising question this: How do science and religion stand with respect to final truth?

Science and Final Truth

This part of our question is indeed forbidding. It would be hopeless to attempt to answer without delimiting the field of our discussion. Then let us confine our attention to the foundation sciences, to those sciences having a history of development, and with their procedures well established. And let us ask: What kind of interest has science, so delimited, in nature?

Judging by their results the scientists involved are interested (1) in time, mass, position, velocity, pressure, volume, temperature, force, energy, wave length, and electric charge. They are interested (2) in establishing these properties with respect to solid bodies, gases, molecules, atoms, protons, mesons, electrons, neutrons, and

photons. Of course the case is not so simple. The real secret is that
(3) they are interested in measurement; or, more accurately, they
are interested in patterns of thought based on measurement. The
properties mentioned above are measurable, and so are of interest
to science. One could say with a fair chance of upholding the
saying: If the operation does not yield numerical values it is not
of interest to science. But (4) the purely scientific factor does not
lie in merely accumulating numbers, but in gaining formulae. The
formulae are general shapes, relations among the items on our first
list, and relations of such a kind that they are implicitly mathematical. That is, (5) when the X's, Y's, P's, V's T's, E's, etc. (which
stand for the properties of the first list) in the formulae are replaced
by the appropriate numerical values, an equation results which
allows a new numerical value as its solution. And the point is
so to relate these first five elements that significant numerical relations can be achieved; and the point of such relations is (6) the
gaining of inferences which are themselves significant, for science
is the triumph of successful inference.

We have twice used the word "significant." Its meaning is different in each usage. To relate numbers significantly is to relate them
in such a way that mathematical work can be done with them; to
relate them in such fashion that in working with this relation one is
within the bounds of some recognized part of the field of mathematics. Something can then be done with this relation; there will be
mathematical procedures by which additional values can be derived. These values will be derived by some formula capable of
extending the discovered proportion to additional numerical relations. To gain any inference one must have a system through which
the reasoning can travel. This system is provided in part by the
number system, letters of the alphabet, and the relevant procedures
of mathematics from ordinary arithmetic through algebra to the
differential, integral, and probability calculus. But the elements of
the formulae must be more than mathematically significant. This
brings us to our second use of the word "significant." The X's, Y's,
P's, V's, T's, and E's must have an extramathematical meaning in
order to allow inferences which will concern something more than
a formal scheme. The additional meanings, contributing to the
system through which inference will travel, are the items in the
first of our foregoing lists: time, mass, position, momentum, velocity,
pressure, volume, temperature, force, energy, wave length, and

electric charge. More exactly, it is some combination of these items which fuse into something more than a formal scheme. If the system is concerned with gases the items of interest are pressure, volume, temperature. In studying the smaller components of our second list, interest centers on energy, wave length, electric charge, heat content, entropy. The relevant items are held together by some discovered proportion, a relational shape, a theory or law — in short, a formula which can be regularly filled in to allow inferences which are significant in our second sense. Given numerical values for these items at one time, or in one state of the system, the values in another state, or at another time, can be inferred. In addition, time and position have a special importance in establishing the framework within which the calculation will take place.

The question leading us through these remarks has been: Has science the final truth? We meant by final truth a statement of the way things really are, an expression which would need no correction at a later time. And we had said that men must work toward this goal from opinion through the self-corrective process of inquiry. The various scientific enterprises show every indication of using a self-corrective process. Yet implicit in what we have said about science is the recognition that the science of our present day does not possess the final truth. There is nothing surprising in saying this. And many reasons can be given to support the contention.

The Formal Scheme and What It Is About

The very fact of a difference between the formal scheme and what it is about, that the two are separate, that one is symbolic and the other is not, always allows the possibility of their being different in some essential manner. Now scientific schemes are formal. They could not be the world, nor do they appear very much like the world of our experience. And in fact many scientific laws state what would happen under ideal conditions which are not found in nature. Are these laws, then, really statements about nature? Again, there is at least one case of critical failure in fitting the scientific entity into the formal scheme. The schemes of science most often relate to the position and velocity of some entity. When the scientist investigates the items on the right hand side of our second list — electrons, mesons, neutrons, photons — in fixing their position he loses the opportunity to know their velocity; and in fixing their velocity he finds it impossible to establish their position.

This was the problem of Heisenberg. Of course, the electron — being so minute and its orbit so confined — can't be going very far anyway. But this is not the point. Failure here may be a critical case of conflict between the formal scheme, and what the scheme is about. The matter is weighty enough that its solution, if found, might well require substantial changes in the orientation of modern science.

The Formulae in Flux

Again, as we have seen, the formulae of the sciences are in a slowly evolving flux. The solution of a given problem usually raises new problems and calls for adjustment in other systems; given enough of this process the set of the whole of science can be given a new direction; and this, too, happens although it is an affair of centuries. Most scientists, then, would be shocked by the charge that they possess in their formulae the final truth of things. Scientists are out to solve their problems efficiently and with elegance. They are aware how often the solution of a given problem is temporary, and provisional.

Measurement

Science puts its reliance in measurement. If science possessed a final truth, it would be a truth about the exact measurement of some property mentioned in our first list. But curiously there is and can be no absolute certainty in scientific measurement. Let anything be measured with any instrument from the yardstick to one 100 times more precise; if the measuring is done carefully each measurement will yield a different numerical value. Indeed, the more sensitive the measuring instrument the surer it is that the measurements will differ. Scientists measure with care; their instruments are incredibly precise; and because of this care and precision, individual scientific measurements will always differ. So certain is this that standard procedures are used to reduce the scattered set of values gained in actual measurements to a single value. Something like the average of the measured values is taken to be the proper measure. One can measure with a yardstick and gain a scattering of values; then one can measure with the instrument 100 times more precise; and although the precision is increased, there is the same scattering of values relative to the new precision that there was before. And this is a reason why the discipline which bases itself upon measurement cannot be said without qualification to possess the final truth.

The Meaning of the Scientific Statement

If final truth is a statement of the way things really are, there is a question about the meaning of the scientific statement. Science does yield general statements about the world; we have certainly learned from science the amazing power of the entities of nature; this has been dramatically, and for that matter tragically, illustrated. But what for one thing are we to make of a statement so simple as that concerning the size of an atom? If the size is 10^{-8} cm., we can know a centimeter to be about ⅖ of an inch; but how can we interpret the figure, .0000000001 cm.? 1 cm. or one billionth cm.; all we know is that both are very small. In a certain sense this may mean that science gives us an uninterpreted, perhaps an uninterpretable, scheme. Scientists, we have said, are interested in a certain limited range of properties of things — the properties which are measurable. And surely these are ideas. Even here there is a qualification; these properties are not merely represented by numbers. The property is blended with its number, is virtually identified with it. Clearly, the more closely space and time are identified with a set of numerical values, the more formal they become, and the less like what we mean by space and time in ordinary experience. The scientist gives minimal meaning to these properties. For these reasons there exists a problem of interpretation, and a question about whether the scientific formula can have a nonmathematical meaning.

Finally it may be suggested that the properties which are measurable are only a small part of the ideas which would be properly included in the final truth could we possess such truth. The techniques of science, even if completely successful, would still be presenting us with no more than a portion of the final truth of things.

We have confined ourselves to the foundation sciences. This was appropriate for obvious reasons. But a thorough analysis would require the addition of other properties to our infamous, and still foregoing, first list, such as valence, nerve impulse, and perhaps some psychological properties. Correspondingly, we should have to extend our list of entities to include elements, cells, chromosomes, and organisms. Many of these additional schemes would seem to be of a different nature from those we have considered. When the system of interest is the animal body, clearly we have the entity before us — not a formal scheme; yet it is the entity which is formalized, and again mathematics is the tool. And in many of these disciplines the space and time of ordinary experience is acceptable, because the center of interest is a system obviously within this space and time, such as the animal body. But with qualifications our comments still hold.

We can say then that, and only that, very likely — indeed, one feels like urging, almost certainly — there are final truths in the achieved science of the present day. But the science of today is not the final truth. The weightiest problems are still unsolved. And even to regard the present state of science as the final truth would be to block the road of further inquiry.

Religion and Final Truth

In turning from science to religion one is struck by the contrast between the two. While no two fields of science cover the same material, there are a number of what might be called foundation religions, or highly developed religions, covering the same — or what appears to be much the same — ground in different ways. It may be noted, too, that these religions contain a stronger claim than the claim of science. It is the typical claim of religion that it possesses, or expresses, or has available for a worshipper to possess and express, some final truth about the universe. This stronger claim must be taken seriously, since the claim is accepted by a great many people. Their whole lives recognize it, are an expression of it. The claim must also be examined. What can be the ground, and what the reasons, for believing the claim to final truth made by religion?

Certain elements are common to these high religions. The religions have sacred scriptures; they have a founder or founders; they have services of worship through which the experience of the worshipper is directed toward the divine being. The scriptures are a group of documents composed at different times and usually handed down from a rather remote past. The founder appears at an appropriate time in history and is intimately related to the divine being who is in some sense creator of heaven and earth; the coming of the founder has a special significance for man; he is a point of contact between man and the divine being. The experience of the worshipper in the religious service is the most intimate point of contact with the tradition, the founder, and directly or indirectly with the divine being.

The final truth of religion would have to be present in one of these three areas. In every high religion there are groups of men who would not allow this question to be asked. There are groups of men who rest this truth upon an unquestioned, unquestionable authority. We have already found the idea of authority to be deficient as a final test for opinion; if an opinion is worth believing there must be some ground other than authority on which this opinion rests.

Let us call X the sacred book which contains the word of the divine being; and Y the founder through whom one can come in contact with this being.

The Sacred Book

X, the sacred book, contains poetry, narrative concerning the early stages of the religion, sayings of the founder, and others related to him or preceding him. How does the sacred book relate to final truth? The problem is difficult.

Sacred books are always written by a large number of people through many generations. Each of them may be contributing statements which are true; but we have no reason for believing that every statement of every person within the group is true, or that every statement of any person in the group is as such true. This would be to argue for an infallible person. We have seen there can be no such argument. The same is true when the authority is a book. Why this book rather than some other as my authority?

The sacred book is a sample of historical writing, concerning a past which is remote. In the less remote regions of history a given document can be compared with other documents and a high probability of its authenticity given; this is less easy for a sacred book. Independent documents verifying what is said are hard to come by; patient inquiry can sometimes find such documents; independent documents sometimes appear dramatically. These can help verify the historical features of such writings. But they help not at all in throwing light upon whether or not the point of view expressed in the writings is a final truth. And at last the one who takes religion to be his guide will find his final truth in the point of view. And concerning this, all one can come to about the book is that it is what the people who wrote these scriptures through time thought to be the case.

The Founder

Y is the founder of the religion. Can one say that the founder has the final truth? The claim is made of every founder; his followers have a feeling of certainty about the matter. But on what does the claim truly rest? Again, the questions are hard. Since the founder is known primarily through the book, there is the problem of knowing whether the founder did indeed say what he is represented as having said; once again, we cannot go back to establish certainty concerning this. Could there be independent manuscripts confirming each other this would add some feeling of reliability. In the case of the Christian founder the gospels seem to be independent manuscripts. But it is the verdict of scholars that the gospels are not independent, their writers having used common sources. And these common sources in turn were written down some years after the death of the founder; and prior to its being written out the substance of the teaching was carried by word of mouth, in preaching. We may have a certainty about the teachings of the gospels, but it is not an historic certainty.

In the case of every founder it is through the haze of the past that we must try to glimpse the outlines of his figure. Now if these founders did say what they are supposed to have said; namely, that through them one can come into contact with the divine being, does this establish a completely proper argument and establish the truth of the point of view of the founder, his relation to the divine being, and the existence of the divine being himself? Would not one have to ask, if interested in finding the foundations of this belief: *Does the fact that a founder expresses his point of view, and states his intimate relation to the divine being, automatically guarantee the truth of the point of view?* This would not follow if it were the statement of any ordinary human being. If it follows this must be because of the uniqueness of the being who is the founder. But we are told of this uniqueness only in the sacred book; and from this we can learn at best only what the writers of that book thought to be the case. And such writers were certainly fallible human beings. From this approach we cannot arrive at certainty concerning the final truth of the point of view contained in the words of the founder. Then how can we so arrive?

The question is put mindful of the fact that millions of people in all religions have found contentment, satisfaction, peace of mind, abiding purposefulness, and balanced useful lives from some one of the sacred books, and have felt a relation to a divine being through some great religious leader and founder. The problem is: Wherein lies the certainty which the worshipper attaches to this relation? How is it known that this is a final truth? Our second effort to state the meaning of "truth" identified truth with what works. Every religion makes the claim: Try this and it will work out well for you! But not only does every religion make this claim; to judge from the lives of their followers, most religions make good upon this claim. The lives of worshippers are often balanced, purposeful, and sometimes — when the devils have been driven out — possessed of an inner serenity. There are such people in all major religions. It is as though the particular words, expressing the point of view, were not of great importance; whatever the final truth, if it lies here, must be capable of being expressed in many ways. If this is not so, then we must have been mistaken, the claim of final truth is to be given up, and the religions are maintaining only that truth is what works for you; and this working is its truth. But then we are back again; since different beliefs are found to be workable, there is no truth for everyone.

The Worship Experience

What then of the experience of the worshipper? If documents from the past can give us no final certainty, if the founder is known only through these documents, what of the worship experience where the certainty of the religious claim is often centered? It is through religious devotion that one comes into contact with the founder, and with the divine being who is the creator. This is the claim and the feeling. Can we rely upon the immediate religious experience? The approach seems more hopeful. In all religions, I suppose, this would be said to be the heart, the most central aspect, of the religion. Our question is: *What in the religious experience itself can serve to guarantee the final truth of the point of view of that religion?* Here we are within the worship experience; we have listened to the words; there is around us silence. What can be found in this experience? Perhaps we have prayed; it was a petition, or a supplication, containing our uncertainties and fears; and now there has come over us this calm; we feel at peace; some apparently hear actual words of response; most of us, I suspect, never have heard these. We have had at most the feeling of being elevated, and the feeling of peace after struggle. We may have also a feeling of being in touch with something beyond ourselves. The calm, the feeling of elation, the feeling — rather formless to tell the truth — of being in touch; it is true that we have these.

The difficulty lies in finding the way from this undeniable feeling of peace to the final truth of the words by which we express the point of view. Often the point of view is expressed in such words as: God lives and is good; I shall be judged; there is a life beyond this life.

Goethe in *Wilhelm Meister* has at one point placed a story within a story. It is titled "Confessions of a Fair Saint." One passage is pertinent here. The heroine of the confessions has become very religious. She comes into a time of great difficulty, caring for her parents through an extended illness. Of this time she wrote:

> It was now that I could try whether the path, which I had chosen, was the path of phantasy or truth; whether I had merely thought as others showed me, or the object of my trust had a reality. To my unspeakable support, I always found the latter. The straight direction of my heart to God . . . I had sought and found; and this was what made all things light to me. As a travel-ler in the dark, my soul, when all was pressing on me from with-out hastened to the place of refuge, and never did it return empty.[4]

Many have reported the same experience. But does an increase of strength imply the presence of some final truth? If so, how so?

I do not claim that it does not. And if we could lay the specter that this undeniably healthful and productive cleansing is nothing more than a self finding its own unity through reflection on ultimate broad perspectives, perhaps the connection might be made more easily. Yet I have never seen the argument which made convincing the transition from personal well-being to final truth. Some will reply: "Exactly; you expect an argument and here the matter goes beyond argument to faith." I am far from dismissing the point out of hand. But the situation turns upon itself. We may admit that faith is an essential part of life. Yet one cannot countenance an un-reasonable faith; for if unreason is what one desires any form of

---

[4] Thomas Carlyle, *Wilhelm Meister's Apprenticeship and Travels,* trans. from the German of Goethe (London: Chapman and Hall Ltd., 1899) Vol. I, p. 426.

nonsense will do. And among the forms of unreason there will be no way of determining the form which is not nonsense unless reason is allowed to help in its determination. At least it is a reasonable faith to which one should adhere. And in support of a reasonable faith, arguments can be given.

If one insists upon this transfer from personal well-being to final truth, at the very least one would have to grant the presence of final truth wherever one finds an increase in personal strength. This would be granting the presence of final truth in all major religions, perhaps in all religions without exception. In addition, to handle apparent contradictions, we would have to say that the final truth in religion does not depend upon the words by which it is expressed. To hold this position, then, one would have to grant to all forms of religious life, which successfully produce in their worshippers an increase of strength, the presence in one way or another of this final truth.

I do not think, really, it would help for us to argue that since our form of religion has endured for such a long time, it must be true. All religions have a tremendous staying power. This may mean they have some truth within them. But again this staying power may be a reflection of the helpfulness of religion in a problematic life. Even if it is more than helpfulness, what we were trying to find was the clear and certain ground for its claim to final truth. And, perhaps due to our lack of vision, we have not yet found that.

Meanwhile the experience of religion, it may be noted, is much like the experience of beauty, the esthetic experience; something like the transport often found in listening to great music, or in poetry, is found again in worship. Indeed, the likeness is close enough that in religious worship great music is commonly employed in order to heighten the religious effect. And when one thinks of it, the great religious literature has something like a poetic form. Religion, poetry, music seem much alike. In the form of religion which we know from the inside, there is an important, added element of moral striving. This does not mean that religion is "morality tinged with emotion." Indeed, we are making no judgment about religion, but only looking for the source of its certainty with respect to final truth. So far as religion is esthetic the problem will be faced in the following chapter; and our final chapter will be concerned with the affirmations of religion.

At least the most promising source for the religious claim is to be found in our direct experience. What we experience directly we have at least experienced; of course, we may be suffering from an illusion; but we have already registered an opinion concerning those who find the rest of the human race laboring under lifelong illusions.

Now if we consider the sacred book and the sayings of the founder to be something like the formal scheme, allowing us to infer something about what the worshipper may experience; and if we consider the experience of the worshipper the observation; then religion and science are comparable disciplines. Offhand, one would note that whatever data may be present in the experience of the worshipper is "softer" — less subject to agreement than some other types of evidence. And yet, on reflection, the entities to which reference is made by the high religions and the foundation sciences would seem to be almost equally remote, intangible, and "occult." The difference is the irrelevance of mathematics, and the relevance of value, to the religious experience. There are other differences. Even the kind of thinking is different; this we shall not explore just now. But there is some similarity; the two are similar enough to be compared. In the comparison we would say:

Science contacts reality at the point where an observation is expected on the basis of a formal scheme, and when the scheme requires something which can in fact be observed. Religion contacts reality at the point of the worshipper's immediate experience. In both cases a number of formal schemes may successfully direct us to this observation or to this experience. In the case of science these will be alternate theories; in the case of religion these will be alternate religions.

In both cases our embarrassment stems from the fact that the observation and the experience do not require a single formal scheme which might then stand some chance of being a final truth about the universe. In both cases, looking back over the history of science and religion, the formal schemes have developed. Science exhibits a more rapid rate of change; but in the larger span of human history the religions, too, have developed, added and refined concepts, and changed the generating ideas of their formal schemes. The self-corrective nature of inquiry is more self-consciously present in science; in science it is an instrument; but in religion, too, the worshipper is engaged in an inquiry — of the greatest importance to himself. His seeking is self-corrective in a general sense, as a corollary of human awareness.

Each of us must decide what is to be made of these facts. I do not see, however, that we can say anything other than this: Neither the religions of the world nor the sciences of the day, taken separately or together, can be said with certainty to be the final truth. Of both one feels like urging, and for the same reasons, that they must contain final truth, are on the way to it by a self-corrective process. But we do not know and cannot know that any single scheme of either religion or science has arrived.

And this is the best we can do, the best outcome we are able to gain. Surely no other area of life is likely to have final truth if it cannot be made out in the sciences and in religion. As we think back over our path it seems that we have accomplished ridiculously little. We were looking for the needle in the haystack, and what we found was the haystack itself. Of course, we may have gotten farther than we think. And even if we have not, a haystack has its uses.

The Summing Up

Let us pull together the questions, scattered along the path our thought has taken: (1) What are the important beliefs of my life? (2) What important belief do I hold which originated within myself, which is truly my own? (3) At what sources in the outer world have these beliefs been gained? (4) On what grounds do they rest? Are they reliable? What is their proof? (5) How should the flux of opinion be ordered? (6) What meaning should be assigned to "Truth"? (7) Can final truth be found through inquiry? (8) Are science and religion sources of final truth?

Could one work his way through these questions, resolving the problems we have met, he would have found his position with respect to truth. And, indeed, no real obstacle blocked our progress until we came upon the later questions. We had found three meanings for truth. The view which seemed appropriate allowed a sense of final truth; at last, truth was to be objective, and part of the nature of things. But every step from that point on furnished us with greater problems. At last we have had to grant our inability to find a final truth.

What can this mean? Perhaps our choice of the third meaning was ill advised; perhaps truth need not be "the set of ordered opinions ultimately fated to be agreed upon by all who pursue inquiry far enough." The second meaning is still available. Must we return to it? If the first and third meanings are awkward, because they assume a view of truth on which we are unable to deliver, the second meaning has an opposite encumbrance. On the first and third meanings, truth becomes quite remote, but on the second it is much too near at hand, common, and familiar; in fact, there is too much of it. And further, we have found the second meaning tending to resolve itself into one of the other two.

These pages form the outline of our problem. We have met with more frustration in this coursing toward the truth, than in either of our other efforts. Seeking truth about the truth, no wonder the problem was more tangled, and our vision less acute. In any case you now inherit our problem; and where do you stand, in truth?

II. Toward the Discovery of Truth

Let us try to find the point to which the discussion has come. The meaning for which I had expressed a preference allowed us to think of truth as absolute, and yet admit the initial bondage of man in the welter of opinion. Summing up the considerations which appeared in our discussion we would say: If it were possible to work our way from opinion to truth, our truth would be a statement of the way things really are. But the statement would not be a blunt assertion of unsupported opinion. It would be a statement in depth. The assertion would follow unavoidably from reasons which could not be denied. And this statement in depth, this formal scheme, would lead us to expect in reality what in fact is observed. The formal scheme would exhibit its nature as a statement of the way things really are by allowing an unlimited number of inferences to the world around us, and these inferences would never disappoint us. And we would begin our journey toward this ideal statement from the clutter of whatever opinion is encased within our lives.

Now we do begin in this manner. Socratic-wise we must begin where we are — slave boy, Sophist, merchant, chief — and the beginning is criticism, testing of our ideas. The problem is our inability to find in any area of life anything which can be known to be a final truth. It would be intolerable if trains had schedules clearly delineating departures, but with no information as to when we might arrive at our destination. And no one would entrain at all if, once on the train, neither you nor anyone else could ever say with confidence that he had at some point arrived at his goal. Yet our analysis suggests this to be the case with the whole human race concerning final truth. Once the matter is put so bluntly is there any way of softening this unhappy conclusion? Could we say that actually, like the little boy in the forest, we know where we are; it is the final truth which seems, for the time, to be lost? Certainly, knowing where we are has its importance. Let us try this gambit.

If in the most direct sense truth is quite remote, might there not be another sense — perhaps one equally important — in which truth is near at hand? Might it not be that every person who seriously probes his life in quest of truth does in a certain personal sense find a final truth? At least he may learn what he truly believes. He knows the final truth that this is what he believes. And beyond any question he could not have been aware of this before he had deeply probed his set of opinions. Before his attempt on final truth he was merely acquainted with the material of belief around him and in him, passively accepting it while irritated, perhaps, by its vagueness and inner conflicts. And is not the discovery of what one shall believe in large part what one is after when he wishes truth? Shall I believe "A" or "B" or "C" to be the proper estimate of this topic? Our suggestion amounts to this: In seeking truth one comes to know himself.

The truth turns out to have two sides, what really is the case, and what one really believes oneself. The first side has proven too elusive for us. Yet in seeking the first we have come upon the second. In the effort to make out the final truth we may discover the truth of what we believe, and gain a solidity not otherwise possible in the foundation of our lives.

If this is so, man's decision to seek truth gives him a double commitment. He is committed to self-discovery, and he is committed to the discovery of the way things really are. The first half of the commitment is a requirement that the one who declares for truth must probe the foundations of his being. The other half, his commitment to truth as the discovery of what really is, requires him to participate in the unfinished adventure of thought. The two commitments modify each other.

I have thought of asking, and you have asked I am sure: What is the use of troubling about something the nature of which one is unable to know with clarity? There was an excuse when we thought final truth might be available; having found the difficulties of the notion why not drop it now? Why not go back to the second meaning for truth? These questions can be answered.

The reason for still holding to the difficult notion of final truth is that by means of this idea man gives himself a point outside the press of opinions. Let him believe that every question has its hard, and difficult truth, and he has a point of criticism for all random doctrines offered for his consumption in this curious world.

For one thing, if he believes in final truth he will not easily confuse his own random opinions with the truth. He must of course at last make up his mind; but if he is, and knows himself to be, on the side of truth, then one may approach him in a spirit of fairness; one may point out additional facts; so the man who seeks truth in all the affairs of life is bound to learn; he is bound to be closer to the truth than the man who does not wish to learn, or who despairs that he can learn, of any truth — immersing himself in whatever partisan opinion may be at hand or to his advantage. We live in an age of rhetoric. There is no escape in the greater part of human life from the pressure of the countless words which assail us from every side. There is no one to whom we can turn for a completely unbiased account of any matter. These being the circumstances, I think it has never been more certain that we need in our philosophy the idea of truth as absolute. There is no alternative. If man is not to bend to the greater pressure, the larger flow, of the rhetoric which plays against his life, he must master the power of word and thought, sifting the logic of events for himself. He must penetrate rhetoric through the power of his own mind; otherwise, he is lost. Why should anyone ever suspend judgment? There is one reason only: because he respects the truth. Let man lose this respect and he will judge by fear, envy, hatred, or a desire to be approved. Even if it cannot be known with certainty, final truth has this use in human life.

It has another related use. Belief in final truth gives man power against the demagogue. In the eyes of any man who respects the truth, the man who urges strongly while offering no adequate reasons is greatly suspect. To say yes or no, to deny or affirm or assert, this is nothing without its reason. Who cannot assert, and what cannot be asserted? Every leap, every gap, every extravagance will serve as warning that this one is intent upon something other than the truth. The man who has trained himself to insist upon adequate reasons will find them here as well; if not in what is said, then in the life of the one who says it, in his real intent. To insist upon reasons is a good defense against the large untruth. These untruths mount in moments of hysteria. But the man who respects truth will not allow his mind to be swept away with words.

If we are to found our lives on this two-sided nature of truth, how should we proceed?

Through Self-examination

In seeking final truth we find the truth of what we can believe; now if this truth is a matter of self-knowledge, the point is both surprising and important. Quite the most important question for a person to ask in his own philosophy is the question of what that person is. This is not an easy question, so hidden is the self, so deviously and variously does it develop. In the moment of critical thinking one is on the verge of self-discovery. How can this be? The insight is as old as Socrates who taught that one could begin to know himself by discovering what he could hold as true. And to discover this meant questioning everything he had been told was true. If we declare for truth we are committed to nothing less than this.

If one is to find the truth of what he believes, if one is to discover his own nature, he must tear himself free from all the things he is said to be; the accepted must become for the time questionable. The need is for a self-examination, probing every depth of life, to find what is worth believing. In its natural course every belief, every attitude, every custom, in the mind of man is turned over (not, as some think, overturned), and examined to determine whether or not it has a proper claim on human life.

The thought may sound forbidding. Certainly, our education does not require this examination; our institutions are content that our people be without it. And the thought may seem forbidding, because there is some personal anguish in this crucial self-examination.

And yet man should be in anguish at one time in his life. We avoid the anguish present in this attempt at self-discovery only at the price of inner confusion. And confusion is a reasonable price for many who are thus able to avoid turning the searchlight of criticism upon themselves, their customs, their beliefs, their superstitions. And yet there is a natural period of criticism just as the youth begins to become a man. Allowed to take its course this criticism will strike at every illusion, semblance, shade, and the nothingness which in us is crusted over with the past stands forth; in that emptiness the youth has room to find himself.

In this examination one must let go for a time all of the safe, easy answers, the obvious because so familiar way of viewing the world, which has been our possession since childhood; and face the problematic character of existence. One must let the old, ultimate questions rise and face them in solitude. One must tear himself away from the group in which so graciously he allows his individuality to be cast down, and struggle with himself to find the strong ideas — the true, authentic ideas — on which he may build a life. In all of this, one is learning to walk alone; and, in the most literal sense, walking alone may help.

If one must let go all of the safe easy answers, the examination also requires what Holmes well called the free market of ideas. Let all ideas be entertained, jostle against each other, interpenetrate; their variety provides material for a wisdom still to come. The conflicts of civilization must pass through the mind of one seeking to find himself as options which might be taken up, as mighty contradictions which must somehow be resolved. The mind of such a person must begin to live the life of the world with a vengeance. And this requires an active, open awareness, a liberality of spirit, a tolerance to opposing ideas. For this person can no longer rely upon the majority opinion of his group; his search is individual; he is in personal struggle with all the facts, data, and theories in the universe. He is engaged in a crucial struggle.

Truth is also a value, and the one who seeks to find what stands against objections, is also engaged in the search for human excellence. To let the illusion fall, to probe behind the semblance, to have the courage to see, really see, the realm of opinion with its false motives scattered here and there, yet with their portion of honest truth. To sense the falseness even in one's self — to score it, cauterize it, burn one's nature not quite uniform, and to accept some even of one's own grossness. To live in this hybrid multiform seeking the genuine, the true. To be willing to take anything so long as it is anything but a lie, to stand to lose even but to stand for truth. This is a force with power to mold authentic values. It is one way in which a man announces his intention to be not one whit less than human. The way to become authentic, we suggest, is to wish the truth with all one's heart, and to make up one's beliefs out of what, after criticism, still stands. No one all your life can require you to care for truth. This is exactly the luxury of desiring truth; to care for something which is not required, which one must require of himself.

And if one probes the beliefs of his life what will he find? He will find part of his nature to be made up of worthless patchwork material; uninteresting, untrue, mediocre. But the issue of the struggle may be a new vision of one's manhood. We have said that in this probing there is anguish. The anguish need not go on forever. Serenity will come as one begins to see the order for his life.

Through Conversation

Second, one may begin to find the basis for his life through conversation. By conversation we do not mean the chit-chat of an ordinary social evening, the choosing up of sides and taking turns to report the events of the daily press, the dress or manner of an associate, polite slander; nor do we here intend the happy faculty of fusing words and their associations in an incongruous and therefore humorous manner. By conversation we mean the revealing of one mind to another through the spoken word. Whatever thought may be it is much like conversation. If one is to know himself he must learn to talk seriously and earnestly with another person, perhaps with many others, concerning the deepest matters. While he is doing so and never before, he begins to understand what he thinks, how and where he differs, on what ground he stands.

This is a simple discovery of the greatest moment; it is, again, part of the discovery of Socrates who talked himself to death; one can come to know himself by searching for the truth in conversation. Indeed, there are some things one can learn in no other manner.

We have said that man is overwhelmed by the pressures of his daily press, the reports and drama of his radio, the spectacle of his television set. But here is a counteragent — the pressure of his own thought. A man in thought saying what he thinks, creates a counterpressure against the pressure of the world, breaks its thrust, and around such a man there opens out the needed elbow room.

To discover himself, one must begin some day saying what he thinks. Let it be wrong, even mendacious; he has checked the pressures of the world. As we have observed, however wrong the thought, he has discovered something absolutely true; this, at least for the moment, is what he thinks! The discovery may surprise him. And once in the public world he may discover, too, his dissatisfaction with this thought; and begin to search for something better.

Note at the next social gathering, how general talk tends to glide across the surface of the world's events while often the width of one paragraph, one sentence, a single phrase, separates this talk from the most profound issues — which we pass without mention. This talk, skittering across the surfaces of things, allows man to fill every void, every uncomfortable silence, and yet avoid the important task. "Let no silence fall" — this is the dictum. "Remember the ever-bouncing ball" — this is the rule. Join one report to the next; weave a pattern unbroken through the evening; but in the silent depths below the pattern, lie the more profound questions, the locus of man's proper quest for truth. Then if we would find ourselves, we must probe beneath that surface.

Through Philosophizing

We come then to the two-sided nature of truth: on one hand, the drive of the individual, our internal questioning and striving, toward the truth of what we shall believe; and on the other hand, the drive of the community toward, the great debate concerning, truth as something ultimate. Long ago we had suggested: The drive of the community of inquirers has been creating since ancient times a developing pattern of thought. Our separate sciences have each elaborated a portion of this pattern. Our philosophies have sought its meaning and unity. The goal of all this effort is the truth as what really is.

We have seen how we have come into this stream of thought obliquely, penetrating from below and at an angle, carried in the direction of its basic current. We have seen how the current may shift and change; and how, prior to our making any judgment about this movement of human thought, much of it must sweep over us. First, we must learn. We were forced to decide, also, that most of us live most of the time in what we may now call a stream of feeling, carrying opinion. To join the two figures, as the Gulf Stream has direction within the larger volume of water which surrounds it, so has the growing pattern of thought direction within the larger volume of mere opinion. And as the power of the Gulf

Stream, within limits, redirects the waters of the ocean, so the power of thought to some like extent redirects opinion.

But the problem returns that knowledge has multiplied beyond the possible understanding of any man; knowledge has been pre-empted by the specialist and even so the conclusions of the specialist, could we master them, are not final.

Now perhaps we must here take a simple, further step beyond our discovery that the truth of what we shall believe is possible for us. In the first place, we can relate ourselves to the drive of the community of inquirers. Our very commitment to this elusive final truth makes the developing pattern of thought, which seeks it, a part of our nature. The concern of inquiry is in one sense the completion of the fabric of our being, could this concern be successful, and could we know of its success. It is in this sense our truth which begins to rise in ancient times, which develops in the Renaissance, and which engages probing minds today. Since it is our truth which is being sought we can take the maxim as our own: Do not block the road of inquiry! That is, the grand enterprise can receive our support even where it reaches beyond our grasp.

But to say this much is not to satisfy the problem. Since the authority of experts can be no final ground, we are required by truth to understand the reasons for the conclusions of experts. Is this not just what we claimed to be impossible? It must be admitted that the situation is desperate, indeed, unless there can be a general understanding which is not a popularization, not merely a thinned-out version of something beyond our understanding.

For the moment I merely suggest this may be possible. And a reason may be advanced to support its possibility. Although our account of science was oversimplified, we did see that the formal schemes of science are very closely associated with mathematical procedures, and mathematical procedures are certain because they are themselves part of a formal scheme, and obviously not anything like the world of our experience. We observed, also, how the ideas, or properties, of interest to scientists were virtually identified with their numerical equivalents so that time, mass, position, velocity, etc., have their meanings as parts of an equation which will yield a number. All we have to assume is that the translation of ideas into numbers, which has so completely fascinated the mentality of the West for close to four centuries, should not be a one-way street. At some time the numbers must be translated back into ideas. This is not a far-fetched assumption. If the numbers do not translate back into ideas to be sure there is a problem for us. But if they will not translate back the expert has an identical problem. There is a question concerning how he can understand what he is about if these numbers cannot be related to the rest of life. If the equations do not translate back into ideas, expressible in words, there is a question about whether science is a meaningless quest. We are going to assume that the quest has meaning. Now ideas expressed in words are familiar to us. And the ideas of science, translated back from equations to words, lose their foreignness, and are sometimes commonplace. Further, when we allow ourselves to ask of science the question, "What does this mean?"; in terms of the general question the detailed answers offer not the indigestible earlier mass, but in many cases only some pertinent suggestions. Still further, from the standpoint of what is meant, the ideas of science change slowly enough that understanding is possible; it is only through centuries that a shift comes in science of such a nature as to require a reshaping within philosophy. And finally, while expressions in words are less precise than expressions in mathematical symbols, such expressions have much greater content. It is properly not a loss, but a gain, to interpret in words the ideas of the special sciences.

At the same time we have seen how the expressions of religion, quite contrary to those of science, have an immense wealth of content, but the vagueness of expression proper to poetry and song. To make precise what is being affirmed, and to evaluate it, interpretation through careful analysis of meaning is required. To put its case in formal terms religion must have recourse to philosophy.

The great philosophies of the West have addressed themselves to this task of interpretation. It now seems that this philosophic enterprise is necessary for the understanding of what we have called the developing pattern of thought. And it is our chance of understanding the conclusions of the special fields, and of evaluating religious practice.

From this standpoint both religion and science require philosophy. And thinking back over what we said final truth, if available, would be, our statement in depth was, except in one respect, very much like the shape of what philosophy attempts to do; for philosophy has through ages worked to frame conclusions about the world following from reasons which cannot be denied. The missing respect is that one does not infer from a philosophy surprising new observations about the world. This is because philosophy does not attempt to do the whole job; it needs as its material the sciences and every other aspect of life, including the religions of the world.

The outcome might be happier. The point does not bring us to final truth; the point merely urges a need for philosophy in understanding the findings of the special sciences and the experience of religion. The point is urging us to include philosophy in the developing pattern which attempts to move toward final truth. It would be better if we could add a single step, one which might make more credible our belief in final truth.

Let us try, cautiously of course, the further step. In our discussion of truth we have had to take account of two things: opinions, and the reality toward which those opinions were directed. Truth was to be a *statement* of the way things really are. The statement spreads a net; and it is to be hoped that the way things are is sometimes caught by such a net. Every formal scheme casts such a net; but we have had trouble with all such schemes; we have found them "on the way" to truth, and nothing more.

Now we may add the concern of philosophy for a general understanding of the world. In a way philosophy spreads the net more widely, and the catch is sometimes curious, indeed. But there is a suggestion in this which may prove of value. Suppose the net of thought spread so widely that, no matter what else is enmeshed, the way things really are will also be caught within our net.

How is the net to be arranged? In our discussion of freedom we spread such a net. At one point in the discussion we had said:

> On either of the two meanings note that we have a critical decision before us. Either it is true that sometimes in the same situation we could have chosen otherwise; or it is true that in no case could we have done otherwise. Either it is true that sometimes we can act in accord with our own unique natures; or it is true that all our actions are a reflection of the world. These two pairs of sentences, these two sets of ideas, are opposed in such a way that we must accept one of them or the other; we cannot take both; and if one is true the other in that pair is false.

If our arrangement of ideas was proper, then anything which can be asserted for or against freedom will fall under one or the other of these two statements. The statements will exhaust the field.

We had thought final truth so far away; yet here it is, surprisingly, caught in one or the other of these two statements. To be sure the sounds and words employed grew out of custom. To be sure, we are supposing that our statements make sense, are neither meaningless or irrelevant. Assuming this, we can know the final truth about man's freedom to lie in one of these two statements. If one of these could be decisively rejected, and the other supported, we should have before us a final truth. I think our discussion did not do this well. But the program might be possible.

I am urging for the last half step that we may know the truth in general through philosophizing, even when we are still in particulars uncertain. And I must add a word of caution: there can be no easy unravelling of the final truth by this route because of a failure within philosophy itself. There are three or four basic philosophies of pervasive interest, and with records of considerable success in ordering opinion. The world can be fairly well ordered by any one of them, and their decisions differ at a number of critical points.

I am urging that the attempt on final truth requires philosophy as a participant in this attempt, and that it is in principle possible to know the final truth of things in general; and since every man is also a philosopher; and since philosophy marshals ideas with care and interprets the findings of special fields, through one's discovery of the truth of what he believes he is relating himself also to the truth which is the goal of the community of inquirers. Then in practical terms it may be said that the truth of what you believe is the path toward truth as ultimate and final.

Chapter Four

Beauty

I. The Problem of Beauty

Most of us, if asked to list the important topics of personal philosophy, would never have thought of including a problem concerning beauty. And this is natural. When the modern world was in the making philosophers tortured themselves over many problems; but in the sixteenth and seventeenth centuries very few raised any question about the nature of the beautiful. For them it was a blind spot, as it is for most of us. Only toward the end of the eighteenth century did the problem assume importance once again. We say "once again" for the problem was posed by the Greeks; Beauty, Truth, and Goodness formed the great triad, three ideals for the guidance of human life. We treat each of the three — in our own way and in its own place. This is not to say that the Greeks have had a monopoly on the appreciation of beauty. Very likely such appreciation is present in the experiences of every man. But if it is part of our experience we should become more aware of the fact; one hears, for example, that the Chinese have several hundred words to express the variations of beauty which we express by "pretty," "beautiful," "sublime," and possibly by "cute."

What is to be meant by "beauty"? Each of our problems is differ-

137

ent and poses its own difficulties. Finally, the answer to this problem must rest upon a sheer appeal to individual experience, for we are working once again with soft data. To slash away at the problem lustily would be to risk gaining no result. But perhaps we can approach the answer cautiously, step by step, and somewhat backhandedly.

I view a sunset complete with fleeting clouds and find it beautiful. I see a painting, a piece of sculpture; listen to a symphony; sit in the gallery and watch ballet; see a play; read a novel, a poem, and find these also beautiful. What is it about these objects of nature, and of art, which makes it appropriate for me to call them beautiful?

We would say that we appreciate or enjoy these things; but not all our experiences of appreciation deserve this term. Receiving the telegram: "As the defeated candidate from the fifth district, let me express my appreciation for your efforts in my behalf," I might know the appreciation to be genuine; and I would certainly not expect my defeated friend to mean that my past efforts were a form of beauty. We must decide which forms of appreciation, or what appreciated things, can be called beautiful.

Suppose that, munching upon a bag of peanuts, and walking through the Louvre, we were to come upon the portrait of Mona Lisa with her tender, and (on one theory) slightly possessive smile. And suppose we were to find ourselves enjoying the peanuts more than the portrait. Still we would hardly think the peanuts more beautiful than the painting. Why? Because all of us fairly much center this experience in sight, hearing, and — in a way — in thought. We do not call tastes and smells beautiful, even when they are appreciated and enjoyed. Sight and sound may predominate in the esthetic experience because these senses are more fully developed; there may be other reasons in addition. Occasionally the rumor goes round that someone is preparing an olfactory symphony. And occasionally the term "beautiful" is applied to the odor of perfume — especially to the more expensive type, having "odeur" instead of odor, and known as "parfum." In the experience of some a perfume, released from its bottle and at work in the world, may deserve to be called beautiful. But the label on the bottle would suggest that the product is intended to be "exciting" rather than merely "beautiful." And certainly, well-prepared food — while appetizing — is not beautiful. As a matter of convenience it will do no harm to follow the common usage, and think of beauty as confined mainly to appreciations of sight and sound.

So far! Beauty concerns things seen and heard — and appreciated. "It must be seen to be appreciated." Also, it must be heard to be appreciated. But still, not all things seen or heard, and appreciated, would be called beautiful.

I may hear some good news, see evidence of its truth, and throb with appreciation; yet the experience may not be regarded by any of us as an experience of beauty. For example, I may hold in my hand a check, representing a substantial increase in salary. I enjoy the sight of the check; I appreciate having it. In a spirit of exuberance I might even exclaim: "What a beautiful sight!" But you would not take me to mean seriously that this check belongs in the class of beautiful things; we place it there only because we are using words loosely and impudently. But why is this not an experience of beauty? The case may have critical importance. What released the adrenalin into my blood stream as the check came into view was the thought of the consequences of the news and the check in my life — a new car, a new house, travel in Europe, maid-service, man-service, the dream of early retirement, security in my old age, and prestige in the financial community. I was not appreciating the immediate experience but its consequences. Now had there been something about the check itself — the engraving, the coloring — which I was appreciating; then the exclamation, "What a beautiful sight!" might be taken seriously.

We are suggesting, then, that in the experience of beauty our appreciation is directly related to the sight or sound. If this is so, then my appreciation of an increase in salary, the pleasure of regarding newly acquired property, my enjoyment in viewing the crackling brown of the Thanksgiving turkey would not be experiences of beauty because my interest would be in certain consequences having to do with spending, using, or eating these things. And if I were with this hypothetically immense salary increase to purchase a painting and, while examining the work, think principally of its resale value, my experience would not be an experience of beauty.

This is a more radical way of limiting the field than was our first decision. Yet I shall assume it to be a proper limitation both because I think we do all make this distinction; and because I cannot recall any philosopher writing on the topic who has not thought this to be the case. Let us try to understand the experience of beauty as an experience of sight, sound, or thought, where our interest is concentrated within the experience itself without regard to personal consequences. Then we could say:

In the experience of beauty we sometimes look; we sometimes listen; or we look and listen together. And we sometimes read, requiring thought, and on the whole more like "listening" than "looking." When we look we are enjoying beauty as "spectacle," figure, that set of ordered parts now opposite us. So beauty is sometimes spatial. When we listen we are experiencing beauty as a succession of sounds with sounds now past as background, the present sound as foreground, and in these together a shadowed anticipation of what is still to come. So beauty is available under the aspect of time as well as of space; we experience it in spectacle and succession. Of our first examples painting and sculpture are instances of spatial beauty. Music is an example of temporal beauty. The dance is spatial and temporal together; and so are drama, and for that matter also the sunset with fleeting clouds. Works of literature generally — the play which is read, the novel, poetry — seem to form a special type of case. Whatever happens is internal to us and yet through our imagination and understanding events fall into our own projected space and time. We listen to a "flow" of words appropriately projecting the events, characters, and scenery called for in the plot. These can be said aloud and truly listened to; some of them can be physically enacted, leaving less to be projected by the viewer.

But the question is: What happens in this looking and listening, this enjoyment of spectacle and succession? The words release an immense number of theories, clamoring to answer. These theories do not particularly stand in opposition to each other; but they adopt different starting points, are perhaps "partial" theories, asserting "partial" truths. And yet one cannot simply put them together and call the whole collection the explanation of beauty.

A Digest of Clamoring Theories

Beauty is skill in representation. The heart of the experience is our admiration of an artist's ability to imitate nature. At one stage in his career, and not in a spirit of admiration, Plato treats beauty as an imitation.

Aristotle, sensing the limitations of this theory, held the beautiful to be an imitation not merely of some actual thing but of some possible things as well. The artist works not alone with what does happen, but with what might happen; he presents a possible or probable unity. Aristotle's immediate discussion concerned drama, especially tragedy. And we do not have the whole of his reflections on the problem; but generalizing from what we do know of his discussion the view might be expressed in these words: *Beauty is the presentation of an organic unity.* In the presentation the parts, whatever they may be, must be so related that a change in any part will alter the quality of the whole; in the presentation there will be nothing inessential, nothing which can be removed without affecting the whole. Here it is form or pattern, some organic unity, which constitutes the beautiful.

Beauty is a quality of splendor sensed in anything which has a unity of the whole. This is the view of Plotinus. And on this view there is beauty everywhere through nature, since to deprive a thing of unity is to deprive it of existence. So in an army, a choric ballet, a building, in any natural unity, organization is to be found; and this quality constitutes our experience of beauty.

Beauty is a quality of consonantia, claritas, integritas in a thing. Consonantia is the harmony of the thing; *claritas* is something like the radiance Plotinus found in the unity of existing things; *integritas* is the unity, the wholeness of the thing, its being distinctively something or other. This is the view of Aquinas; it is these elements in combination which make up our experience of beauty.

Beauty is a sense of harmony induced in us by some perceived form. In this view the heart of the idea of beauty is found not in the thing but more completely in our experience of the thing. Explanations for this harmony run from holding our imagination and understanding to be brought into some kind of unity in this experience (Kant's view), to the notion that the perceived form fits our life-rhythm, or the structure of our bodies (a physiological approach to beauty).

Beauty is truth in sensuous form.

> 'Beauty is truth, truth beauty,' — that is all
> Ye know on earth, and all ye need to know.

In this view truth is meant to include abiding values as well as hard facts. This is the view of Hegel. John Keats, at least when his mind turns toward reflection on Grecian artifacts, adheres to the view as well. And Keats has shaped its popular expression, as given above.

Beauty is the expression of an act of imagination which has gained for us a unique individual something. The imagination strives for the completely individual; the reason, as in science, for example, works toward the universal. A work of art is an expression of the imagination. If we feel its individuality the expression is successful; and this is the core of our appreciation of beauty. This would be the view of Croce.

Beauty is the feeling of an emotion placed in the work by the artist; it is this which stirs us and constitutes the experience of beauty. This is the view of Schopenhauer; in his view beauty can be found also in nature since in everything, because of his view of the world, there is a throbbing will. The modification gained by shearing away nature and confining attention to art so that the beautiful becomes an expression of the artist's emotion, is popular with a number of modern writers.

The beautiful is a quality of life, encompassing "the highest and best feelings to which men have risen," and presented in works of art in order to help guide mankind toward perfection. This is Tolstoy's view; but it must be said at once that Tolstoy would not welcome our calling this his conception of the *beautiful.* He puts aside the idea of "beauty" as much too vague. And confining himself to art his language is in harmony with the meaning immediately preceding — that in art the feeling and experience of the artist are transmitted. This aversion to the word "beauty" is difficult to understand. In any case there is a rather common view which tends to identify beauty with goodness in the above manner. And for Tolstoy any work of art lacking the above quality is false art. The view raises the question of censorship. Should false art be controlled?

By the term "beautiful" one can only mean the objects which give him pleasure through sight and sound. Whatever these may be, and of course there is no disputing about taste, we objectify our pleasure, place it in these objects, and call the objects beautiful. This would be the view of Santayana.

The heart of the beautiful is a sexual impulse, repressed by the artist, sublimated, and becoming overt in his art. The problem of identification is here left to the reader.

Beauty is significant form. This, so brief as to be unintelligible, stands as our most successful digest. The view belongs to Clive Bell. And if we ask what is meant by significant form Mr. Bell tells us that a significant form is any form which strikes us as beautiful. If this seems faintly circular to the reader, let him be patient until we see whether something can be rescued from this point of view.

Certainly, there are theories enough to suit any taste. There are perhaps as many levels and types of appreciation as there are theories about beauty. And, curiously, there are elements which ring true in most of these theories. We are sometimes charmed by an artist's skill in representing some natural object. We do feel the need for organic unity; and we label a musical composition, novel, or play poor when we discover that it does not "hold together." There is something to be said for unity and harmony in the objects we call beautiful. In many artistic compositions we do recognize something like "truth." Perhaps we revere a Hamlet because he is a unique individual, unforgettably himself, and for this reason having universal overtones. And who has not felt the emotion in a piece of music, or in the throbbing paintings of van Gogh when all of nature seems to be stirring dynamically? And certainly we are pleased by the things we think beautiful.

Perhaps, then, most of these theories accurately explain something of the nature of art, including natural artistry. Perhaps there are artists, and arts, to fit all of these theories. But it is hardly satisfactory to set down a cascade of theories and call it a day. We must raise the question: Which of these theories have elements to be found in our own experience?

A number of our theories stressed the need for a unified variety in the experience of beauty — an organic unity, a harmony, a wholeness. And one often hears that every form of beauty presents a unity in variety. Now is there something here which must be included in our thinking? Perhaps there is.

Unity in Variety

Suppose that the New York Philharmonic has set up its stands in your living room with a full panoply of musicians, the instruments perfectly tuned, and with great precision, clarity of tone, and unwavering volume, plays the note of middle C for the length of a full-blown (and, of course, full-fiddled) symphony — say, for one hour and fifteen minutes. However great the skill of the musicians, or of their conductor, you would be displeased. You would be experiencing a great amount of unity of tone and purpose, but no variety whatever. Apparently, in the experience of beauty there must be variety in the sight, sound, and thought.

Or suppose the cacophony of unorganized sound which greets us when an orchestra is tuning up were to be called a symphony. Suppose this were to continue with great gusto for the hour and fifteen minutes. You would be irritated. Yet certainly there would be immense variety in this performance. Apparently, in the experience of beauty we can hold to the need for unity in the sight, sound, and thought.

We may generalize the conclusion, applying it to all esthetic experience, and say that the experience of beauty must contain a unity in variety.

But is it proper to speak of beauty in nature, as well as in art?

The Pervasiveness of Beauty

We have been assuming that beauty can properly be spoken of in referring both to art and nature. Certainly, in common speech the term is applied to both of these areas. And yet many of our theories apply only to art. Beauty as Imitation, as Imagination, as Emotion (in the dilute version), as Sublimation: such theories are directed toward works of art, and can be applied to nature, if at all, only with considerable awkwardness.

Can we restrict our sense of beauty to art alone? To confine it so seems very strange. The man who finds value in art is very likely also one who is impressed by nature. The more one reflects upon the point the clearer it seems that no reason can be found for such restriction. Indeed, whatever the elusive thing is which we find in works of art can be found quite widely in our whole experience.

And I think we can convince ourselves of this by posing a question which seems at first beside the point: *Where in our experience do we find an example of absolute ugliness?* I do not insist such examples are completely missing from our lives — that the slate, on which experience writes, is a total blank in this respect — but where would we look?

Earlier we had insisted, somewhat ungraciously, upon the pres-

ence of ugliness in your community — a street-power-line-archi-
tectural ugliness. Then select the ugliest building there, whether it
be the mayor's house or the modest establishment of a teacher.
And raise the question: *Is this esthetically displeasing in every
way?* If your experience is anything like mine, or like that of my
acquaintances, you will find something pleasing in this selected
house, in an arch, a column, or — to begin to speak of the teacher's house — the angle of a broken shutter. And if to make the test
still more convincing, we were to seek out such an unlikely spot
for beauty as the city dump (with apologies to all those superin-
tendents among our readers whose work we are now discussing)
and ask if this cluttered example of "Nature morte" (and with a
vengeance) is esthetically displeasing in every way, we would find
that it is not. Despite ourselves, the visual aspect of this sheer collection would begin to present unities pleasing to the eye. (Happily,
we have already confined our attention to sight and sound alone.)
It is reported to me that a bombed-out area, even though its former
unity is gone, gains even through destruction new and pleasing
visual aspects. The example which we seek might have to be beyond any experience we have had — a chaos "without form, and
void," a state before creation.

But if this is so we would expect to find beauty in nature, as well
as art. We have found one condition for beauty in the presence of
form, unity in variety. And surprisingly, one condition for existence
is likewise form. Do we experience anything which is really formless? Part at least of Plotinus' point seems very true: existent things
do have unity — definite lines and facets. Trees do not simply flop
across the landscape. Existence does not present us with sheer
monotony or with chaos. It would not then be surprising should
we begin to find beauty widely spread through nature, for nature
has form in great abundance. Perhaps any appreciation of nature
is an appreciation of beauty; for confront it, and it is the surfaces of
things, their visual aspects, their forms, which enter our experience.

More generally, if we begin to look for flashes of beauty, we
begin to find them all around us — in light and shadow, in the jux-
taposition of interesting forms, in the surfaces and relations among
things. Of course, we may be living in our own illusion. But if we
ask why beauty is to be found here, or there, or somewhere else, the
answer must be that the beauty is at least as much present there as
in some work of art. Of course, it would not have been there had not

human beings been here to observe it; nor would the work of art be there. But we are here, and this may bring beauty, too.

If the argument is convincing we have reason to eliminate any theory which cannot explain the presence of beauty in the whole range of our experience, in nature as well as in art.

The Imitation Theory Rejected

This alone would lead us to look with suspicion upon the Imitation theory. But there are other reasons for suspicion, too.

Often in art, as has been said, we do admire skill in representing, or imitating, nature. But, certainly, the beauty we experience in nature cannot be an imitation of nature; so far the theory is defective. Some paintings and sculpture, but not all, represent nature. Symphony, ballet, architecture, plays, novels, poetry seem not to be imitating nature. Perhaps music is developed from the sounds of nature, but the symphony has here improved upon the natural product. The occasional melody of nature has been transformed into melody through and through. In the dance our sometimes graceful, sometimes awkward bumbling movement, has become sheer patterned grace. In drama, the novel, poetry, our occasionally expressive, often stumbling, conversation with its delayed reactions and sheer confusion, has given way to an ever-expressive and graceful form. And architecture certainly seems a transformation of the structure of nature. Each art through its own excellence transforms, rather than imitates, nature: painting through line, mass, and color; dancing through the patterned grace of human movement; sculpture through form and mass and the play of light. Architecture through colossal dimensions of form and mass. The play, novel, and poetry through presenting out of words some larger whole — a pattern, a form, which the words support for a perceiving mind. Music through ordered tones, and rhythms, a material invisible, but very real, falling on the ear.

Nature, then, furnishes the material for beauty. And in art the material is transformed. This seems to be true even when we view some natural scene. "But look at the landscape from this perspective." "Come up here. Now let the fringe of trees serve as frame." The imitation theory does not have sufficient power to explain this experience.

We can say, then, that the material of tone, line, mass, color, rhythm, motion, perspective, and meaning is the means for presenting this unity in variety. But still something should be said which has not been said. Through this material there is presented a unity in variety — of what?

The Remaining Theories Examined

Our emotions are stirred through works of art and natural artistry. pressed by this unity in variety — emotion, imagination, goodness, truth, significant form.

Our emotions are stirred through works of art and natural artistry. But it seems doubtful that this should be made the heart of the experience. Nor do we really mean to say the emotion is *in* the work of art or in the natural scene; this is more easily explained as our response. But certainly in the appreciation of beauty both our emotions and our reason are included in the experience, not excluded as is emotion in the sciences.

And Croce clearly scores with his talk about imagination. Obviously, imagination is important in art; is it, however, more important here than in works of reason? Probably not. Yet Croce is right in stressing the drive of reason toward something universal, while the imaginativeness of art is moving toward the individual. Science produces general schemes for our understanding. Art produces this figure, that sonata, this building, that particular pattern of grace and motion. The excellence of the scientific scheme lies in its generality; the excellence of the art object lies in its individuality. The contrast can be overstated; the work of art, well done, has universal overtones simply because it is so unforgettably itself. Hamlet is so completely individual that he is in one sense the universal man. And any scientific finding is at last written down as a single work. Yet the difference Croce finds is present and is important.

It would seem, though, that the beauty lies in the individual nature of the object rather than in the imagination which produced it. In art this individuality is the work of imagination. But in nature one finds the individual, too. And it would be forcing things to insist there is in nature the same kind of imagination that one finds in works of art. The secret of beauty then is in the individual. This takes us back to our theme of unity in variety.

Is some moral perspective, some aspect of the Good, the point of the experience of beauty? Apparently not; the essence of beauty is often pointedly amoral. The feelings engendered by classical music are not particularly feelings reflecting moral worth. In neither Greek nor Shakespearian tragedy is the tragic figure engaged in a morality play. In the comedies the case is clearer still. And while paintings often represent something, the presentation is, as often as not, morally neutral. Nor in ballet is one presented with a passion play, although there may run through it a play of passion. Indeed, if we find some work of art which has a moral lesson as its sole reason for existing, this is enough, we rightly feel, to justify our marking down the value of the work. It does seem obvious that the breadth and sweep of art go far beyond the kind of situation in which it is appropriate to speak of good and evil, when we think of music, the dance, painting, sculpture, architecture, poetry, the novel, and the rest. And when we include the experience of nature, it is clear that moral distinctions distinguish nothing through much of this field.

Even if the theory of sublimation is true, this would tell us only why some people are artists; it would not explain beauty to us. And the theory that the beautiful consists only of the objects in which we perchance take pleasure, true as far as it goes, depends upon whether this taking pleasure is really *per* chance; it stands as a kind of last resort.

We have left: Beauty is truth in sensuous form; and Beauty is significant form.

To identify Beauty with Truth or Knowledge, however much the meaning of these terms may be altered, is not quite satisfactory. I find the sunset beautiful. One does not carry away a vastly increased store of knowledge after having viewed a sunset, although in the experience one does perhaps feel a heightened awareness. This sense of keener awareness may be the source of the notion that Truth or Knowledge is the point of the experience. But this heightened awareness is an awareness of what? Of the setting sun? Of myself? Of height? For all the attention one may address to a Beethoven symphony, a Chopin nocturne, a Grieg concerto, has one the reward of a single atom of factual data to weld into a molecular statement? Knowledge-wise, what a paucity of information is to be gained from the arts! More knowledge of David, one would presume, is to be found in reading the Books of First and Second Samuel, than in viewing the inspiring figure created by Michelangelo. And if, in poetry and novel, one may learn something of the appearance of London, or of France in revolution, these facts are more conveniently ordered in a Baedeker, and a history of France. Knowledge, or truth, is not as such the point of the experience. There is a sense of increased awareness, but it seems to be without Truth or Knowledge in any discoverable sense. Art then tells us nothing as such. And even where something definite is imparted this is not the point of the work so far as it is art. The facts, so necessary for modern life, are conspicuously absent here. Even when information is conveyed, as in a novel, this is not the point of the reading, or of its having been written.

This awareness without knowledge in the usual sense, in fact, reminds us of beauty as significant form. Our attention is caught and held; whether or not a definite truth is conveyed to us, yet the object of this awareness seems to hold significance for us. Can the view of Mr. Bell provide us with an answer to the question of the nature of this unity in variety?

The phrase used is so mysterious, and the possibility of an answer to our problem so important, that it might be well to spend some time in gaining an entry to his point of view. Here, then, at some length, is the significant form of Mr. Bell.

Significant Form

The Aesthetic Hypothesis

What I have to say is this: the rapt philosopher, and he who contemplates a work of art, inhabit a world with an intense and peculiar significance of its own; that significance is unrelated to the significance of life. In this world the emotions of life find no place. It is a world with emotions of its own. . . .

Before a work of art people who feel little or no emotion for pure form find themselves at a loss. They are deaf men at a concert. They know that they are in the presence of something great, but they lack the power of apprehending it. They know that they ought to feel for it a tremendous emotion, but it happens that the particular kind of emotion it can raise is one that they can feel hardly or not at all. And so they read into the forms of the work those facts and ideas for which they are capable of feeling emotion, and feel for them the emotions that they can feel — the ordinary emotions of life. When confronted by a picture, instinctively they refer back its forms to the world from which they came. They treat created form as though it were imitated form, a picture as though it were a photograph. Instead of going out on the stream of art into a new world of aesthetic experience, they turn a sharp corner and come straight home to the world of human interests. For them the significance of a work of art depends on what they bring to it; no new thing is added to their lives, only the old material is stirred. A good work of visual art carries a person who is capable of appreciating it out of life into ecstasy: to use art as a means to the emotions of life is to use a telescope for reading the news.

To make his meaning clearer, Mr. Bell gives an account of his own condition with respect to music, an art form he does not claim to understand.

My opinion about music is not worth having. Yet, sometimes, at a concert, though my appreciation of the music is limited and humble, it is pure. Sometimes, though I have a poor understanding, I have a clean palate. Consequently, when I am feeling bright and clear and intent, at the beginning of a concert for instance, when something that I can grasp is being played, I get from music that pure aesthetic emotion that I get from visual art. It is less intense, and the rapture is evanescent; I understand music too ill for music to transport me far into the world of pure aesthetic ecstasy. But at moments I do appreciate music as pure musical form, as sounds combined according to the laws of a mysterious necessity, as pure art with a tremendous significance of its own and no relation whatever to the significance of life; and in those moments I lose myself in that infinitely sublime state of mind to which pure visual form transports me. How inferior is my normal state of mind at a concert. Tired or perplexed, I let slip my sense of form, my aesthetic emotion collapses, and I begin weaving into the harmonies that I cannot grasp the ideas of life. Incapable of feeling the austere emotions of art, I begin to read into the musical forms human emotions of terror and mystery, love and hate, and spend the minutes, pleasantly enough, in a world of turbid and inferior feeling. . . . I know very well what has happened. I have been using art as a means to the emotions of life and reading into it the ideas of life. I have been cutting blocks with a razor. I have tumbled from the superb peaks of aesthetic exaltation to the snug foothills of warm humanity. It is a jolly country. No one need be ashamed of enjoying himself there. Only no one who has ever been on the heights can help feeling a little crestfallen in the cosy valleys. And let no one imagine, because he has made merry in the warm tilth and quaint nooks of romance, that he can even guess at the austere and thrilling raptures of those who have climbed the cold, white peaks of art.

The Metaphysical Hypothesis

Now to see objects as pure forms is to see them as ends in themselves. . . . What is the significance of anything as an end in itself? What is that which is left when we have stripped a thing of all its associations, of all its significance as a means? What is left to provoke our emotion? What but that which philosophers used to call "the thing in itself" and now call "ultimate reality"? Shall I be altogether fantastic in suggesting, what some of the profoundest thinkers have believed, that the significance of the thing in itself is the significance of Reality? Is it possible that the answer to my question, "Why are we so profoundly moved by certain combinations of lines and colours?" should be, "Because artists can express in combinations of lines and colours an emotion felt for reality which reveals itself through line and colour"?

If this suggestion were accepted it would follow that "significant form" was form behind which we catch a sense of ultimate reality. There would be good reason for supposing that the emotions which artists feel in their moments of inspiration, that others feel in the rare moments when they see objects artistically, and that many of us feel when we contemplate works of art, are the same in kind. All would be emotions felt for reality revealing itself through pure form. . . .

What, then, is the conclusion of the whole matter? No more than this, I think. The contemplation of pure form leads to a state of extraordinary exaltation and complete detachment from the concerns of life: of so much, speaking for myself, I am sure. It is tempting to suppose that the emotion which exalts has been transmitted through the forms we contemplate by the artist who created them. If this be so, the transmitted emotion, whatever it may be, must be of such a kind that it can be expressed in any sort of form — in pictures, sculptures, buildings, pots, textiles, etc., etc. Now the emotion that artists express comes to some of them, so they tell us, from the apprehension of the formal significance of material things; and the formal significance of any material thing is the significance of that thing considered as an end in itself. But if an object considered as an end in itself moves us more profoundly (*i.e.* has greater significance) than the same object considered as a means to practical ends or as a thing related to human interests — and this undoubtedly is the case — we can only suppose that when we consider anything as an end in itself we become aware of that in it which is of greater moment than any qualities it may have acquired from keeping company with human beings. Instead of recognising its accidental and conditioned importance, we become aware of its essential reality, of the God in everything, of the universal in the particular, of the all-pervading rhythm. Call it by what name you will, the thing that I am talking about is that which lies behind the appearance of all things — that which gives to all things their individual significance, the thing in itself, the ultimate reality. And if a more or less unconscious apprehension of this latent reality of material things be, indeed, the cause of that strange emotion, a passion to express which is the inspiration of many artists, it seems reasonable to suppose that those who, unaided by material objects, experience the same emotion have come by another road to the same country.

The Conclusion

My aesthetic hypothesis — that the essential quality in a work of art is significant form — was based on my aesthetic experience. Of my aesthetic experiences I am sure. About my second hypothesis, that significant form is the expression of a peculiar emotion felt for reality — I am far from confident. However, I assume it to be true, and go on to suggest that this sense of reality leads men to attach greater importance to the spiritual than to the material significance of the universe, that it disposes men to feel things as ends instead of merely recognising them as means, that a sense of reality is, in fact, the essence of spiritual health. If this be so, we shall expect to find that ages in which the creation of significant form is checked are ages in which the sense of reality is dim, and that these are ages of spiritual poverty.[1]

We have been offered a broad-ranging point of view. The isolation from the affairs of life of Bell's "significant form" places the experience of the beautiful on a somewhat misty, somewhat mystical peak. He does in fact admit a relationship between this experience, and the mystical type of religious experience. The elevation of this

---

[1] Clive Bell, *Art* (New York: Frederick A. Stokes Co., and London: Chatto & Windus, Ltd., 1913). I have selected the relevant passages from pages 27, 29–30, 30–33, 53–54, 68–70, 100–101.

experience above the affairs of life is reminiscent of Plato's handling of Beauty, if not of art. The doctrine is presented partly as a reading of his own experience. He does not translate this significance into words; it is untranslatable. At the same time he finds an important function for this experience in human life; it can purify our emotions, and turn our attention to "spiritual" (broadly conceived) ends. Somewhat less certainly he proposes the experience of significant form as the means of opening a path toward ultimate reality. Here in the esthetic experience, he seems to suggest, is a possible relation to final truth. And this possible relation could help account, one would suppose, for the "significance" of significant form.

But are you, along with me, both impressed and perplexed by this doctrine? Do you wonder, as I do, why this significance will not translate into words? Are words, perhaps, too imprecise to carry the meaning of this experience? But if between the significance of ordinary words and meanings, and the significance of form, the isolation is complete, how can this experience be significant for us? Of what is it significant? What does it signify? The missing element is missing still. If in the experience of beauty we are presented with a unity in variety of significant form, one is disposed to ask, "Significant of what?" And if the answer is, "Significant of ultimate reality," at least we must come to understand this answer — an answer which seems not to lend itself readily to understanding.

It might be possible for us to check this view by turning abruptly from it. Let us turn back to our experience, and for a test case, we may elect the art furthest from words. If in such an art form we can find "significance," we have found it everywhere.

A Test Case

Suppose we listen to Chopin played sensitively. Here is a theme without words — but identifiable (later, you may catch yourself humming it, just as you might recall at a later time the ideas in an article you have read); here are certain related themes which logically seem to develop the main theme; and here are contrasts and repetitions. The basic theme comes back, altered and augmented, just as the basic thesis of an argument gains new qualities and continues to develop through many printed pages. And here are you listening to an articulation of melody and harmony. Your practical nature is in abeyance; your intellect is not at work in its usual manner, and yet you are alert. You are confronted with a richness of quality which comes and goes, arrives at endings and new beginnings, comes to conflicts and resolves them; but all without the words, which give us wordy creatures something to which to hold, having any relevance.

Beauty as a Sign of Something

What is happening, indeed? Unless we want to rule this organized quality, and rhythm, and expectant articulateness into the limbo of the meaningless, we had better let it stand as a sign of something. To say this is little enough, except that saying it explains our expectancy. We always attend to signs — signs of the time, of rain, of distress, of joy. Man spends much of his time attending to signs of various kinds. This volume, for example, is nothing save wood pulp and an immense number of signs to which you are paying more or less attention; the same is true of the morning newspaper, the racing form, recipe books, letters; but still more, one attends to stop signs, go signs, neon signs which flash or flutter, highway markers, the indicators of the automobile panel which warn of temperature, oil, speed, and electric voltage; price markers at the grocery store; and still more, one takes as signs a cloudy sky, a cry of pain, the roar of an approaching motor, the troubled countenance of a friend, the pressure of a handclasp, a broken twig, a footprint. Indeed, even a listing of the kinds of things which we look upon as signs of something could be completed only with great difficulty. For man the world is packed with signs. And let us note that a sign always leads us on to something else. The cloudy sky may lead us to expect rain, the roar of a motor may lead us to expect the sight of a car, the footprint may lead us to expect the proximity of another human being, a cry of pain may lead us to expect the presence of a suffering and living thing nearby. Many signs lead us to expect certain happenings or to believe in certain states of affairs. The signs on this page, in newspapers, in letters, lead us to meanings of various sorts. These are often called symbols — signs with an agreed-upon meaning. Man's interest in such signs accounts for his having been well called a "symbolific creature."

Let us regard this music as a sign of something. But this kind of sign is not like any yet discussed. We are not led to expect another kind of happening, but just more music. And if we are led on to meanings, it has to be in a very personal way for tones and harmonies do not have agreed-upon meanings as have words, our more ordinary symbols. Suzanne Langer seems to me to have begun the answer to this problem when she says of music:

> . . . *music at its highest, though clearly a symbolic form, is an unconsummated symbol.* Articulation is its life, but not assertion; expressiveness, not expression. The actual function of meaning, which calls for permanent contents, is not fulfilled; for the *assignment* of one rather than another possible meaning to each form is never explicitly made.[2]

Let us appropriate this insight, used by Langer to explain music, and apply the thought to beauty anywhere.

Here then in Chopin, we would say, a complicated scheme is articulated. In its own way something like a thesis is announced and unerringly developed toward conclusions; what we at least take to be urgency, striving, compulsion, gaiety, austere melancholy, peacefulness, contemplativeness, spiritedness, somberness, sweep us through and through; not separately, and not in themselves, but in their own movement toward whatever end will complete the thesis, and without verbal content.

What one finds in Chopin is not so different from what one experiences when he really sees so commonplace an object as, say, a lowly sumac. A sumac is appropriate for several reasons: First, there is one outside my window (beside the broken shutter); second, a sumac is apparently good for nothing; it produces no shade, no lumber. Yet with a light stirring in its leaves is it not, too, an articulation which tells us nothing verbal? Its scheme is complex; its movement is from trunk to topmost leaf; it divides and subdivides to substitute slender branches for the mass of trunk; it ends in foliage more complex than a Calder mobile, weaving patterns of varying complexity before our eyes. Its complexity, its articulation of its own substance, is this not its purpose here?

And if the play, Hamlet, is not designed to give us information about Denmark, then is it not too an articulation about life in which the main point is not the geography of Denmark, or the nature of

---

[2] Suzanne K. Langer, *Philosophy in a New Key* (Cambridge: Harvard University Press, 1942), p. 240.

the person, Hamlet, or courtly life; but the ordered whole silently (behind the noises of sentries, soliloquies, and guilt-stricken nobles) exfoliating from an initial situation into its precise components, and through their working — along an action natural to the parts, toward a completion called for by the parts — achieving precisely the ordered whole which is here so neatly appropriate?

In all the arts, and even in things with natural artistry, there is, I think, an articulation of whatever materials are at hand — tone, substance, word, character, color, motion — of an initial "given" (a situation, a sketch, a bloc of material), in space, or time, or both. And this articulation, which is all I name it so far, stands to us as a sign, an unbound sign. I mean that even where words are used, signs bound to dictionary meaning as in a novel — "bound" signs, then — the point is not the "bound" signs, but the larger unity which includes the whole of this artistic expression, and which is not itself expressed or expressible in any single set of words.

Here the appeal must be to your experience, for how can one say convincingly in words what already has been granted to be something other than a set of words? But this can be said; it is in answer to the eyebrow lifted when I held that whatever is articulated, it is not expressible in words. It can at least be said that artists generally do profess their arts not to be reducible to words. With this in mind we have said the signs are free, are as Langer holds to be the case with music. No playwright would hold that the plot is the same as the play. But more generally we mean there is no exception to the statement that all art has an indefinite connotation. Aristotle long ago suggested metaphor as the life of poetry. Now what is a metaphor? It is a figure of speech in which two meanings are fused together. "John is five feet tall" is not a metaphorical expression (although once there was something metaphorical about it, this measure of distance being the king's foot). "John is a fox" is a metaphorical expression. The first is definite; the second is rich in possible meanings but indefinite. One would need several statements: "John is cunning," "John is sly," "John is deceptive," "John is . . ." what? Cowardly, backhanded, untrustworthy? to get out the meaning present in the single metaphor; and one would not be sure of having gotten all of it.

Or, again, consider the little verse of Sandburg:

> The fog comes
> on little cat feet.

It sits looking
over harbor and city
on silent haunches
and then moves on.[3]

Words are used; each has a dictionary meaning; but the words are being used in another sense than when one gives full weight to dictionary meanings. To get out the meanings one would have to hold again to a number of statements: "The fog is pervasive," "The fog comes and leaves silently," "The fog is amazingly noiseless for so major a phenomenon." And have we yet expressed all the meanings which Sandburg's metaphor may hold for some mind somewhere? The signs are arranged so as to be free signs, delimited to be sure. It would be inappropriate to think of "fire" in this context, and discourteous to think of "smog." But within the appropriate limits we are encouraged to think of many things.

Now it is notable that when two clear meanings are fused, the result is not simply a third clear meaning, but a range of meanings. What is meant is delimited, but not described. And whatever meaning you find within the limits set, is as appropriate as any other. If even in those art forms which use words directly the meaning is essentially indefinite, then in art as such the signs, it would seem, are "free," are not "definite," delimit but do not prescribe.

A poet is not unhappy when we find a meaning he had not seen or intended in his poem. And if what happens when the public visits art galleries be given any weight — namely, that to this composition, so perfectly precise in its own way the visitor adds whatever meanings he may find appropriate from the meanings in his experience — then here, too, the sign is free and will support a multiplicity of meanings, only the limits of which are demarked.

And what is the point of all this? We have decided that beauty is present in nature as well as in art, that the experience of beauty is the experience of some kind of unified variety, that art works a transformation upon nature, that appreciation of beauty is appreciation of the individual, and that in the experience of beauty forms become significant to us, standing as signs which delimit without prescribing, presenting a matrix yielding insight only with our help, a context waiting as it were to be fitted to the context of our lives.

[3] "Fog," from *Chicago Poems* by Carl Sandburg. Copyright, 1916, by Henry Holt and Company, Inc. Copyright, 1944, by Carl Sandburg. By permission of the publishers.

Our analysis differs from that of Mr. Bell. He had found significant form unrelated to the rest of life. We find it related, standing
as an unbound sign, providing man with freedom from the tailored
symbols which surround us. Beginning with our experience in the
arts, the principal matter seemed this calling out of our attention,
our following out the parts expectantly as one led to and required
another; and the likeness between this, and our comparable behavior
in the presence of those other signs, called "symbols." But the difference in the expectancies had also to be noted; hence, my monstrous
phrases, "indefinite connotation," "nonverbal articulation," and the
rest. There would seem to be two points which must be acceptable,
if the view is to be accepted. (1) We can follow a logic of development without symbols. And this may be why a logic of symbols,
symbolic logic, is even possible. We have, then, two levels, as it
were, of discourse. In discourse with each other we use significant
symbols. In the appreciation of the beautiful — both in art and
nature — we attend to significant forms. (2) There exists a contrast,
almost a conflict, between these complex forms, and ordinary meanings. From the side of ordinary meanings these forms are indefinite
telling us, as we have said, nothing as such; clusters of ordinary
meanings may be applied, perhaps must be applied, in drawing out
the significance of such forms. From the side of these "significant
forms," each is precisely what it is — but language is imprecise, and
can only endlessly approximate these forms; and the clusters of
meaning are man's attempt to reduce to symbols what is other than
symbolic.

But we have not faced the question: Why are any forms "significant"? Admittedly, we do attend expectantly to objects of art and
nature, but why? Must we come at last to say with Mr. Bell: In this
experience we grasp, or seek to grasp, ultimate reality? But this is
a strangely closed-end kind of saying; after this has been said, what
can be added? Only an index! For this reason I should prefer to
defer such ultimate answers, until we reach the ultimate questions
of our final chapter.

A less ultimate kind of answer might be this: Why are any forms
"significant"? Newton, while helping to initiate modern science,
included in his *Principia* the delightful suggestion that the universe
is the "sensorium" of God. Perhaps the answer to our question is
simply: In the experience of beauty man takes the place of Newton's
God; and the world — as beautiful — becomes a human sensorium.

You may not allow this statement as an answer. In the second half of our discussion we may be forced to go beyond this answer. The statement may have something in it; even if not, it may be sufficiently mystifying to require a halt in our reflections. As you may have noted, we have not proceeded, in the present case, in our accustomed manner.

It has been our custom to produce the horrid problem, reflect upon its possibilities, ponder its difficulties, and then to suspend operations — for rest, refreshment, and in the hope of preserving a kind of positive neutrality. It is not my wish to bring you bag and baggage into any philosophical camp other than your own. Our whole enterprise is directed toward finding where we stand. For this reason I have rather hoped for a double solution to every problem — yours, and mine. Only should we be fortunate enough to encounter truth would I expect our answers to be the same. Apart from this hope — and we have already reflected on the remote nature of this bright possibility — your resolution of our problem must be your own. It has been our custom, likewise, to let you know the direction in which the discussion has been leading me; to this end, and toward the end of a discussion, I have dropped the posture of neutrality, and have continued — possibly all alone — toward an answer to the problem which seemed to me indicated by the argument, and therefore not unreasonable.

In the present case, hardly knowing how to state the problem, we had simply begun at large; we drew a number of distinctions, and from a great catalogue of competing views funnelled in to a kind of "symbolific" or "signific" view of beauty. This was the position which remained after an irenic, and not too extended, period of criticism.

Your task is, of course, to find your view; and it may be nothing like the view which stands in partial outline. But do you share my estimate of the elements of our catalogue of theories? Does the phrase "unity in variety" contain an element essential to the beautiful? Do you find beauty as pervasive as do I? What importance have imitation, emotion, imagination, goodness, and truth in your thought about our problem? And where have I gone astray in centering this experience in one version of "significant form"?

Once again, I shall join issue with the problem, and perhaps with you, in the latter part of our discussion. But here is your chance, by careful and independent thinking, to break away — should my line of resolution seem not too promising — before I further extend the line which I have chosen.

II. Toward an Appreciation of Beauty

So we have gained a tentative conclusion; spindly, gangling, lacking in development, requiring further nourishment, yet it exists! This gives us the privilege of beginning from a somewhat different point. Should we be able to arrive — and without strain — at something like the same conclusion, it might be evidence of our having found the truth. Again, it might be evidence of a clever manipulation of ideas, held together by the flow of rhetoric. In either case my attention is drawn to a kind of variant counsel I have heard concerning the use of beauty. One would suppose the experience of beauty to have some use in human life. And yet, as we have seen, those most intimate with our subject join together in telling us we must forget utility in preparing ourselves for the possibility of this experience. We shall begin by raising a question about the use of beauty.

The Use of Beauty

If in the experience of beauty we are to forget utility, then this experience is strikingly at variance with the major drift of an essentially practical culture. If we live in such a culture it would be easy to understand why some of us are mystified by this nonutile experience which artists, at least occasionally, picture as having importance. Now we have seen that in our society a heavy stress is laid on utility, on instrumental values, on instruments; indeed, an important philosophy, arising from the American scene, was called Instrumentalism. We are naturally at ease among instrumental values — productions which lead to further production. We understand instrumental thinking and do it efficiently. One *could* conceive of everything in terms of its utility. If one did so, it would be natural to believe that a thing which has no use is useless; and if useless, then also worthless. And if such a person were to ask: If it has no use, what is it worth? the question, since for such a man, *use* is the only kind of *worth,* is asking: If it is not an instrument for some further purpose, then for what further purpose can it be the instrument?

No one can answer the question put in this way. The answer, which cannot be given in terms of the asker, is: The experience of beauty is not intended for use and is its own worth. And this is to understand the experience of beauty, the esthetic experience, not as an instrument but as an end. If it has any value, its value is not instrumental but intrinsic. That we must have instrumental values, the more the better, is obvious to Americans. That instrumental values require intrinsic values in order even for the instruments to fulfill their instrumental promise, should be equally obvious.

Preoccupation with this useless type of endeavor, I am pleased to argue, has matchless worth and is an essential ingredient in the life of any thoughtful man. It does seem reasonable to find something of great importance as the goal of art. Consider the immense energy spent in its behalf. It is surely surpassed only by the energy expended, among similar pursuits, by those engaged in science. It seems unreasonable to regard the paying out of this immense sum of energy as a payment upon some oddity or trivia of life, or for escape, or even to gain pleasure which might be gained in some less tiring manner. But rather, where art is at its finest, men would seem to be engaged in matters of the greatest moment.

And what are these matters? No Renaissance has ever been accomplished in human life, no period with a tremendous upsurge of human energies, individuality, and vividness in the total life, without its having as part of it a great burst of artistic endeavor. This leads me to take very seriously the notion that art has an essential relation to any renaissance which may occur either in the life of a culture or of an individual. Its purpose should be one of arousal; it should mark an awakening.

If this is so then, since man lives so meagerly, since often we are little more than half alive, what better could we do than try to find ourselves through forms of beauty? Strange prescription for Americans: a formula for becoming less active! How we do pound away to solve our problems; but pounding will not touch this problem. With lesser problems we can pretend that we are really going somewhere, very busily adjust one thing to another, take trips, fly around the world, and claim that finally we have "gotten somewhere." But in fact one does not really *go* anywhere in moving from place to place. For seventy years we are fixed within this universe with no *where* to go. Perhaps the only sense in which we can truly advance is to interrupt the feverish trips which take us here and there, stand quietly and — for one thing — in beauty learn how we may grow as is proper to a man.

If beauty has this function we must try to describe it. And we are dealing here with an experience which is intrinsic in its value. To find an experience intrinsically satisfying is to interrupt one's web-woven sequence of means-end-means-end-means with every end itself a means to further ends, to interrupt this with a final end.

We interrupt the mean-end-means sequence in sleep; but then we are in no position to profit from the interruption. It may be granted that one's state in the experience of art is sometimes much like sleep. There are other times when the web of means and end is interrupted. It is interrupted in play, and yet in play one is apt to submerge himself again within a social group and substitute another means-end sequence.

In the experience of beauty, because it is our own unique experience, we cannot submerge ourselves within some social group; and if we really interrupt the sequence of our lives, we cannot in this experience substitute another means-end sequence. What happens then when one breaks the means-end sequence of his life and stands erect — apart now from his purposes, his instruments and property, his wallet, and all the other impedimenta of his ordered life? It is, of course, possible that nothing will happen; it is possible — as we have noted — that one will fall asleep. But it does not seem to me likely, I must confess, that the great expenditure of artistic energy through the ages has been directed toward a drugless, non-habit-forming, barbiturate-free cure for insomnia.

Quite the contrary, beauty must furnish an awakening! Man can, in a moment, lift his head in contemplation, break the means-end sequence of his life, and live in the articulation of some sign which is not verbal. So — what? James Joyce has a word which may be important for us; it is in his *Portrait of an Artist as a Young Man;* the speaker is Stephen:

> The mind in that mysterious instant Shelley likened beautifully to a fading coal. The instant wherein that supreme quality of beauty, the clear radiance of the esthetic image, is apprehended luminously by the mind which has been arrested by its wholeness and fascinated by its harmony is the luminous silent *stasis* of esthetic pleasure, a spiritual state very like to that cardiac condi-

tion which . . . Luigi Galvani, using a phrase almost as beautiful as Shelley's, called the enchantment of the heart.[4]

I have set this passage down in order to gain the word *"stasis."* A *stasis* is a stopping, a halt, an interruption. We have come upon this halting of other activities before, and have found it a condition for the appreciation of beauty. I should now like to suggest that this *stasis* has great importance just because of all we have so far said.

When we spoke of freedom, reference was made to the nature of time — time as it is for us. Let us do so once again. Do you remember how time dragged in childhood? Not only were rooms larger and people bigger; days were longer, years were longer. To provide filling for a single day, or rather, to do justice to the inevitable filling of a single day, immense energy was required; even summer would drag, until we began to catch sight of school not many weeks ahead. Then of course it began to scamper because, by contrast, nine months was so nearly infinite. But consider time for an adult. How quickly the weeks and months fly along; how short a year which seems a decade to the child. The greater the number of projects which we have to accomplish, the more quickly time makes its march. Time, for us, moves with the speed of our busy lives, as we complete old sequences and begin new ones. But in beauty sequences are interrupted; we have an end not means to any other.

We are searching for the concept to attach to *stasis*. And Newton regards the spatial universe as the "sensorium" of God. In the moment of *stasis*, we now suggest, man takes the place of Newton's God; and the world becomes a human sensorium. But what meaning can be drawn from this display of rhetoric? Certainly, I must grant the nebulous aura which surrounds my present language. And I am willing to entertain the possibility that I am talking nonsense. But I think there is a meaning here much like the final and uncertain step taken by Mr. Bell. In short, could the vagueness be dispelled, I think the consequences of our thought would be the following: Any present moment has a great depth if only we can become aware of it. This is what we feel in the experience of beauty. It is an articulation of the depth of reality from which all words are mere abstractions, handling only part. In the esthetic *stasis* one's own authentic self

---

[4] James Joyce, *A Portrait of the Artist as a Young Man*, (New York: The Viking Press, and London: Jonathan Cape, Ltd., 1956), p. 213.

has time to expand, to become itself again, to regain its own depth and proper form. Our rush through time flattens it out, as well as speeding it up, squeezes away its proper depth — much as a fire hose is flattened when rolled back on its spindle. And when we stop its rapid flux — in *stasis* — through halting our pursuit of projects, the world springs back with the depth which it properly has. The intrinsic value of beauty, our "feel" of the proper world, squeezed out when the sumac was only an object left in the wake of a purposeful, fleeting car, now returns — and leaves us in wonder.

And now if we will put *stasis* alongside our notion of the unbound sign in art and natural beauty, viewing them together, I think our goal will be in sight. Sartre, the French philosopher who writes unhappy novels, rightly insists that no one can tell you what you ought to do; one is left by himself in the struggle over any important decision. The point rings true! If we decide to ask advice of another we must first pick the person from whom we shall gain this advice; and in picking the person we are already deciding for ourselves. But there is a circle here, because — not knowing what we ought to do — we wished advice from another. How can the circle be broken?

We come back to the injunction: "Be natural, be yourself!" But what is natural? What is oneself? One cannot be told. What we are to do may be commanded by another, but then what we do is false, external, not ours. And if we have not the words, what we are to do cannot come from a telling of oneself. But here is the rhythm of one's life, and here the conditions of that life; hard, illy arranged, lacking in inner unity.

And here, too, are all the nonverbal articulations of the arts which in no case leave their materials as they had found them. The initial situation yielded to another by what must have been development, and that to another, and still another, until a theme was found; then confidently the interplay began until a finished whole was wrought.

If we cannot tell ourselves what we do not know, and if command cannot help, perhaps we can only look to beauty which in all its forms is an articulation which is not verbal, a logic which does not take words as its pattern but is rather the kind of patterning which led first even to the forming of languages. For we are holding that beauty has a use without being an instrument; for beauty is the use and the result at once. Its use is one's personal articulation of self.

This is finally why one must learn to follow the articulation of a Chopin nocturne, of Hamlet, of a ballet, of a sumac tree. Let one live in these articulations, those as refined and difficult as he can bear. And without command — for this cannot help — but as catalyst these may start the articulation of one's own proper life.

Great art, a product of some renaissance, can lead one to his own personal renaissance. For this reason one should not adopt a pose concerning beauty. I am quite certain, although unable to frame the argument, that a difference of better and worse really exists with regard to works of art. But let no one strain his appreciations into some accepted form, pretending to like what he thinks a person of his capacity and station should approve. One cannot now avoid liking what he likes. Then like it proudly, yet learn to understand it. And if what is liked be something mongrel, a profanation of beauty, one's understanding will lead him beyond the profanation to the authentic beauty which had been profaned.

The experience of beauty is important because it can direct us to our own depth in a life which we allow to become too flat. The subtlety of a tree, a play, a piano concerto, can be a plea for the development of your own proper quality; for every work of art is replete with qualities, is nothing but qualities of color, tone, line, character, and plot. One goes no *where* really in fleeting through space, but one may be able to see and foster his own being in the *stasis* provided by any great work of art, or any object of natural artistry. If this is so, the energy spent by artists is well spent; and our energy in learning to respond to their subtleties will be likewise well spent; for it may lead us to the possibility of living as an art with its own intrinsic satisfactions.

But this is not all. Many of us have our purposes, have gone with them a little way, and then have come flush against our inability to know the further step. This too is the function of the arts: not to teach escape, but merely to articulate their proper metier, that we may live in these and learn from ourselves the next genuine true step.

And this restores once more the bond of art with nature; for a man in the throes, as we say, of decision will seek the solitude of nature; in the quiet of a garden, the wilderness, the sea. Perhaps we have been drawn to this experience for so long, because it can help us to decide. It was curious that we had to argue for the presence of the beautiful, not in art alone but in the natural world as well. For in fact every form of art is also natural. The purity of tone, sound, rhythm, light and shadow, color, and the rest, are functions of natural materials — proper to this universe, employing its character, and wrought by men who are also part of nature.

For many persons, we need not ask the reason, a sense of foreignness hangs over nature. And yet our basic dependence has always been upon this natural world. John Dewey catches the point in a neat phrase, saying that breathing — the constant fluctuation in man's breast — is as much a function of the air we breathe as of our lungs; and hearing is as much a function of the air as of the ear. In the same way seeing is as much a function of nature's light as of the eyes. And since looking and listening are the dominant modes of perceiving beauty, here is still another indication that we must not sever art from nature. And our own physical motion from one place to another is a joint product of the earth on which we stand, the pull of gravity, the continuity of space, all of these, and our own musculature and will to move. And our inner life, our self, has as its platform the same electronic impulse as has any part of nature. There is no foreignness between man and nature. He is rather a focal point in nature's vast continuum, a structure built from its materials. One becomes this single focus of the world out of the matrix of his past, and the conditions of his present life. To mix in one image the themes we are seeking to combine, the individual man comes forth from the natural world as the painting comes forth from its materials. Man is natural; he is of nature's substance. The collision and tension of the forces of nature in its storms and gigantic upheavals have the same basis as the forces colliding in man in his own storms and inner upheaval. Not even in the city does man separate himself from nature; the city is only nature rearranged by man with some of its most striking effects, its life and fragrance, ruled out in the rearrangement. In a way, man being natural, it is not his own house but all of nature which is his home; this is his element, the extension of his life, the whole of which he is part.

Since this is so, it is regrettable that we do in fact bind ourselves so much to other people and miss the freeing influence which an appreciation of nature (which we now grant to be an appreciation of beauty) might bring. We gain support from people, and ignore too much the support of nature. Yet profound men have always turned their attention to nature, finding in this larger world a source of strength and insight.

Jefferson sensed this power in nature, and Rousseau, and Emerson; indeed, Emerson often lumbered out into nature to collect fresh thoughts; many poets and artists have done the same. Jefferson and Rousseau felt together the need of a bond with nature to keep man from becoming decadent, to enable him to renew himself. And this renewal, whether found in art or nature, is, we now maintain, the use of beauty.

It has been often said there is a danger in courting the sense of beauty. And, indeed, there is. For a man with only imposed purposes, the sense of beauty is irrelevant, since he is an Instrumental Man. But for a man with no purposes, no real self driving out from his being, the sense of beauty can be dangerous. He can become a dilettante; he can toy with all the pleasing aspects of experience, his refined appreciations leading him nowhere and softening his whole life. He can live in an immediate moment, but without its depth, a beating of time without filling, the catalyst precipitating no reaction.

What one needs in life is finally one's finished whole; the arc which has begun — your life — needs its proper extension and completion; it needs its unity such that to remove any part would affect the quality of the whole. And this pre-eminently is what any work of art does; it furnishes its unity out of itself. It should then be an invitation to face reality and through beauty, the art of man and nature's art, develop artfully — that is, out of one's self, one's situation, and conditions — the portion of reality which will become your life. And this, I think, is the role of art, both of the looking, and of the listening, and of the looking and listening together.

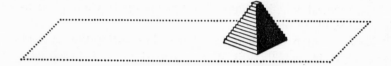

Chapter Five

Ethics

I. The Problem of Right and Wrong

What is the rule of conduct, the strategy, for achieving the good as a social being? This is one way of putting our question. But many questions might be asked about our question. Is not this the question of the good? If so, it has been dealt with; now, especially, we should refrain from double-dealing. Do we need rules of conduct? Do we not already have rules of conduct? Are not all rules of conduct arbitrary? Will not attention to this aspect of our lives probably curtail still more our freedom, introduce into life a perspective which cannot be taken seriously, stand us in danger of becoming "do-gooders," "good Samaritans," and turn us from the main business of living with its emphasis upon the development of our persons? The answer to all of these questions about our question is, "Perhaps." But let us take them in order.

Have we not already discussed the good? The saying is correct, and yet, as we have also noted, the term has at least two senses. We lean back and sigh, "Ah, but life is good"; and the good of which we speak is something like "richness of value." Our statement means: Life is filled with value. There are other times. Reflecting upon some portion of our settled past, we lean forward worriedly, sigh again but in a different manner, and reflect: That was not a good thing for me to do. Or we might have said: It was not proper for me to have done that. Or: I ought not to have done that. Or, more simply: It was not right. In another age we might have torn our hair or put on sackcloth. And sometimes the word "good" is used in the sense of "richness of value." At other times it means "rightness of conduct." We have come to one of those times. It is the second meaning which is before us. Our question, so understood, is the ethical question; we are to think about the "right," or the "ethically good." To avoid confusion we shall use these terms, reserving the single word "good" for "richness of value."

Do we need rules of conduct? The problem of right and wrong turns our attention to the tremendous fact of the overlap in human life. What do we mean by the overlap? In its crudest sense, instances are to be found wherever people meet and jostle. "Excuse me." "Beg pardon." "So sorry." "How thoughtless of me; take my handkerchief; I had no idea the umbrella was still up." "Out on three, please." All of these are recognitions of the overlap. But to come from manners to morals, there is a very powerful sense in which we are fate to each other; the actions of any man will help provide the context in which others make out their lives. Unhappily, the word "action" no longer reveals its inner drama. But we are speaking of that exercise of power which makes into fact what was the material of wish, whim, idea, or dream before. By means of human action the line between private and public is crossed. Men must act; and as the line is crossed, the world becomes settled not only for themselves, but for others in the bargain. We act, and consequences follow. Should the consequences be disastrous, much more is now involved than a simple change of mind or purpose; we must act again, setting up new consequences to oppose and block those earlier creatures of our minds. This is the fact which has from time to time provided the occasion for some very bad poetry about the spoken word, the released arrow; and there are instances of this fact too fearful for poetic treatment; a case in point — the missile — once risen from its launching pad. I am trying to express the sense of fatefulness involved in human life and action. This is the fact requiring concern from each of us about our present problem. Without this fact there would be no conflict of value, requiring arbitration; perhaps we would not speak of the "right" as anything different from the "good." We wish the good; we hope to achieve it by following the right — if only we can come to know the right. The right, then, is — as we have said — a strategy for achieving the good as social beings. The question of the right takes account of the overlap in human life, and is required at the many points where we are fate to each other. Because of the overlap some rule of conduct, some strategy, is needed.

Do we not already have rules of conduct? Indeed, we have; so many! On the grand tour, and unsure of your behavior among sophisticated Europeans, an acquaintance, having made the tour before, suggested helpfully: *When in Rome do as the Romans do.* In times of uncertainty the advice given is often this: *Let your conscience be your guide.* Is anyone completely unacquainted with the tension between these two rules? No other form of words in our Western world has been more often quoted as *the* rule of conduct than this: *Do unto others as you would have others do unto you.* Having stepped across the line, having told the immense untruth, watching with horror as your gentle vocables reap the whirlwind, well-wishers comfort you with the maxim that after all: *Honesty is the best policy.* And if I have carelessly poised myself to leap without looking, a bystander might remark (in some possible world): *Look before you leap.* Or if you should sometime be at the fatal point of squandering your largesse shortsightedly, a maiden aunt — should one happen to be at hand — will remark, as so many maiden aunts have remarked: *Count the cost!* Or in a different context, if your proposed act should be likely to have suspicious side effects, you might have heard: *Avoid the very appearance of evil.* And let us not forget the phrase we employ so often when it is not a question of the principle of the thing, but of the money, namely: *It is not the money; it's the principle of the thing.*

There are rules enough; but is any one of them — and, if so, which one — *the* rule of conduct? And once again, they are a heritage from childhood; even more — once more — a heritage of the race, delivered by tradition to your being. These many rules are as many strategies for achieving the good as social beings. And often we apply these rules with confidence, as though possessing knowledge concerning right and wrong. Apparently — let us be thankful — we are not always perplexed about the matter. And certainly our conduct will be right, if it conforms to a rule which properly distinguishes the right. But not only must we ask about the rightness of our conduct; we must ask also about the rightness of our rule.

If we could work out the nature of the rightness of our rules, with how much greater assurance we might approach the point of overlap where we are fate to each other.

But are not all these rules of conduct arbitrary? This is a specter capable, I predict, of haunting us. You may feel with Steinbeck's Casy, although you would not express it in his language:

The hell with it!
There ain't [sic] no [sic] sin
And there ain't [sic] no [sic] virtue.
There's just stuff people do.[1]

People adopt different attitudes, and do different things, calling what they prefer "right," and other behavior "wrong"; but at heart there is no difference; there is "just stuff people do." This would be to hold to the utter flexibility of right and wrong. The view may be regarded as a kind of last resort. The Kwakiutls push their mothers out of trees; the Samoans in the simplicity of their liquid consciousness hold a drink-of-water theory concerning sex; what is approved in one part of the world is disapproved in another; the "right" in one time will be "wrong" in another. All of this may be true. But I for one would be disappointed should this be the conclusion to which we come; and at the very least we must try the problem; we must have reasons for coming to this, or any other, conclusion.

And will not any discovery which we may make concerning right and wrong curtail our freedom, and stand in the way of our development? I do feel something of the force of this reaction; for certainly our current problem is different in tone from those which have preceded it. Our earlier problems had been concerned with ourselves; and oddly enough this concern has a strange fascination for each of us; while here the concerns of others unmistakably intrude. And yet part of our development — and of our freedom — may relate to this aspect of the good.

Whatever other questions you may have about the right, let me insist upon one point: The problem is inescapable. The manner in which each of us responds to life finds us in some sense distin-

---

[1] John Steinbeck, *Grapes of Wrath* (New York: The Viking Press, and London: William Heinemann Ltd., 1939), pp. 31–32. In addition to breaking the lines I have taken the liberty, for the protection of the young, of partially sicating the material.

guishing right and wrong, better and worse, good and bad. Even if we should think ourselves quite emancipated persons, beyond both good and evil, I have no doubt but what we approve some things, while disapproving others; and upon reflection the only final adjective we could apply to these judgments is that we think them right — or wrong.

The Discovery of a Rule

There is, then, nothing trumped up about our problem; we are simply after the most cogent explanation of what we are constantly doing. Apparently, as in the case of truth, our judgments about right and wrong stem from custom, our initial youthful shaping, authority, and — of course — experience. And we hope for something close to the truth concerning right and wrong. And we have learned that custom, the view which happens to be imposed upon one, and authority must yield to the offering of reasons. This requires separating "experience" from the rest. But experience, that magic word, tells us nothing as such. We must take some judgments to it in order to gain a judgment from it.

Now we may have come to this moment, having kept ourselves immersed in action, attending only to the particulars of conduct, having made our decisions merely by noting the likeness between a proposed act, and others in the past which have borne a stamp of rightness. In short, we may have no more than feelings of rightness with respect to conduct. Even so; this must be our starting point. Such feelings, when expressed, become opinions about the rightness or wrongness of individual human actions.

How should we proceed to find our rule of conduct? Each of us might conduct a survey of his own opinions. As a result of brilliant introspection one might bring together for his Institute of Personal Opinion, some or most or all of the judgments in which he terms individual actions, dispositions to act, and perhaps beliefs, right or wrong. The place to begin is with the actual material of our lives. And if this could be collected — of course, it is a personal task — then the questioning can begin.

Once the immense welter of judgments we have made concerning right and wrong has been assembled, a question can be posed: What do you find common to the judgments which seem so right to you? And what property is common to the things appearing

wrong to you? If one can discern a common quality in the judgments which seem to him to contain the right, then a statement is
possible which will stand as a kind of theory about the right. You
may be amazed to learn you have an ethic. You may also be amazed
to learn the nature of the ethic which is yours. It might be different
from everything you have heard about the right. And let us remember: We are working with appearance. We are risking error in a
gamble, perhaps, for later truth. When a general statement has
been gained, our thinking can be to some purpose; objections can
be raised, reasons can be furnished; the statement can be revised,
if need be. Can you discern the common quality? It may be evident at once, lying on the surface of your judgments.

It may be hidden; and if it is, our repeated question might be of
value here. You might concentrate upon a single act within its
context — one you have judged to contain the right — and ask:
Why is this right? Your answer would be a more general kind of
statement. Of this statement you might ask again "Why is this
right?" eliciting a further answer. The chain would reach its final
link when you had reached the point of saying: This is right, because
it is right. One would expect the repeated question to work here
quite as well as it did for final values; and perhaps it will so work.
In my hands, I must confess, the repeated question seemed rather
frail, leading me to forms of words with little meaning. You may
have better fortune; or you may find it less cumbersome to ask the
single question: What is common to all the judgments I have made
concerning right and wrong?

In whatever manner it is possible, we need to find a statement, a
rule, concerning our manner of distinguishing right from wrong.
It would be ideal could each of us, having made his analysis apart,
compare the results which we have gained. Since this is scarcely
possible, once again I must estimate, must proceed by sheer con-
jecture, must construct a framework which might contain something
like your answer. In short, by impersonal means I must contribute
to the resolution of a personal issue.

Criticism of the Rule

The result of this inner searching will be a general statement, a
standard or rule of action, derived from the judgments we have
made, general enough to include them, while excluding what is

common to the judgments we have thought improper. The next step is to test our rule; this, as we have seen, requires a search for reasons which will reveal the supportable — or insupportable — nature of our rule.

But I have nothing more than suspicions concerning the statement you have gained. Of course, we are all aware of the many rules of conduct, scattered through our common speech, present in the "culture" which surrounds our lives. And, to be sure, every finding to this point suggests the likelihood of some influence between our personal decisions and these rules. We had begun a list of the most common of these expressions. While I cannot know if one or more of these resembles the common quality which you have found, the chance exists, and directs me to these rules as a substitute for yours.

What is the rule of conduct by which we do in fact distinguish right from wrong? Is it anything like the common rules which we have mentioned? If so, then any weakness we may find will provide an opportunity for our advance. If not, at least we shall have gained a sample of the kind of ordeal our rules must be prepared to pass. In considering such rules, and along with them our personal statements, we may come to ultimate issues, capable of adding point and refinement to the rule of right.

When in Rome do as the Romans do. This is saying that our rule should be whatever rules are present — written, unwritten, spoken, unspeakable — in our society. It is the easy and (if for once you will permit a personal comment) utterly idiotic answer to the question: What should be the rule of human life? Thus can one remain utterly unthinking and yet have rules to guide him.

One is not often in Rome; but quite excitingly the rule also means: When in Paris do as the Parisians do; and, more placidly, perhaps more primly: When in London do as the British do. But one might easily breakfast in Rome, lunch in Paris, and dine in London. Indeed, Europeans would consider this quite normal for an American doing his grand tour. Could one vary so much in a single day? Or, better, should one? And if we should try, what of character with its bent toward unity of action? And what of the sense of order in the good life?

The proper rule for living is expressed by the awesome and celebrated voice of the group; such is the contention. Three comments are in order concerning this celebrated voice. First, the voice of the group is not a single voice. Its speech holds many accents — not alone Italian, French, and British. Today it speaks with many voices, and they are in conflict. This conflict, and its attendant confusion, will enter the life of any man, the principal guide of whose conduct is this surface of his outer world. Second, while the voice of the group is also the voice of experience, yet "experience" as used here is not a neat and tidy concept. Included in the human judgment and fixed in custom are man's hates, fears, self-interest, prejudice, love of status, blindness, quite as prominently as his love, hope, altruism, insight, and good will. Yet, strangely, the belief is more widely spread than one would care to think that any binding elements are good just because they bind, as though mortar could be accused of wisdom, or binder twine of justice. Granted, there is some wisdom, some justice, in any set of customs; the quality of the mixture is not startlingly high. Third, while the voice of the group is always powerful (more powerful than ever today), yet it is not always benign. Does not its power tend to reduce all to obedience? It seeks its own level. Is not this level too often the dead level of mediocrity? My conclusion is plain: Let no one assume he finds the proper foundation for his life in the cadence of this voice. Here is no counsel of despair. It is merely a pointing to the fact, a fact which is the basic ground for every urge toward self-improvement, that man is not yet truly man in what one might call his natural state — casual, uninspired, indifferent man, man in the mass. This is, perhaps, where every man begins; it is not his final and proper end.

And yet even this unruly type of rule has its point. Certainly, there must be some tolerance in a rule for living, some taking account of changing situations as one moves from Rome, to Paris, to London. But a rule which counsels us to adapt completely is no rule at all. And if the group does not speak with a single voice, then man must be the measure. Again, we say: Then, let man measure!

Let your conscience be your guide. If it will not do to be a Roman, can one say: Man is able to measure right and wrong by means of conscience? Immediately, an improvement may be noticed. At least this rule asks a man to make his own decisions. The rule of conduct comes from within, or so it seems. Of course, we must admit that while this seems to be the case, yet the rule may be coming from without — from a single prized and cherished group — behavior impressed upon us which we impress again upon the world. But perhaps, once more, even if this is, it need not be, the case.

And yet so many things have been done in the name of conscience, whether honestly in its name or not, that one cannot rest easily in dealing with one who lets his conscience be his guide, unless he knows the conscience in question to be a sensitive instrument, strongly oriented to the "right." Conscience, then, is not itself the answer to our problem. But if "conscience" can lead one astray, we who praise the modern world must remember the modern origin of this appeal to conscience. Recourse to private conscience, anticipated in the inner warning voice of Socrates, becomes a common bit of mental furniture much later. It is the inwardness of the Reformation and the Renaissance which allows conscience to act as a court of appeal from public, established, authoritative opinion. If these historic movements have set anything right, then something is right about conscience. And yet in referring to conscience, one refers to whatever rules do in his experience separate right from wrong. And we are thus directed beyond conscience to the more precise rules by which it ought to function.

Do unto others as you would have others do unto you. These often-quoted words are not able, indeed were not intended, to stand by themselves as the rule of conduct. As a rule these words presume we have knowledge of the right, and wish the right to be done to us. Assuming this knowledge and these wishes, the very sane counsel is offered that we behave toward others in the same way. And indeed everyone practices this kind of reciprocity. But a difficulty stands in our way. One who does not know what is right practices this rule equally with those who do. And if you do not want the right, neither will the right be present in what you do. And if one should have confused right with wrong, and this is what he wants, what then is the counsel? Do unto others as you would have others do unto you.

If we suppose everyone really wishing the good to be done to himself (even if what he thinks he wants, what he wants on the surface, is evil), then the rule is saying he should behave toward others on the basis of this good of which he is not aware. And this is the whole point which the given rule does not help us to resolve:

In the overlap what should we want, what should we desire? The rule needs an additive; the person needs an awareness he does not have. The problem is the same as with the rule of conscience. The golden rule also points beyond itself to something more.

Yet this, too, brings us a step closer to what is needed. There is the sense here that whatever the right may be, it includes at least two persons, and requires a common standard. At least, this rule wishes to take seriously the problem of the overlap.

Honesty is the best policy.   Notice the difference between this rule, and those which have gone before. The others apply to everything in general; this concentrates upon a single virtue. Indeed, it is a single and separate judgment, something like the judgments with which we began our search for a rule. Much of our thinking about right and wrong may stay on the level of maxims such as these, which fix and laud certain kinds of conduct as the core of virtue. There is no end to the number of such maxims in common speech. Mr. Franklin's Poor Richard is the authority here, and in following them — this seems to be Franklin's point — Richard will cease to be poor. Yet it would not be fair to regard such maxims as leading to expediency as a rule.

"Honesty is the best policy" might or might not, depending upon how we understand the statement. This statement might be made part of the rules already criticized. It might be one of the maxims to which a sensitive conscience would refer; or it might be part of what one wishes for himself, and so should will for others. It might even be attached to: "When in London do as the British do" (or used to do) — to take the most appropriate case. And possibly one might believe the saying, and be unable to attach it to any given rule.

Much of our common morality is carried not by general rules, but by individual maxims; and the sum of these maxims is expected to constitute the right. Allowing our minds to run freely over the kinds of behavior thought by us to be right, each of us achieved, or could have achieved, a set of statements, pointing out a particular line of conduct which is to be approved. In doing so we were declaring something of this sort: It is right to tell the truth, to keep one's promises, to be faithful to trusts, to respect the wishes of others, to avoid gossip and ridicule, to help others, to preserve life, to respect property rights.

And as we took our second step, asking for the rule which would include these judgments, we may have come to one of the rules already given. On the other hand, we may not have discerned a rule; we may have tried the repeated question: Why is it right to do these things? and we might have been very puzzled, even by the asking of the question. You may have decided that the right simply exists in these individual statements. And if you decided so, you would have on your side the massive opinion of the race. There is nothing puzzling about our puzzlement. These judgments have come to us from custom. Custom, the great deceiver, is also the great resource. It has furnished the balance wheel of our lives which, otherwise, might have gotten out of hand — which, otherwise, have indeed gotten out of hand. (Do you remember the time when, after reading anthropology, you went against all custom?) But times arrive when men can no longer guide themselves simply by custom. At all times there are some men who can no longer accept customary judgments as self-evidently true; then they must take thought about their lives. In this day, for increasing numbers, the accustomed ways have lost their sanctity. When we confront ourselves with the question: Why this? our puzzlement is no wonder; for in the question we are being called upon to justify something which we had never dreamed needed to be justified.

A related point may now be mentioned. In fact none of us expects such maxims and individual judgments always to lead us to the right. Should someone ask about the items on our list one by one, and allow us time to think about them:

> Is it ever right to tell a lie?
> Is it ever right to break a promise?
> Is it ever right to betray a trust?
> Is it ever right to exaggerate?
> Is it ever right to ridicule?
> Is it ever right to refuse one in genuine need, if we have the resources to meet that need?
> Is it ever right to kill?
> Is it ever right to steal?

most of us would tend to answer: Yes, it is sometimes right to behave in this opposite way. How amazing! We know what is right; and yet, sometimes, the very opposite is right instead.

Of course, it is right to help others, and yet there are times when we are tempted to say, or at least to act out: Every man for himself and the devil take the hindmost! Unquestionably there are times when one's personal ship of state, vocational or social, has such a decided list that, supposing the women and children safe, we would be apt to defend the saying or the doing: Every man for himself! And for every statement on our list, there are situations in which we would approve the very opposite of what these statements urge.

Consider even the revered Ten Commandments. Whether they derive from Moses, or Hammurabi, going through them one by one can we not envision times when, with the exception of one, or possibly two, we would be certain of serving the right by doing just the opposite? Our considered actions reveal the times when we think the opposite of these commandments to be perfectly right. It is not right to steal — and yet, if in poverty with hungry children, and the bottle of milk sitting at the rich man's door. . . . It is not right to kill; and yet in warfare, or under personal conditions, when it has become a question of your life or the life of your assailant. . . . And so with the rest.

If no actions, or virtually none, are *right* at all times under all conditions, then these individual injunctions cannot outline the right. What they require of us may be right in the main; but we must try to find why they are sometimes right and sometimes not. In any event we cannot be satisfied with the mere feeling of their rightness.

We can no longer accept these particular maxims, commandments, and individual statements at face value. We must ask the question, Why? Why is honesty the best policy? Why is it never right to tell a lie?

Let us return to the maxim with which we had begun. Why is honesty the best policy? If we can overcome our puzzlement and force an answer from ourselves, and if we do not find it natural to answer in terms of one of the rules already in our wake, then I think our answer will have to be a statement similar to one of our two remaining rules.

You may answer: Honesty is the best policy because its consequences are best. And then we would have to ask: If the consequences of honesty in a given case are bad — that is, unpleasant, unfortunate, or what you will — then should one lie? In the answer to this question we shall find a basic difference of opinion. Some would say: "Yes, then we should lie." For such people, "Honesty is the best policy" is nothing final. And others would respond: "No! Even when the consequences are unfortunate the truth should be told." With these people we must continue the conversation: "In the name of common sense, why?" The answer might be of this nature: "It is something beyond common sense. It is a basic principle that truth be told, and has nothing to do with consequences." Here, too, something beyond honesty has been cited.

This is an interesting pair of answers because each leads, and respectively, to one of our last two sets of rules. The next rule on our list, expressed in imperatives such as "Count the cost!" "Look before you leap!" and "Avoid the very appearance of evil!", counselling prudence for the whole of life, might be put: *Let your decision about a given act rest upon the consequences which will follow from that act; calculate these before you choose.* And our final rule, invoked as we had said, when it is a question of the money, announces one's stand on *the principle of the thing.*

Now it was exactly these two rules toward which we found ourselves turning when puzzled by the rightness of the maxims which surround us. And now I begin to think every rule so far given can be resolved, if we push our questions far enough, into a view relying on consequences, or one supporting principle. And if this is so, then I suggest it is also true of the rule you gained from introspection. Some of our rules turn naturally to the citing of consequences; others into the statement of principles. However far apart may have been the initial statement of our rules, from this point we can proceed together, for any rule — this is my claim — turns either to the citing of consequences or to principles; and any of our statements, when tested, turns into a rule which looks to the consequences, or a rule which rests on principle. You should test this claim of mine; and we shall test it in a way together as we take the next step which promises to add some insight to the problem of distinguishing right from wrong. Let us concentrate more precisely on principle versus consequences.

Principle versus Consequences

How often have you heard this fragment of conversation?
"I know that this is right; and I am going to stand on principle."
"But look at the consequences!!!"
Indeed, can you not recall occasions when you were standing, as

you said, on principle; and other times when you were busy counting up the consequences in the most exacting manner? If this point to which we have been led should turn out to be basic, we would need to learn what exactly is being traced when one traces consequences; and we would need to ask on what one is standing when he stands on principle.

I think one has only to become sensitive to this distinction, and he will discover such conflicts in his daily newspaper, in the conversation of friends, and in his own experience. Any one of us could produce a list of instances where one person seems to be tracing consequences, and the other standing on principle.

For example, in the Platonic dialogue, *Crito,* we are introduced to the following situation: Socrates is in prison, awaiting the execution of his sentence — more simply, awaiting execution. Without Socrates' knowledge his friend, Crito, has prepared a plan of escape. Socrates believes it would not be proper for him to avoid the judgment of the court. They discuss this question in unbelievable calm. In accepting the judgment of the court, Crito holds, Socrates will be playing into the hands of his enemies, deserting his children, and allowing the world to believe the friends of Socrates to be deficient in courage. Crito continues: "See now, Socrates, how sad and discreditable are the *consequences,* both to us and to you." In Socrates' immediate reply are these words: "The *principles* which I have hitherto honoured and revered I still honour, and unless we can at once find other and better principles, I am certain not to agree with you; no, not even if the power of the multitude could inflict many more imprisonments, confiscations, deaths, frightening us like children with hobgoblin terrors." [2]

Crito is very sensitive to the consequences of the situation. Socrates is sensitive to something else; he calls them the "principles" which are at issue. Here then is a conflict between consequences and principle, a conflict between two rules of action. Is this kind of conflict widely spread through our experience; or is this an occasional, an exceptional, clash? At least on the surface, it is widely spread.

A young married couple is discussing the tendency of the husband's father to air his anti-Negro prejudices. The husband remarks: "To keep peace in the family, I don't say anything when he

[2] Plato, *Crito, op. cit.,* Vol. I, par. 46. Italics mine.

talks that way; it does no good." His charming young wife replies: "I'm sorry, but as a matter of principle I must speak up when he gets on that track."

A university president is conversing at a dinner party with some of the university family (otherwise known as "faculty"). The president remarks: I am unable to see why a professor who is not a Communist would ever be unwilling to say he is not a Communist before a duly constituted Congressional Committee. He knows how unhappy the consequences will be for himself, his college, (his President?), and the position of colleges generally." One of the family, a professor, replies: "I think I understand why a professor might be unwilling to testify. If the questions he is asked are not those which can be put properly to a citizen in a free country, he may refuse on principle."

Those who have been exposed to the virus of the university will recall the perennial dispute over fraternities. One student will oppose the American fraternity on principle, because of its restrictive covenants governing certain racial and religious groups. The other, typically, will admit these as unfortunate, and yet point out how nearly the polishing action of the fraternity appliance, the comradeship, the future contacts, outweigh the fact.

Socrates stayed in prison and drank the hemlock. Aristotle under somewhat similar conditions fled into exile "lest," he is said to have remarked, "Athens sin twice against philosophy."

"Regardless of what it may do for our country," says one man, "giving aid to, or making alliances with, countries fascistic and dictatorial in nature, is not to be countenanced." "Regardless of some abstract principle," replies the other, "such alliances are necessary to our position in the world."

The Northerner, not involved in the difficulties of integration, is apt to say of the current phase of our long internal struggle of race: "Integration is the only principle by which democratic peoples can live together in one society." The Southerner, lashing out against outside interference, insisting on time "to handle the problem in our own way" is in effect saying: "but look at the consequences. . . ." This, I think, is the case even when verbally the clash is one of two different principles; for this seems not to be a real collision. The Southerner does not as a rule (although he may) deny the northern principles; he takes his stand on a different level with a different principle, states' rights and local autonomy. What is this but saying,

"Let us handle the problem in our own way"? Basically, here too we have a clash of principle and consequences.

In each of these examples, one party has been adhering to what he calls "principle," while the other has called attention to the "consequences." When one looks for it the world seems filled with this dispute. And if I am right this conflict is discerned not alone in the modern world, and in the encounters of individuals. This is the conflict between the Stoics and Epicureans of later Greek and Roman times; it is the conflict of recent times between Immanuel Kant and the Utilitarians. It is a tenacious, enduring, recurrent conflict. And if it is all of this we had better take it seriously. Since we wish to know the right, and since it might be found through tracing consequences, let us first examine what is involved in the strategy which would have us trace out the consequences before we act. And now the way swings off into increasing difficulties; and yet I think we are on the track, the "right" track without question.

The Right as a Tracing Out of Consequences

What is one doing when tracing consequences? He is being rational. He is looking to the future; it would be backward, indeed, to refuse to do so. And it would be quite advantageous to be able to solve ethical questions by means of the general foresight we use elsewhere.

To find what is involved, let us take an example from some area of life; a game will do. Why have I given up the game of chess? The game moves too slowly, I may say, because of the many involved consequences which must be traced through additional moves and counter moves before one can be reasonably certain that the move he has in mind is, compared to others, the "right" move to make. We had begun to consider the tracing of consequences and stumbled at once upon the word "right." But has "right," when one is discovering the "right" move in chess, the same meaning as when one is trying to discover whether a proposed act can be part of the strategy for achieving the good as a social being? Let us see.

A move is right in chess if it does not cause you a greater sacrifice than it causes your opponent, and if it brings your opponent closer to checkmate. That is, a move is right in chess if it supports the purpose you have in mind. The main point of tracing out consequences, generally, is to determine whether or not a given line of action is apt to succeed. This is highly important, because success in this is success in implementing any purpose.

Now is success of this kind exactly the concern of ethics? Surely, if it is my goal in life to bring all of my opponents to checkmate, success in this would not be widely thought to make of me an ethical person; quite the contrary. To settle such foresight into an ethical frame, something must be added.

To estimate the probable success of my act, I must have in mind not only the act itself, but the purpose it is to serve — checkmate or whatever. With these two things in mind I seem to be able to project the situation which includes my possible action. And in a curious way of "seeing" I can see whether or not the act will fulfill the purpose for which it is intended. And thus far the discussion, we have said, is ethically neutral. What does this mean? Is it impossible to "see" the rightness of an act by setting out the consequences? If so, this whole view forfeits its claim upon us.

We should work carefully here in determining what we have before us. Let us see if we can bring the purpose of checkmate into life, building up a situation where "right" and "wrong" retain their usual, and ethical, meanings. Suppose in life I really intend to checkmate an opponent; I intend for him to lose his pawns, his castle, even his queen. My nefarious purpose stated, we want to learn how, by looking to consequences, the wrong-headedness of my purpose and its attendant acts can be "seen." I would be able, one imagines, to envision a number of actions which would bring about my purpose. I could detail many of the consequences of so acting. My opponent will lose money; I shall gain a great deal of it. The enemies of my opponent will applaud; his friends will weep. Some men will be pleased and others displeased. We can even estimate the likelihood of this displeasure leading some men to interfere with our future plans. Now, can anything be seen in all of this which marks the act as "wrong" — or "right"? Nothing, I think.

The act, its purpose, success in achieving this purpose, the reactions of other people: these are the only elements to be seen in this curious way of seeing. The first three are neutral and present in all foresight. Could the final element, the reactions of other people, have anything to do with right and wrong? Crito was troubled partly by what others would think of his allowing Socrates to die. At least to a certain extent, all of those in our examples who traced out consequences seem to have had in mind the pleasure or displeasure of those whom their act would touch. Since the reaction of others, their pleasure or displeasure, can be rather easily foreseen, it would be absurdly easy to settle upon this as the mark by which consequences are to be viewed in determining right and wrong. But here is the point, and it is important; we must first decide upon this as *the* mark by which right and wrong are to be distinguished. When we act "in the light of the consequences," any ethical light in the situation has been imported by ourselves. There is no virtue merely in gazing at consequences. There is something more to this problem than *merely* looking before we leap. And now we can discern this "something more." The consequences must be viewed in, or from, some respect. What has to be imported into this prudential foresight, in order to gain an ethical framework, is the respect from which consequences are to be viewed.

But suppose we accept the "reactions of others" as the mark to be used in tracing out consequences. Would this provide us with a rule for conduct? If this is the respect in which consequences are to be viewed, then here is our rule. *A proposed act is wrong if the act and its consequences are unpleasant to those affected by it; a proposed act is right, if pleasant to those concerned.* If we accepted this as the mark, how would we defend our viewing the consequences in this, rather than in some other, way? We might point out that this is the way in which people do behave. And, while mingling with a given group, one does try generally to avoid an act which will bring down upon his head the displeasure of the group; one does tend rather to do the thing which will yield pleasure. All people do this some of the time — even when it means qualifying their honest opinions. Even philosophers, I am sorry to report, have been known to trim their behavior in this manner. Some people do so all of the time. And then the fact becomes troublesome. A man who practices duplicity, who is largely self-seeking, will always qualify his behavior in order not to irritate but to please those with whom he is face to face. Since all men act in this way part of the time, and since some men — the villains in particular — act in this way all of the time, are we therefore to settle upon this as the mark by which right and wrong are to be distinguished? Or is this merely an amendment to the rule of right

— indeed, perhaps no more than a slight qualification, introduced at times to reduce the conflict at some of the less important points where we are fate to each other? If it should be the latter, a man would be tragically mistaken in taking it to be the former.

But I find this rule somehow familiar. Consider! If people are most often pleased by behavior which follows an accepted pattern, the rule can be put in a second manner: *Whatever is accepted by society, at least the society of those concerned, is right; and what is not so accepted is wrong.* Of course, this rephrasing is permitted only by assuming one of two things: Either some ways of acting become accepted and habitual because they give pleasure to the individuals within the group; or else customary ways are pleasing because they have become accepted and habitual. In either case we could come to know what will please those around us through learning what has been accepted in the past, and fixed in custom. And with the rule so stated, its recognition comes. Is this not a more sophisticated form of the popular rule: *When in Rome do as the Romans do?* That rule was telling us we were free to practice what the group practiced; and we were to prohibit in ourselves what the group prohibited. Is this not the same as choosing what pleases while avoiding what displeases, or choosing what is accepted by while avoiding what is not accepted by, the group around us? In any of these versions, has not the voice of the group, fixed by its collective pleasure or displeasure, determined right and wrong? Our present identification can be taken as one bit of evidence, supporting my claim that the rules with which we began can be reduced either to looking at the consequences, or standing on principle. When the voice of the group determines right and wrong, and this is the end of the matter, we have gone back to the view which is our last resort; this is holding to the specter of utter flexibility, which has already begun to haunt us.

But if we think back to our examples, those citing consequences were not thinking merely of the pleasure and displeasure of others, but also of a somewhat different notion: the actual pain and pleasure to be occasioned by the act. Crito is aware of the actual pain in store for Socrates and his family. The university president is likely to include in his estimate the pain and difficulty in store both for the professor and his family, and for the university. The fraternity member is certainly including the feeling of his own future pleasure in being more adept socially, in having a wide range of spiritual brothers in Detroit, Kansas City, and Abilene. And Aristotle must have noticed how staying in Athens would involve a certain amount of physical discomfort on his part. And so with the rest; on the basis of what people do, a case could be made for saying that it is not merely the pleasure and displeasure of others which is to be considered; but the total amount of pleasure and pain involved. Both of our former statements of the rule failed to take account of one person who is at least as vitally concerned as any other — namely, the person using the rule.

A slight modification will correct this oversight, making the rule more efficient and clear-cut than it was before. For pleasure and displeasure (the surface reading of consequences), substitute pleasure and pain (including our own), and here is the rule. *Whatever act yields the greatest sum of pleasure, and the least amount of pain, in a given situation is right. Any other act is wrong.* "Agreement with others" has been replaced by "the greatest sum of pleasure"; and now our own pleasures are to be cast into the calculation along with those of others. We can even imagine a kind of balance, a curious pleasure-pain scale, into which we place or pour the expected pains and pleasures of the actions we propose. The pans tremble uncertainly as units of pleasure or pain clatter, click, splash softly pear-shaped (whichever description is appropriate), and as one pan or the other settles, we learn the difference between right and wrong: the greatest yield of pleasure or the smallest yield of pain. The appropriate act is the one providing the greatest balance of pleasure over pain.

This rule is more powerful than its former versions. If the good is pleasure and pleasure is the good, this rule will point us toward "the greatest good for the greatest number." Nor has this modification led us to an imagined point of view. We have been led to a conclusion about the right actually held by Jeremy Bentham, erstwhile, and most aggressive, member of a nineteenth-century group called the Utilitarians. Utilitarianism was shaped as a weapon against flagrant social abuse; and it performed when called upon.

> The golf links lie so near the mill
> That almost every day
> The laboring children can look out
> And see the men at play.[3]

[3] Sarah N. Cleghorn, "The Golf Links," *A Little Treasury of Modern Poetry,* ed. Oscar Williams (New York: Charles Scribner's Sons, 1946), p. 441.

In this kind of situation the rule and the scale worked with power on human minds. The pain of workers, including children from the age of six, laboring from fourteen to sixteen hours daily, when put into the imaginary scale against the pleasure in the life of a single golfing, yachting, and conspicuously idle employer (even including the pleasures of his family of two or three, scattered in splendid isolation through the echoing rooms of his palatial home), would outweigh that little sum of pleasure. Right as the greatest sum of pleasure, the least amount of pain, could reveal dramatically in this context that the times were out of joint.

And now I think we have reached a definitive form of the rule we were approaching all along by means of Romans, social acceptance, pleasure and displeasure. Is it acceptable to you as *the* method of distinguishing right and wrong?

This view, we may notice first of all, is not entirely different from its earlier versions. Its intellectual content is not quite the same as an insistence upon conforming to the group, since our own pleasures count for something. And where the group is very small, including only two or three, the greatest sum of pleasure will require an action satisfying all concerned; in such intimate groupings a way can be found which will allow my own desires their satisfaction along with those of others. All of us, I am sure, make this kind of adjustment in our face-to-face relations. On the other hand, most ethical questions include a larger group; the larger the group, the more nearly by this rule must my ethical will be determined by that group, and the more nearly does this rule merge back into the former rules from which it was derived. The mark of pleasure-pain, it may next be noticed, is not superbly clear in meaning. Without any explanation I know what pain is and wish to avoid it; in the same manner I know what pleasure is, and am not averse to it. But all shades of pain and pleasure become part of this account. Displeasure is a kind of pain. The pain of an affront to my ego must be included along with the pain of physical injury; and the pleasure of successful deception along with the pleasure of health, or physical well-being. The mark of pleasure-pain cannot be sharply sundered from the pleasure-displeasure of our preceding rule. The two observations seem to blend. On the more important questions this rule, too, asks us to conform, to accept the judgment of the group. And in the diversity of human customs it leads us once again toward the utter flexibility of right and wrong, our view of last resort.

Let us not reject the rule out of hand, simply because it shares this tendency with its predecessors. It would be more charitable to ask after its defense. Our rule, clarified and somewhat strengthened, insists upon pleasure-and-pain as the respect from which we are to view the consequences. How can the picking out of this respect be defended? We have already noticed one manner of defense. It can be claimed that people do behave in the given manner. The claim is easily countered: Even if people do seek pleasure, total the pleasures and pains before they act, this is not to say they *should* do so; we are after the respect from which consequences should be viewed. This answer is adequate unless a stronger claim is made. Bentham makes a much stronger claim. It is worth while to take this issue to Bentham's principal work; in so doing we may come to a better understanding of what is involved in any procedure of tracing out consequences.

Bentham Revisited

Taking as his slogan "the greatest good for the greatest number," and understanding by greatest good "the greatest sum of pleasure," Bentham makes this claim:

> Nature has placed mankind under the governance of two sovereign masters, *pain* and *pleasure*. It is for them alone to point out what we ought to do, as well as to determine what we shall do. On the one hand the standard of right and wrong, on the other the chain of causes and effects, are fastened to their throne. They govern us in all we do, in all we say, in all we think: every effort we can make to throw off our subjection, will serve but to demonstrate and confirm it. In words a man may pretend to abjure their empire: but in reality he will remain subject to it all the while. The *principle of utility* recognises this subjection, and assumes it for the foundation of that system. . . . Systems which attempt to question it, deal in sounds instead of sense, in caprice instead of reason, in darkness instead of light.[4]

Not only do men seek pleasure and avoid pain; they can do no other; and even to deny the claim is to engage in pretense, and is only verbal — sound, caprice, and darkness. No one would wish to deal in sound, caprice, and darkness, could he exchange such

---

[4] Jeremy Bentham, *An Introduction to the Principles of Morals and Legislation* (Oxford: The Clarendon Press, 1876), Chap. I, Par. I.

doubtful values for sense, reason, and light. Since men can do no other, pleasure-pain becomes the respect from which consequences should and must be viewed in determining right and wrong. The only problem lies in learning how to determine this greatest sum of pleasure. And to this end Bentham introduces seven considerations; he calls them the seven "dimensions" of value. We are to consider:

(1) the intensity of the pleasure or pain
(2) the duration of the pleasure or pain
(3) the certainty or uncertainty of the pleasure or pain
(4) the propinquity or remoteness of the pleasure or pain
(5) the fecundity of the pleasure or pain: "the chance it has of being followed by sensations of the *same* kind: that is, pleasures, if it be a pleasure: pains, if it be a pain."
(6) the purity of the pleasure or pain: "the chance it has of *not* being followed by sensations of the *opposite* kind: that is, pains, if it be a pleasure: pleasure, if it be a pain."
(7) the extent of the pleasure or pain: "that is, the number of persons to whom it *extends;* or (in other words) who are affected by it." [5]

The "process" of thought which would include and apply these considerations is to be kept in view always, but "need not be pursued previously to every moral judgement" — for which we can be grateful. Clearly, Bentham is providing a way to estimate the quantity of pleasure in the consequences. These considerations are offered in order to allow a more particular estimate of the greatest sum of pleasure. But in adding clarity to the method, the difficulties present in its use stand out more clearly. Bentham wants to find the right by estimating the quantity, or sum, of pleasure involved in any given act. But I would have expected the good, and so the right as well, to stand for a quality of life; and I should not have expected qualities to be so easily reducible to quantities of any sort. And I feel a second difficulty. We are to look to the consequences; but the consequences extend beyond the point where we can possibly look. How, beyond our possible knowledge, can we judge of the intensity, duration, certainty, propinquity, fecundity, purity, and extent of the pleasures and pain which may follow from any given act?

We shall defer the question in order to consider the two parts of

[5] *Ibid.*, Chap. IV, Par. IV.

Bentham's extraordinary claim: (1) Men can do no other than seek pleasure. (2) All other views — when the sound, caprice, and darkness are removed — reduce to this single calculus of pleasure-pain. The second part of his contention holds greater significance for us than does the first.

We have already met the first contention: Men are compelled to seek pleasure by virtue of the nature of their human nature. Epicurus introduced us to this view. And his contention was met by our counterclaim of a plastic human nature. Epicurus, we had said, was merely entering pleasure as one more candidate for the final value of human life. In the same way pleasure, we may hold, is really Bentham's final value rather than, as he insists, the sovereign power of human nature. Regarding the matter so, an interesting skein of relations comes into view. Bentham holds pleasure to be the final goal of human striving, having "governance" over all we do; he calls his rule a "principle of utility"; and this use of "utility" comes from David Hume. If one looks into Hume's *An Enquiry Concerning the Principles of Morals* he will find the useful several times equated with the agreeable. Section Five of this work is titled "Why Utility Pleases"; in Part II of this section, usefulness is identified with what contributes to human happiness; and in the same paragraph an instructive footnote informs us how happiness and misery are to be understood in terms of pleasure and pain. And, as we have noted, long before these philosophers had begun to compose their footnotes, Epicurus had presented pleasure as the final value of human life. The skein becomes a kind of pattern. These men, called the Utilitarians, are the intellectual heirs of Epicurus for whom pleasure was the key to human value. The first extraordinary claim comes down to little more than this suggestion. If pleasure is your final value then by all means consider whether pleasure-pain may not be the respect, amenable to your person, from which consequences should be viewed in separating right from wrong. The suggestion gives rise, in turn, to a thought of somewhat greater breadth, and possibly of greater interest. If one for whom pleasure is the final value may choose that as the respect from which consequences should be viewed, why may not we — supposing our final value to be other than his — substitute our own as the critical respect for judging among the consequences?

We are now in position to make a mild discovery. Earlier, we had noticed the ease with which the pleasure and displeasure of others can be observed in the consequences of an act. But we found the decision to settle upon this observable feature of the world as *the* way to distinguish right from wrong originating within ourselves. The mild discovery is this: Any other final value can be "seen" in the consequences quite as plainly as pleasure-pain. If one knows what he means by a given value word, he can find wisdom and ignorance, beauty and ugliness, love and hate, happiness and misery, peace of mind and anguish, self-realization and self-destruction, power and weakness, efficiency and inefficiency, in the expected consequences. Something further now appears, our second mild discovery within a paragraph: Many of the traditional ethical views can be expressed by "plugging in" to the consideration of consequences the proper judgmental values. We might try to demonstrate this claim by citing a number of such views. Also, you might experiment with the first modest discovery of the paragraph; you might attempt to see if your final value, related to the consequences, does indeed distinguish right from wrong in action, as you would wish them to be distinguished. If so, you may be approaching a solution to our problem.

But something is happening to the orderly pattern of our advance, for we still have Bentham's second contention to consider. There is nothing for it but to consider all of these matters, as terms in jail are sometimes served, concurrently. All other views reduce to pleasure-pain; such is Bentham's interesting claim. Then suppose we try the experiment of expressing additional views in terms of consequences to see under what conditions, if any, these views reduce to pleasure-pain. Meanwhile, increasing the variety of points of view may turn up some respect which you will recognize as belonging to your standard for judging right and wrong.

The Concurrent Discussion of a Number of Issues

To select at random, quite the most important value for Spinoza was wisdom. Since he believed the gaining of wisdom to be the final purpose of society it is proper to say for him: *Whichever of a set of possible acts leads to encouraging the greatest amount of wisdom, the least amount of ignorance, is right; and the others are wrong.*[6] And one comes at least fairly close to Aristotle by taking

[6] Spinoza, *Essay on the Improvement of the Understanding, passim.*

the Greek value of "moderation" as the critical mark. Aristotle's golden mean, between the extremes of too little (deficiency) and too much (excess), leads out into a set of value relations where *courage*, the mean, lies between the too little of *cowardice* and the too much of *foolhardiness; temperance* similarly lies between *insensibility* and *licentiousness; liberality* lies between *stinginess* and *prodigality; magnificence* lies between *meanness* and *vulgarity; highmindedness* lies between *mean-mindedness* and *conceitedness; good temper* lies between the *phlegmatic* and the *irritable; friendliness* lies between being *obsequious* and being *surly; truthtelling* lies between *false modesty* and *boastfulness; wit* lies between *boorishness* and *buffoonery;* and *justice* lies between the *injustice of demanding too little,* and the *injustice of demanding too much.*[7] Some of these relations strike their mark; and others seem appalling nonsense. But one can certainly imagine Aristotle, or any other Greek of the classical period, saying: Look to the consequences of your behavior; and if it is leading you to extremes, pull back! *Whichever, of a number of possible actions, contributes most to a life of moderation is right; whatever fails in this respect is wrong;* so might the rule have been stated.

But to leave the philosophers; if our problem were to be introduced to any group of sensitive and sensible people, up to that point uncorrupted by philosophy, very few of them, I am sure, would pick pleasure-pain as the critical mark. I think, too, there would be a strange unanimity in their choice. If they were to use our present language, by and large they would answer: *Calculate the consequences, and judge that act to be right which does most to help, and least to harm, those affected* — taking oneself into account along with others.

Many ethical views have come from taking some important value as the norm from which to judge the consequences of our actions; this much seems clear. And the proper norm for you may turn out to be one of your important values; from this a standard can be built which will apply to conduct, and allow decisions concerning right and wrong. But the claim of Bentham is that, even when we seek to use another standard, we are using his in fact. How can this be? Let us take the standard of those uncorrupted by philosophy, and see if a case can be made for Bentham. If we are to use helpfulness-and-harm as the critical mark, we must first learn how to use this

[7]Aristotle, *Nicomachean Ethics, passim.*

mark; we must know when we are helping and when we are harming. This is clear enough when a family is starving, being led before a firing squad, without housing due to damage by wind, rain, storm, foreclosure, or any other act of God. It is much more difficult to know the difference when, as a parent, one is struggling with the problems of growing children; then, as all of us know, our attempts at helpfulness are sometimes harmful.

In fact, we often accept what the person concerned thinks helpful or harmful. And permissive parents do so with the problems of their children — to the dismay of the neighborhood.[8] But we cannot always accept the opinions of those concerned; a would-be suicide thinks it helpful to be given a gun; a narcotics addict thinks it helpful to be given dope; and the children of permissive parents think discipline of any kind harmful. Whenever we accept the verdict of those concerned, this rule is no different from Bentham's sum of pleasures, for by "helpful" will now be meant what is pleasing, and by "harmful" what is displeasing, to those concerned. More generally, whether the given respect be wisdom, moderation, or helpfulness, if we accept the verdict of those concerned — their versions of wisdom, moderation, and helpfulness — Bentham is right; and all respects come out the same; the right is what pleases the people concerned.

Bentham's conclusion can be avoided only if we can speak sensibly of what is really helpful and harmful, no matter what people think; that is, helping and harming must depend on something beyond mere inclination. Looking back to our discussion of values the most appropriate term in understanding helpfulness would seem to be "self-realization." We could mean by helping, "providing conditions for self-realization"; and by harming, a failure to provide, or a destruction of, those conditions. And in explaining this one would be driven back to the development of the capacities of the individual, mentioned in our first and faraway discussion.

More generally, we should have to contend that we can talk sensibly of acts producing real wisdom and moderation, as well as helpfulness. If this is not possible, Bentham is right and every respect is another way of attending to the inclinations, pleasures, satisfactions, and accepted ways of those concerned. And admittedly

---

[8] I think it should be discerned by a sociological study if there is, as I suspect, a direct correlation between the number of permissive parents in any neighborhood, and the local price of shinguards.

it is difficult to find the ground for the assertion that in addition to what people think wise, courageous, moderate, helpful, and whatever else, there are real wisdom, courage, moderation, and helpfulness; and what people are willing to accept is sometimes different from that upon which they should insist in these matters. This is the question, once again, of "is" and "ought." Certainly this "oughtness" is not written down anywhere in the universe — or at least not very plainly. Yet in fact we have tried to defend its nature in our discussion of values; possibly, we succeeded. If the point can be defended, Bentham's second claim will fall; and other views need not reduce to pleasure-pain.

Of course, we cannot ride upon our wishes; and your best thought is needed in pondering this decision. But is Bentham really serious in allowing the greatest sum of pleasure, no matter what the nature of those pleasures, to determine right and wrong? At the very least, we may timidly ask, are not some pleasures better than others? Is not, we may say, the pleasure in an act of kindness better than the pleasure of taking dope? Bentham's answer is not altogether clear. The pleasure of ill will is, he tells us, considered in itself (before the consequences return upon the person indulging in this pleasure), as good as any other. Considered in itself, then, Bentham would say: No, the pleasure in an act of kindness is not better than the pleasure of taking dope. But, of course, we are not interested in an act "considered in itself." We are interested in a standard to guide us where human lives overlap. We are interested, at the moment, in actions considered in the light of their consequences. And Bentham, when considering the consequences of ill will, calls it a "wretched pleasure" — likely to be faint, short, and impure.[9] Is not this admission all we need? When considering the consequences, pleasures may be judged by the seven dimensions of value, as Bentham came to call them. The pleasure of the kindly act, similarly, we may urge, is more enduring, more fecund, more pure, and can have greater breadth or extent; for these reasons it is more desirable. Now, of course, by "desirable" we can mean only that if a person follows such conduct he will come to desire it, and to prefer it to the other. And, in fact, we have used the term in just this sense in our earlier discussion. And having gained this point, we might go on to urge that even in a society where everyone takes dope, and no one engages in acts of kindness, the act of kindness

---

[9] Jeremy Bentham, *op. cit.*, Chap. X, Par. II, fn.

remains preferable, since — if it were tried — it would excel the other in most of the seven dimensions. Bentham makes the admissions, which we are now choosing to regard as fatal; but most of the time he writes as though the whole matter of right and wrong depended on whatever now pleases those concerned. And so the matter must be brought to this conclusion.

Either —

Either Bentham is going to let anything pleasing to anyone determine what should be done (and then we have to throw away the seven dimensions); then it is right for the Coliseum set in the intensity of its pleasure to condemn poor, quaking slaves to their deaths; and it may be right for narcotics addicts to stay on the needle, if they keep to themselves; and it may be right to eliminate minorities (especially where painless methods are at hand — recall the gas chamber, and the millions of Warsaw Jews) if this will hugely please the majority. If he takes this path, then his rule merges back into its predecessors, even into "When in Rome do as the Romans do"; and into the utterly flexible extreme concerning right and wrong. If his view should follow such a course, an Argument from Strangeness can be used against him. How strange, we may say, that the rule of right and wrong should come to this; for if this is the final issue of our thought anything whatever can turn out to be right under some conditions. Exactly opposite judgments can be right at the same time for different groups, and at different times for the same groups. Initially, we had turned to this problem in order to find our way out of the conflict of opinions, the opposing judgments of different groups with respect to right and wrong, the urge toward conformity without reason, and thoughtless individual judgments. And we were willing to seek this right, even should it be a difficult matter to achieve it, even should it mean piling upon ourselves duties and responsibilities. And now we are being told in effect: If you wish to know the right, find what pleases those whom this act touches. In short, find what pleases the majority. And this might require asking our Instrumental Man, the very one who refuses to pile upon himself any notable duties and responsibilities, who may never have raised this problem in his mind, to look up from his work and reveal to us the nature of the right in human conduct, so far as it touches his life. And this conclusion, we might say, is strange, indeed! If this is where your standard leads, we are as well off without a standard. And we might feel like quoting Casy: "The hell with it." In this case there is no right and wrong. "There's just stuff people do." And indeed to have this standard is the same as having none. The argument is a kind of reduction to absurdity, and seems to me to dispose of Bentham, should this be his point of view.

Or —

Or Bentham will keep the seven dimensions, and modify his rule. Following what he says about ill will, there will be a difference between superior and inferior pleasures. Now in fact John Stuart Mill, who followed Bentham as leader of the English Utilitarians, was troubled exactly as we have been troubled, and introduced the very qualification which alone can rescue Bentham's rule. We are suggesting the qualification is already implicit in Bentham's seven dimensions of value. Is it better to be Socrates dissatisfied than a pig satisfied? Mill thought it was better; the seven dimensions show it to be better; and if it is better, the good no longer reduces, simply, to sums of pleasure. Of course, this change makes it almost beyond the powers of imagination to focus coolly upon the imaginary scale. While plumping down the relevant units, blocs, or droplets of pleasure, we are asked to prefer those which are "higher." Even with this way of understanding Bentham, the possible pleasures which might be experienced are, of course, the sole consideration in determining what must now be called "the ideal greatest sum of pleasure." And yet we have arrived without question at a moment of transition, and are moving toward the statement of a somewhat different kind of rule. A note of "ought-ness," for example, is present in this ideal sum of pleasures. And as a matter of fact it makes little difference whether or not we call these ideal experiences, these values which ought to be preferred, by the name of pleasures; we have already noticed the vagueness of our topmost value terms. Once the qualification is introduced, the notion of pleasure has become so "iffy," tenuous, and ideal, that such experiences might equally well be termed pleasures, instances of happiness, self-realization, satisfaction, or what one will. The notion of preference, of "oughtness," has been admitted; no longer will the rule model itself upon the opinions of those concerned; this is our point.

And so a new statement is in order. Upon reflection, one finds these higher preferred experiences which mark the good to be, without exception, what we have called intrinsic values. One way of stating our qualified Benthamic rule; and, indeed, one way of putting the view of John Stuart Mill in consequential terms is this: *The right action of a number of possible actions is that one which satisfies the greatest sum of intrinsic values whatever.*

The image of the teetering balance with its pans of pleasure is no longer quite appropriate. And once we have reached this point in our ascent, there can be no reason for denying the candidacy of any proffered value, which you may judge to be the pivot in encouraging this "greatest sum" of final values.

We can say: *Whichever of a set of possible acts leads to the greatest amount of wisdom, and the least amount of ignorance, is right; and the others are wrong.*

We can say: *Whichever of a set of possible acts leads to the greatest amount of moderation, or self-control, is right; and the others are wrong.*

We can say: *Whichever of a set of possible acts does most to help, and least to harm, those affected, is the right act in that situation.*

We can substitute any other important value as the respect for judging consequences, because we have learned that, supposing knowledge of what we mean, any of these values can be found in the consequences; and we have discovered that values do not reduce, simply, to what pleases. On the contrary, pleasures themselves separate out into the more and less admirable. And "good" no longer means simply "pleasant."

And now the way is open to construct your standard in terms of consequences, choosing pleasure or any other value, which in your experience adds cogency to the making of ethical distinctions. Whatever your choice, it can yield a rule which will not merely echo the opinions of those concerned. Our need is for a rule of sufficient power that it can be applied to concrete situations and produce results; the rule applied to the case, a directive for our conduct should emerge. Let me suppose that, thinking in terms of consequences, you have succeeded in framing such a rule, and so have I; and we have chosen different values as the mark for distinguishing right and wrong in terms of consequences.

A troubling question now occurs, a cloud no bigger than one's hand. We have allowed differences in our sets of values, reflecting what we find upon inspection of our lives. We have allowed them to rest on preference, as I suppose they must. And yet, to keep all marks from reducing to inclination, we find ourselves insisting upon the objective nature of wisdom, moderation, helpfulness, and the like. The question is: Will not our judgments differ if consequences are judged by wisdom rather than helpfulness, or moderation rather than — say — the will-to-power? They will. But what does this mean? Should they differ? And if they differ, can the different respects be equally right? It would be disappointing to come to a final disagreement, concerning the means of deciding what should be done in those cases where we are fate to each other. But how can this be avoided when some respect or other must be laid down, and that respect for me must be one of my important values; and when my valuations depend upon what I am able to appreciate? I suppose it cannot be avoided for any view which says: Look to the consequences!

The edge of disagreement can be blunted somewhat. The lack of agreement can be made less objectionable by the conclusion we had gained much earlier; final values, we had learned, after all do form a consistent whole. And while with different standards we must sometimes disagree, yet often the result of applying these standards to conduct would lead to agreement; they would dictate the same kind of decision. And this I think is the best we can do so long as our gaze is fixed on consequences. And it is not a small achievement! To find a rule which consistently yields the right for you is to extend considerably the scope of one's understanding, and the orderliness of one's life.

But there is a second question of greater import than our first. It is the question we had posed when considering the view of Bentham, while deferring the attempt to gain an answer, since any view which builds on consequences is included in its scope. Taking any respect whatever, we can estimate the likelihood of different acts producing consequences which will embody this respect. But since the balance of pleasure and pain, wisdom and ignorance, and the like, is final only when all the consequences have been accounted for, this balance requires the total future. "Look to the consequences," we cry. And yet, as we have said, the consequences extend beyond the point where we can possibly look. When the problem is momentous, what follows from this fact is most distressing.

Let us suppose an argument between two citizens of a state

where it is the pleasant custom to eliminate by execution, imprisonment, or forced labor, all who adhere to the capitalistic system;
the object of this behavior is to gain a perfect society, where the
family communism in which everyone believes spreads out to include everyone and everything; in this sense society is to become
a single family (and Big Brother will be watching you!). My example is designed to allow us to preserve the neutrality proper to
theoretical capitalists, even as we follow the dispute of these theoretical communists. Both citizens accept the stated goal; and we
shall have them agree upon pleasure-pain as the mark for distinguishing right from wrong. But Mr. X-sky also defends the custom
we have mentioned. Mr. Y-sky insists that even though the goal is
good, persuasion is the only proper means of progress; force in
such matters is to be avoided, is wrong if you will. Mr. Y-sky will
then appeal to the consequences for support. He will point out the
consequences of this behavior for those concerned — all who live
within the state; the direct suffering of the ill-fated ones and of their
families; the sympathetic anguish of their friends; the unpleasant
fear and uncertainty in the minds of citizens generally, as they
come to know that men like themselves, guilty of no overt treason,
have been dealt with so severely; he might refer to the paralysis
this may occasion in the body politic, and the probable growth of
a reluctance to serve the new order wholeheartedly. Against all this
pain and displeasure there is the pleasure of only a hatful of disciplined leaders in the knowledge that the pattern of history is
forming. Put in this way it does appear as though, in terms of
consequences, the balance of pleasure and pain shows the policy
to be clearly and decisively wrong.

But if we think so we have underestimated Mr. X-sky. He has
only to regard these as the immediate consequences, and to appeal
beyond them. Taking the same mark of value, he can claim that
in the long run the pleasure of the citizenry, and indeed of mankind, will be served by eliminating the capitalist element by whatever means are necessary. A reign of harmonious pleasure will
follow this necessary violence (and Big Brother will no longer need
to be watching you).

Deny what he has said if you will; you cannot refute him by
citing consequences. Since the consequences, which might prove
one view and refute the other, are all in the future, and since the
future is essentially uncertain, it seems the argument serves no
purpose. This is very strange, because we have not presented a

situation where different rules are being used; the same rule is being applied, and there is agreement on the end to be achieved, but still we reach an impasse! The purpose of the rule was to be able to reason more effectively about the issues of right and wrong. And yet not only when Communists disagree, but wherever there is serious disagreement, this impasse will appear. Looking to the consequences, it seems, can give us a conclusion concerning what we are to do only in the cases where we do not need to estimate the long-range future. There are such cases. If my decision concerns whether or not to be dishonest in commenting upon my wife's new hat, the consequences of honesty and dishonesty need not be traced very far. The consequences are easily predicted, dramatic in nature, and compelling to me personally. This would seem to mean that the rule can be applied to unimportant matters, but not to the very critical long-term issues on which we so badly need ethical decisions.

What other answer might Mr. Y-sky give to the man defending violence on this occasion? Only one other kind of answer comes to mind. And each of us has heard, perhaps has used, this general type of answer at just this point when engaged by serious disagreements. One is apt to hear or make this kind of statement: Consequences or not, violence is self-defeating, and will never lead to anything else. Pick up one end of a stick, and you get the other with it! What kind of statement have we made? It does not mention pleasure and pain; at least it is a departure from that simple rule. If this view grounds itself on consequences, it is as much in doubt as the rule we were trying to shore up by its means. But, in fact, the response turns away from consequences. And in form it partly resembles the maxims which we found leading, if not to consequences, then to principle. But if this is supposed to be the statement of a basic principle, we are saving the consequences' view by means of a stand on principle — which admits its insufficiency.

So far as I can determine, then, we have found a case of failure in applying the view which looks to consequences. It seems the failure cannot be overcome save by departing from the view itself.

A Question of Principle

When one looks to consequences, we have learned, he must have in mind some mark by which to judge them; any important value can serve as this mark; but there is no way of showing that one value rather than another is *the* respect from which consequences should be viewed. And even where there is agreement on the mark, in any serious conflict of opinion there will be disagreement concerning what the consequences will at last reveal; and we have found no way of resolving the impasse which ensues. In serious conflicts we prove our case only to ourselves, and those like-minded, not a very convincing kind of proof.

It would be well if we could approach the right in some way which would put less weight upon the consequences which roll out beyond our human view. In any case equal time must be provided to the man who supports himself by principle; and so we come to the question: When a man stands on principle, on what does he stand?

The Meaning of "Principle"

What can be meant by principle? It seems the word is, or may be, used in every definable area of life. There are principles of business and of advertising. I have heard it said that the most effective principle of advertising is: Tell the customer what he wants to hear! Offhand, this seems a very unprincipled type of principle. There are principles of football, handball, and every other sport. There are principles of medicine, law, and every other art. There are principles of painting, sculpture, and ballet. What is meant in speaking of the principles of these activities?

In every case the principle seems to be a way of proceeding which is particularly appropriate to the activity in question, almost certain of guiding the activity better than it would go without the use of these procedures. Well, the word "better" has occurred. What does it mean this time? It seems to mean only that, if this procedure is followed, the activity will more surely reach its goal.

We have then an activity, a goal, and a prescribed means of reaching it. And the principles are the means which can help us reach this goal. We have the operations of business, the goal of profit (to accept what is heard on every side), and the principles which will more certainly enable us to reach this end. We have the sport of football, an activity (to put it mildly); the goal of victory; and principles of punting, blocking, tackling, and moving in formation, the use of which by any team will make more likely the reaching of the goal — often enough to achieve its goal of victory; victory will be much more likely than would be the case for an

utterly unprincipled group of men. The ball is to be kicked from the
top of the metatarsal arch, slightly back of center and with a slight
spinning impetus, foot meeting ball at the moment of greatest potential impact (or something of this sort). In any case, the established principles of punting could be described; and can be demonstrated, fall and spring. There are ways in which this act is
properly done. In some of the better established athletic circles
principles of clipping, one is given to understand, have been discovered; and principles of falling in a dead faint to stop the clock
(akin to the principles of drama, one imagines). And certainly in
medicine, or in surgery, there are well-established and well-founded
principles: they concern sanitation, operating techniques, the tieing
off of veins, and the like.

But if the ethical principle is like these, have we not examined
many possible statements of this principle? The activity is more
general than any we have mentioned. It is living in a social context;
the goal is the good; and our principles are the prescribed means
which can help us to reach this goal. If a principle is a rule of
conduct which outlines a path to the goal in a peculiarly appropriate
manner, then every rule so far offered has been a principle; and has
been thought to be *the* principle peculiarly appropriate for our
guidance in reaching this goal. But in the ethical principles so far
announced, everyone seemed capable of prescribing his own method
for reaching the good; and we have found no grounds from which
to argue for the superior quality of any method.

The suggested principles of other areas of life are in better case.
In other areas one can talk about the "true" principles of the area,
and mean by this the rules which guide the activity better than
any other known rules. Such principles can be tested by experience;
they develop slowly through time; they are "improved" by men
intimately connected with the given pursuit, and who understand it.
And by improvement and development would be meant bringing
the activity more certainly, and perhaps more quickly, to its goal.
Such principles are only relatively changeless; they change as better
means of profiteering, sculpting, and dancing are discovered. In
some sense, it can be said, they have in them the wisdom of the past;
they result from theorizing about the given activity; they are also
a result of experiment, as the various ways have been tested.

Now can we theorize about and develop, test by experience and
experiment, the principles that the greatest amount of pleasure,

wisdom, helpfulness, or moderation in the consequences distinguish right from wrong? The situation for ethical principles seems to be closed-end. We have only the claims and counterclaims touting X, Y, or Z as the proper mark. Where are the experiences which make a difference, the experiment and testing? Is it because the goal in question is so general, and so variously conceived, that it is impossible to show one means to be better than another? In each case we had seen how part of the good was taken as the mark by which to judge the consequences. If you want the good, then you had better seek the right in your social relations; and if you want the right, then you must use this critically important part of the good to evaluate the consequences of your actions.

But the train of thought is rather different in other areas. If you want victory, then your team must train to punt in this manner, block in that, pass in such a way, and learn to coordinate their movements precisely in this set of complex plays. In both cases, it is presumed, some necessity has intervened: If you want this, then you must do that. It is a necessity, the binding force of which is measured by the strength of one's desire for the goal, and having at hand the proper means to reach that goal. Although the two kinds of principles are comparable in announcing this hypothetical necessity, there are important differences. Principle in nonethical activities, we see, is plural; there is not a single rule, but a set of procedures to be followed to insure the goal. And this is true in football, medicine, painting — perhaps even in advertising.

Since these goals can be achieved in a relatively short time, their procedures can be tested. One cannot avoid knowing if the victory has been won, the jury convinced, the patient restored to health, and the product sold. To be sure, if the goal of painting, sculpture, and ballet, is beauty, we can't be so certain that prescribed means have achieved this goal. We can know of the success of a painting with a given audience; but this kind of success, one presumes, is not a proof of "beauty." And in this respect the achievement of the good, according to our discussion, is much like painting. One can know what prescribed means will satisfy himself; but there seems to be no way of knowing if this is the best means, or even the proper means, of reaching the good through distinguishing right and wrong in conduct. Part of the difficulty may be that achieving the good takes a lifetime of maturing appreciations. Since this is

so, we never have a clear-cut verdict of good or evil in the consequences by which we can reshape our principle.

The Stand on Principle

But perhaps we have missed something; let us turn back to
our examples once again to see if something can be learned from
those who claim to stand on principle. Socrates said, "The principles
I have hitherto honored and revered, I still honor, and unless we can
at once find other and better principles, I am certain not to agree
with you. . . ." But he referred to "principles." Twice the plural
was used. Apparently, Socrates is standing on a set of principles,
just as one might stand on the principles of medicine or law. The
professor held that a man may refuse on principle to answer a
Congressional Committee "if the questions put to him are not those
which can be put properly to a citizen in a free country." Socrates
adhered to some principles which he would not give up until a
"better" set — still better, one presumes — is found. Our professor
held some questions to be proper, and other questions improper,
when put to a citizen in a free society; the notion of the "proper"
again suggests a difference between what "ought" and what "ought
not" be done. Both relate "oughtness" to social conduct. In both
cases one wonders what these principles might be. When thinking
about the singular principles, which may light up consequences,
we had said their concern was merely "living in a social context."
And now we may have a clue. Put all of this together, and it spells,
not "Mother," but a suggestion that the set of principles will define,
mark out, and make up, a theory of what society ought to be.

The suggestion may have struck, or missed, its mark. But think
through our examples; each person who took his stand on principle
would have been ready to discuss the kinds of relations which ought
to obtain among men. Our suggestion is that a stand on principle
has implicit within it a theory of what society ought to be. The
suggestion is, further, that when a man discovers he is involved in
a question of principle, he has discerned a given way of acting to
be consistent with, and its opposite to be inconsistent with, some
theory of what society ought to be.

If the suggestion has merit, we should be able to confront a man
who claims to stand on principle, and by questioning him, discover
behind his stand something like a theory of society. Perhaps each

of us should try to do this, independently (while avoiding, if possible, the usual cup of hemlock). But together let us take from our list any example of a man who stands on principle, and see if we can reasonably move to a theory of society lying behind his stand.

Take any case! Suppose you picked the man who said: "Integration is the only principle by which democratic peoples can live together in one society." We might ask this person: Where did you get such an idea? How do you know this to be so? Since he called his statement a principle, I suspect we should be given, in answer, some other related principles. I can't know exactly what these would be; but in the course of the discussion, I would guess, a theory of democratic society, much like that of Thomas Jefferson, would emerge. At any rate, if one were to read through even a portable Jefferson, he would encounter a set of basic ideas which might be cited in support of integration. Here are some of those ideas, taken from both his letters and formal documents; and of course they show signs, as does any theory, of having been gained by Jefferson from many earlier sources.

(1) Sovereignty can reside nowhere other than in the whole people; for this reason the will of the people should rule. (2) Further, men may be trusted to govern themselves. They are no more bestial and selfish than rational and benevolent. Which they become depends upon their opportunities for education and the social institutions in which they live. When their capacities are developed by education, they are able to govern themselves by reason and truth, discerning the common good which is their enlightened will. The most reliable index of that will is to be found through use of the majority principle. (3) And yet it is true that power tends to corrupt; this does allow selfishness, rather than the common good, to be the source of rule; because this fateful power is necessarily present in any central government, the state should have the right to criticize and annul federal action. (4) All men are created equal; this is to say they have natural rights which belong to them as human beings, which cannot be taken away by any society. For this reason they must be equal before the law. As they are created equal, so they are created free. (5) Since freedom belongs to all men, some of the more central freedoms, as freedom of religion, of press, trial by jury, and permanent habeas corpus, must be guaranteed by legal means. The principle is that each man should enjoy as much liberty as he can exercise without injury to the equal liberty of his

fellow men. (6) Although men are equal in the sense of having equal rights, it is impractical to make equal the conditions under which they live. Even so, their inequality of condition should be kept within bounds by imaginative legislative programs. (7) The natural community is one in which men live in democratic simplicity, recognizing their equality of rights, and where they are nearly equal in condition, and secure in their persons.

I am positive our man of principle would have come out with at least three or four of these ideas; and he might say that, believing these, he had to believe also in the principle of integration. The defense of his stand would lie in pointing out how one line of conduct is consistent with these ideas; and its opposite inconsistent with them.

But we would need to ask further questions of this man. We would want to know of the whole set of ideas: How do you know these to be true? What supports the whole theory?

We might be told: Experience. And in some sense, I would imagine, these social principles do come from experience, as do the principles of medicine and law. But as there can be disagreements among schools of medicine and law, so we might find disagreement here. It would seem, then, that experience is not the only consideration. Looking over the Jeffersonian principles, we might well agree that the points relate to each other rather well; but the consistency of a theory is not enough to make it true. Some of the points in the list aren't very clear. We might, for example, want to know why sovereignty must reside in the whole people; and we might be given a reason for this which would make the whole theory more convincing. And some of the points are such that digging up facts would help us to test their truth or falsity. But after we had related all of the available facts to the theory, we could not avoid noticing how many of these ideas seem not to be touched by facts. Words like "should," "ought," and "must" are being used; even when the plain ordinary connective "to be" is used, it often has the sense of "should." One can assemble facts to test the truth of an assertion that something "is" or "is not." But how do facts test the claim that something "should" or "should not" be? Now, to go back to the start of our discussion, we had gotten into the toils of this problem by noticing ourselves talking about right and wrong, "should" and "should not," "ought," and "ought not." We wanted to know what lay behind these judgments. We tried the way of consequences and, while learning a good deal, finally ran into difficulty. We tried to understand what it meant to stand on principle; here we seemed to find the stand on principle looking, not to consequences, but to a theory of society; we examined one theory of society (in brief) and found a liberal use of the very terms "should" and "should not" which started us on our problem.

Have we, like one lost in a forest, drifted around in a huge circle to find ourselves back at the starting point? Either we have done so, or else we shall say: Even if a theory of society stands behind one's stand on principle, still something stands behind this theory which gives the sense of "oughtness" to it; and we haven't begun to find what this might be.

Merely to keep one's conduct in harmony with a consistent theory of society is no final solution to the problem of right and wrong. There are many theories of what society ought to be — and they do not agree. Can two men stand on principle, and disagree? They can!

Jefferson had presented a doctrine of states' rights; and that doctrine is also presented by those in disagreement with our man of principle. The doctrine, we had said, can mean merely, "Let us handle the problem in our own way." But it can also be one idea in a set of ideas, making up a theory of what society should be in opposition to the theory held by Jefferson. To find the whole set we might refer to a man who mightily opposed the principles of Jefferson, John C. Calhoun. Once again drawing out the basic notions from a sheaf of material, we might summarize his view in this way:

(1) Democracy, in its truer sense, is a partnership among equals only, and these are the superior people; sovereignty resides in the superior. (2) Since every man is selfish no common good, or will of the people, is to be found; among the competing interests of society there can only be a will of the majority. And the will of the majority can result in tyranny, as complete as any in history. (3) Protection against this tyranny, in addition to other checks and balances, lies in the right of states to have final authority over the measures which will bind them. (4) All facts support the proposition that men are not created equal, as they are not created free. (5) Liberty is an indispensable condition of progress; but since men are unequal, only those who deserve liberty are entitled to it. (6) Those who have gained liberty, and the means proper to a free man, must show their virtue by enter-

ing a co-partnership to care for those not entitled to liberty, the inferior members of society. Society thus divides naturally into two groups; and every great society in the past has recognized this division of superior and inferior, of free and slave classes. Civilization can progress only when some men are freed from toil, living on the labor of their inferiors. (7) But this slavery can take several forms; there is wage slavery, and bond slavery; the latter is preferable, being more humane and responsible, generating natural communities of superior and inferior in which each fulfills his proper responsibilities toward the other.

Here is a second theory of society. And, unhappily, our two theories of society oppose each other point by point. They agree on one idea, the doctrine of states' rights, but to some extent they disagree on the reasons for its inclusion. Every step of our analysis would allow Calhoun, or another so inclined, to oppose integration on principle, standing on this theory of the nature of society.

If men can stand on principle, and completely disagree, while the theories of society they defend oppose each other point for point, how can a stand on principle furnish the means for an advance? Whatever progress we have made in working out this question, the stand on principle is now in exactly the same position as was the stand on consequences; when a man stands on principle he may be merely exhibiting his personal feelings to the public view, backed by a theory of society shaped to express these feelings. Principles are man's most cherished prejudices. Must this be our conclusion?

It must be our conclusion, unless there are insights still to come. Those who took a stand on principle did seem to be relying on sets of principles which together would constitute some theory about society. Yet even a quick glance at the theories of society we have sketched will reveal how much these theories omit of what we ordinarily mean by "right." The basic maxims of our lives, phrased cryptically — "It is right to tell the truth, to keep one's promises, to be faithful to trusts, to respect the wishes of others, to avoid gossip and ridicule, to help others, to preserve life, to respect property rights" — are touched upon only slightly by these theories of society, the contents of which we must assume to be typical of any theory of society. The absence of such judgments in our theories does suggest the need for some other part to the working out of the nature of principle.

But what step will reveal the rest? Our sets of principles in medicine, law, football, and wherever else, prescribed means for reaching a goal. Similarly, our sets of principles defining theories of society are prescribing means for the reaching of some goal. Long ago we had said the goal is to achieve the good in a social context. I see no way to improve upon this as the goal. But what of the "good"? Could we learn more about the nature of this good, not only might it fill in whatever judgments may be lacking in our theories of society; it could possibly furnish a lever by which to judge among competing theories; it might throw light upon the problem of disagreement among men of principle.

Was this not precisely where we failed in trying to measure right and wrong by consequences? It was. The specific nature of the good seemed individual. And, in our discussion of value, we had some evidence of a common good; but in our self-examination differences appeared among us in our most basic judgments about this good. Is there any point in returning to the scene of our failures? None, unless — as all hopeless folk affirm — the third time is somehow charmed.

Our second failure came as we were attempting to apply a bundle of rules, each of which was seeking by way of consequences to find the greatest amount of some selected value. On the supposition that the rule would lead us to the good, each was seeking to find the greatest good for the greatest number. But our man of principle is not inclined toward this close scrutinizing of the consequences; even though it is supposed to lead — if all goes well — to the greatest good. Indeed, although he may be wrong, the man of principle is a bit contemptuous of those who spend their time totting up the consequences. If he believes a certain stand to be a matter of principle, he does not feel the need to learn how others will respond to the action he proposes. Right is right, no matter what the consequences! This is oftentimes his attitude — and indeed the point to which we came, when considering the view which rests on consequences. It is as though this man knew the good, had no question about its nature, his only question revolving around the means for the drawing of this good into the world. We owe our man of principle the courtesy of trying to understand how, if at all, the good may be known apart from consequences. Certainly we have learned to our sorrow how slight is the instruction to be gained from staring at the consequences!

Since he does not even try to consult the greatest number, has no interest in polls of public opinion, certainly he is not after a greatest good for the greatest number. But he must have as his goal the good; and this object of his concern is obviously not thought by him to be merely his own individual good. What is left? Perhaps the man of principle, without particularly trying to find the reactions of others, is — mysteriously — after the greatest good for all. Should this be his goal — let us not decide offhand — and if there can be a good for all, then surely any set of principles, guiding us toward this good, would be guiding us more certainly than others to the right.

The man who stands on principle might be after a different kind of good, not a good for the greatest number merely, but a good for all. But while some theories of society assume there is a good for all, others assume there can be nothing beyond the "greatest good for the greatest number." And we cannot cancel out the conflict of opposing principles by fiat, deciding arbitrarily that theories of society must be governed by a "good for all." You may have sensed this danger fifty lines ago, and muttered to yourself: "But on this point Jefferson and Calhoun disagree. Jefferson believed there was a common good which would be good for all; Calhoun believed there could be nothing beyond a majority good, and this could not be good for all. Are we not dangerously close to begging the question?" Agreed. But if principle requires one of these views and denies the other, this must bear even upon the conflict between Jefferson and Calhoun. The point is: Our argument must be independent of our present conflict, must go behind it to see if it can be somehow resolved.

In our first assault on the good, by questioning ourselves about the happenings and decisions of our lives, we were able to come to values which were final; we had used the name "intrinsic." You remember the partial listing which had contained wisdom, courage, temperance, justice, and the like. Examining such values, we had learned they could be shared, were noncompetitive, and were not diminished by the sharing. More important, we had discovered a kind of unity, implicit in these value attitudes, which allowed us to argue that they were not wholly arbitrary. Join these slight discoveries to our desperate need for discovering a path to the determination of right and wrong, these insights, against a background of despair, become positively luminous. It is evidence of a sort that the good is, or at least can be, common.

The Common Good?

Our discovery had its less hopeful side. We were able to reach these final values only through inspection of our lives; and even though each of us gained a sense of final values we had learned — without surprise — of the disagreement among men over the value, if any, which is chief of all; and over the relative importance of every value. And this was one of the two stumbling blocks in the way of attempting to spell out the right through consequences.

Now, we seem to have evidence for, and evidence against, the possibility of a common good — a good for all. Not knowing any better move, we might simply accept this result. The evidence is mixed; then let us regard the situation which produced this evidence as also mixed. In life, we shall say, in one sense there are common goods; in other senses there are not. In one sense the presence of common goods is almost certain. If the unity of society is not in every way coercive, and it is not, then there must be a common good in some way shared among its members. At the same time — so far as we know — any common good must be of the nature of some intrinsic value; the common good is an "ought to be," a thing to be discovered, to be produced, to be achieved. Men can exist without it, or without much of it. Its not existing baldly in the world leads to the sense in which, so far as we know practically, goods are not completely common. In this mood, it seems, nothing is to be learned about the good, except what will satisfy me, and lead on my development; and what will do the same for you. When we attempted to find a mark to use in judging consequences, this was our conclusion. But why not make a virtue of this necessity? Where men are in agreement there is a common element among them; and where they agree upon a final value, we may call this element a common good. And where men disagree, each wants . . . what? Each wants to go his own way, regardless of the other, to achieve his individual good. Then let the wish be granted; and have we not established, or discovered, a common element even here? Where there is nothing common in the ends to be pursued, one can still speak of a common agreement in the means by which these divergent ends are gained; where there is no agreement as to the end, there can be an authorization of liberty. This second kind of common element is different from the other; it is an agreement which sets up boundaries; they are like the boundaries of one's property, except that we carry them with us — and they surround each person. But this is a social principle phrased by Jefferson: Each man should enjoy as much liberty as each may exercise without injury to the equal liberty of his fellows. And the point was precisely stated in the French Declaration of Rights. At least, we have discovered a possible common element even where there is no agreement on the ends to be pursued. This makes more promising the discovery of those steps by which a common good can be established, or discovered.

The Man of Principle

What will happen if we suppose a common good to be possible in each of these two senses? How, apart from simple questioning, can those attitudes be found which are mutually supporting, consistent with each other, and capable of being shared without diminution? If we can find such attitudes, the right will be the kind of conduct which comports with the good. We have found the meanings of intrinsic values to be consistent with each other; but, we had said, should one try to substitute "duplicity" for "integrity" he would find duplicity strangely at variance with the rest. While this would be equally true in substituting "ignorance" for "wisdom" or "cowardice" for "courage," it might have been good fortune which supplied the words we in fact had used. Let us take up the thought. The same meaning is given to "man of principle" and "man of integrity." If we ask how such a man is to be described, one of the appropriate remarks would be that he is consistent. And we might cast about for the meaning of the term. When one becomes something definable out of the flux of feeling, sensation, emotion, purpose, and idea, he gains, we say, a certain consistency of behavior. If things go properly this "consistency" can develop into what we call character. Whatever else, this consistency makes the person dependable; what he will do can be predicted, up to a certain point. Is this all we mean by the consistency we find in such a person — that we can have advance knowledge of what he will do?

We must learn more about this "consistency." He has gained a definition of himself, so to speak. Having gained this, he will either keep it in all of his relations with others, or else he will lose the identity he had found. He has found in himself these value attributes. And how will he behave toward other men? He will be himself; that is, he will extend to others the grounds from which he acts. It is not saying too much to hold he must do this; he cannot retain his own unity of character unless he treats all alike. So acting, a consistency through time is gained. But there is more to the problem than we have yet discerned. Consistency through time is possible even for an unjust man.

We may come at this through a very much paraphrased passage in the Republic. Glaucon and Adeimantus are presenting an argument; the most advantageous posture in life, they argue, comes from combining the appearance of justice with the reality of injustice. The graphic portrait of the man described contains these elements: The perfectly unjust man, who appears perfectly just, will have mastered the art of deceit; he will lie, thieve, even kill, to gain his unjust ends. Partly by persuasion, and partly by force, he will make unlawful gains and not be punished. Everything he does will be to his own interest. Through his appearance of justice, and his increasing power, he will be influential in the community; he will be able to marry whom he likes; in business enterprises he will always profit at the expense of others; when he enters upon public office he will use his position for personal profit; at the same time he will have many friends because he will use his office to benefit his friends; he will get the better of all who oppose him, profiting at their expense, plotting harm against his enemies and giving presents to his friends. Out of his gains he will give liberally to religious and charitable organizations, and will be highly honored because of his beneficence. And so he will live and die, honored by gods and men.

In the Republic this man is called "perfectly unjust." His most essential feature is the contrast between an outward appearance of honesty, trustworthiness, helpfulness, and active benevolence; and an inner reality of dishonesty, a capacity to betray any trust, and active ill will or malevolence. He seems to have the better of both worlds; depending upon what is to his advantage, he is able to falsify or tell the truth, keep or betray a trust, help or harm an acquaintance, support the greatest values, or the greatest evils. There is a double nature to this man.

All the same I suppose there would be in this man a certain consistency through time. If we were able to become well enough acquainted with him, and could survive to tell about it, we would be able to predict how he would act in a given situation. But the consistency of his selected purpose, looking to his own advantage, has in fact resulted in a striking contrast, a general inconsistency, between the façade and the inner man. And this kind of inconsistency is what we call "duplicity."

Ethical Consistency

Clearly, "being predictable" does not reach the kind of consistency which is meant when one speaks of a man of "character." The life of any man of purpose will be predictable to some extent, perhaps to a great extent. Yet there is a difference between a "man of purpose" and a "man of character." Given a fixed purpose, and a familiar situation, what a person will do can be known in advance. What he does will be consistent with what he had done before; then, what he will do can be predicted. But while this does include our man of character, it also includes the man of double nature. If we remove the general inconsistency between the façade and the inner nature of our double-natured man, he will be characterized by a new kind of consistency — an internal-external consistency. There will be a consistency between his act and the motive from which it proceeds. What is the nature of this change? I think he has become a "man of character."

But since we may have been mistaken, let us consider the man of double nature, asking how his general inconsistency can be removed. There are two ways. In the first place he can be candid about his personal motivations; he can shape his external appearance to reflect his inner nature. He can confess his wish for power and the gratification of his senses. He would be able to gain an inner-outer consistency if, openly, he were to lie, betray trusts, and harm those in his way. But should he do so, his behavior will be very ill-suited to his goal; for his lies and betrayals, without the appearance of truth and trust, will bring him no advantage. Nor am I certain that one can speak with sense of "lying" and "betrayal," done openly. Glaucon and Adeimantus are right; "perfect" injustice requires a contrast between an outward appearance of honesty, trustworthiness, helpfulness, active benevolence; and the inner reality of dishonesty, untrustworthiness, active ill will, or malevolence. Only such a man could profit from his deceptions.

Duplicity seems to be required for the success of certain actions. I tell you a lie, and am immediately caught in this internal-external contradiction. The lie I present to you must be tricked out with all the external features of the truth; it must be accompanied by the firm jaw, the clear-eyed unblinking glint of sincerity, the warmth of trust and friendship, and it must be plausible — a statement which could be true. I am positively willing for you to accept it as the truth. At the same time it is my inner will deliberately to falsify. I cannot gain the advantage of my lie if I am honest with you, saying: "Now, pay close attention; I am going to tell a lie." In the same way, to betray a trust successfully I must have you believing up to the last moment — the moment before betrayal — in my trustworthiness.

There is, then, a practical impossibility in removing the general inconsistency from our man by shaping his behavior to fit his inner motive. This way restores nothing to him; and deprives him of what he otherwise might have gained.

In the second way he will not except his inner nature from the requirements of his speech; let him tell the truth, keep trusts, be generally helpful, and support the good (the mutually supporting attitudes). The double nature will be gone without reduction of the man to utter impotence. But in removing this general inconsistency we have changed the nature of our man. We have given him character, or integrity. And if this is the path toward the right then we would be saying: The good is made up of those common elements which are found within us when, upon questioning our lives, we come to ways of behaving desired for themselves alone; and the right is simply action directed toward the good with a singleness of mind beyond mere consistency through time; a consistency of purpose among these sharable values is required, running from the appearance of the act back through the most hidden sources of our motivation. It is a consistency which does not except oneself — even in a hidden, inner way — from the values which are in question.

The Discovery of a Rule

Not only have we defined a man of character; we are approaching the statement of a different kind of rule. An act is wrong if it requires duplicity. And this is a mark which one can "see" without looking to consequences. An act is "right" if there is an inner-outer consistency in the act, the man, and the motivation for his act. We might well catch up the point in a general rule: *Do not except your inner nature from the principle which your act presents to others.* At least the rule does apply to the maxims of our early list: it ap-

plies to lying, betrayal of trusts, harming under the guise of helping, and supporting evil under the semblance of good.

Insofar as there is a common good, and we can come to know it,
this rule, applied to our conduct, can help us introduce this good
into the world. But we have found this good to exist only in a way,
and up to a certain point; in another way the common element is
no more than an agreement to disagree, an agreement to authorize
the pursuit of individual goods. Our present rule does not cover
this aspect of the problem.

Its Second Phrasing

Now in fact something further is contained in the rule which is
before us. Why did our "perfectly unjust" man lie, cheat, betray
trusts, thieve, and kill? We had said it was for his personal gratification. And what, in relation to him, were the people who felt the
effects of his duplicity? They were means to an end, instruments
of his will. We might say: One is acting wrongly when men are
treated as the instruments of another's will. And this brings us to a
second statement of our rule: *Treat every man as an end in himself,
and not as a means to some private end which is your own.* The
same conclusion might be gained in another way. Why should we
have any concern to keep transparency within, and duplicity without, our lives? Why should we have any concern to avoid presenting a false appearance to others? We must do so, we had said, if
we are to retain our unity of character. But in doing so, note this,
we are placing others on a footing equal to ourselves; we are extending to them the same respect and consideration which we
feel toward our own lives. Now, we look upon ourselves with
some finality; we are the final arbiter of our values, the final end
of our striving. Intrinsic values, in a peculiarly intimate manner,
stand for aspects of man's own development. We are their source
and sanction. In seeking wisdom or beauty our developed self is
the end of such striving. The respect we grant to others is a respect for them as, equally with ourselves, the source of final values.
This is saying that man's life has (can have, or should have) intrinsic value. Just as we found intrinsic values, upon inspection, to
be the ends of life, so — to furnish other words — man in his developed form is an end, and not an instrument. And once again we
would come to the statement of the rule, equating right action
with the treatment of men as ends, and wrong action with their

treatment as means. Note how the rules tie in to our distinction of instrumental and intrinsic values. We are now saying: Men are treated properly when viewed as having intrinsic value; men are being treated wrongly when viewed as having only the value of an instrument — instrumental value, then.

Our present manner of expression allows the rule to cut more deeply still. This rule, too, can be applied to cases, and without looking very hard to consequences. We can separate out the conduct in which men are treated as instruments of another's will; and that which grants to men a final value. But does the rule now cut too deeply for us? In our discussion of value the final values appeared beyond the instruments of life as a goal to be achieved, an ideal, a point allowing some control over our instrumental striving. But now it is being said that quite the proper manner of relating ourselves to others is in terms of the final values where personal integrity, sharing, and cooperation replace the oppositions where each is used as instrument of the other's will.

Now the relation of the first way of putting the rule to the second is this: If, in keeping with the first statement, one has chosen integrity for himself, no other behavior toward others than the behavior expressed in our second statement can be in accord with this integrity. And when one judges his actions by our first rule, then he is committed to viewing those around him under the conception of the second rule. And now a surprising insight comes: The first rule applies to the good, so far as a common good exists and can be found. The second rule applies not only to the common good, but to that considerable area where each must go his way with the common liberty which must be granted men who are not viewed, and do not view themselves, as instruments, but as ends.

How shall the problem of the overlap in human life be solved? It can be done in two ways. One way is to make the area of overlap into a common will, where we do not need to collide because our wills are mutually supporting. But where we disagree, where our wills are in fact in conflict, there is another way: to let the liberty of each extend up to the point of conflict and no further. Thus does the autonomy of each provide a natural limitation upon the liberty of all.

Its Third Statement

If the first statement underlines how men must act if they are to establish the common good; and if the second statement describes the relation in which such men must stand to each other, then clearly something is implied about the character which should be present in society as a whole. Ethical questions aside, the overlap in human life has been handled in at least two ways.

Let us imagine a society in which some men are expected to be the instruments of another's will. Commands will be issued, and those commanded will obey. We have knowledge of societies based on command; the arrangement can be called culture by command. Imagine another arrangement where the basis is not command, where "command" has been replaced by "law." What is the difference between "command" and "law"?

Sweep the floor! Wash the dishes! Put down that comic book and do your calculus! These are commands. Should I command you to sweep the floor, all within earshot would understand the statement, which included you, which was directed toward you, to exclude me. You are to sweep the floor, not I! And for a long time societies developed with the fact rather obvious that some were to command, others were to sweep the floor! Certain people were privileged to give the commands; certain other people were to obey these commands. If a general commands his men to advance, he himself — I have been told — is not compelled by this command to advance beside them. Of course, he may require this of himself. If a king commands that all the world be taxed, he is not thereby compelled to pay taxes. The commands may be pleasant or unpleasant, wise or foolish, useful or harmful; but one has culture by command whenever the requirement issues from one person or group, and is binding upon another person or group.

As one thing leads to another, a different arrangement is possible: an arrangement in which no one is exempt from the command, where it bears on all alike. The command is here cut loose from its arbitrary human moorings, and floats freely — as it were — over the whole group, binding all alike, and thus changing in its nature. A new entity has emerged; it is the appearance of a law. This happened in Greece, and had its flowering in Rome; it happened in western Europe; and in a somewhat different way it happened, and continues to happen, in our own southland. Culture by command gives way to culture by law.

A command issues forth from some commander; but what is the source of a law? It issues from both commander and commanded.

In this new arrangement men command themselves, and the gulf between commander and commanded disappears. Any command is expected to yield some good for the one commanding. And in the case of law men command themselves; the law, then, issues from all — and if this kind of command yields some good for those from whom it issues, then the law should be a good for all. But not all laws are of this nature? You are right, of course. At least, we sometimes have no desire to obey a given law; and it is possible to have bad laws. Yet we are not speaking of what we desire, or of what is undesirable. We are trying to think about what is desirable for us. There are types of conduct desirable for us which we do not now desire; this has been granted. And if we have drawn our lines properly, law should represent what is desirable for all and, therefore, good for all. But are we not stepping beyond our mixed evidence? Any law will come from the people; must it not come from what they desire? How, then, does the desirable enter our consideration?

It can come in only if there is a common good at least partly known, and certainly knowable; and only when we will the good. If there are such times, then every man is legislator and sovereign, as well as subject. In particular, he may desire almost anything; but in addition to his particular desires, whatever they may be, he desires the good for all — what is desirable for all; and this desire provides the foundation of the idea of law. It can be put in other language. There is a common will at the base of society. This is the true source of laws, a source which can and should contribute the ordering principles of our social life. If all of this is allowed, the principle can be stated a third way: *Recognize in every man that he is sovereign, as well as subject, in the realm of ends which is the good society.*

Accept the principle, and it follows that all men should be guaranteed equality before the law, for they are jointly its source. And all men have equal rights, for they are equally sovereign. Our third statement provides the notion of equality, needed to gain the principle of liberty. The third statement views man in his capacity as a member of society, as a citizen.

The same view has been expressed in three different ways; but each expression has furnished a somewhat different insight; and each statement has developed the insight present in its predecessor. Together they provide a sphere of cooperation, a sphere of liberty, and a set of rights with a premise of equality.

We may seem to have moved some distance from our basic question of right and wrong; but every step has been forced upon us. We wanted to know what was behind the statement of the man who claims to stand on principle; the answer seemed to be that a theory of what society ought to be lay behind his stand. But we found opposing theories of society. This led us once more to the question of the unity of values, and to the question of character. Probing these, we found a rule which could help establish the good, so far as it is common; the first rule led to a second, establishing the good so far as it is individual; these two rules together gave us a basis for law and for society. Now we can say that the theory of society, upon which one stands when he stands on principle, must be in accord with our third statement; and the third statement of our rule provides an immediate support for the set of principles in terms of which some theories of society have been expressed.

The movement of our thought, being somehow backwards, may have concealed the unity of this conception. We began with the sets of principles constituting theories about the nature of society; and through questioning we arrived at a set of still more basic principles, the basic standpoint of them all being the single requirement: Be consistent! We can reverse the movement. We can begin with the rule: Do not except yourself from the principle which your act requires of others. We can continue: Treat every man as an end in himself, and not as a means to some private end which is your own. Still further, we can say: Recognize in every man that he is sovereign, as well as subject, in the realm of ends which is the good society. And from this statement we can move to that elaboration of the principles upon which a man of principle will stand. Unless I am very much mistaken these principles will be much more like those of Jefferson than like those of his opponent. And now these principles may be said to have a foundation. Indeed, we can claim: Accept these, or be inconsistent! Only such principles can preserve a means-end, inner-outer consistency in human life.

In the stand on principle, at an earlier stage of our discussion, we had noticed a lack of comment on questions of personal ethics. If we have found the explanation of principle, this gap is now filled in. Referring to our list of questions, this view is telling us: It is never right to tell a lie, to break a promise, to betray a trust, to exaggerate, to ridicule, to refuse one in genuine need, to kill, or steal. It is telling us, further, that it is never right to adopt an attitude of superiority, or to use another as an instrument, to use a friend; it is never right to circumvent the law which is above the law, to deny a person due process of the law, to deny a person, as person, those rights which lay down natural boundary lines among us. It is telling us many things about right and wrong; too many, you may think. Here, you may say, is a view too strict for ordinary use. But if we have gotten the view out properly, we can now say that when two men, both of them standing on principle, disagree one of them is wrong, has not probed far enough into the underlying basis of his stand.

The Unveiling of I. Kant

From the time of our arrival at the first statement of our rule I have been drawing covertly on the three rules for ethics of the German philosopher, Immanuel Kant. But since two of his three rules have been given somewhat different treatment, and since there is disagreement over what his rules require, and what they mean, I did not identify him at the time. The first rule, called by him the Categorical Imperative, states: "Act as if the maxim of thy act were to become by thy will a universal law of nature." I am not certain one would know, in most cases, how to act at all if he acted only as he would if the principle of his act were to become a universal law of nature. I am certain of our ability to know when we are making an exception of ourselves; and Kant clearly says that these two ways of putting it come to the same thing. The second rule, called the Practical Imperative, was stated: "Act so that you treat humanity, whether in your own person, or in that of another, always as an end and never as a means only." This is almost identical with our statement, except for Kant's interesting qualification. On his way of putting the second rule, it is acceptable to use men as instruments if we do not do so exclusively. But our stronger statement follows directly from the first imperative; his is a weakened form. Although Kant discusses a third way of putting his principle, he gives us no distinctive form of words for its expression. Our statement of it does relate to his discussion; the following paragraph is to the point:

The concept of each rational being as a being that must regard itself as giving universal law through all the maxims of its will, so that it may judge itself and its actions from this standpoint, leads to a very fruitful concept, namely, that of a *realm of ends*.[10]

And so our third statement was presented as an ordering principle for society; and in its discussion we employed some of the phrases of Rousseau, including his "general will."

It would not desolate me to learn that this is not in all respects what Kant intended; we have gained our distinctions from the argument; they stand or fall alone. But a slight defense of this as Kant's general meaning might be offered. In the first place we know how Kant admired Rousseau, thinking him possessed of the deepest understanding of human nature in the eighteenth century. And we know of the immense influence which Rousseau's *Social Contract*, a defense of law as against command, had in his adopted country, France. Kant was able to watch from Prussia the bubbling of ideas and events as the French Revolution was in preparation. Shortly after Kant published his important writings in ethics the revolution did occur. The first act of the successful revolutionaries was to begin the preparation of a code of law which, while completed only under Napoleon and bearing the name, "The Napoleonic Code," was the fruit of this revolution. The revolution, happening during Kant's lifetime, replaced absolutism with its arbitrary power to command, allowing Louis XVI to insist in the manner of his predecessor, "The state, it is I!," with a constitution and legality. We know how Kant deplored the violence involved in the shift toward a new basis of society; but we also know of his defense of these ideals in his lectures at the University of Königsberg. He stood somewhat alone in a rising tide of Prussian nationalism. Jefferson in a similar situation, at about the same time, was defending the French Revolution in America. And this revolution marked a shift from culture by command to culture by law. The conclusion of all this seems clear enough: There is something about this particular cultural change which has great bearing upon the ideas of right and wrong, as Kant envisioned them; the basis of his ethic is the new kind of idea which can work its way into a culture.

[10] Immanuel Kant, *Foundations of the Metaphysics of Morals*, in *Critique of Practical Reason and Other Writings in Moral Philosophy*, trans. and ed. L. W. Beck (Chicago: University of Chicago Press, 1949), pp. 90–91. Copyright 1949 by the University of Chicago.

Objections to the View

We had found two objections to the Consequences view which we were unable to resolve. First, we could find no way to determine a single respect from which consequences should be viewed; and we were left with a final disagreement concerning what this proper respect might be. Second, even when two men are using the same rule there can be disagreement, since all the consequences are in the future and if they disagree over these expected consequences, what one will call wrong, the other may call right; and we were able to find no means by which either could prove his case to his opponent.

Taking the second objection first, clearly this objection does not apply to the stand on principle. If two men are agreed upon the view of principle, as it has come out in our discussion, they could not disagree on the rightness or wrongness of a proposal to liquidate a given social class. Both of them would have to grant: "The proposal is wrong; it employs duplicity; it uses men as instruments; it deprives men of their rights."

And to come to the first objection, the question would be: Can two men stand on principle, and yet disagree about the rightness or wrongness of an act? The issue was joined between Calhoun and Jefferson. If we have hit the mark in developing the idea of principle, then we have strong reason to believe that no two men can stand on principle and disagree. Almost every proposition in Calhoun's list falls when viewed from the standpoint of our present theory. He is willing to see men used as instruments; he supports the basis of command in society; he does not accord men equal rights. And if one should say, "But I think principle has a different base," we would wish to know the nature of this different base. He might have another way of spelling out the stand on principle; on the other hand, he might have nothing but words to offer us. Until we know his argument, we would have to say that men, who understand what they are about, cannot stand on principle and disagree.

But there are two huge waves coming which may damage what we have been able to build, calling it the stand on principle. There are two further objections of great power, attacking our view from opposite sides.

A man could read very carefully our discussion of principle, and could reply, after thinking it over: "This view is judging some kinds of behavior to be always wrong. I certainly don't get this from common sense. And when we tried to find ways of acting which were always wrong, we found no ways of acting which might not be, in some circumstances, right. This view completely ignores our common feeling. I can think of times when telling a lie would save a life, while telling the truth would forfeit life. If you are telling me it is wrong to lie at such times and right to tell the truth, I don't think much of your ethic. And what is true of this is also true of theft, keeping or betraying trusts, and preserving or taking life. I don't quite see how to argue against the view, but it seems to me much too strict."

Situations arise in which following principle would result in evil; such is the claim. The view which looks away from consequences would have one draw the lines of right and wrong in a much too rigid manner. I feel the force of this objection, believing there are times when it is not wrong to tell a lie. If you feel its force as well, we had better let the objection stand as a problem for the view which takes its stand on principle.

Curiously, there is another objection which registers an opposite complaint: The rule is not too strict, but it has no content. After reflecting on the present view, a man might say: "Let me see, the whole meaning of right and wrong seems to go back to not excepting oneself from the rule one's conduct presents to others. If only this is required, to be sure lying, stealing, and betraying trusts are ruled out; but I can retain this inner-outer consistency while practicing abstinence or social drinking, taking dope or refusing to take dope, adhering to free love or chastity, holding to polygamy or monogamy, believing in private property or the holding of property in common. According to the view, as given, any of these actions can be right."

There are many kinds of behavior with respect to which this rule gives no guidance; such is the claim. Hegel was the first to frame this objection: The Categorical Imperative has no content, because so many ways of living can be universalized. Whether or not we have a ready answer to this objection depends upon how we understand our view. Kant tended to believe that one could not be a drifter, and remain consistent; while excepting himself from the development of his capacities, he would be expecting of others the continual development of their talents to provide the quality and conveniences of social living. If the point is acceptable, then the taking of narcotics cannot be right. And if his premise of self-realization is granted, one might argue for a context of monogamy, chastity, and no more than social drinking. But such questions bring us into an area of semidarkness; we do not have clear cases of inner contradiction here; and our questions must be posed in terms of the consequences which will "best" achieve this quality or that. And to allow this is to admit a consideration of consequences into the stand on principle. Neither is the second objection easy to overcome. Together these objections may reveal a weakness in the view itself.

What we want in all of this is some manner of separating out right and wrong in conduct. We have posed the question, run through a number of typical answers; we have found these falling into a stand on consequences and a stand on principle; we have found helpful and promising features in both views; we have found weighty objections to each. The objections to the stand on consequences came down to saying that on this view the right is subjective; the objections to the stand on principle came down to saying that in some cases the view may be too rigid; in others it offers us no guidance.

We have worked long and hard, and have ended with objections on our hands. But after all, we do not believe in the logic of fatigue; we do not believe that working long and hard means we have proved something. At least our discussion has posed the problem: How are right and wrong in conduct to be distinguished? At the very start we tried to gain an awareness of whatever rule controlled the practice of our lives. And every step since then has had to do with the testing, refining, and strengthening of this rule. Having made our way through many pages, once again the problem returns to you. And I shall continue on, doing for myself what each of us must do — attempting to gain its answer.

II. Toward Principle in Life

I propose that our two approaches be compared in order to understand what each demands, while reviewing their most solid features and greatest difficulties. We should be prepared to retain the former, and to meet, if possible, the latter. The stand on consequences required, at last, something like principle to shore it up; and we seemed to find in Kant a covert looking to the consequences, as his three-way principle was extended from the more to the less obvious cases. Do these findings, which suggest the inability of these views to stand alone, also suggest between the views some relations of importance? A convenient beginning point will be the question: Do principles and consequences require each other?

Principle and Consequence Compared

"Look at the consequences!" We have learned one of several things is being done in so looking. We are asking how others will be pleased or displeased by the act, or to what extent others will find the act wise, moderate, helpful, or whatever else. Or we are asking to what extent the act "ought" to please them, to what extent it encourages real wisdom, moderation, self-realization, or whatever mark has been held to be the norm. In the second case something besides consequences is needed to furnish this mark, to gain its meaning, to keep it from being an arbitrary choice; this something we could not furnish from within the view itself.

In either of these cases our first approach holds to a rule and notes the consequences for those affected by the act. In either case we must look directly at what happens to those affected by it. We have already noted the flexibility in this approach.

Now it is also natural for a person standing on principle to say or think: "What will be the consequences of my so acting?" Then are those standing on principle also tracing out consequences? There is evidence of some kind of looking to the consequences when Socrates, in the remainder of the *Crito*, points out that escape will mean denying the laws and institutions of the state, and breaking an implicit contract which has grown throughout his life between his society and himself. Are not these consequences? Here a ray of light breaks in. Consequences they are, but logical consequences! Our first view gravitated always around and toward personal, practical, physical consequences. This view moves the other way. Even if all such consequences are satisfactory, in terms of logical consequences the act might be most unsatisfactory. When the man who stands on principle asks about the consequences of his act, he is asking: "What are the implications in this act for the structure of society? What nature does this act give society? What idea of society does this act contain?"

And yet principle is not unrelated to physical consequences. There are at least two ways in which physical consequences relate to the stand on principle. Even if the person who invokes principle were to claim that, regardless of the nature of any of the consequences you can cite, a certain path should be followed, still we would expect him to believe that in following this path the good will be achieved. And this must mean that the consequences of standing on principle are better than those following from any other course. Both of these ways of making decisions relate themselves to consequences in this general sense. But what we have called the way of consequences does, in addition, decide what is right by reference to these consequences. Does the way of principle do this also?

Since any stand on principle is at last a stand upon a set of principles, spelling out the relations which ought to obtain among men, the question is whether these principles, developing what "ought to be," can be unrelated to consequences? Certainly if one is thinking of any single principle of medicine, law, or football, it is true that unfortunate consequences may require a revision of principle — so consequences can and do qualify principles, at least in all other applications of the word. And when one is considering the relations which ought to obtain more generally among us, a so-called principle which consistently made the worse appear the better cause, would come to be known, I am quite certain, as a false principle, and such principles would be drastically revised. But this is not the same as saying that consequences have determined what should be done. If consequences merely qualify the stand on principle, this is because there are in addition to the unfortunate consequences which might reveal the presence of a false principle, all the other principles in the set. And if we follow the lead of natural speech about principles in special fields then, of course, we would have to admit that every principle in the set has come from "experience" — what other source could one suggest? But this is not quite the same as saying such principles are statements of the customs of the race. We have already discovered the untidy manner in which custom contains the experience of the race. There are grounds for saying that we are now concerned with custom or experience, clarified and sharpened by reason. Certainly, if one stands on principle, he is willing to state a reason. His reason will be some idea concerning the nature of man or of society; and in this reason is the germ of a theory about society. It is on the ground of this theory that one stands when he stands on principle. A stand on principle arises, at least in part, from a consideration of society; it is freighted with the experience of the past, made intelligible and enlightened by the human mind, containing the clarity of mental decision which has struck away any irrelevant features, and developed the essential beyond the burden of past experience. The set of principles is a theory; the theory is an interpretation of the nature of man, of his function and his place. The theory fits the facts, or fails to fit those facts. It is proper to ask whether or not the interpretation is biased, whether it fits the facts neatly or with a twist, whether or not important facets of experience, which would rule out parts of the given theory, have been overlooked and omitted.

The theory of society implicit in any stand on principle will not often be spelled out. Often, one cannot state even to himself the nature of this larger whole. One does in fact usually have only a more or less clearly felt intuition about the larger whole to which his principles belong. But on the basis of his principles, bonded to his continuing experience, one works both ways: toward the view of society they imply, and toward decisions concerning specific actions. And standing, as it does, just between the individual and his social life, this set of principles can serve at once as a critique of both — of a society which has not arrived at principle, and of any individual who has not achieved integrity.

As we discovered when looking to the Calhoun-Jefferson contrast, principles are not merely descriptions of what has happened; there is a sense of "ought" about and within so many of these principles that no facts can reach them altogether. This aspect of our principle cannot come from looking to consequences, because consequences will merely produce more facts. We had decided provisionally that this "oughtness" could be supplied by the three rules which seemed unavoidable upon reflection.

What we conclude from this is that, while a stand on principle must use every available factual consequence in the shaping of social principles, there is another shaping which requires that these principles have not only plain logical consistency, but also the consistency of integrity.

Facts are important in both shapings. What the total past reveals about our social life is highly important. A man who stands on principle must plunge studiously, I should think, into the reading and understanding of our total human history. One danger of the stand on principle is that the view of society may be too narrowly fitted, may not look out from an acquaintance with man's spirit with the appropriate breadth and depth. The movement of history may teach him how to make his way from knowledge of the manner in which people do respond to knowledge of how they should respond; the deeper his acquaintance with the human spirit the more likely he will sense the common good.

The discussion helps us to see how our two views differ with respect to consequences. The first appeals for its data to the sum total of the individuals who are affected by the act. The other appeals to the common element in human striving, data for which may be found in our total human history. The first can handle with efficiency only the short-run future whose details are subject to the human estimate; the second speculates in a sense about the total human future by looking to the total human past.

There is a sense in which the rule of consequences, and the rule of principle, are in accord. One will define his rightness in terms of the greatest good for all. Where it is possible he will seek that good. Where it is not possible, he will take the second best, the greatest good for the greatest number; but still he will understand the right in terms of this good-for-all.

But if we are to define rightness in terms of principle, using consequences where they apply — as a subordinate principle, a principle of the diplomacy of action — this supposes principle to be adequate to define the right; and the supposition is possible, only if we can answer the two major unanswered objections facing the stand on principle. Can these be answered?

The Two Objections to a
Stand on Principle

One objection to this view complains of the strictness of the rule; the other objection finds the rule much too lax, and lacking content. If only the objectors could agree! Let us try to see the substance of these objections.

Is the rule too strict? There is no question in my mind about the rule of principle requiring us as individuals to hold that it is never right to lie, break promises, betray trusts, ridicule, refuse those in genuine need, kill, or steal; and it is never right to use another as an instrument. Then the rule requires too much?

If the rule demands too much, let us try to estimate how much too much by putting its demands as vividly as possible in a picture, including in our picture even some attachments of the sentiment which is found replete in human life. So let us suppose, as is often supposed against the stand on principle, that you are a citizen of a police state in good standing, and because your mother — yes, do not laugh, your mother (so goes the normal illustration of this objection) — has criticized the state for its persecution of minorities, the secret police are on her trail; if they seize her the result will be certain imprisonment and, very probably, death. Mother has sought refuge in your home; you have hidden her upstairs. Now as you sit with false composure in your living room — (Has not duplicity, false appearance, already entered this domestic scene?) — you hear a knocking at the door, a most compelling, vigorous knocking. You answer; it is the local commandant of the local secret police. You are in high esteem within the councils of state, and your word will be accepted at face value. The commandant bows politely, clicks his heels smartly (this is an essential point), and asks if your mother is in the house. If you say "No, she is not here," the house will not be searched, and your mother's life will have been saved. If you say "Yes" you will be responsible for your mother's certain imprisonment, and almost certain death. The choice is before you. What would you do?

Let me answer for you. You would lie; of course, you would — at least, I hope you would! But, according to the stand on principle, it is never right to lie. Does this example, then, refute the stand on principle? As a matter of fact the case is still more desperate. If you lie you have been guilty of duplicity, and duplicity is denied you by this view. If you tell the truth you have been guilty of taking human life — your mother's at that — and the taking of human life is denied you by this view. But you must either lie or tell the truth; hence, by the most antiseptic and surgically clean dilemmatic reasoning . . . the conclusion follows. No matter what you do, you will do violence to the way of principle.

The same kind of forced situation is before one when, as we had suggested, it is a matter of starvation or theft, killing or being killed, fighting or being enslaved. One can think of many such forced situations in human life, and possibly call more than one from memory. Whenever they occur the way of principle seems no longer to furnish guidance for our lives. And the question is: Do these dilemmas, which undeniably do occur, prove the bankruptcy of this way of distinguishing right from wrong?

Let us turn back to the melodrama of the mother, her stalwart son, and the commandant. It is right to tell the truth; it is right to preserve life. How can the situation have become so twisted that to follow either right action means one will violate the right in the other case? But is not this our point? It *is* the situation which is twisted. Indeed. The situation is without integrity. It is no marvel that one can be trapped embarrassingly, tragically, in trying under these circumstances to do the right! Now, in such twisted situations, where integrity is lacking, is the stand on principle powerless to guide our lives? Well, if the stand on principle will not work, looking to consequences performs no better; would one rely on the greatest sum of pleasure, wisdom or helpfulness; would one consider consequences rolling out into the future? I think not. One would simply, and immediately, lie. Has one ground to lie in this situation? I think there is ground, and it is the ground of principle. One should take whatever action will restore the situation to one where truth can be told, and at the same time human life can be preserved — or whatever other rights had been caught up in this dilemma. The stand on principle yields a directive even here: *Let the situation be restored to one where ethical behavior is possible.*

What has happened in this twisted situation? We have come upon a case where the rule to avoid duplicity cannot apply; the rule to treat men as ends cannot apply (someone will be used as the instrument of another); what can apply, however, is the third imperative which defines society as the realm in which sovereignty, rights, and safeguards are to be provided for the individual. And this kind of society is needed in order for men to avoid duplicity, to avoid treating other men as instruments. The directive comes from our third rule; what must be restored is the goal of the third imperative that the first and second may function once again.

And in regaining a situation where integrity is possible, when this is the goal, then indeed one will have ample use for consequences; strategy is of the essence; and sometimes the duplicity of the underground is called for.

I think something like this must be said. Where one is caught — in the cases where it is a matter of lying or taking life, stealing or starvation, killing or being killed, fighting or being enslaved, it is all right (that is to say, merely acceptable) to lie, steal, kill, and fight — but it is not right! There are cases where one simply can not be right; whatever course one takes, something right is violated. But surely, right is not less right, simply because in a given case there is no right for us to do. Is it not, indeed, a more realistic view of life to admit the presence of times when one must do wrong — whatever one does? And is this not the point of our speaking, sometimes, of "taking the lesser of two evils?" And so of warfare, does it not put the matter in perspective to say that at times perhaps we must engage in warfare, and yet it is not right? This would be one case where wrong must be done. But what would be perfectly right is the achievement of a world where men might live perpetually in peace.

One might wish to argue with this conclusion; one might say that since one must act in such tangled situations, the lesser of the two evils should be considered perfectly right. One might be able to apply some ethical view, perhaps that of consequences, to such dilemmas, and gain the conclusion that it is at times perfectly right to lie, steal, kill, and fight. But can we be satisfied with this? Can we even believe it? I think it would be perfectly right if the tangled situation did not occur. And so, I claim, while one can lie to save his skin, he cannot lie on principle. While one can kill to protect his home, steal to feed his family, and all the rest, he cannot do these things on principle.

The answer to the first objection, then, is to admit it. And this is saying that the ethical view of life, resting on principle, is somewhat austere; at times it rises far above the peak of common action; perhaps it is in some respects always above the peak of possible common action. This admission does not, in my eyes, cast any shadow on the doctrine. It is not intended to be a blueprint of what people do; it is a blueprint of the right. The reflection it casts is upon life as we know it; and by reflection we find our common life to be often less than good.

To insist that the path of integrity sometimes requires a surface lie in order to preserve a more profound integrity of purpose, or to restore integrity of purpose, or to restore integrity to a situation, has its dangers, and yet I think it is the truth. Among those with vicious intent who will to gain some personal goal through sacrificing

others, one had better lie. The lie will not achieve the good; but
it may keep the situation less evil than it might have been. The
thrust of an evil situation, when met with a convincing lie, may be
restored a bit closer to integrity, even though this sacrifices for the
time your own integrity. And this does not change the right. Nor
would a good man wish to lie; he will not do so habitually; he will
seek other means of handling the twisted situation. But at whatever
level it is possible, he will support integrity of purpose.

Nor is the twisted situation to be found only in circumstances
markedly exceptional. The public level is hardly ever the proper
level. Is there not something of the twisted semblance almost everywhere? Even so, the rule should be to depart from principle only
with great reluctance, and for the shortest possible time. To some
extent one must fight out his life on whatever level is dictated by
the course of events. Men descend to meet and join in conflict.
But the descent must not be accompanied by forgetfulness. Men
must ascend to meet on the level of common good. One ought
to work eagerly toward this ascent. One can see the ethical insight, even though in practice a thousand hindrances prevent our
following it in any purity.

The Second Objection Handily Refuted

The second objection insisted upon the lack of content in our
present view. First, we must try to understand what the objection
does and does not urge. The claim cannot apply to the second imperative or the third. The objector must intend to apply his objection to our first imperative. Should his objection be fatal, then
the overlap in human life would be handled by allowing the pursuit of individual goods. The first rule would be void; and the second must carry all the weight. But each man as his own end still
leads to society as a realm of ends with equal rights. Anything
whatever can be part of the common good; this must be his claim.
If the claim is true, the first imperative gives us no guidance. The
claim is at least partially false. The kinds of behavior where one
is caught in a contradiction cannot possibly be nonexceptive types
of action. Lying, theft, murder can never be part of the right on
our present view. Then the claim must be reduced to saying that,
apart from the stable and constant elements of right action, there is
yet much latitude in what one may claim for himself, and make

part of his set of principles. And in this portion of our conduct the imperative yields no guidance.

What shall we say to this? Boldly, we shall again admit the objection; no, we must insist upon it! Does one wish his rule of right to encompass every action in his life? And perhaps Kant stretched the scope of this imperative too far. It is more in keeping with what one can get out of the stand on principle to say that, beyond a certain range of actions, latitude is allowed. The universal content lies in what man most inevitably wills, what he cannot avoid willing: that truth be told, that one keep his word, that life be protected and preserved. After all, the presence of some latitude may not detract, but render the view more admirable. Latitude must exist, we might claim, because we cannot be certain of the good in all respects; and even to differ, to disagree, is also part of the common good of life. This good is both discovery and construction. There is latitude in the first imperative because a man can only follow his best insight; he can will himself, just that! If this disagrees with another's will, at least it is an honest disagreement — and the second imperative takes over. Just as one should not try to do what is not one's own, so one should not try to stand for what is not oneself. And if your self, your deepest nature, wills a different kind of act from that of someone else in this area of latitude, you fall into a double will if you try to emulate this other person. Your real will is one thing; and his another.

Nor am I certain of Kant's disagreement even at this far point. The question, Kant once said, is this:

> Can I will that my maxim become a universal law? If not, it must be rejected, not because of any disadvantage accruing to myself or even to others, but because it cannot enter as a principle into a possible universal legislation, and reason extorts from me an immediate respect for such legislation.[11]

The sense of the good as a construction is, at least, suggested by the passage. As I understand our view, there is no reason why one who believes in principle need hold his principles to be universal absolutely. Even if universality is not the point, neither are these principles simply arbitrary.

[11] *Ibid.,* p. 64.

And, finally, to those who claim our first imperative is void of content, let this be said: One is never without content to be worked. And, indeed, one does not choose this content. It is set by the relations among men in one's society; it is recorded in their customary ways. Here is unavoidable content; it is this which one must work into one's unity of character, striking out an element here, transforming one there, transvaluing its values, seeking final values, the common good, using experiences of achievement and frustration to gain insight into the good. And as one's insight grows, our three imperatives will be busy, shaping these common elements into the unity of a critically aware set of social principles. But for a reason already mentioned, each age and culture — indeed, each individual — must find its or his own set of principles, simply because the context changes; and an age or a man is the individual locus of its or his own actions. And yet it will be surprising, once one works his conduct into the form of character, my view insists, how large the area of the common good turns out to be.

And if latitude is proper, in following the right one is commanded to be most himself. Such a rule does not bind, but frees; it furnishes a command to free one from commands which are external; and the command is to be yourself. In asking you to be yourself the way of principle restores in ethics the freedom one tends to lose as a social being. On the other hand every ethical point of view which understands the right in terms of a society outside oneself allows still another area of life to slip away from the realm of freedom.

If principle and consequence are related, and if principle is adequate to define the right, then it remains for us to apply to our persons whatever we have learned about the way of principle. Let us make this application through a series of suggestions.

The Suggestions

First, one will not spend all his life looking at the consequences. In the deepest sense, as we have seen, these consequences illumine not the right, but the strategy for gaining, retaining, and increasing that right. The diplomacy of action will require sharp attention to these consequences; but our beliefs about the right must be more deeply based. Indeed, the two relate as do Plato's upward and downward ways. To consider consequences is on the way down to life and action; discovery of principle requires an upward way toward theory. The way down should always be molded by the prior shaping of this upward way. And though the point is somewhat moot, let me suggest that the view which spends all its time looking to consequences is for the safe, secure, gradually constructive days. In times of peril it is integrity that counts. And there are such times. This is, of course, jut the reverse of what we most often hear; unhappily, integrity is often thought a luxury for the safe and pleasant days when nothing threatens; an anxious weighing of consequences is selected as the needed instrument for times of danger. There is some small element of truth to this; and we have discovered times when principle does not apply, or applies somehow almost in reverse. But even here our goal is defined in terms of principle. And I suspect those who have done most to save what can be saved within an age — those called heroes, saints, and martyrs — have been able to command themselves, even in dangerous times and despite the consequences to themselves, to stand on principle.

Second, if one is to stand on principle, he must sift out the data of his life to find these principles. They are not written in some book of law. They are in the world, and in oneself, but only partly so; discovery is often wanting, but always wanted here. There will be no trouble in finding those ways of acting, the contrary of which would force you or anyone into duplicity. You can simply run through the possible kinds of behavior, making our guaranteed ten-second duplicity test. But where inconsistency seems not to present itself either if one does, or refrains from doing, a certain thing, what then? One could try these developing principles against our second imperative: Do they make one man a means to another's will? The question might reveal some doubleness, even in actions with no apparent inconsistency. And when this does not tell us quite enough? We might take the question to experience. We wish the common good; then we might act to see if there are consequences which, despite our troubles with the concept, reveal anything about this act as part of the common element in human striving. Beyond all this, I think we are privileged to turn to our most intimate knowledge, to what we most deeply affirm, especially to our most final values, and build our principles of conduct from within. What, after all, does one want in life? A chance to be himself, to develop whatever powers he has, to contribute — as we say — significantly, to feel a sense of worth. All of these will help to set the principles in terms of which a man of principle will act.

The goal in our social life is one which would find all false principles exchanged for true. If we could imagine such a goal, we would know with certainty the common basis which supports our individual striving. It is known in part at present, but in part alone. What one can do now is to preserve his own integrity, to affirm himself, and not deny to another the grounds on which his affirmation rests. Much of the rightness of things can be enlightened by testing a proposed act against our three imperatives. Surprisingly, just in being oneself most fully and completely, in affirming one's nature, in coming to recognize duplicity — the semblance of things, appearance — not as anyone's nature but as a façade erected over human nature, one is contributing to his knowledge of the right.

Third, if no man should be an instrument, a common relation among us just as men, a common bond, is at once established. And no one has the right to shrug off a personal relationship; acceptance of another's friendship entails the responsibility to see that person through. Much more attention is deserved by persons than by things — lest we make men our instruments.

Fourth, as we learn of the sovereign nature of our fellows, we must likewise learn to rise above the level of command. We need not, therefore, be permissive with our children. But commands of status, thundered down from some imagined height, these we must learn to do without. There is in each of us sufficient love of status, and sense of our angelic nature, to stand us in danger of aspiring to become the moral keeper of all the world. But in rising above the level of command one begins to know he is not (in this sense) his brother's keeper. To be a keeper is to command; but your life belongs to you, and your brother's life to him; neither is keeper or commander. It is principle alone which can command, once this stage is reached. If anyone is still wondering the extent to which he should compel other human beings, he may lay this intellectual burden down. One keeps himself, of course — and this is quite enough. There are more wholesome means of entertainment, more worth-while avenues of personal release, than attempting to control the lives of those about you.

Fifth, these suggestions may be rounded out more clearly; and along the way — if a slight essay roundabout may be allowed — we can gain a conclusion of importance about a quality of life which needs to be achieved. My essay will begin with the recollection of a point of view, having almost nothing to do with the conclusion to be gained. Several persons, writing recently in philosophy, have suggested that when I say to you, "You ought to be honest," my statement is in fact a veiled command: "Be honest!" or "Sweep the floor!" And in the command — so they believe — is veiled a threat which will be carried out in case you are not honest, or will not sweep the floor. So be it! Without question the rules of ethics must begin on the level of command, since culture generally so begins. The question is: Must they also end on such a level?

Men have differed widely in their ways of determining the right. Men have differed widely because, allowing entrance here to human freedom, more than one basis is available for choice. And more than one has understood the right to be a veiled command. But I cannot forget how frequently we have found philosophers, and ourselves as well, insisting upon steps to be surmounted, levels of wisdom, truth, and beauty. If development is in order elsewhere, why not here as well? We have already spoken of human culture, beginning on the level of command — where a man may command what is pleasing to him — and progressing to the point where command gives way to law.

We are agreed, then, in believing ethical rules to have their origin in command. But such rules begin as open commands, and then are slightly and increasingly veiled. And yet, thinking in terms of levels, our whole discussion requires us to insist upon such rules turning into principles, furnishing an absolute for all our relativities, and yet allowing their vast areas of freedom. Movement from the level of command to that of principle, whatever the intermediate steps may be, involves a great leap, which embodies the concept of true culture. And this is the leap, taken by a society when it moves from the level of command — its tribal origin — to law as a new entity swinging freely over the heads of all alike, for law can have no other base than principle. It is in culture the leap from patriarchate to constitutionality, from the level of superstition, through the opening wedge of tradition, to rationality where custom is reshaped and ordered. This is a leap we have taken in our culture, but not so clearly in our personal lives.

For the description we have given of a culture likewise fits the individual. Every man begins his ethical life on the level of command, indeed as the object of command, but no man need end there.

And from this point one faces, I suggest, an arduous climb to principle. His first ethical patterns are the commands which have been impressed upon him, made internal, veiled. Man also begins on the level of pleasure-pain. Perhaps his first ethical advance consists in learning to make the calculus of the pleasurable and painful consequences affecting both himself and others. In practicing reciprocity he begins to seek the common elements in human life. And along the way he may learn that self-control is helpful, the value of moderation, Aristotle's avoidance of extremes; he can begin to formulate the difference between what "is" and "ought to be." Through all of this he can be discovering the path of his own high integrity, the unity of self on which he is willing to stand. These lesser rules may be merely steps in the climb from the level of pleasure-pain to the level of integrity, from the level of command to the ethical plateau where the tendency and desire to command have dropped away.

Within a culture this last step is a magnificent giant step toward reason and the idea of law. And this step requires of the people, the common elements of whose striving form the platform of their law, that they be a particular kind of people — people who have found intrinsic worth within their lives, who are capable of self-discipline, and freedom. The connection is very close between this achievement in a culture, and within an individual life. The transition from the first to the second imperative, Kant remarks in passing, involves granting intrinsic worth to persons. But, of course, this is completely wrong. Such worth cannot be granted; it must be gained. And yet the whole movement depends upon the level of intrinsic worth, for only such actions can be common. But when this step is taken, men become the source and center of value. The essay has reached the quality I had in mind. Earlier, through words alone we had changed the character of a perfectly unjust man. Anyone who begins to see and gain the right will find this transformation, more than words, within his life. After a sufficient "building through experience," a man can in a moment take this crucial leap; in some experience, he can discern principle to stiffen his backbone; he can see dramatically the difference between duplicity and singleness of character; he can gain release from the level of mere command, and chart his course by means of that subtle and important concept, the common good. At this point our man does not need to crawl; he stands erect. He will not avoid the eyes of other persons, but confront them. He will not practice duplicity;

his value is integrity. But this was our description of the free man. Admit freedom, and we can use this language: One has reached the stage of integrity when his will can have a principle which, detaching itself from his common inclinations and the general desire for pleasure, begins to stand — like a law — over his being, not a command to another, but something he recognizes as a law for himself, while not withholding the ground of this affirmation from others. And if in gaining freedom one affirms his nature, then ethical decision helps to implement man's freedom; perhaps this is the point of our puzzling fourth meaning for freedom: A man is free when doing what he ought to do. The "ought to be" of principle does support man's freedom; but many other "oughtnesses" limit, or destroy, its possibilities in human life.

Sixth, a comment on the long dispute between "do-gooders" on the one hand, and the apostles of universal selfishness on the other: Nothing could be more wrong-headed than this dispute. Given any example of apparently large-minded, and generous, action, the former will regard it as an act of genuine altruism; the latter will find it filled with self-regarding motives. The former regard some acts as altruistic, and some as self-regarding; the latter find everyone always acting from a selfish motive. The contention of universal selfishness starts from the undeniably true statement that all action is done in terms of one's self. But we have seen how the self is a compound of feeling, sensation, idea, and purpose. One may have a narrow range of loyalties or purposes; another may have an extremely wide range; whatever the range, they are part of, and define the limits of, one's self. And to be sure, one is always acting in terms of the interests of this self. The doctrine of self-interest is innocent enough, until it is confused with selfishness. At this point "selfishness" should refer only to selves which support a very narrow range of loyalties; the difficulty comes when an undeniable self-interest is identified with ministering to a narrow range of purposes, and when it is claimed that everyone tends this narrow range above all else.

The dispute touches our problem, when we speak of man presenting to himself the common good as a duty to be followed against his inclinations. Against all inclination? The claim sounds like a paradox; for one who has set himself this duty will be inclined to follow it. In fact we have no tangle here; granting human freedom, we must allow a time, as man exchanges his narrow for broader interests, when he is acting against the established inclinations of his life. But the time passes, and then his inclination is to the common good; this fits exactly the solution we had gained to the problem of our freedom. Finally, from the argument over selfishness and self-interest, only this modest statement can emerge: Man *can* act from selfish motives shading all his actions; and man can act from more general motives; in either case he will be acting from self-interest; but he may not be acting selfishly. And, of course, action directed toward the common good, seeking its achievement, production, or discovery, will force our lives to encompass the broader range of interests. In general our man of principle cannot be "selfish," cannot sustain his life by a narrow range of interests.

Seventh, if the values of life lie in our affirmation of common principles and not within their consequences, it is more important for us to be active in certain ways rather than to be anxiously watching their results. The important thing is to have our minds filled with content, to have searching minds, to be increasing in artistic appreciation, to be developing more social sensitivity, character and courage, to be cultivating patience and with it humor, to be living a life filled with intrinsic worth, than to be establishing a rank among intellects, artists, industrialists, financiers, or whomever else. Strangely, the point impels me to say: It is more important to be writing a book than to be publishing it. And in the same sense one kind of personal ambition becomes the last false flame to burn out of the human breast. I understand this claim no better than the other; nor am I certain of the degree of irony which invests the thought. But both have a sense of urgency and ultimacy about them. And it should not surprise me to find a related issue in our final problem, our attempt on first and last things.

Eighth, if the common good is at once an object of discovery, of achievement, and of construction, the right is not a set of static rules. Nor do we return to the utter flexibility of our view of last resort. In this respect progress may be our most important product. Development is occurring — in the right, or in ourselves, or both — and one must not fall asleep if he expects to find and do the right. If development is in order here, it is not the end of rightness, or of righteousness, to leave conditions as we find them. The conditions of life are subject to reordering, and not as a matter of inclination only, but sometimes as a positive, ethical duty. And finally, if we have begun to describe the right, it would seem that the way to the good as "richness of value," one's articulation of his personal values, is through the good as "rightness of conduct." Not that the two are the same; but we have seen so often how nearly the intrinsic values stand as those which are, or can be, common. One hardly achieves richness of value in isolation from, or in essential opposition to, our common humanity. Upon the common and developing base of rectitude, one builds the further values of his personal life. The common base provides a needed platform for the main business of living with its development of our persons.

Chapter Six

Principle in Society

I. The Question of Your Social Philosophy

The subject of our discussion, then, is society. And if you should suppress a sigh at the thought, please know that I have sighed before you in just these circumstances, and sigh again with you now. But the subject is clearly of importance, and cannot be avoided if we are to probe the salient features of our personal philosophies. And in any case it is not enough to work out in splendid isolation the parts and principles of one's philosophy, to decide upon one's values, to contemplate one's freedom or its lack, and work out some preferred approach to right and wrong. The support of one's life, or the alien framework which will confine or crush it, is this composite life-of-others with which our lives partly merge. And any "truth" within one's own philosophy is in some sense a truth about society. At least, if one is to be himself, this truth must be allowed by his society.

But "society" is a term so vague, and refers to a "something" so massive, multiple, and encompassing, with no clear boundaries anywhere; perhaps you feel it will not be possible to decide what it is that we are talking about; unable to decide this, naturally one could not know what to say about it. Our first problem then is to reduce, if possible, the vagueness of the term. Concentrating on the word itself, by "society" — as an obvious preface to the point — we cannot mean the antisocial, self-isolating group which appropriates this term to describe its weary rituals. Instead, we have to mean all the others who are not members of "society" in this sense, the people whom God loved, according to Abraham Lincoln, because he made so many of them. What then are the limits of society? This depends upon the limitations we wish to place upon the term.

In the meaning of our term we could include only those who touch our lives directly and constantly. We could add to this small group others who touch our lives directly, but infrequently. Finally, we might include all who are involved in our lives, even if indirectly. And in this sense, just as "environment" means the total other-than-oneself which touches us, society would mean the total human other-than-oneself which touches our lives. If we include in our notion of society those involved in our lives, even if indirectly, then the whole globe would seem to be one society. But we know that it is not; and this knowledge forces the meaning of the word into some more definite shape, drawing us back toward a more explicit kind of unity. We must say only that these interconnections provide the material out of which a single society might someday form. We are being drawn toward those partly autonomous units where human decisions have described boundaries around "society," taken in the broadest sense, and human decision has imposed its more particular unity within the boundary lines. Governments draw somewhat arbitrary lines through a portion of this vast whole, and then work very hard to make the severed portion more explicitly one society. If, then, by "society" we should mean an organized community, one clear instance is the unity men impose upon themselves through the development of government. But this cannot be *the* meaning, for any national life is made up of almost countless organized, or somewhat organized, communities. They are, of course, dependent in many ways upon the order brought by government; but, within the nation, consider the many other units, even apart from those smaller images of government — state, county, and municipal: the family, the church, the political party, the corporation, the academic community, the civic group, even alleged high "society" as reported in the rotogravure sections (here, too, there is an organized community, at least a social chairman, her smiling likeness evidencing her existence every spring). And of these societies, some — the church, some corporations, the academic community — extend beyond the boundaries of the nation; national boundaries have no real significance for these communities. Families, political parties, most corporations, civic groups, and high "society" are partial groupings within the nation. The presence of these curious overlappings, the confusing inclusions and exclusions of organized communities, does pose a certain problem in analysis.

In what follows we shall take as our touchstone for the word "society" the clear instance of an organized community where there exists a national government; but as the need arises we shall speak of those organized groups both within and extending beyond the demarcations of our touchstone meaning. We shall be trying to determine our relation to society mostly through organized groups culminating in the nation; we shall find occasion to speak of families of nations with similar cultural shaping. And in particular our questions will be directed toward the Western world in which, so fortunately, our lives have been cast!

The idea of culture has just been mentioned; it is an idea of large proportions — in its range extending toward one of the more inclusive meanings of the indefinite term which is before us. In an proportions — in its range extending toward one of the more in-Western culture coloring all those "Western" nations which have drawn lines around a portion of the human race. Culture includes the families of languages, bodies of knowledge, art forms, techniques, political ideas, philosophies, and the insights of developing religious structures, of those who stimulate each other, both within organized societies, and across wide areas in time and space, having something to do with the nature of each other's lives. Developing knowledge, arts, philosophies, and the like, are developing culture; making contributions to these fields is contributing to human culture. The limits of shared culture, excluding isolated pockets, extend only slightly beyond the whole of mankind.

So far! We have struggled with the meaning of a word. And this slight struggle leads us to a more formidable encounter. We wish to learn how our lives relate to this massive human other-than-oneself. And clearly, as social animals we relate to it in many ways. Our lives are lived within its boundaries, and composed of its materials; we are members of society; we belong to it, or it to us.

The Sense of Being Included in Society

Let us return to the awareness of a context around our lives, mentioned in the first words of our discussion. You are seated at your desk, or in an easy chair. Your attention is riveted on these words, and you have been intensely interested for five chapters. Or at least your interest would have been sustained had the chair not been so easy, your wife so importunate, the writing so cumbersome. No, you are (my dream insists) awake and eager, although the last chapter was somewhat tiresome. The rest of your mind has been likewise active, suggesting vagaries which carried you a million miles or so from the page which was before you. And with all of this you have been aware of the passage of time, its silent, heartbeat flow, and of the contents of its passage. You are aware of the room around you. In a less definite sense you are aware of the house around your room, and the place of your house on its block. (If you are one of the more fortunate citizens, your house will be like every other house — ranch-style, so called, with everything automatic except the owner; and day by day he feels a trifle more mechanical. If you are either less, or still more, fortunate, there will be some welcome difference in the size and appearance of the houses on your block.) A bit more dimly you are aware of the position of your block within the community, of the community surrounded by countryside and joined to other communities by lines of communication, both of wire and asphalt; while separated from them by farming areas; and you are aware of the larger urban-rural complex comprising your state (the heart of the nation), and of the states comprising a nation as rooms comprise a house. And from where you sit — awake, as I say, and eager — you are related to all of this.

But how do you relate to all of this? Given a map of sufficient size you — sitting where you are, the light slanting across these pages — would be at least a tiny dot on the map of your community within the larger map, standing for the nation. But geographical inclusion is quite external, detailing only the surfaces of things, and too static for our purposes. We have not yet caught the force, the flow and movement, in society and in ourselves. Consider, then, only your community, a part of this whole which we have broken off at the boundary of a nation; and for the moment take but a fraction of this community: Main Street at the rush hour. What a sea of walking and riding purposes comes flooding down the street at this hour, edging forward even against the light, as counter-thrusting purposes go charging through the other way; edging forward to break through as the light begins to turn. And you are aware of purposes within yourself, inevitably requiring and including others. Wherever we find people we find purposes, astounding insight! And the purposes, beginning in the past, required completion in a future still to come. Your purpose, your striving, is part of the sum total of all striving; in you there is movement (you are awake, eager), a "going somewhere." And every society is a sum of human purposes, some portion of the sea of all humanity. The purposes are trivial and important; they include pleasures sought and pain avoided, errors and truths firmly held, emotion in all its varieties, love and deep hatred, concern and astounding un-concern, charging the lives of these people charging down Main Street. Of course, we had selected Main Street only by way of illustration. There are also the people sitting at desks doing sums, standing at assembly lines, bent over washing windshields, display-ing goods, selling merchandise, working in gardens, preparing meals. Many purposes are being fulfilled as humans fit themselves into this larger context, carrying all their philosophy along, trying to fit their ideals of life into life itself — sometimes fitting, sometimes mis-fitting; we have the fits and the misfits, the Edwards' and the Jukes'. Some have a large sense of life; some are waiting for the main chance. And out of all these ingredients a community is made. And in the larger summation a nation is made, that organization of society which begins to impose upon human purposes a purpose of its own.

In the lesser sense our question now becomes: How do your pur-poses relate to the purposes of other people? In the larger sense: How do your purposes relate to the purpose of a nation? How is it that each of us is not only his own individual but a member of society? Or once again: What could possibly provide the unity for all of this variety?

There is design in your community: The flanking, patterned houses, row on row; the patterned streets, block on block, sometimes called the arteries of the city (containing packaged hemoglobin, happily and usually, despite the impression of total mayhem con-veyed by the evening news report); the industrial center which provides the substance of life; the shopping center with its jangling cash registers ("Carry out, please!"); halls of administration, courts of justice; churches; schools for the preparation of the very young; hospitals for the repair of the human vehicle; garages for the repair of the nonhuman vehicle; mortuaries and junkyards, depending on the vehicle, for the reception of the very old; the interweaving of values, instrumental and intrinsic, through all of this; and making up these centers the hundreds, or thousands, or hundreds of thousands, of humans as intense and full of purpose as yourself. Purposes within purposes, but can we find an inclusive purpose?

We return to Main Street once again, viewing its throngs of people as throngs of purposes, and ask: Where are they going? To some perfectly definite place, most of them, however chaotic the street may seem just now. If we watch these streams of purposes, we shall notice their movement from one center to another — business, church, the focal points of municipal, state, and federal government, centers of education, and home again. These centers, out of which and into which our human lives radiate, these centers of our striving, may be called in a general way "institutions." We are by and large, whatever else, institutional creatures. And if there is power in these purposes, hurling themselves along Main Street, there is some multiple of this power in the agglutinative centers of power around which human beings shape their lives.

One quite definite answer to the question, "How do we relate to society?" is "We relate to society through our membership in institutions." An important part of our lives is this complex thatch of our set relations to institutions. And much of the informal context of our lives is formed by our brushing against other institutions.

And if you were now to detail the whole list of institutions to which you belong, or which somehow affect your person, would this detailed list satisfy our problem? Certainly you would have found many of the relations which obtain between your life and this social other. If one of us were to compose a list, setting forth his institutional commitments, showing himself to be a Lion or an Elk, a Moslem or a Methodist, a member in good standing of the young Republicans or the old Democrats, of the P.T.A., the P.E.O., the A.D.A., D.A.R., or C.I.O., he would sense something of the complexity of his life, and of the interdependence and intertwining in human lives generally.

But we might learn more by turning from the great range of

organizations to the institutions, the centers, of greatest power upon our lives. If we should try, generally, to name these centers, I think they would be: business, government, the church, and the many centers of education. And should we ask, further, which of these have greatest power, I think the answer would be: business and government. In terms of the number of times we are related to these forceful institutions, there is no question but what they are today the dominant ones. The other two, religion and education, may have greater final importance, but this is not our present topic. Consider the many-sided nature of our relations with these two aspects of society!

Business touches our lives in the stop at the gas station on the way to work, the parking lot for one's car (if you came by subway yours was a contact with — municipal government?), the job itself, lunch at the restaurant, the purchase of a paper at the corner, the shopping jaunt in downtown stores, the stop at the supermarket to purchase one's favorite foods while listening to soft music and walking through doors untouched by human hands, the bowling alley, the local triple D baseball game, the musical comedy, at last the sleeping pill. So much of life moves through channels which are devoted to business with its purposes — whatever they may be.

The control of government is, possibly, less obtrusive day by day. But the policeman is on the corner; repair crews move down the street, tamping in odds and ends of asphalt to fill the pockmarks in the pavement; the mailman comes, knocking once or twice; the children go off to school; the fire hydrant stands red before your house; the postal box — more patriotic now — stands red, white, and blue; a siren is heard, increasing in volume, and with relief you hear its tone lowering in the distance (someone else's trouble); the sometimes unobtrusive taxes appear in every contact with the business world; above all, there is the obtrusive income tax. In addition, you belong to a political party, perhaps attend a political rally (Victory in November!), and whenever you have the opportunity you (had better) vote.

If the answer to our curiously open-ended question: How do we relate to society? is "Through our involvements with institutions," we should be able to learn something about our social philosophy in coming to understand these institutions. And if business and government are the two major institutions of our time in the number of their day-by-day impingements upon our lives, the question might be neatly channeled into a consideration of these two institutions, as representative of the rest.

But what would an understanding of business and government be like? Certainly, we could gain a kind of understanding of these institutions by purchasing the latest almanac (a contact with industry), and memorizing all the statistical information between its covers; most of this information would pertain to business and government. And yet this information, could we assimilate it, would not meet our needs. Such information has been vastly compounded in recent decades. And this increase of information has not been accompanied by a vastly heightened increase in the understanding of our relations to society. Clearly, it is a more original inquiry which should be ours, and which confronts us even now.

One fact, which must be recognized, and toward which we have been moving, is the fact that, for whatever reason, many of us feel lost within society. The understanding which we seek is one which would remove this feeling. No amount of facts can do this! One manner of coming upon the kind of understanding which we need is through paying attention to this sense of feeling lost in relation to society. I think you will not deny the feeling. And you may defend the point; you may say: "It is no great wonder, this feeling lost within society. Lapped as we were in dreams; held in the warm, close confines of the family; and then that hurling of ourselves, or being hurled, into a world where none of this remained, where alien purposes stand against our own, where in the mere business of living we are caught within vast impersonal structures, pitted against impersonal forces, yet feeling the necessity of making our way. We are caught in some mysterious current, and without a compass. Our feeling lost, then, is to be expected."

Let us address ourselves to the point. One can become lost in the woods, I learn from the more hardy among my acquaintances. One may be unable to see the forest for the trees; this is the brilliant way they put it. Now, one may also feel a sense of being lost within a great, impersonal city. And as one can feel lost in the city, so one can feel lost within society. As a matter of fact, in all three cases the sense of being lost is much the same. Now what is it to be lost? I think we might say: When one is lost what is really lost is one's sense of direction. This is to say, one's sense of relationship, one's orientation, to what surrounds him, is missing. The only way, I think, to avoid feeling lost in relation to any of these larger wholes is to discern an order in its immensity which we can understand. The word has occurred again. What does it mean? In this sense, to understand the relations among the parts, or institutions, of one's society is to gain a sense of direction in order to find one's way. To understand this relation is to begin to feel at home in one's society. When one begins to discern the forest, in addition to the trees, one begins to feel at home, because now at least one knows that he can find his home. But in the case of society our home is, and must be, within its great immensity. Finally, then, I think one will not feel at home in society until, and unless, he can discern an order in society with a direction and a goal which one recognizes also as his own. Then it becomes his society in truth. And, since society is composed of persons, it is not completely beyond all question to hope that one might *find* himself in a society organized by men who are somewhat like himself. And yet, how would this finding be possible? Institutions have a history, as men have a history; they have begun in the remote past, and have been subject to development. And certainly there is in a sense purpose in a nation, or in a national life. There are change and movement, and at least in the shorter span it seems that, as a nation, we are sometimes going somewhere. It is your nation; you are its citizen. It has claims upon you; you have claims upon it. There must be important relations between the two.

But of course! These are the areas of life governed by principle in the ordinary sense. And we have just learned how our lives are, or can be, governed by principle in the extraordinary ethical sense. In asking how we relate to society, we are asking how our principles relate to the principles of society. And now it becomes clear why memorizing the World Almanac cannot solve our problem. If we are in search of social principles, we wish to learn not only what is but what ought to be the case. And a factual study will reveal only what is, and not what ought to be.

What are the principles governing the institutions to which I belong? And how do they relate to the principles of my life? How does my purpose relate to the purpose of a nation? How do my principles relate to the principles of society? What is the bond between the development of my life and the movement of society? This is the kind of question which is before us.

Our new question could, and should, be asked of all the institutions in which we have a stake. But if we can gain some insight concerning the two major institutions, it would throw light upon every other. And it should be kept in mind that any relation we may find will be a correlation — between the movement of an individual life and the movement of a segment, or even of the whole, of a society.

Very well, we have come to this point: If we can find some identity between our lives and the movement of society, which is its corporate life, we are no longer lost within society. And should this discovery be an identity among developing principles within ourselves and within society, and should the principles be good, then we would be on the edge of a discovery about the good society. And, indeed, since the whole problem concerns movement and development on either side, probably we can never relate comfortably to any society just as it is; the unfinished nature of every society, when taken in cross-section, requires us to think in a complicated manner. We seek the complicated relation between society as it is and ought to be; and our personal lives as they are and ought to be.

All that I have said may be utter nonsense; it may seem so to you; and yet we cannot be sure until the sequel. And so, as I ask "What are your social principles?" I do not expect you to be able to set them down at once. I would expect some people to be unable to set them down at all. For I am clearly asking not only how society is, but how it ought to be, arranged. Of this question you might justifiably say that while you are reasonably certain of discovering something of the relations which obtain between yourself and the rest of society, still as a man, fixed somewhere in its immensity, you cannot possibly see the nature of the whole; you will speak from where you are and what you are. And if you cannot say objectively even what society *is*, how can you say anything concerning what it ought to be?

The argument has some point, and admittedly the question is difficult. And the use of this argument would be an admission that you feel lost within society — as do I. And yet I cannot avoid a dark suspicion about this feeling which is ours. For one thing the feeling is not limited to ourselves; it is widespread in the Western world. It is a pervasive fact, which might be called the Western paralysis in social thought. The paralysis is a sign that the "nerve" of social action among us is almost severed. We find ourselves today less certain about what society ought to be than we have been for centuries. By "we" I mean anyone like yourself who — in all these centuries — has been willing to face the question. And my dark suspicion is that it is not at all the vagueness of the terms, or the difficulties of the problem, which keep us from an answer, but — something else. When man understands a thing, he begins to act on what he understands. If for some reason, lacking confidence in ourselves, we cannot bring ourselves to act, we might well claim — to explain our indecision — an inability to understand. By claiming that the problem simply cannot be made out, we free our minds of all responsibility. And yet, if I am right, we cannot in this age have satisfactory personal philosophies until the Western paralysis, which has halted the discussion of what society "ought to be," is overcome. And certainly we cannot take a further step in the discovery of our social principles, since the subject has been broached, until we accept or reject the contention I have made.

The Western Paralysis

What keeps us from confronting the important questions of our social philosophy? The Western paralysis, one might say. But what is this paralysis? I think it concerns a double tendency, cutting rather deeply into our apparent motivations. On the one hand we, as finite earthbound (although possibly not for long) creatures, have come onto the scene somewhere in the middle of a long development of social forms. Initially, out of the mystery of man's origin, societies formed without a rational plan. And yet it was reasonable, because necessary, that they should form. But it does not follow, and we know it does not, that all the parts of the pattern — falling into place through centuries of growth — are likewise reasonable. And yet there is in us a respect for the past, a feeling that the response to crises, in which our social forms developed, has in some sense a reasonableness beyond our own. Here in the West I think our most deeply rooted feeling is that our societies should be allowed to develop naturally; that is, in the course of things, without disciplined planning, and without coercion. For from two to eight centuries, depending on the object of our reference, we have had deep confidence in the propriety of adhering to a "natural" evolution of social forms. We believe in the working of an unplanned plan which produces naturally, or perhaps it is accidentally, a pattern for society. And if we were to verbalize our argument for the feeling, we would say that we are most likely to come out well by allowing change to occur thus slowly and by persuasion through a kind of social evolution. The arts of life — medicine, law, economics, and the like — are not immune to change; but their patterns change slowly, and not by coercion; they change as men gain insight, and adapt their ways to newer methods and "better" goals. The argument would be that all society, including its overall pattern, should change in the same manner.

On the other hand, mixed with this thought and feeling is a different tendency. We are, somehow, aware of man's genius lying in his ability to plan, to look before and after. We tend naturally as men to consider how anything ought to be planned, and this does not exclude the social whole. It is also natural for man to consider the planned society as his goal. But even as I state this other tendency, after accepting the statement for the slightest instant, we almost as quickly find within ourselves an inner recoil from the thought of thus applying human reason. This recoil in our minds contains a clue to the paralysis in Western thought. There have been times when the planned society has been a dominant motive among us — taking the referent of "us" as broadly as the life of Western man. And yet in the drawing back we find our other motive, still more deeply rooted, and confirmed — as we think — by experience: We are suspicious of the planned society.

In practice we compromise these twin drives by planning, but only around the edges of society. We plan as a result of crises, and for the purpose of meeting crises. This is a statement of our double tendency; but of itself this tendency would not produce a paralysis in our social thought. If change is to occur slowly, and by evolution, we still have the obligation of finding some way to think about "better" and "worse" in society, to learn the nature of our social principles, to be willing to adduce reasons for them, to be willing to alter these principles as new insights appear, to be willing to formulate new principles. It is, even on this view, our obligation to find our way around the social whole by learning to carve properly at the joints. Not even our deeply founded (whether well or illy founded) bias against the planned society, is the reason for our modern refusal to work our way in thought through the problems of what society ought to be.

Can this refusal be explained, as we explain so very much, by pointing to our practicality as a people? We are more interested, it is true, in what is going to be done to solve the specific problems which we face than in reflecting upon majestic social principles. And this emphasis is not altogether out of place; we have many problems to be solved. But how are practical problems solved? You will answer that such problems are to be resolved in terms of certain objectives; for example, peace, prosperity, full employment, a "sound" return on investments, a healthy citizenry, and due process of law. And you may conclude: It is in terms of objectives such as these that we decide what is to be done in a given situation. These very objectives demonstrate that to decide a practical problem we must have more in view than awareness of the problem. We need objectives; and these are goals more general than the details of our specific problem; nor did these objectives just float in from some impersonal void; they belong to a set of general notions, or principles. Even to solve our practical problems we need a set of principles with objective worth, some validity or cogency, which can generate more particular attitudes, which can be set against our practical problems, directing us to their resolution.

We have already discerned how the active intelligence of man needs — in addition to the facts — a set of principles in terms of which the practical problems of life can be settled. In exactly the same sense a nation, some settled portion of society conscious of its unity, needs a set of principles in terms of which the problems of ordering, coordinating, and uniting the society can be viewed; and these principles in turn have much to do with the manner in which practical problems are resolved. Now a set of principles of this kind is usually called a social philosophy. We are looking in short for social principles which will be a result of human insight, which are only relatively changeless, which can improve as time and experience dictate, and which can form the unity of a nation.

Since even practicality requires decision on general principles, this emphasis among us can serve as the explanation of our refusal, only if we admit to the general charge of dullness, or of sloth; and this charge I am loathe to grant.

The Fear of a Word

Our current refusal, I rather think, stems from a different source; this source is, surprisingly, nothing more than fear of a word. The word is "revolution." Now, perhaps it is the case that we no longer believe in, although we were born in, revolution. Would it be fair to say that the world's richest nation now denies, and should be expected to deny, the right of revolution? Certainly, it is long since I have heard it mentioned in the streets. I have heard it said that to advocate violent overthrow of one's government, apparently under any conditions and no matter how bad one's government might become, is treason. Of course it is — by definition! And a society begun in revolution will define treason like the rest. But once upon a time we did believe in man's possession of a right which went beyond society, and this was a right of revolution. Even today "treason" may have a double edge; there are times when a man betrays either himself or society, when the choice is sharp and cutting at either edge. But this would not seem to be the case for Americans, not now; we are enjoying too much our holiday from seething unrest. It has been a nice holiday. Of course, there may be some risk in such a holiday, perhaps a risk of drifting into social forms which are meaningless, or of becoming gross and vulgar because we have failed to think out the destiny which should be ours, and thus cannot have a sense of direction investing the social change which is, nonetheless, occurring.

Certainly one can understand our fear of this word. It was once a term of hope, this word of fear. And to be sure any revolution has fear trembling in it as well as hope. Excess is never wholly foreign to it. And some revolutions ought to be feared absolutely. Now, I think it is fear of this word which causes our quick checking of the mental impulse, which otherwise might lead to thinking out our social principles.

And possibly all revolution should be feared — absolutely; quite the final word to be spoken in this connection may be the claim imbedded in our deeply rooted feeling: Society must develop according to the unplanned plan! But if this is the final word, then we come close to believing that "Whatever is, is right." At least, whatever cannot be developed slowly and naturally is wrong. Further, if we do not want revolution, surely we cannot want the stratified society which is pre- or anti- (and sometimes post-) revolutionary. Were it not for our current fear the matter might be put (once it would have been so put): If the natural and evolutionary changes of the unplanned plan lead always to the stratified society, there is a point beyond which Americans believe in revolution.

But with this fear, and our uncertainty, we are led to a kind of suspended animation or, to change the figure, in answer to the question: Where do we stand in our social philosophy? I must say: We don't stand; we're all sitting down, and we have been for some time! But I suggest we cannot forever refuse to think. Unless I am mistaken, our posture has something to do with our feeling lost; our lives are an active movement; and we must find some identity between ourselves and our society. Unless I am mistaken, the fact that we are sitting down means we have no object sufficient for our energies, and are thus much less alive than we need to be; we live less richly, experience less deeply. At least, let us probe the parts of this double tendency.

Let us put aside for the time our fear of words, and begin an earnest search for the identity between our lives and the movement of society. To look for this identity requires us to discover the direction which society has been taking. We shall begin, generally, with the institution of government, and let us see whether there may be the beginning of an insight in this double tendency of our lives, relating to the planned and unplanned plans of social ordering. In this connection, then, let us notice two very obvious facts.

Two Obvious Facts

The first is this: If one looks around the world ever so slightly, he will discover that the kings are mostly gone. Two centuries ago they were all there; today, some wait on the Riviera for time to reverse its irreversible course; one reigns without ruling; in slighter kingdoms there may even be some ruling; but generally we are now post-royalty. This is a striking change, and has occurred within a relatively short time. It is a change, reflected through so many nations, that one must suspect the fact of having great importance.

Now the king ruled from the top of a pyramid, supported by a class supported by the people — and from this point it was people all the way down. What has happened cannot be understood without admitting the appearance of a new social principle in human life, a principle which required an alteration in the pyramid. To dramatize this in a picture I shall use the geometrical figure of the pyramid, and oppose to it another; that of the plane; or if the term "pyramid" leads one to think of those eternal structures near the Nile, then I speak of the pyramid as against the "plain."

Let us admit, then, what must be admitted; society, in its earliest and most recurrent form, assumes the shape of a pyramid. It was so in the most primitive societies; some group, the aged, those with prowess, those able to placate the gods, were granted, or else assumed, the power to keep order within the larger group; around such men the life of each society was ordered. And most of our Western history has reflected this pyramidal structure. Where should sovereignty reside if not in the sovereign? What is the source of power, if not the powerful? Still more broadly, spanning East and West, this has been the expected form for society. How often has society become rigid, frozen into a pyramid — untouchables, slaves, serfs providing the base; brahmans, kings, princes, and their attendant nobility composing the top (or, decomposing at the top?)!

But this figure of the pyramid has not stood unopposed. The obvious fact to which we have pointed suggests an opposing figure. The reality behind this opposing figure is something like the idea of law, providing in a sense a plain where each man stands the height of any other, so far as sovereignty and the power of government are concerned.

Among the Greeks, I think no earlier, the notion of the equality of men before the law, did remove in some times and places — and temporarily — part of this pyramid with its power flowing down from above. In Rome, once again for a time, a republican form of government and a lofty conception of the equality of citizens before the law (among Stoics, who were not infrequently lawyers, the equality of all men before the law) gave something of the figure of the plain to the Republic of Rome — to the city if not to the Empire — and of course only for a time, chiefly among citizens. Indeed, if we are to apply these contrasting figures to social realities, we shall have to say that the plain of democratic action here rests upon a blunted social pyramid. How mixed the metaphor now becomes, combining the lore of East and West, ancient and modern, times! My almost universal figure requires us to imagine one of the pyramids of Egypt, sliced through somewhere near its apex by a sharp and cutting sheet of metallic stuff with the strength of one of our better things for better living, yet moving like a Baghdad magic carpet. The universal metaphor has been presented. We would have left a blunted pyramid, and at the top a little plain created by the cut. Apply this to the social whole; the society is still a pyramid but those in control, the citizens, act upon a plain for the whole society to determine questions of the public good. So it was with Greece and Rome; democratic processes, so far and so long as they were observed, rested upon a base of slavery. The society required the distinction of superior and inferior to implement its necessary functions. In the following period of time, known as the Feudal Ages, the Middle Ages, or even as the Dark Ages (although the darkness in every age keeps the phrase from being quite appropriate), society had once again its pyramidal shape. Superior and inferior were related in bonds of privilege and servitude throughout the social structure; and it rose from its broad base through many levels toward an apex, slightly blurred through multiple exposure, representing monarch, church, or God himself. The revolutions of later times, the Glorious Revolution of 1688, the American Revolution of '76, the French of '89, the Russian of 1917, all had as their goal a transformation of this pyramid. The English retained the apex, swinging beneath it a platform on which some men might meet as equals; today only a broken, ceremonial line marks out the apex of their ancient pyramid. Now, is it clear to you what the Americans were about? Did they wish, like the Greeks, to lop off the little pyramidal top, leaving a plain of free discussion, the rest of the structure unchanged? Some among us thought this to be our proper goal. Or was it in them to accomplish something more? At least the French wished more than this in '89. Their cry was "Liberty, Equality, and Fraternity." For some? They seemed to mean it was for all. What was finally accomplished — and it took more than one effort to gain so much — was, once more, a lopping off of the pyramidal top to leave a plain of self-determination. The revolution of 1917 had as its goal the dream of Marx; here, again, was the wish to transform the social pyramid, to introduce the plain. And what was the result of this revolution, less furious than the French in its initial stages but much more devastating? A pyramid as complete as any yet devised, the monolithic state, its power concentrated at the apex, its control from above.

Concerning the Americans once again, does anyone really believe that the ideas which motivated them had as their goal no more than a slicing of the top from their social pyramid? We shall come back to this again; but whatever gave Americans the power, I suggest, to remove king and noble from the social pyramid, required of them — at a later time — something more. Hidden in the argument and counterargument, and indeed in the drift of history, was the proposition that men, created equal, remain equal in their social rights. Thus, we could not forever allow the apex of king and noble on our pyramid. The notion of a superior class had to go; and it went by revolution. Unless I mistake the matter, it was the same ideal and the same logic which, almost a century later, required of us a second act. If there can be no superior class by right, neither can there be an inferior class at the base of the social pyramid. The slaves were freed. I think this act, however intertwined with other issues, was simply the continued working of the initial principle which gave us being as a people.

Whatever else be said, and on this subject everyone has much to say, the three revolutions — the French, the American, and the Russian — have, even against our conscious inclinations, a common goal. The goal is social equality. I said "have" a common goal because — in the working of history — such a principle cannot express itself in a year or in a decade. I may be wrong about the goal; but I cannot otherwise make sense of our history, or of modern history. And if you see the matter otherwise, then your best thought on the subject should be brought forward to counter these mistaken thoughts of mine.

It does not disturb my thesis that the grand French Revolution ended in the Imperate of Napoleon Bonaparte, in the monarchy of Louis Philippe, and today in the Fourth or Fifth or Sixth Republic; or that the Russian Revolution ended in the monolithic state; or that the American Revolution, almost a hundred years after its second stage, is still taking slow and hesitant steps to implement the insight of that act. These things are part of the deceptiveness and irony of history; they are marks of its precarious nature, and of the massive grasp of the past upon the present.

If the ideal of social equality requires that each man as a member of society be the equal of any other before the law, and in his rights and opportunities, it is no wonder that the principle has required time to make its way, and is still today reflected so imperfectly in the three societies which have fallen under its sway more or less completely.

In this complex fact about our history, or in the principle it contains, we may discover a sense of identity, a common element in our personal philosophies, and in the society to which we belong, from which we are derived. But even if we find it so, there is another fact — quite as obvious — which runs counter to the one before us. It is not important to dwell upon the origin of this fact; I do not know that it is a matter of "cultural lag" or "a vestige of primitive life"; but it is very different from the complex fact to which we have been attending.

The Second Fact

The second fact is this: There is among us, within us, a sense of status. It is something we have, or lack; it is something we can gain, and apparently something many of us wish, much of the time, to gain. In a somewhat mysterious way we feel ourselves within a social structure where some are our superiors, and quite a few are inferior to ourselves. It is reflected in our speech: "There is always room at the top." "Don't worry about that boy; he is on his way up." "Unhappily (or happily) he is on the way down." "The higher they climb the harder they fall!" But where is this top? Which way is up?

However "democratic" you may be, is not this sense of looking down and up part of your nature? And has not financial power some connection with your judgment? Do not all heads turn when any person who is at the "top," wherever that is, enters the room at any social gathering? Have you never found yourself paying a kind of homage to such an one? Do you not hesitate to dispute his opinion? Does not anyone further "down" hesitate to speak against him? Does not your forthright manner alter; does not something of the "yes man," ever affirmative, enter your responses? Why should this happen? Do you defer to him because he might use his influence to do you some favor? But of course, he won't; the occasion will very likely not arise. Then do you defer to him because he might use his influence to do you harm? Probably, he would not do that either; the occasion, once more, would almost certainly not arise. But do we not regard him as one able to command; and do we not think of him, in ordinary circumstances, as above command? Why, then, he seems to occupy the place once held by royalty — and we are all such courtiers at heart!

What we have cast out of our social thought remains within our social pattern. We tend to look upon society, in some dimly conscious manner, as a pyramid, containing the superior, the inferior, and ourselves who are Mr. In Between. We tend to fix ourselves somewhere in this pyramidal structure. We recognize superiors and inferiors. And since this pyramid is a kind of mental thing, here is one case where thinking makes it so. At least, by thinking so we make the pyramid real enough to be effective.

The change which has occurred, far from destroying the social pyramid, has thus far merely made it more flexible. We must herald the unofficial, new-flex pyramid of modern times. In the new style a man can work his way to royalty, and — as in the olden times — a prince can be deposed. This fact is new only in a general sense. It was true in the 1890's, and some centuries prior to that. Edward Bellamy expresses this sense within society so clearly that we might look in on his account; he is pretending to look back upon the 90's from the year 2000. This is how the end of the nineteenth century appeared to him:

> . . . I cannot do better than to compare society as it then was to a prodigious coach which the masses of humanity were harnessed to and dragged toilsomely along a very hilly and sandy road. The driver was hunger, and permitted no lagging, though the pace was necessarily very slow. Despite the difficulty of drawing the coach at all along so hard a road, the top was covered with passengers who never got down, even at the steepest ascents. These seats on top were very breezy and comfortable. Well up out of the dust, their occupants could enjoy the scenery at their leisure, or critically discuss the merits of the straining team. Naturally such places were in great demand and the competition for them was keen, everyone seeking as the first end in life to secure a seat on the coach for himself and to leave it to his child after him. By the rule of the coach a man could leave his seat to whom he wished, but on the other hand there were many accidents by which it might at any time be wholly lost. For all that they were so easy, the seats were very insecure, and at every sudden jolt of the coach persons were slipping out of them and falling to the ground, where they were instantly compelled to take hold of the rope and help to drag the coach on which they had before ridden so pleasantly. It was naturally regarded as a terrible misfortune to lose one's seat, and the apprehension that this might happen to them or their friends was a constant cloud upon the happiness of those who rode.
>
> But did they think only of themselves? you ask. Was not their very luxury rendered intolerable to them by comparison with the lot of their brothers and sisters in the harness, and the knowl-

edge that their own weight added to their toil? Had they no compassion for fellow beings from whom fortune only distinguished them? Oh, yes; commiseration was frequently expressed by those who rode for those who had to pull the coach, especially when the vehicle came to a bad place in the road, as it was constantly doing, or to a particularly steep hill. At such times, the desperate straining of the team, their agonized leaping and plunging under the pitiless lashing of hunger, the many who fainted at the rope and were trampled in the mire, made a very distressing spectacle, which often called forth highly creditable displays of feeling on the top of the coach. At such times the passengers would call down encouragingly to the toilers of the rope, exhorting them to patience, and holding out hopes of possible compensation in another world for the hardness of their lot, while others contributed to buy salves and liniments for the crippled and injured. It was agreed that it was a great pity that the coach should be so hard to pull, and there was a sense of general relief when the specially bad piece of road was gotten over. This relief was not, indeed, wholly on account of the team, for there was always some danger at these bad places of a general overturn in which all would lose their seats.

It must in truth be admitted that the main effect of the spectacle of the misery of the toilers at the rope was to enhance the passengers' sense of the value of their seats upon the coach, and to cause them to hold on to them more desperately than before. If the passengers could only have felt assured that neither they nor their friends would ever fall from the top, it is probable that, beyond contributing to the funds for liniments and bandages, they would have troubled themselves extremely little about those who dragged the coach.

I am well aware that this will appear to the men and women of the twentieth century an incredible inhumanity, but there are two facts, both very curious, which partly explain it. In the first place, it was firmly and sincerely believed that there was no other way in which Society could get along, except the many pulled at the rope and the few rode, and not only this, but that no very radical improvement even was possible, either in the harness, the coach, the roadway, or the distribution of the toil. It had always been as it was, and it always would be so. It was a pity, but it could not be helped, and philosophy forbade wasting compassion on what was beyond remedy.

The other fact is yet more curious, consisting in a singular hallucination which those on the top of the coach generally shared, that they were not exactly like their brothers and sisters who pulled at the rope, but of finer clay, in some way belonging to a higher order of beings who might justly expect to be drawn. This seems unaccountable, but, as I once rode on this very coach and shared that very hallucination, I ought to be believed. The strangest thing about the hallucination was that those who had but just climbed up from the ground, before they had outgrown the marks of the rope upon their hands, began to fall under its influence. As for those whose parents and grandparents before them had been so fortunate as to keep their seats on the top, the conviction they cherished of the essential difference between their sort of humanity and the common article was absolute. The effect of such a delusion in moderating fellow feeling for the sufferings of the mass of men into a distant and philosophical compassion is obvious. To it I refer as the only extenuation I can offer for the indifference which, at the period I write of, marked my own attitude toward the misery of my brothers.[1]

Is the description unfair? It is difficult to know. But are we not aware of the inner pertinence of this account? Let me admit it, if you will not. I am aware, then, of a pyramid of status — despite my best intentions — framing my "position" in the world. I find myself looking up and down, and the position — sometimes only the posture — of those to whom I look determines whether I think I am looking down or up. And yet, within, I think it should not be so. At times cannot you, as I, consider men only in their humanity, see all as equal; and for a considerable time refuse to bow and scrape? But the social "facts" come back upon us; those who have a vested interest somehow arouse our special interest. You say: That's only human nature! The point, exactly: Human nature constructs a pyramid of status. The danger is that, having said it is natural to build a pyramid, we shall go on to regard it as the right and proper thing to do.

But let us pursue the point a bit more closely. Where are we looking when looking "up"? The meaning is not exactly clear. We do not ordinarily think of those at the "top" as ethically superior to the rest. Nor do we think them intellectually our betters. It is not uncommon to hear confidential and whispered remarks about them in both respects — and the deference continues. What meaning have we for "superior"? By their superiority, I suggest, we

---

[1] Edward Bellamy, *Looking Backward* (Boston: Houghton Mifflin and Co., 1888) pp. 10–13.

mean very simply their control of the financial resources of the community.

Now, I remember, this is what "society" inside quotation marks purports to be, the families of those in control of the financial resources of the community. This may not be obvious at once. Have not these "societal" circles an origin in the past, before the community gained its present form with its present, ever-present, financial market place? Indeed, so. These groups are celebrating customs going back at least to Neanderthal man. If so, participation in the control of the financial resources of the community is the modern form of something to be found in all societies. And all these centuries we have gone Neanderthaling along, perhaps in much the same way. We need only ask, more generally, what this common feature might be, and the answer suggests itself: To possess financial power in the modern world is to control the decision-making power of a portion of society. In all ages men have meant by the inside-quotes "society": The leisure-time activities of those fortunate members of a community, holding the decision-making power for themselves and their relations. In different ages this power has gained its authority from force of arms, and control of landed estates, as well as by control of the financial resources, the capital (sometimes mistaken for the "capitol") of a community.

By the power to make decisions is not meant the right to vote. The right to vote is, of course, part of the occasional decision-making power granted to all adults in any society where the plain has altered an ancient pyramid. But in the new-flex modern pyramid to hold part of the decision-making power is to exercise a day-by-day direct control, helping to shape the events which illuminate our time, making up the history of a community, a society, and a nation. For this reason accession to high office, and its decision-making power, is automatically accession to "society." And for this reason there was shock in the country when Thomas Jefferson would not accept his role as a member of "society."

Now, we must notice the fact that while in one way status is earned, in another it is society — we, ourselves — who grant status to the privileged members of a community.

In one sense status is earned. It is the reverse side of the coin standing for an individual's financial power; the two sides together mean that the resources of the community are at the disposal of this man, and of his family. And the goal is attractive enough for most of the red-blooded males of our society. One begins in the new-flex social pyramid at the status-level established by his parents. The thrill of any sport (for example, mountain-climbing) is present here, and the pitfalls in the bargain. Teamwork, fair play, ruthlessness mingled with occasional chivalry, the strong in-feeling of all for one and one for all: These values are present in the miniature reflections of the contest for status. And, after all, the sport of kings has always been — sport!

In another sense status is granted by the community. It is, after all, the rest of society who decide when they are looking down and up. And so, beside the sense of fulfillment in making one's way in the financial realm, there is added a kind of fame (It is not inconsiderable to be the object of an upward glance). Here are to be found the values of reputation and prestige; and must not that man have been much impressed with the sense of status who proclaimed: "He who steals my name steals all"? He said he would rather lose his purse. He had better keep them both. If the foregoing is correct, the second has some mysterious connection with the first.

I think the most graphic phrase applying to the social pyramid is already in our language. One hears of a kind of person called a "social climber." What a picture this brings to mind! Can you not almost see this man on our human pyramid, inching up, planting a heel as lever in the face of one below who clings both ways for balance, fearful of losing his own and dearly won position; hands grasping and pulling; a handy elbow to insure sufficient elbow room? Up he goes, or does he? At least we may suppose his progress plain enough to be noted from above. And then? A heel in the face to put him back (Or her? In some circles one hears the fault lies mostly with "her") to the spot where he belongs, to show him, as is said, his place. The figure is fantastic, and the doctrine as well — a heel-in-the-face theory of social adjustment; but those who have climbed the social pyramid, and lived to tell about it, assure me of its happening. Why this heel in the face? Who is the social climber to be treated so? Is he not the one who has presumed above the status he has fairly gained?

I would not defend every detail of this picture. Indeed, the whole claim is fantastic. And yet there is a social pyramid; and beyond the needs of life men struggle upward. Upward? Well, upward in our figure. Where are they going? It would seem they move toward the spot left vacant by the ancient kings. I do not mean to present this goal as one toward which they head in open consciousness. They know themselves, when successful, to be heading toward an increase of their power, to a position of control over the conditions of human life; indeed, to an increase of their freedom — as they think, at least. And there is something to this, because the alternatives increase as they increase in power (If only the contest did not render its contestants insensitive along the way!). Successful participation in the adult contest for status often has as its reward a clear-headed incisiveness, an ability to command, a quickness of decision more admirable in many ways than the deliberate, sometimes hesitant and always interminable pondering through endless implications of the thinker, so maladjusted to the world of action. (But we must not fail to mention, too, the desire and sense of status in the professor, busy also in a kind of social pyramid, not at all impeded by his robes and hood and cap, rising "higher," the ladder of truth by no means his single instrument of advance.) Successful participation in the adult contest for status may develop, true enough, an unctuousness of manner, an appearance indistinguishable from the façade of the man with an inner-outer tangle in his life, stretching every bit of information to its limit, as though there were not many precious items. And yet these are, possibly, accidental products; the princely qualities are also there.

So far, then! We have presented the two facts, pervasive and underlying in their nature. Although somewhere in all of this there may have been a misstatement, an overstatement (or an understatement?), which I urge you to correct, still in some form these two facts about our society, ourselves, and our relation to society, cannot be denied. Further, these two facts contain opposing principles, or sets of principles. The more my reflection continues the more distressing does this continuing conflict become for me, amounting to something like a contradiction within myself. This conflict, since I assume you feel it too, may furnish the occasion for our present attempt to advance our topic.

In one or the other of the members in this opposition you may sense a principle, or a set of principles, in which you recognize something basic to your point of view. On the other hand you may recognize, as I, both points of view within your nature; the problem then would be to find your way around this conflict. In either case more than recognition is in order. If we are to philosophize about this mixture and contradiction in our being, we must find and test the reasons which might be used to support the notion of the pyramid, and the other reasons which support the plain.

The figure of the plain is related to the idea of law, constitutions, sovereignty as imbedded in the whole society, and social equality. The figure of the ancient pyramid was related to the idea of command, arbitrary rule, power belonging to those at the apex, and a recognition of social inequality. And we have hinted at a modern form of this ancient pyramid.

In any case we wish to see if the opposition in our feelings is reflected by an opposition in our world. And we may begin with the plain, since it is this which furnished a challenge to the ancient pyramid. How then was it that the plain began to challenge the natural pyramid of social ordering? And what were the doctrines, carving out for society a kind of plain, allowing new loyalties and a new kind of man — a plainsman — ready to oppose the inherited pyramidal order?

If one were to follow out the history of the idea of sovereignty from the fifteenth to the eighteenth centuries, he would observe the pyramid deflating, almost before his eyes. The sovereign, at the beginning of this period was the head of state, the ruler, the elect of God, standing at the apex of the pyramid. And the sovereign power was his power, whether exercised by him in person and immediately, or by any other man acting in his name, under his sign, and according to his will. Before the end of this period the doctrine had been transformed into something like its opposite. Who is the sovereign? At the beginning of this time the answer was, "The monarch!" By its end the answer was, "The people!" Sovereignty, the power of the state, resides in the people. And by this time our Western world had, in effect, disavowed the principle that one man has the right to rule a community. The new principle in its various forms required that the people shall rule. We may never have gotten the notion exactly right in practice, but in principle it is unmistakable. For a change so great must there not have been a powerful instrument of persuasion? Indeed, so! And, indeed, I think there was. One very powerful instrument was the celebrated social contract view; it has taken many forms; it has been called impossible and invalid, and yet has had power over many Western minds. Let us note in passing how ideas, in addition to standing as candidates for the truth, stand also as instruments of persuasion. And it is not necessary for a set of ideas to be logically unassailable in order to exercise its power in the minds of men, and thus to have power in the world. And if we wish to understand the principles of the plain, now in some sense part of our persons, we had better deliberate upon the notion of the social contract, becoming familiar with a portion of the spate of treatises, working out its nature.

The Social Contract

Organized societies are bound together, this is the notion, by an unwritten contract, "containing" responsibilities and privileges for sovereign and people alike. I do not know the origin of this notion. There exists a hint of it in the *Crito*, already mentioned; having accepted the benefits of Athenian society through many years, Socrates feels the presence of an implicit contract, an obligation to the state. It would be impious of him now to escape and, in escaping, stand against the laws and judgments of his Athenian city-state. There is a hint of this doctrine in the *Republic* of Plato; to some of his discussion we shall return. And in the actual practice of Greek city-states one can see the working of this social contract where wise men are commissioned to frame constitutions, and the people in assembly accept them for the rule of their society; here is clearly a contract among the people. Underlying these explicit acts is, of course, the double reference: Men exist not only as individuals but as members of society, the source of power and sovereignty, as well as those to be governed by its power. But the doctrine was never phrased so clearly in these early years. Its real development has taken place in recent centuries.

Some of the elements around which most such doctrines turned are these: The origin of a society is marked by the social contract. One can imagine man's "natural" existence before the contract was drawn; and often his natural state was "pictured." One could also write about the drawing up of the social contract. And as a result of these imagined pictures, one might conclude with a description of the actual society which was emerging. The authors of the social contract theory were dealing with one real entity in three. And even the third, providing some control over human imaginations, was a blend of what society then was, and what they thought it ought to be. The state before the contract had been drawn was man's natural state, the state of nature; the parties to the contract were the people and their sovereign; in some accounts this meant the people as individuals, and the people as a sovereign whole. From the contract came the organized society, the state, civil law, and the powers necessary to fulfill the conditions of the contract. And in the contrast between the natural and the civil state, and in the conditions of the contract itself, a new contrast made its appearance; one could talk about the difference between natural and civil rights. Having set up the theory in this manner it was possible to insist upon rights for man which went beyond, which were prior (both in time and logic) to the civil rights granted men by law; this provided some control over civil law. And the rights to which we are referring were considered "natural rights," rights belonging to man as such, rights which any civil society must respect, which the civil order was designed to protect, and the abridgment of which called forth another right, the right of revolution, allowing the state to be directed once again toward its proper ends.

But, of course, great differences are to be found among the men who advanced the social contract theory. Let us remind ourselves of two or three of the principal figures.

Thomas Hobbes

The pronouncements of this English philosopher were no more than a delaying action on the side of the absolute monarch. Here the state of nature is a state of war; every man is naturally at war with every other. At last, in Hobbes I find one natural right, the right to preserve one's self, one's being. This is the first of three for Locke, the right of "life." Self-preservation is the basic drive of man, natural to him even as a member of society. Now when the compact is made, Hobbes would have it made with a natural sovereign, a man capable of quelling the war of every man against every other. Curiously, once made, the compact (and apparently the working of history to establish a man as sovereign is equivalent to a compact) cannot be broken. The people have committed themselves to the care of the sovereign; they have given up the right of using force to gain their ends, and now must gain by peaceful means — that is, ingenuity and stealth — what otherwise they might have gained by force. The sovereign guarantees order within the state, and the continued existence of the state itself. The rights of the citizens are civil rights, granted by the state. The natural right of "life" cannot be signed away. Man has the right to preserve his life even against the whim of the sovereign. He does not have the right of revolution for, strangely, this somewhat one-sided contract cannot be terminated by the people. It ends only with the failure of the sovereign to keep the contract; it ends, that is, with the breakdown of order in the state.

In this view, clearly enough, the pyramid is retained with only the slightest change. Another thing is clear: what one thinks of man will help to shape his social thought. Hobbes thought of man in terms of egoism and a narrow self-interest; he thought life "nasty, brutish, and short." The thought helped to shape his conclusions. Still, one of Hobbes' pronouncements is worth some pondering. He claims to be able to show us where the state of nature still exists, unchanged. Excluded from the nation by the social contract, it exists in the relations of national states among themselves; here is a war of each against all, and peace is only an uneasy truce.

John Locke

For John Locke, to contrast one Englishman with another, man is a reasonable creature; and cooperation is natural to him. The state of nature, it follows, is not vastly different from the civil order; it is only less convenient. Men enter into societies to avoid the inconveniences of a less settled way of life. They form societies in order to protect the basic rights which belong to them as men. For this reason the contract with the sovereign, whoever — or however many — he may be, is not without conditions. The sovereign power remains with the people always, and only its administering is delegated to the sovereign. And if the state should fail to provide for man his natural rights, or if these rights should be abridged, the people have a final right, the right of revolution. For Locke the end of government is framed according to a set of natural rights, which also provides the pattern for any civil rights which may be added; and to preserve these natural rights man has the right of revolution. Various statements have been given of these natural rights. The listing formed by Locke, and often repeated by others (see almost any section of our constitution!) enshrines Life, Liberty, and Property, as the basic and natural rights. Notice how for Locke the conception of what society ought to be is already implicit in human nature. Naturally, then, just where Hobbes discerned the war of each against all, Locke would discern a natural justice, still implicit, and resting on man's essentially reasonable and sympathetic nature. Locke's way of viewing the contract as conditional was the typical manner among plainsmen of treating the relation between government and the society it governs.

Whether one considers Hobbes or Locke, one is put into a frame of mind in which, moving back and forth between the actual conditions of one's society, and an imaginary state of nature, one is almost led to believe in the existence, somewhere or sometime, of this state. I think this was not really intended by our theorists; I think they were concerned with a hypothetical state of nature in the large. While in the Greek city-states, and in Geneva, to mention a few of the many instances, such contracts did occur, what they replaced was not a state of nature, but an earlier societal arrangement which was not initiated in this manner.

Jean Jacques Rousseau

The description which almosts fits the facts is the social contract as given by Rousseau. For Rousseau it is in the first place not a contract between the members of society and a sovereign person; it is a contract between part and whole, a contract between myself as an individual and the whole society. As for Locke, so for Rousseau, the sovereign power remains in the whole society. But what is the state of nature for Rousseau? Unhappily, the doctrine is developed in more than one manner; but I take it that his central thought can be stated in this way: Man gives himself to society as an individual, and receives himself back as a citizen. In this transfer we have something like the contrast between the now familiar state of nature and the civil state. In developing this contrast Rousseau works at the issue with profundity. Rousseau's natural man is an authentic picture of what man nonsocialized — without the benefits of social development — would be. And in his description it is equally appropriate to consider the social contract to be something which has been developing through the ages, an implicit agreement with the state made by each man as he grows to maturity (so that the description also fits Socrates' discussion of the matter), or an explicit contract made by naturalized citizens. All of these aspects of the problem are covered by his analysis. The coming into being of the social contract substitutes intelligent for more primitive animal-like behavior; justice replaces instinct, the idea of duty or morality replaces impulse, reason replaces our sheer inclinations, property replaces possessions, and an equality by convention replaces our physical inequality. Without society the basis of animal-man's life is the impulse toward self-preservation. Within society the basis of human life is reason. The transfer from the state of nature to society is something like a transition from Hobbes to Locke. I think it cannot be doubted that man's social life does effect this kind of transformation.

As a result of the social contract man's nature becomes more complex. Not only is one his own individual self; in addition, he has become a member of society and part of its sovereign power. He has still his individual will and his aggressiveness; and yet he must participate in the more general will of his society. Surely, Rousseau is partly right in this conception; if we can speak of what we will as individuals, we can also speak of the kind of compound willing which is the judgment of society. But Rousseau would not allow the general will to be gained so simply; for him it is not "the will of the majority." And even though the compound will of a society is often taken to be the will of the majority, he saw the general will (and this makes the concept tantalizingly difficult), as what society ought to will, a common good on which all men can agree, and would in fact agree, if they knew the situation and their own natures thoroughly. His principle amounts to the belief that for every problem facing a nation there is a possible decision which, had we the wit to see and act upon it, would, while solving the problem, also preserve all that is most important in our individual willing. One aspect of man's nature concerns his private inclinations; the other concerns his social duties and responsibilities; in a sense the second stands over the first, for in his second aspect man is participating in the general will. In another sense, the second aspect might be said to underlie the first, because the general will of a society contributes, and for the first time allows, freedom to the members of society. Similarly, but in fact perhaps this is a case of identity, man's sense of duty and "oughtness" supports his individual striving, giving it point and direction, and so increasing his personal freedom. In short, through Rousseau one is able to find a means of moving from the problems of ethics to those of social philosophy.

The French Declaration

We were led to the social contract theory in an effort to discover whatever principles may be involved in the idea of the plain which has been at work altering the pyramid of status. A number of relevant principles have appeared. And, in fact, turning to our Declaration of Independence and our Bill of Rights, one finds these principles at work. For the sake of variety I propose a glance at the French "Declaration of the Rights of Man and of the Citizen." This declaration prefaced the Constitution of 1791 and so, no less than ours, must stand as a document of revolution. We can observe the social contract in operation if we look to the first eleven rights. The document begins:

> The representatives of the French people, organized in the National Assembly, considering that ignorance, forgetfulness or contempt of the rights of man are the sole cause of the public miseries and of the corruption of governments, have resolved to set forth in a solemn declaration the natural, inalienable, and sacred rights of man, in order that this declaration, being ever present to all the members of the social body, may unceasingly remind them of their rights and duties. . . .

It then goes on to list the "simple and incontestable principles" upon which society rests.

1. Men are born and remain free and equal in rights. Social distinctions can be based only upon public utility.
2. The aim of every political association is the preservation of the natural and imprescriptible rights of man. These rights are liberty, property, security, and resistance to oppression.
3. The source of all sovereignty is essentially in the nation; no body, no individual can exercise authority that does not proceed from it in plain terms.
4. Liberty consists in the power to do anything that does not injure others; accordingly, the exercise of the natural rights of each man has for its only limits those that secure to the other members of society the enjoyment of these same rights. These limits can be determined only by law.
5. The law has the right to forbid only such actions as are injurious to society. Nothing can be forbidden that is not interdicted by the law, and no one can be constrained to do that which it does not order.
6. Law is the expression of the general will. All citizens have the right to take part personally or by their representatives in its formation. It must be the same for all, whether it protects or punishes. All citizens being equal in its eyes, are equally eligible to

all public dignities, places, and employments, according to their capacities, and without other distinctions than that of their virtues and their talents.

7. No man can be accused, arrested, or detained except in the cases determined by the law and according to the forms that it has prescribed. Those who procure, expedite, execute, or cause to be executed arbitrary orders ought to be punished; but every citizen summoned or seized in virtue of the law ought to render instant obedience; he makes himself guilty by resistance.

8. The law ought to establish only penalties that are strictly and obviously necessary and no one can be punished except in virtue of a law established and promulgated prior to the offence and legally applied.

9. Every man being presumed innocent until he has been pronounced guilty, if it is thought indispensable to arrest him, all severity that may not be necessary to secure his person ought to be strictly suppressed by law.

10. No one ought to be disturbed on account of his opinions, even religious, provided their manifestation does not derange the public order established by law.

11. The free communication of ideas and opinions is one of the most precious of the rights of man; every citizen then can freely speak, write, and print, subject to responsibility for the abuse of this freedom in the cases determined by law.[2]

The whole document is worthy of attention. And now, if we consider this application of the social contract, together with the theories of society advanced by Locke and Rousseau, we can discover the parts, or principles, necessary to the view from the plain.

We are dealing with society, once it has passed from the level of command to that of law. Sovereignty resides, then, in the whole people. A constitutional frame is necessary for this canvas. Natural, or basic, rights are presupposed. Liberty and equality are the most frequently mentioned of these rights. There is the premise of the common good, serving as the basis of society's laws, and the need for legislative, executive, and judicial functions to discover and implement this good.

[2] F. M. Anderson, *The Constitutions and Other Select Documents Illustrative of the History of France (1789–1901)* (New York: H. W. Wilson Company, 1904), pp. 58–60. Used by permission of the H. W. Wilson Company. The same version is reprinted in Leo Gershoy, *The French Revolution and Napoleon* (New York: Appleton-Century-Crofts, Inc., 1947), pp. 142–143.

The Principles of the Social Contract

These are the basic elements of the doctrine which opposed the ancient social pyramids. And each of us can estimate how nearly in his life it is the plain which allows an identity between his own nature and the nature of society. Strangely, the arguments for the point of view are not in every case compelling. We have already noticed the imaginary elements in the "picture" of the social contract.

Sovereignty

Why should the power of rule lie within the whole people? One argument for this is in Rousseau's *Social Contract*. It should, because "force does not create right" and "we are obliged to obey only legitimate powers." [3] Now if right comes into being only by agreement, and in our former discussion we had admitted much of this, then the right of rule, the sovereign power, must reside in some agreement among the people concerning their society. The argument comes to the idea of sovereign power from the imaginary social contract. Is the argument compelling?

Natural Rights

Not only Hobbes, but every other theorist, singles out a right to life. Locke presents life, liberty, and property as man's natural rights. One wonders why Jefferson, in framing our declaration, scratched out "property" and scratched in "happiness" to form our triad: Life, liberty, and the pursuit of happiness. The Declaration of the French insists upon the imprescriptible rights of "liberty, property, security, and resistance to oppression." And in the flaming declaration of the boulevards the rights were: Liberty, Equality, and Fraternity. In fact, human equality is singled out by Jefferson as well, "equality" standing but thirteen words away from the triad we have mentioned. And in Locke's *Second Treatise* the state of nature, the source of other rights, is held to be a state of equality. Thus, there is much agreement among our authors concerning the basic human rights. And the newest list of human rights, that of the United Nations, includes all of these and many more.

[3] Jean Jacques Rousseau, *Social Contract*, Bk. I, Chap. 3.

But what is the support for natural rights? They derive of course from the imaginary state of nature. The best argument I have heard in their support is the one employed by Locke; it is short and simple: These rights are the gift of God. Now, what one has received as a gift cannot properly be taken away. If life, liberty, property, the pursuit of happiness, security, resistance to oppression, equality, and fraternity (to combine the lists) are a gift of God, they are securely and rightfully our own. But is the argument convincing?

Equality

The assertion of equality is very important to the doctrines of the plain. Assert the inequality of men, and some special class or group will always rise, claiming to be superior to the rest, and assuming special privileges. With such privileges the show of superiority can be carried off convincingly. Assert equality, meaning it, and such posturing can be known for what it is. Only if men are in some sense equal can there be a constitution, rightly binding all. If men are equal no man has the right to deprive another of his liberty. Equality seems to be a principle, founded in man's love of liberty, and in his respect for law. It does not rest on fact alone. But the defense of "liberty" and "lawfulness" is doubtful, unless the equality of men can be defended, too.

Yet it is not a simple thing to find the sense in which men are equal. It is easy enough to find our inequalities. We are unequal in strength, intellect, personal appeal, emotional intensity, property, influence, beauty, and in the ability to express ourselves. No defense of equality is to be found in any facts of physiology, psychology, sociology, or history; the facts of these disciplines always support human inequality. Is the equality of men another bit of make-believe?

Thomas Hobbes could see equality only in the fact that no man is so wise or powerful that his life could not be taken by a group of other men; we are equally at the fate of other men. This incredibly slight equality is not enough to support the doctrines of the plain. The only argument for equality known to me has been expressed in at least two forms; it was used by Locke and Jefferson. We are equal before God, who sees in us his image; I suppose this means that beyond the "surface" inequalities God is able to discern our basic humanity. I suppose this means that we are equally men; our inequalities of capacity having less importance than the equal humanity which we share with other men. Men were viewed as equal by the Stoic thinkers of late Greek and early Roman times, because each man contained a spark of the universal reason which controlled the universe, and this identity in man was more important than the differences among them. If men are equal before God, or equally share in a universal reason, then they ought also to be equal before the law, and in each other's eyes.

For the time we shall let the argument rest. But has the argument sufficient power to establish this most important point?

Liberty

The description of liberty in the French Declaration is clear enough: "Liberty consists in the power to do anything that does not injure others; accordingly, the exercise of the natural rights of each man has for its only limits those that secure to the other members of society the enjoyment of these same rights." No restriction shall be placed upon human thought or action, except the restriction imposed by the rights of others. In this doctrine we come again upon the natural barriers of our last discussion, allowing each his needed elbow room.

Perhaps the most appropriate expression of the point of view is that of John Stuart Mill:

> This, then, is the appropriate region of human liberty. It comprises, *first,* the inward domain of consciousness; demanding liberty of conscience in the most comprehensive sense; liberty of thought and feeling; absolute freedom of opinion and sentiment on all subjects, practical or speculative, scientific, moral, or theological. The liberty of expressing and publishing opinions may seem to fall under a different principle, since it belongs to that part of the conduct of an individual which concerns other people; but, being almost of as much importance as the liberty of thought itself, and resting in great part on the same reasons, is practically inseparable from it. *Secondly,* the principle requires liberty of tastes and pursuits; of framing the plan of our life to suit our own character; of doing as we like, subject to such consequences as may follow: without impediment from our fellow creatures, so long as what we do does not harm them, even though they should think our conduct foolish, perverse, or wrong. *Thirdly,* from this liberty of each individual, follows the liberty, within the same limits, of combination among individuals; free-

dom to unite, for any purpose not involving harm to others: the persons combining being supposed to be of full age, and not forced or deceived.

No society in which these liberties are not, on the whole, respected, is free, whatever may be its form of government; and none is completely free in which they do not exist absolute and unqualified. The only freedom which deserves the name, is that of pursuing our own good in our own way, so long as we do not attempt to deprive others of theirs, or impede their efforts to obtain it. Each is the proper guardian of his own health, whether bodily, or mental and spiritual. Mankind are greater gainers by suffering each other to live as seems good to themselves, than by compelling each to live as seems good to the rest.[4]

To invade the domain of individual liberty is to rob the human race. Where an individual opinion is suppressed, the action makes impossible the discovery of truth. If the opinion is false, its falsehood cannot now be determined. If the opinion is true, since truth can be determined only by means of free discussion, we are separated from the knowledge of this truth. If in the conflict of opinion between suppressed and suppressor, each should have part of a larger truth, mixed with error, the whole truth can be discovered only by allowing both, and insisting upon the clash of these adverse opinions. If truth is important, here is an argument for human liberty. Where the liberty of individual action is controlled, we deprive men of their individuality; but this is the quality which allows development in human life and in society. If development, if progress, is important, this is an argument for human liberty.

I am satisfied with the argument; it fits so well the conclusions of our first discussions. Is the argument convincing to you?

Revolution

What, then, of revolution, the right standing behind the rest, their guarantee, the word so fearful to our minds? In the first place it is doubtful that a people can deny their origin, and we were born in revolution. In the second place, let us recall the meaning of the word. All that is meant by revolution is a major turning of the power of the state from the ends to which it has been directed, and toward other ends. The word we fear is, hence, a neutral word. If the power of the state has been directed toward improper ends,

[4] John Stuart Mill, *On Liberty* (London: W. Scott, 1901), Chap. 1.

the major turning of this power to proper ends is positively good. If the power of the state has been directed toward proper ends, the revolution which redirects this power improperly is positively bad. If the power of the state has been directed toward improper ends, and by insurrection someone else assumes the power to direct the state to ends which are still improper, this is no revolution, because there has been no major redirection. These are the little coups and countercoups, the *coups de main, coups d'état,* the fluttering in the political dovecote, the so-called palace revolutions, the slight scuffling and shuffling within the pyramid of status, replacing a bad head of state with another quite as bad.

If the social contract describes society when it is ordered toward the good; and if we wish and need the good society, then, should the ordering of our society be improper, we would be right in working toward the reordering of this society. As long as a state is sensitive to the need for change, and as long as change can take place through its normal deliberative and executive agencies, the need for redirection can be satisfied by many minor redirections. When this is possible we do not need the right, which stands behind all other rights. But the fact is this: If we are not insensitive to the good society, we must believe in revolution as our final right. No other consideration can change this fact, or the nature of our commitment. And there is nothing inconsistent about believing in revolution and in a government of law. Indeed, the appearance of law is part of the meaning of the good society, part of the substance this final right must guarantee.

And this brings us to a nice distinction. We may distinguish an authentic from a spurious revolution. We may believe in the former and deny the latter. The authentic revolution will be directed toward an increase in human rights and liberties. The spurious revolution will lead not to an increase, but to a decrease in these rights. One should fear, indeed, any revolution which is not authentic. The question is whether we do not fear them both. The troublesome thought is that we might be just unwilling to see a state unhinged for the sake of human rights and liberties. And yet Americans find within themselves a feeling of identity with those peoples in revolution around the world, where the issue is a challenge to some ancient social pyramid (although some may feel slightly guilty about this feeling). Why the feeling of identity? We sense, I think, the presence of an authentic revolution. If the social contract describes the good society, here is an argument for a final right of revolution.

We have presented, briefly, the principles of the plain, along with the arguments — good, bad, and indifferent — which might be used, and have been used, to defend these principles. They have had power in recent centuries; and yet they serve as nothing more than raw material for our thinking. Not every point is apt; but in some of them your own philosophy, or mine, may have been expressed.

The Functional Pyramid

And abruptly we must turn from this important aspect of our heritage not to the political pyramids of ancient times, now in a condition of disuse, but to the functional pyramids of our modern world. We had touched upon the curious fact that, while the kings are gone, a kind of social pyramid remains. As it presents itself in the felt ordering of a community, the pyramid of status is only a matter of the feelings of men. There is, however, a more substantial kind of pyramidal fact. The more substantial fact is this: The pyramid has gained a function within our modern world, and this is enough to give it a place in the hearts of functional modern men. Indeed, the pyramid has found its most effective form in modern life. The name for this most effective form of modern pyramid is: the Corporation. One has only to examine the diagram of its structure to observe its unmistakably pyramidal form. And, in fact, the pyramid of words is possible, only because it is backed by a pyramid of power. After all, someone must be in charge if anything is to be accomplished; someone must rule, make decisions, take upon himself the responsibilities of command; hence, others must obey; they must, if the functions of society are to be carried out efficiently. When someone takes charge the functional pyramid springs into existence, and the flow of power goes down to the lowliest functionary. The governing pyramids of ancient times have been transformed into the functional pyramids of the modern world.

Here is a functioning and functional structure, employing the level of command; although it may not be in conflict with, certainly it presents a contrast to, the theory we have been considering; its serried ranks of obligation and of privilege have an appearance most like, although more efficient than, the feudal structure, which fell when locked in conflict with our planar principles.

What is it about our purposes which so inevitably frames the functional pyramid in human life? For these pyramids are, of course, compounded human purposes, given permanence through legal pronouncements, and given power through the number of human wills involved. If our earlier analysis is to be trusted, the purpose would seem to be a desire for status, power, control. Mr. Tawney found reason in this connection to claim that we are acquisitive men in an acquisitive age. This would be to say that the functional pyramids are energized by human greed. And should this be their purpose, I suppose we would have to say the same of the throngs of purposes on Main Street, edging forward even against the light, at last breaking through — as we had said — their patience hardly lasting sixty seconds. And this downtown area of hard sidewalks and dilute carbon monoxide gas, these down-cut canyons from three to 183 floors in depth, this territory of the corporations, we should have to say, is dedicated to the proposition that all men are creatures of a narrow self-interest. But must we say so much? Must we view these great buildings as monuments to human greed?

It is, perhaps, better to think of the goal as a better life. Men engage in this activity to improve themselves. They have accepted responsibilities on which they must perform. And when we were attempting to name what is most descriptive of our age, we had said:

> This is the age in which man is manufacturing, processing, packaging, transporting, advertising, wholesaling, retailing, and in these ways earning money to buy, several thousands of varieties of aids to living which were unknown to the most exceptionally elite one century back. More than that, this is the particular time and place in which whole portions of the world have been raising the human level to a new height. . . . This . . . is the age in which industry has made available to whole peoples the means to an existence in which machines are heating, cooling, toasting, stirring, washing, rinsing, drying, lighting, perking, cleansing, polishing, entertaining, conveying, and disposing — all for man's purposes, to satisfy this or that whim, desire, or need. Man's life has been altered, and the indications are that this will continue.

The purpose of the monuments, structures, and functions to which we have called attention is, we can as easily say, to accomplish this raising of the human level. The saying is much more kind.

Put either way, we are concerned with a major activity of twentieth-century Western man, a concern not with beauty, truth, and goodness but with commodities, a different kind of good, and yet essential in providing a platform for our lives. In terms of basic physical conditions, we have already claimed, whole peoples have succeeded to the position once held by those at the top of the ruling pyramid, those in the position of command.

What are the elements of this activity, and what is its goal? By what social principles is it guided? What are money, profit, interest, and price? Although important, the questions seem not very philosophic. In covering the topic, perhaps we can use the device employed by Plato, when he had come to the edge of his philosophic thought. We can substitute for analysis a kind of fable. Here then is:

The Briefer History of Economic Life from Paleolithic Times to the Present

Already at the dawn of history buyers, sellers, products, and media of exchange were in existence. How did this happen? One can only imagine. Therefore, let us imagine.

A great advance toward our modern world was made on the day a Paleolithic brute proved his manhood by trading a pile of fish for a pile of skins. Barter, an astounding invention, added comfort and variety to the life of this man, providing better things for better living, and to the lives of those who aped (or Paleolithed) his bright inventiveness. As time dragged on, not only were finished products exchanged — caught fish, scraped skins — but the instruments of production in addition; that is, capital goods: the finished bones for scraping skins, and the nets for catching fish. The second great advance came when scraping bones, a capital good, became the standard for barter; that is, it became the Medium of exchange. The value of scraped skins and caught fish came to be figured in terms of scraping bones. This was the discovery of Price. In this simple brutish state the value of a product depended upon the amount of labor necessary to ready this product for its market; in another sense it depended even then upon how badly the product was needed or wanted by those who were without it. Sometimes a product could be purchased in one place where the scraping bone price was low, and carried to another place where the scraping bone price was high; in this way, one might accumulate a pile of scraping bones; and the only work involved was the carrying of the product from one place to another. Thus, the trader, importer, and merchants were born. But there was risk involved in such transactions; it became known as the scraping bone risk. The scraping bone price might drop while the goods were in transit; or some uncivilized lout (i.e., one who did not understand about scraping bones) might set upon one along the way, eliminating the need for any medium of exchange, bartering unilaterally through an exercise of man's scarcely latent talent for aggression. It was obviously proper for the buyer to stand some of this scraping bone risk. The difference between the number of scraping bones required to make, or buy, the product, and the scraping bones it would bring upon the open market (all markets were open in this day) came to be known as Profit.

Gradually, men's desires turned from the needed goods and products to the scraping bones themselves; a group of scraping bone enthusiasts arose, the Paleolithicis, and it was one of their number who discovered the real miracle of the scraping bone. Happily and thoughtlessly engaging in exchange with a pile of scraping bones, he found one day his pile of scraping bones had doubled; two piles of scraping bones lay where but one had been before. Meditating darkly upon this surprising fact, he made the great discovery within a month and a half. The scraping bone is alive; it reproduces; and the *mana* in all living things is in it, too; it has then a value in its own right. To confirm his discovery he loaned his second pile of scraping bones to a boneless friend; and after one moon (it was a harvest moon), his friend had two piles of scraping bones as well. The Paleolithicis, our early financiers, drew the obvious conclusion: The loan of a pile of scraping bones for a moon or two must be repaid by a pile-and-a-half. The amazing thing was this: Both parties were better off because of such a loan; and it is hard to discover if anyone was worse off. The scraping bone could reproduce; thus was Interest born. And the economic ingredients which would transform themselves into the modern world had made their appearance.

When we come to recorded history (which shows that such accounts as this are fables written backwards; and mine is by no means the only one!) scraping bones had been exchanged for metals which men had begun to prize — instead of scraping bones or the pebbles on the beach; and the age of metals had begun to change the world. Technology, wisdom applied to practical affairs through commerce, had likewise begun; there was a lot of talk about a wheel someone had invented; the old men all agreed it would never replace the brush rack. But, of course, it did; and the liaison between commerce and technology began. The account, should anyone be wondering, is not at all historical, and yet the elements of this complex must have formed in some such manner. And there is a scraping bone magic, the scarcely understood "multiplier effect" of money, no less mysterious than the "Doppler effect" of physics. My account is nonhistorical because the magic of the scraping bone had its triumph only at the origin of our modern world. For at least two thousand years man's religious and ethical insights had been at war with the custom of using money to make money. The practice was often opposed in legal pronouncements. But the taking of interest was a necessary part of the function of exchange — and interest won.

Then came the Renaissance with fresh, and growing, knowledge about the world; and with it came the new economy, applying this knowledge in the intimate union of commerce with technology, packaging bits of knowledge into machines capable of producing goods in more abundance. We had come to the point where it was for the first time possible to raise the level of human life, transforming the people of the West from agrarian to urban folk, and in the process, changing their lives, their values, and their loyalties.

The account is not yet finished. As goods began to multiply, as mass markets developed, a new entity arose, an economic person not to be confused with any man, and yet with powers as mysterious as the reproducing scraping bone. This person is the corporation, responsible before the law, and thus limiting the responsibilities of any person sharing in its corporate life, a hypothetical man and yet a legal person, able to act and grow, to accumulate wealth, to gather resources much greater than those of any person, a superperson whose hypothetical welfare is sometimes identified with the welfare of the state. And in whatever measure we desire the goods which have contributed to the raising of the human level, in that measure this hypothetical person holds our respect and elicits our protection.

This, then, is the briefer history of economic life. We are inter\
ested in its consequences upon our persons, and in the social aspects
of our philosophies. In terms more sharply drawn we wish to
know to what extent the attitudes engendered by the functional
pyramids are in conflict with the principles of ordinary plainsmen.

To determine the question, one further item must be set down.
When the great commotion, called the Industrial Revolution, had
fairly started to change forever the contours of our world, slowly
there began to dawn in the consciousness even of philosophers a
premonition that something was afoot, or abroad, or even ahead,
in the land, deserving of attention. Now to attend to something is
to try to understand. And for philosophers to understand, it is
necessary, first, to build a discipline, a system of ideas, to provide
the foundations of a science, a scheme capable of providing a foot-
hold on the subject matter, and enabling one to look before and
after. The most economical kind of concept is the statement of a
law. "What Newton has done for physics, we shall do for man's
propensities to buy and sell." But man is much less tidy than an
atom, a planet, or the subjects of other lawlike disciplines, his purposes are so multiple his ends of action so diverse, how discover
lawlike behavior here? This, I take it, was their problem. And its
answer was elegant, indeed. We shall invent a hypothetical man
as standard as an atom; and with such an entity, and the proper
formal scheme, our new science can begin, aspiring even to prediction. Although fabulous, this is no longer the statement of a
fable.

The Hypothetical Economic Man

For some time this doctrine of a hypothetical economic man
hovered among the pages of philosopher-economists without explicit statement. This is the case, I think, with the writings of Adam
Smith. At last and, as we say, in due course, the statement was
made. The earliest explicit statement known to me is present in
John Stuart Mill's first treatise on economics, the *Essays on Some
Unsettled Questions of Political Economy*. Because of the light it
throws upon our subject, let me quote at length:

'Political Economy' . . . does not treat of the whole of man's
nature as modified by the social state, nor of the whole conduct
of man in society. *It is concerned with him solely as a being who*

desires to possess wealth, and who is capable of judging of the comparative efficacy of means for obtaining that end. It predicts only such of the phenomena of the social state as take place in consequence of the pursuit of wealth. It makes entire abstraction of every other human passion or motive; except those which may be regarded as perpetually antagonizing principles to the desire of wealth, namely, aversion to labour, and desire of the present enjoyment of costly indulgences. These it takes, to a certain extent, into its calculations, because these do not merely, like other desires, occasionally conflict with the pursuit of wealth, but accompany it always as a drag, or impediment, and are therefore inseparably mixed up in the consideration of it. *Political Economy considers mankind as occupied solely in acquiring and consuming wealth;* and aims at showing what is the course of action into which mankind, living in a state of society, would be impelled, if that motive, except in the degree in which it is checked by the two perpetual counter-motives above adverted to, were absolute ruler of all their actions. Under the influence of this desire, it shows mankind accumulating wealth, and employing that wealth in the production of other wealth; sanctioning by mutual agreement the institution of property; establishing laws to prevent individuals from encroaching upon the property of others by force or fraud; adopting various contrivances for increasing the productiveness of their labour; settling the division of the produce by agreement, under the influence of competition (competition itself being governed by certain laws, which laws are therefore the ultimate regulators of the division of the produce); and employing certain expedients (as money, credit, &c.) to facilitate the distribution. . . . The science then proceeds to investigate the laws which govern these several operations, under the supposition that man *is a being who is determined, by the necessity of his nature, to prefer a greater portion of wealth to a smaller in all cases,* without any other exception than that constituted by the two counter-motives already specified. . . . *The manner in which it necessarily proceeds is that of treating the main and acknowledged end as if it were the sole end; which, of all hypotheses equally simple, is the nearest to the truth.* The political economist inquires, what are the actions which would be produced by this desire, if, within the departments in question, it were unimpeded by any other. In this way a nearer approximation is obtained than would otherwise be practicable, to the real order of human affairs in those departments. This approximation is then to be corrected by making proper allowance for the effects of any impulses of a different description, which can be shown to interfere with the result in any particular case. . . .

Political Economy, then, may be defined as follows: And the definition seems to be complete: —

'The science which traces the laws of such of the phenomena of society as arise from the combined operations of mankind for the production of wealth, in so far as those phenomena are not modified by the pursuit of any other object.' [5]

The idea of an economic man is presented by Mill as an hypothetical notion. No actual man, he tells us more than once, is so motivated throughout all the areas of his life. And yet the hypothetical man is to some extent what man actually is; with respect to buying and selling this is man's "main and acknowledged" motive; but, more important, the hypothetical economic man is needed in order to gain the framework of a science. In a paragraph, happily omitted, Mill compared his procedure with the approach of astronomers to their science. The abstraction of economic man, along with other abstractions, can enable us to predict how man will behave in society. Among the elements of the burgeoning science are: The economic man, property, labor, competition, produce, money, credit, and whatever is contained in "&c." I think we can supply one of the things included in "&c." Mill had spoken of "competition" as governed by "certain laws, which laws are therefore the ultimate regulators of the division of the produce." Not much reflection is needed in order to discover that one of the laws to which he here refers is the famous law of supply and demand.

Clearly, we are not talking about a real man when this hypothetical economic man is mentioned; for a real man seeks wisdom, has honor, is charitable in what he does. We are speaking of a fiction. The hypothetical economic man will turn to profit as naturally as a flower turns its leaves to the sun. He will buy as cheaply, and sell as dearly, as he can, always at a profit — to the right man at the right time in the right place for the right (that is, highest) price. He will always calculate to increase his property, or to minimize his losses; as his goods increase his wants will multiply. And he will so conduct his life not to reach any final goal; but merely as the habit of his total life. It is not alone, however, the consumer and the merchant who are to be understood in these

[5] John Stuart Mill, *Essays on Some Unsettled Questions of Political Economy* (London: Longmans, Green, and Co., 1877), pp. 137–141. Italics mine.

terms. The producer is included; and the laborer, wishing to sell his labor as dearly as he can in order to benefit the more from the consumer market. Apparently, we are to think of a hypothetical society, composed of equally hypothetical economic men.

The Economic Scheme

Now, this imagined man is, indeed, as standard as an atom, interacting with its colleagues in some atomic context. Given our entity, and its economic nature, we are in a position to draw some conclusions. When the supply of goods is scarce, we can expect the price of goods to be high; when the supply is abundant, the price will drop. The more plentiful the supply of goods, the more economic man as seller will find his propensity to sell dearly, checked by economic man as buyer. The more scarce the supply, the more will economic man as buyer find his propensity to buy cheaply, checked by economic man as seller. And, indeed, men do tend to sell as dearly, and buy as cheaply, as they can. Just so! At times there will be a buyer's market; at other times a seller's market. The scheme applies to merchants; it applies also to producers. In our society of economic men, where there are many sellers as well as buyers, the price of a commodity will reach its "natural" level. If one man is selling too dearly, the market will go to another. If one is selling too cheaply . . . well, bankruptcy ends this game! The cost of labor and raw materials provides a lower level of price. And the wages of labor are controlled, at least in part, by these same considerations of supply and demand.

I can understand how the hypothetical economic man helped philosophers and economists to think about buying and selling, just as the social contract theory helped philosophers and political scientists to think about society. Indeed, the scheme is elegant, and can furnish a set of principles. One of them is clearly this: The end of economic life is private profit. Procedures could be stated, ways of acting to attain this end. And this set of principles would not, I think, be much in conflict with the theory of the social contract — so long as our economic man is merely hypothetical. But it would be tedious and fruitless to derive this set of principles. Without question, something has gone wrong with the scheme, and with its famous law. Indeed, there is some question concerning whether the professors, who shaped the law, were describing the new economy, or the simpler economy of Paleolithic times.

In truth, when goods began to multiply, the purposes of buyers, sellers, merchants, traders, and financiers all tended to interfere with the working of this law. The purpose, it seemed, was not to bring prices to a natural level, but to drive competition from the market; competitors should be bought out, or forced to sell; financial interests, this seemed to be the goal, should not exist as separate and competing forces; they should be merged — for bigness is not necessarily bad, and badness often comes in very small packages.

The Economic Superperson

Where did the scheme go wrong? What has happened to the law? Whatever happened, the result — I claim — was to place the functional pyramid in conflict with the principles of the plain. The scheme had taken account of economic man; but, of course, did not anticipate the other, bloodless kind of economic person, stranger than its fictions. The result of merging economic interests was the large and powerful corporation, our legal person. And the breakdown of the scheme had something to do with the coalescing tendency of financial interests, and with the voice of this economic superperson; for the corporation had gained the power of speech. It was a limited kind of speech, to be sure, yet dulcet in its tones, honeyed but insistent. The speech is called Advertising. In the main its utterances took a single form: a request to buy, a request for others to buy. Its speech fulfilled the end of the corporation in harmony with the economic law, and the end of economic man. The speech of corporations was designed to sell its product, the product furnished by a corporate team in keeping with the law of supply and demand. And yet, as we shall see, this added factor caused the law to be honored only in the breach.

To speak with candor, our hypothetical economic man, as originally conceived, was a creature extremely cunning in buying at the lowest, and selling at the highest, price. But he was not possessed of much discrimination concerning what he was to buy, or the wants he was to satisfy. He would buy what he wanted but, beyond a few necessities, it was not at all clear to him what it was he wanted. This being the situation, a master stroke was prepared by those whose lives were molded within the corporation. Instead of merely finding out what was demanded by these economic men, and meeting the demand with the needed supply of goods, it might be possible, in the first instance, to create the demand. Since man's wants were supposed to multiply as he increased his supply of goods, it might be possible to shape these wants by rhetoric through the corporate speech. The pen, it had long been said, is mightier than the sword. And here was a chance to test the saying. And although the economic law called for competition, it might be possible to shape these wants into a demand for the very product the corporation had to sell. Of course, if this could happen, its happening would completely wreck the law, for then the seller would control both the supply and the demand. It could happen, and the law was wrecked!

And now for competition to continue among the giants it was necessary for every corporation to have its say, directing the people to buy the goods which every corporation had to sell. This speech was, of course, a request; it could not be a command. And one would expect, offhand, to find in advertising a factual statement about a product; and in the accepted scheme the price should be the most compelling aspect of this request to buy. But the expected and accepted are not enough if the demand for goods is to be controlled in addition to their supply. The request could be put in a very compelling way: If you want to be happy, successful, beautiful or handsome, the darling of "society," the envy of your neighbors; if you aspire, that is, to the role of the ancient prince (or princess), you had better use X (at this point one will fill in the name of the product to be sold). Or it could be put the other way around: If you do not wish to be an outcast, that is, malodorous in body and breath, hair falling out or breaking off, dentures slipping and nail polish peeling, lipstick cracking and crow's feet forming, energy going, head throbbing; if you do not desire to be an untouchable, use X.

Curiously, neither of these ways of putting the matter makes a valid argument. The whole procedure is illogical; and yet it worked — and works. But the consequences of its working are not exactly happy ones. Our inner lives have been invaded, and are being shaped, by an influence which stands in conflict with our social principles. The triad of values we found among the Greeks was Truth, Beauty, Goodness. Consider Truth! If the principle of advertising is: "Tell the customer what he wants to hear!" we should not expect in advertising a statement of facts about a product. Indeed, in the hysteria of competing claims, the cause of truth drops out of sight. A federal board now functions to compel the discontinuance of outright lies ("misleading claims") in the competition for the market. Appeals to passion have been heard before; indeed, the subject of discussion is Rhetoric, the art of saying pleasing things. Aristotle wrote a treatise on the subject, describing how to go about its use; and no other discipline has had a more fulsome career. But before the present age such appeals were understood to have their use in moving an assembly toward action at a moment of national or municipal crisis, or to preserve one's being in moments of personal danger, or in the peroration of a sermon. The modern rhetoricians, who claim the field of advertising, put rhetoric in the place of logic as a permanent substitute for sound reasoning and factual declarations. One must sell, even at the cost of truth: this seems to be the notion. In this new ideal, for truth there is substituted propaganda. Consider Beauty! Repetition enhances the esthetic value of any musical, pictorial, or poetic theme; no esthetic principle is better founded. Sixty seconds spent in listening to any acceptable bit of music will reveal how essential is repetition to the subtle qualities of musical art. Through repetition a net is woven in which the enchanting values of the art are caught. Modern advertising, with no deeper urge than to sell a product, adopts this esthetic principle, denuded of esthetic purpose, and through the sheer pressure of repetition weaves a net in which not enchanting values but we, ourselves, are caught. There is built into us a sense of value, welded to this product, not as we have seen by argument or fact, but through the urgency of the dinning. This is an essential deceit, for repetition has no place in such paltry contexts. Esthetic value has been cribbed and cramped into an instrumental role. We have seen how repetition in artistic form contributes to our freedom; but repetition here would seem to have at least a mild enslavement as its goal.[6] In this new ideal the beautiful has been replaced by "psychological appeal." Con-

---

[6] The word and the phrase — "enslavement" and "being caught within a net" — are not mere poetic overstatement. Were the goal something less than this, who could have given a moment's thought to the devices for subliminal projection? But if we have stated, rather than overstating, the goal a train of thought can be imagined in defense of this projection: Since the force of advertising is irrational, accomplishing its work through the shaping of man's unconscious motivations, would it not be better to pitch the whole enterprise on the irrational level which lies below man's conscious awareness? Then the message can do its work; the victim can be caught, or "hooked," or "gaffed" without interfering with his pleasures, and without even ruffling the surface of his conscious being.

sider Goodness! Goodness has two meanings. In the place of goodness as the end of life, our modern substitute for final value would seem to be an Elysian place in the pyramid of status, surrounded by every gleaming product of our modern art, including a plan for annual replacement to avoid "planned obsolescence." And in the place of the "right" our modern substitute demands, I think, conformity. One can not attribute this to advertising by itself. After all, if the pyramid is to function as a corporate person, teamwork is essential. It will be more important from the standpoint of the functional pyramid for one to be a good team man than to be an individual. This statement is a modern commonplace. And Darwinian principles, operating within the functional pyramid, will explain the sudden appearance of the mutant form, *homo teamiensus*, who in the struggle for existence within a corporate society exhibits such marked capacity to survive — and prosper! This one will be a team man to his finger tips; part of his power to survive will depend from his ability to take on the coloration of his environment. In all of this he becomes somehow standardized, and his wife as well if what one hears of "corporation wives," as well as "corporation husbands," has any point. Of course, there are many other pressures, and conditions bringing pressure, upon our lives which might be mentioned in the explanation of our modern tendency to conform. But it is curious that, along with the multiplication and standardization of goods, there has come a standardization of men — a mass man, a standardized man, to produce, market, and buy the mass and standard product. This simultaneous appearance is not entirely accidental. It has something to do with the requirements of the functional pyramid, with the urgency of its voice, the consistency of its expression no matter what the corporate source may be, and of our uniform response as we turn on the lathe of its continual shaping. In this new ideal, for goodness we will tend to substitute conformity, aspiring in conformity toward the apex of the pyramid of status. Think of these together, and the contrast is startling. Propaganda, Psychological Appeal, Conformity! Are these our modern substitutes for Beauty, Truth, and Goodness?

I am not completely serious about this modern triad. And yet we do ourselves no service, following these leading strings toward instrumental values, confining our aspirations to those commodities offered by the corporations, observing this filling of the minds of our young with the commercial copy of our day, furnishing their speech, their song, their purposes (to say nothing of their role as ancillary agents, wishing with all their hearts, and forcing their parents out of love — or sheer fatigue — to buy the useless product). There is such a thing as mental hygiene, and the better things for human living are nonmaterial. The consequences of our great success now call for deep reflection; in this age the functional pyramid has gained a disproportionate power, an influence in excess of its human value. The two possible motives for the functional pyramid, it is now clear, are not exclusive. It has in fact made possible the raising of the human level. And the raising of this vital level has been accomplished by means of and, in the bargain, reinforcing man's natural drive for acquisition. The functional pyramid has always been directed toward a narrow self-interest, accepting as its pattern the hypothetical economic man. For those who work within this pyramid the goal is personal profit. The rest of society, who must endure its voice, who stand to it as possible sources of its drive for profit, are served a different version of the selfsame end; they are encouraged to aspire greatly toward a commanding place in the pyramid of status.

My point is this: For the reasons given, the initially hypothetical economic man has risen in flesh and blood over wide areas of our industrial society, putting considerations of profit before all else, understanding all value in terms of price, and bending toward this meager concept every aspect of our world. I do not contend that economic men began to exist only with the statement of the economic law, or with the founding of the modern pyramid, any more than I would place the origin of gravitation in the time of Isaac Newton. Gravitation had operated unceasingly before Newton essayed its description; men naturally calculating profit and loss had also "operated" before economic man was described. But economy was not then the major fact of human life which is the case today. The rising of the level in the life of Western man has meant more goods for ever larger numbers; the production and distribution of these goods have given men sufficient scope to spend all their lives calculating solely in the terms which belong to "economic man." In earlier days every man became an economic man during the harvest season, when he had goods for exchange or sale; but his descendants can function as economic men all the year around, unremittingly and unceasingly. They can spend every minute of every hour of every day throughout the year, calculating in terms of profit and (unhappily) of loss. Whether or not this is now a permanent feature of our culture it has been, is, and will be, a permanent feature of our individual lives. The functional pyramid has thus breathed life into the initially hypothetical economic man.

And so, as it turns out, we Americans have been busy building, consciously we have been contriving, the largest, highest, most elaborate platform for human living the world has ever known. But what is it for? What is its purpose? What are we to do with it? Most of our energy for a century has gone into the building of this platform. Can the end of life for us concern the platform only so that almost everybody's labor is absorbed in pushing up the structure one more story, the children building on the foundation of their fathers? But then our lives never reach their completion, the means never reaches to its end. One can often see the inner nature of a man in some outer work; the skyscraper seems to be the mirror which reflects our inner drives. Up it goes, dedicated to the proposition that the higher it is the better; and the good life will begin one floor above our present striving — a penthouse theory of human excellence. It is not enough to build a platform. One must also learn to live upon it; and in this we have not yet schooled ourselves.

In the realm of ends, everything has either a *price* or a *dignity*. Whatever has a price can be replaced by something else as its equivalent; on the other hand, whatever is above all price, and therefore admits of no equivalent, has a dignity. . . . Thus morality and humanity, so far as it is capable of morality, alone have dignity.[7]

Whatever has dignity is not subject to the conditions of exchange; so wrote Immanuel Kant, whose insights we have called upon before. What if, because of the influence of our economic life, we have produced a commercial civilization which fails at last to recognize the priceless value of human dignity, unable in its appreciations to respond to any other motives than those of price? What if we move toward the conclusion that everything has a price and nothing a value? Should this be even possible it is time for a stern warning. One analyst of society a century ago, as the parts of the functional pyramid were falling into place, issued his warning. The man was Karl Marx; the analysis is to be found in his early economic and philosophic manuscripts; I offer it in the summary of Helmut Kuhn:

[7] Immanuel Kant, *Foundations of Morals*, from L. W. Beck, *op. cit.*, p. 92.

Society . . . is the essential unity of man and nature. Society produces the true man. But man must work in order to live, wresting a livelihood from an as yet unreconciled nature. In working and making things, he externalizes himself. What exists first as thought and plan in his mind, a part of himself, becomes an object outside himself. So work is self-estrangement: the thing becomes the maker's. As though it were a bit of his self, he claims it as his own, to the exclusion of claims which might be made upon it by his fellows. But thereby he, the maker, comes under the sway of the thing made. As a manifestation of the cleavage in his mind, private property arises, and the individual falls away from society. The process of estrangement begins. Capitalism is the consummation of this process: the perfection of private property and total estrangement. Everything now has a price, nothing a value. The victim of estrangement is the proletarian, man in the role of a commodity. His life is a "filled nothing" which at any moment threatens to fall into the "total nothingness" of annihilation. But the curse of estrangement afflicts all members of society, even those who find it enjoyable. It estranges man from man, and man from his world. Instead of his physical and spiritual senses, he has one sense only which holds the others in subjection: the sense of having, which is the estrangement of all senses and the reduction of man to a status of absolute poverty.

A man working on an assembly line, making he knows not what for he knows not whom, nor caring in the least, next to his elbow a fellow worker whom he does not know (tomorrow it will be someone else), earning just enough to enable him to rise in the morning to return to his place on the assembly line, enough also to make him shoulder, hour by hour, all the empty time that is still ahead of him, and to throw away as much of this burden as he can upon unenjoyable pleasures, his cheap narcotics. . . . This is the unadorned void. The gilt void meanwhile haunts the luxurious office, the suburban mansion, the opera house where a singer sells his voice at so high a price that he can afford to forget about that which is priceless in music. [8]

The analysis is not acceptable in all respects; moderate the claim, then, in some fitting manner; allow fifty per cent of it, or only twenty; still, some point remains. At least we must agree in this: The life of the economic man is a "filled nothing" — a void, gilt or unadorned — because he has forfeited the human sense of proper

[8] Reprinted from *Encounter With Nothingness*, by Helmut Kuhn, copyright 1950 by Henry Regnery Company. Pp. 38–39.

value. A kind of obtuse barbarism, then, must be his lot; he is fit for nothing more exalted than raising the platform one more story. And possibly the twentieth-century feeling of the meaninglessness of life, recorded by the most sensitive among our modern instruments — the poets and the artists — is their precise sensing of the nothingness of life when every value is understood in terms of price.

And if at last we are to ask about the principles of the functional pyramid, the end of profit remains unchanged from the simpler economic days. To this end, efficiency and mass production are required. Perhaps the principle of advertising is what they say: "Tell the customer what he wants to hear!" Are these in conflict with our planar principles? Possibly not! It is difficult to say. But if we ask: "Are the consequences of the functioning of this pyramid, according to its principles in conflict with the principles of the plain?" it may be possible to gain an answer.

The principles of the plain concern liberty, equality, the sovereignty of the individual man, and devotion to the common good. No pyramid in history has concerned itself with human liberty. The functional pyramid supports the claims of status; status yields privilege; privilege reflects itself in differences among the factual conditions of our lives; and the more extreme these differences, the less is it possible to maintain even a semblance of equality among the citizens of a state; thus, in effect, the pyramid admits the claim of inequality. And if in the modern scene the economic man has come to life, this is a conception far different from that of the sovereign individual. Mass production requires man to take his place as one of an aggregate of functions, together shaping the mass and standard product; as a result man at work necessarily becomes an instrument, one of the interchangeable parts or functions of the vast machine. When man through most of his purposeful life is forced to an instrumental conception of himself, when he is as much an instrument as a stamping tool, it is difficult to sustain the thought that his value is intrinsic, and his power the sovereign power of his society. And wherever value has been exchanged for price, the goods of life are gained through competition; there exists then no common good to stand as the object of our devotion, furnishing the bond of social unity. Hence, our economic pyramids naturally engender attitudes in conflict with the plain at every point.

The Summing Up

We must find a way of resolving, not avoiding or ignoring, this conflict within our lives. Until we find a way of doing this, I think we cannot have sound personal philosophies in this day. It was our plan to reflect upon the two most forceful institutions of our world; we had expected them to reveal the general problem of our age, and to take us beyond the terms of our analysis. In a sense the plan has been successful. The pyramids of business have continued to grow until this moment. Their power has increased steadily for a century. But the bigness is more general! Big government has become a fact, partly to meet the thrust of the growing economic pyramids. Big government finds its own pyramidal form. The bigness of labor makes its appearance to meet the pressures of these other pyramids. The form of the pyramid fits all three. And that part of government, often slightingly termed "bureaucracy," is the part shaped most like the pyramids of business and by its pressures. I am not certain exactly what it is in modern life which requires the bigness of its operations, the complexity of its concerns, its constantly accelerating pace. But it is surely a fact that in our world one concern accelerates another until the pace is frantic and frenetic.

Meanwhile, one wonders if the principles of the social contract, still working — as I claim — with hidden power, can be made consistent with our modern surge toward pyramidal bigness. In any case the contemporary pyramids are a necessary part of modern life. And if you find within yourself a strange allegiance to the planar principles, not only must you find a resolution of the conflict we have noted; you must look to the defense of the principles themselves. However powerful has been the working of this social contract theory, it referred back to an imaginary state; and in the modern mood a point of view, resting on an imaginary base, becomes an imaginary point of view. You have no escape. If you wish these principles you must find a more powerful support than did our ancestral plainsmen. And is this even possible?

Our social philosophy must have strength in its conception, and in its relation to the facts. And if our personal lives are to be significant; if we are to avoid the sense of feeling ourselves adrift, or lost within society, this conception must be capable of directing us toward the next step in our social development. So we complete our survey of the problem. And having raised the problem — with its host of lesser problems — the problem of your social philosophy, your much-needed set of social principles, is left to you.

II. Toward Principle in Society

What shall we do with the problem? For one thing we can ignore it. Many philosophers have done just this. But if we are to be equal to the issues of our day we had better elaborate our social principles, see to their defense, and exercise in both respects an attitude approaching "infinite" care. And should an identity appear, relating our thought to the movement of some portion of our social world, the discovery would add to the sense of purpose and meaning in our lives.

The principles which follow from the "social contract" seem to me indispensable, even if the contract is an imaginary thing. And so, whatever the present direction of your thought, I must attend to these principles, coming to some decision about their strength. But how can an imaginary contract bind our lives? It cannot. Is there another way of coming to the same conclusions as those to which our imaginary contract led? Let us see.

Search for a Basic Social Principle

Plato, reasoning closely and brilliantly in the opening books of his *Republic*, demonstrated to the satisfaction of his contrived audience, and doubtless to the satisfaction of many of the countless readers of this work, that the end of all art is the good of its subject matter. The principal figure of the dialogue is Socrates, and in his name the view is advanced. Socrates' opponent is Thrasymachus, the Sophist. The object of the discussion is the end of the art of ruling a city-state. In Thrasymachus' opinion the end of the art of rule is the interest of the ruler. Socrates counters with his claim. The claim is: The end of any art, including the art of rule, is the good of the subject matter. Socrates means by art not only the fine arts, but all practical activities issuing in any making or doing. He cites examples from all areas of our common life. The end of medicine, insofar as the physician is acting as a physician, is *only* the good of the patient. It would seem to follow that a physician, whose interest in his patient is financial, is — to the extent of his financial interest — not really a physician, but a man exploiting the art of medicine. In the same way the end of the pilot is safe navigation; that is, the good of the passengers. The end of gymnastic, and so of the physical trainer, is a healthy body. At one point Thrasymachus seems to win a victory, taunting Socrates with this argument: If what Socrates says is true, then the end of the shepherd is the good of the sheep, when anyone should know the true end of the shepherd to lie in the eventual destruction of the sheep, fattening them, as he is, for the kill. It is possible to feel slightly ill as Thrasymachus counters the Socratic claim. But within a few pages Socrates has turned the thrust. He needed only to refer to an earlier contention of his opponent.

Near the start of the discussion Thrasymachus had been forced to insist upon strict definitions for words such as "ruler," "physician," and the like. And he had been forced to this by difficulties present in two possible meanings of his initial principle. He had understood the end of any art to be the interest of the person engaging in the activities belonging to the art. From the side of common sense this would mean no more than what a person *thinks* is to his interest. And in this sense, when a person has mistaken his true interest, the principle of Thrasymachus would be holding the end of any art, and so the end of rule, to be what in fact is contrary to the interest of the person engaging in the art. Socrates had revealed this problem; and Thrasymachus had covered by insisting upon strict definitions; the ruler as ruler, the physician as physician, will act according to his true interest; he can be mistaken as a man but not insofar as he is truly a ruler or physician; the end of any art will be what is, indeed, to the interest of the person making or doing within the boundaries of this activity. Here is the entry of an "ought to be." Socrates now returns to this admission. He reminds Thrasymachus of their decision to use strict definitions; as with the ruler and the physician, so with the shepherd; insofar as one considers the shepherd as shepherd, his sole end is the good of the sheep, their care and their well-being. It is possible to think Socrates a juggler of words as he turns the thrust. And Socrates was nothing if not adept at the art of using words. But it is in fact not the art of the shepherd, but part of the economic art, which attends to the destruction of the sheep; and the end of this art centers not upon the well-being of any sheep, but on the well-being of one aspect of our human lives. In short, I think Socrates has come by valid means to a valid point. And from the discussion a principle ensues which may be of help in relation to our problem: The end of any art is the good of its subject matter. And every artist will attend to this above all else, allowing nothing else to compete with this consideration.

From the conclusion one would be led to conceive of our social life as a complex set of arts, following the principles required for their proper functioning. And surely society is less alien, and more intelligible, when understood as a set of arts, each with its function within society, meeting needs, performing needed services, and understood in terms of the functions and services they perform. And ruling, as an art, the art of our political life, can then have nothing other than the good of the people as its end. So far I have not swerved from the Socratic line of thought.

If the end of any art is the good of its subject matter, this includes the art of rule; and the proper ordering of our social life will be, must be, the good of the people, its proper subject matter. We have gained the conclusion which was drawn from the imaginary social contract without having to carry along the impossible question: How can an imaginary agreement possibly bind our lives? Without the figure of the social contract we have come to the important conclusion: There are conditions of principle governing the structure of society.

From this conclusion I wish to move, and not in company with Socrates, Plato, or any other Greek, to the details of our planar principles. "But," you may object, "Plato gained his initial principle, and with its help began to build a planned and rational society, functioning in pyramidal fashion through the rule of philosopher kings. And the liberty, equality, and sovereign individuality of the plain are notable only by their absence." The objection is to be admitted; and yet Plato's principle does allow us two important social principles: The end of social ordering is the good of the people, and there exists a common good to provide the unity of the social whole. Like the plainsman, Plato believes in the planned society, but with a difference. He works according to a different plan. What, then, is this difference? In making it out, one point must be allowed: If I see the power of his initial principle, the one on which he builds to gain the rest, it is as reasonable for me to use this principle as it was for him; and beginning so, I cannot be required to hold the rest of his conclusions for — at the stage of this discovery — the others had not been derived. And they do not follow from this principle by itself. So far! What then led from the initial principle to Plato's pyramidal, planned society? The answer cannot be avoided: Plato had accepted the inequality of men. Given this second principle, the rest of his *Republic* begins to follow. Unless we can avoid the conclusion of a radical human inequality, some pyramidal form will result from any set of social principles. And you will remember the difficulty surrounding the planar view in this regard. In what sense can we believe in the principle of equality?

Equality

We have found no factual way of arguing for human equality. We can, of course, argue for the approximate justice of this principle. Assuming it as a bit of make-believe, we can say, brings society out closer to the facts than admitting the inequality in fact. If men are not equal, at least the inequalities of station in any pyramid of status will simply fail to correspond to the inequalities in fact. Is one person qualitatively better than another? Of course, but what has this to do with inequalities of station, the possession of different quantities of goods, power, prestige, influence, and the like? Our pyramids always reflect differences in power, wealth, and goods, quite the opposite of differences in the qualities of human life. That we differ, one may properly argue, provides no reason for the building of a pyramid of status. If men are not equal in fact, still their inequality is not self-chosen; if one is superior, it is not appropriate to praise him for this accident; and if one is inferior, it is not appropriate to point a finger of blame. If men are not in fact equal, still one cannot say in advance who is superior and who inferior. To assert their equality, even if it is a lie, serves the purpose of allowing them to find themselves without prejudice. If men are not equal in fact, still the lack of superiority of any given class is a fact. And if men are not in fact equal, still there is more promise to be found in human life than most of us suspect. Let them believe in their equality, and they will believe in themselves. Let them believe in themselves, and they will realize their possibilities more completely.

The argument has power; it also supposes a very tangled situation among our concepts. The assertion of equality, although false in fact, is a more productive principle for the social order, having consequences closer to the facts of human nature, than those following from the opposite principle which, in fact, is true; this is what the argument supposes. Could this be so? Even if it is the case, we have just succeeded in eliminating an imaginary element from the planar theory. Why should we cancel out this gain by admitting another element of helpful make-believe? I think we cannot take this course.

If, within a paragraph or two, we were to find a smashing good argument for our equality-in-fact, to what would this lead us? It would lead, I think, to this conclusion: If men are in fact equal, then our goal should be to reproduce that equality in the physical conditions of their lives; then they should be equal in property, in financial security, and in power. Indeed, although not reflected in the Russian pyramid, the more severe revolution was empowered by a more literal, if less realistic, reading of the principle of equality; this was the source of their anxiety over property relations. But we cannot find a basis for equality in the facts of human nature.

Surely a third alternative exists; we cannot support our principle by the factual inequalities among our humankind; nor can it be defended if the principle is a bit of make-believe. Equality has no basis in fact! The very bluntness of this claim, its not requiring to be qualified in any way, leads to one conclusion: The right of equality, if capable of defense, will not be of the kind which requires an equalizing of the factual conditions, the physical conditions, of human life.

How, then, are we to think of equality? We are the intellectual posterity of those who have spoken of our equality in the eyes of God, our equality before the law, and sometimes — in more recent years — of an equality of opportunity. None of these requires an equality in the physical aspects of our lives. The concept suggests not a flat, but at least a gently rolling, plain. These weaker statements require at least the open society, and the presence of opportunities for its members; but, no more than the literal reading of equality, could it allow the pyramid of status.

And how is even this lesser claim to be defended? We are after the statement of a principle; a principle is not a set of facts, but a mixture of fact with value. It is the proper mastery of an art which directs the art toward the good of its subject matter. And it would be some kind of propriety in human relations which has our kind of equality as its end. Perhaps we are dealing with an ethical question. Possibly the answer to our question lies ready, having been worked out many pages back in our discussions of right and wrong. How did we state the principle of ethics?

Do not except your inner nature from the principle which your act presents to others! Treat every man as an end in himself, and not as a means to some private end which is your own! Recognize in every man that he is sovereign as well as subject in the realm of ends which is the good society! These were our three ways of stating the principle of ethics. If these are acceptable, a principle of equality must be accepted. The principle is this: *Men are to be equal before the law, and in their rights and opportunities.* Our principle requires not a factual, but a moral, equality. It does rest upon a fact. The fact we had discovered in the same discussion. The fact is that men cannot build a unity of character, and deny to others equal status with themselves as men; they must grant to others the grounds from which they act, or they are cut off from the more subtle kinds of value and achievement.

Is the weaker principle of equality the expression of a weak-kneed, weakened view? Does our principle, refusing a factual equality, condone the pyramids in our midst? At least it would downgrade the importance of our struggle on any pyramid. But if it is not the end of the principle of equality to furnish a flat, non-undulating plain, still the principle provides a clear directive for the ordering of society. Here is the reason! Let the factual inequalities among the conditions of our lives become extreme, and equality of opportunity becomes a semblance; the greater the factual inequalities in number and degree, the less will it be possible to preserve equality before the law and in our rights and opportunities. This is, I think, the inner reason for our common concern about the extremes in our actual pyramids of status — the extremes of excessive wealth and excessive poverty.

We have gained a second principle; and it separates our view decisively from Plato's planned society. And in the argument we begin to sense still other elements of the plain.

Liberty

Mill presented a convincing argument for liberty. The argument, in brief, was this: If we are committed to truth, we are committed to liberty as well; touch liberty, and this at once limits the possibilities of gaining truth.

More important for our purposes, the principle of liberty follows from the principle of equality, and the principle that the end of government lies in human good. Sometimes the good is universal. At other times, and very often, the good is individual; at these times we can find a common basis only through following out the notion of that individual good which requires for its attainment the presence of "natural" boundaries between our lives. And if men are justly equal in their rights and opportunities, this equal treatment leads to liberty as a social principle: *The freedom of each man must be allowed to extend to the point where it would interfere with the freedom of another.*

The Sovereign Individual, the Right of Revolution, and the Common Good

And now we can achieve two further principles almost at once. If the end of society is the good of its members, if equality is proper along with human liberty, we are close to the conception of a sovereign person. If we add to these the further conception of law, deriving from the will of the members of society — another aspect of our ethical reflection — the new principle will follow. Certainly the other alternative, with its level of command, is quite incompatible with the principles of liberty and equality. Now if men are the origin of social laws, they must likewise be their sanction. At once sovereignty devolves upon men. And the power necessary for administering the functions of the state must be understood as delegated power, a conditional grant by a sovereign people. *Sovereignty resides in the people:* this is the statement of the principle.

Accept this much, and we cannot disbelieve in any revolution directed toward the increase of human rights and liberties. If men are the sovereign power within society, the source and sanction of their law, and if this law is to reflect their common good, the principle of the authentic revolution follows: *When the sovereign power within a state has been misdirected, man has the right by whatever means are necessary to redirect this power toward the increase of human rights and liberties.*

But both of these principles require the idea of the common good; and our sovereign man requires a double nature (but not duplicity); the sovereign aspect of our citizen is something like the "general will" of Rousseau. Can we accept this notion?

It is a natural condition of undisciplined man to seek what pleases, while avoiding what displeases him. It is a natural condition of society to seek by and large what is pleasing to its members, to have its basis in the pleasing and displeasing. And by a natural process society offers back its verdict to the individual concerning what ought to please and displease, concerning what is to be sought and what avoided. If our planar principles follow without any alteration this natural sequence of affirmation and response, the end toward which they point, and the meaning of the common good, is caught within the statement: Give the people what they want! When a representative does nothing more than represent the wishes of his people, he is understanding democratic functioning in this manner. When a lobbyist represents the wishes of his corporation, he is following a more alarming concept of democratic functioning: Give the corporation what it wants! But if this alone is the end we seek, one wonders why all this hue and cry about social principles.

But the end we are to seek in common is the common good. And this good cannot be any random bundle of desires which happens to possess our being. It stands for the wishes which should be ours, even when we do not wish them; we have more than once sensed the "ought to be" within the common good. For this reason the statement, "Give the people what they want," is a terribly false form of the principle we are seeking. We should have lost our balance on the other side should we think our principle to be: "Give the people what they ought to want!" This statement contains the sense of forcing men into a semblance of democracy; and men cannot be forced to be free. Rousseau, unless we misinterpret his intentions (a likely possibility), held that men could and should be forced into this freedom. Now our right to an authentic revolution is evidence enough of a final relationship between force and freedom. But while this is our final right as plainsmen, it is not part of the scheme of democratic functioning. Is it possible within our scheme to mediate between what people want, and what they ought to want, and not by force, or by a flattening of the good into a shapeless mediocrity?

In sketching the social theory of Rousseau, we came upon his mystifying concept of the "general will." When one reflects, gathers himself up, and gains a unified will, the result of this willing is not necessarily what "ought to be." And yet through individual reflection a sense of "oughtness" can emerge for us as individuals. Similarly for society: Sometimes in the deliberations of a parliament (or of a Congress), an "ought to be" different from the individual wills brought to the assembly may emerge through its deliberations. Doubtless, our assemblies proceed most of the time on a basis of the will of the majority, and sometimes follow the will of a minority through pork-barrel legislation, lobbying, pressure groups, and their like. But the inner meaning and function of any parliament in relation to our planar principles is this: It is the means by which, beginning with what the people will, and by means of careful consideration and discussion, what they ought to will — that is, the common good — may be discerned. And because this is their function, the members of a parliament should be men of principle; not every action of their official lives should be determined with the ballot box in view. Of course, they may be brought to heel. But why is it never pointed out that defeat, linked to truth, is a greater good than victory, when the victory has no greater good in view? Such defeat can be part of the testing of the common good, the "ought-to-be," discerned through debate within a parliament. At least, let us honor defeated statesmen above victorious politicians. The world, as it happens, is just too old for mediocrity or chicane in this important aspect of our lives. Even the campaign for re-election has its inner meaning. It provides the scene for interpreting to the sovereign body the bridge of reasons by which we move from what we wish through the issues of our day to the insights concerning what we ought to will in common. Thus, we have an instrument of advance — if only we would use it! But we cannot advance if the debate, within an assembly or before a people, is too largely a display of rhetoric, the material of advertising. Sound argument, the presentation of the reasons, is more essential than we seem to understand. Otherwise, the attempt to interpret and persuade will be only propaganda; it will have its end, as well, in the manipulation of our persons; and manipulation will not contribute to our freedom, or to our advance; nor will it preserve on any issue the integral context necessary to the discovery of the common good.

The common good in any situation is the ideal insight, capable of resolving whatever problem called it forth, and in a manner which will continue and strengthen the support of our individual striving. And the man who seeks, and begins to find this good is, surprisingly, our sovereign man. The principle which makes a group its own sovereign guide calls for members who are also sovereign. A sovereign people must be composed of sovereign persons. A new concept of person is demanded — a man who can live freely and with the kingly quality, recognizing no absolute, earthly master. Instrumental values will be properly subordinate to those which are intrinsic; he will seek the truth, respond to beauty, have breadth and sensitivity within his appreciations; he will seek a general and not merely his individual good; he will grant to every man the social rights he has discerned; and the "general will" appears within his nature. And is not this the picture of what we must become, if domocracy is to work, according to its promise? In his *Republic* Plato wrote:

> Until philosophers are kings, or the kings and princes of this world have the spirit and power of philosophy, and political greatness and wisdom meet in one, and those commoner natures who pursue either to the exclusion of the other are compelled to stand aside, cities will never have rest from their evils, — no, nor the human race, as I believe — and then only will this our State have a possibility of life and behold the light of day.[9]

When, three centuries ago, the social contract placed sovereignty within the people, the meaning of these words took a surprising turn. The people are sovereign. With this there opens a whole new and immense perspective. It is the people, then, who must gain the spirit and power of philosophy. This is the insight, and from this there can be no turning back. Our people must become in the proper sense (not in the academic sense) philosophers. We must become capable of wisdom in our decisions; we must become willing and able to sense the common good beyond the particular goods for which we strive; we must gain the largeness of view proper to one who is sovereign, as well as subject, within society. You say this is impossible? In more than one of my half-dozen moods, I quite agree. But it is also impossible for a nation to survive forever; and it is impossible for a democracy to survive unless it can make wise decisions, unless it can at least live according to

[9] Plato, *The Republic, op. cit.*, Bk. V, Par. 473.

its principles. In no other nation is the popular will so quickly reflected on the highest levels. There is no alternative. This "will" must be extremely wise. For us, more than for those living within any other social framework, becoming a philosophic people is part of our design. We must try to become a people of genuine culture, living at the height of the Western world.

The Role of Government

And from all of this it is possible to speak of the role of government; for government is nothing more than the social form of this general aspect of our lives. The comment must be tempered by the size and power of governments in our time. As the society to be governed increases in size and power, the government will increase, too, in both of these respects. About this we have no choice. But we do have a choice concerning what government should do. For quite a long time we have talked among ourselves of the two possible roles which a government might assume. Either, it was said, a government will be of the type which governs least; or, if it becomes big, to the extent of its size and actions, it will control the lives, and limit the freedom, of its people. But today, although some still repeat these words, any government which follows the principle of least action will be incompetent. Does there remain the single type? There are two types, still. And I agree with the analysis in this: Only two general types of government are possible today. At the moment I am concerned with our choice between these types. One of these is the big government of our earlier thought.

It is possible for a powerful government to rest upon the people, controlling all their actions; and then the level of command has returned upon us, its form the ultimate pyramid of functions. It is important to remember that for the first time a real police state is possible. It was not possible in absolute form before our present age. And if it is possible in one section of the world, it is possible in another. It becomes a question for humanity everywhere, when any state can so efficiently control its citizens in all their actions, even — when to its purposes — extending this control to the private thoughts flitting through the inner darkness of their brains. When this is possible, what happens to our principle of the proper superiority of man, anywhere and everywhere, to his state? What is man's defense when barricades in streets have little more effect than words on paper? Literally, your barricade is paper-thin! Free men, it seems, had better unite against the possibility of the ultimate pyramid of power; it would be well for them to insure the society in which they believe, against whatever trends — even long range trends — may lead one day to the frightening consequence which has been mentioned.

But government must remain powerful; and so we seek its other possible form. We can approach this form by referring once again to the delightful and urbane common sense of John Locke. In his second treatise on government, having begun with his lovely notion of God's gift of the world to men in common, he explains the right of property. Men add their labor to some portion of this common grant, and that on which they labor becomes their own. Here are his words:

> Thus the grass my horse has bit, the turfs my servant has cut, and the ore I have digged in any place where I have a right to them in common with others, become my property without the assignation or consent of anybody. The labour that was mine, removing them out of that common state they were in, hath fixed my property in them.[10]

The reference to "the turfs my servant has cut" is a bit surprising. By Locke's argument the turfs would seem to belong to the servant. But this is not my point. The discussion moves to a consideration of the ownership of land. Locke is still imagining his state of nature. The first settlers arrive, take possession, add their labor to the land, and the miracle of property makes its appearance. No problem exists so long as "there was still enough and as good left" for the settlers still to come. But Locke, it is clear, has some anxious thoughts about the state of nature when there is no longer enough and as good, when what is left is marginal in its value. Plainly, he is worried about the last settlers who have the same natural rights as the first, and yet the commons are gone. After perhaps a dozen inconsequential pages Locke changes the subject.

But in an age of last settlers it is not well to change the subject; and, indeed, according to our principles, an answer to the problem is forthcoming. The state of nature for Locke was in fact a set of opportunities for development in human life. If we are plainsmen every man must have his state of nature, equal opportunity for his

---

10 John Locke, *The Second Treatise of Civil Government*, Chap. V, Sec. 28.

own development. And what if these opportunities are no longer present in the common meaning of the natural state? There is but a single answer: They must be provided. By whom? By men so far as they are members of an enterprise which seeks the common good. Do men belong to such an enterprise? They do, insofar as they are members of society, and citizens of a state. The other type of government is this: One which builds a platform for the people. Government then becomes the platform for our free development. And certainly this is part of the common good, the general will which can support our individual striving. Only in this role is the bigness of government in keeping with the principles of the plain. It keeps us equal, insures our liberty; we in turn work toward the achievement of the common good, thus strengthening our bonds of union.

I have given my arguments for, along with a development of, the principles of the plain. They seem to me without exception capable of defense.

The Pyramids

But if our social principles can be defended, and if they are in conflict with the tendency and nature of our economic pyramids, what then? Well, let us see. It is impossible to have variant principles for these two important and forceful aspects of our lives. How will the pyramids fare against our established social principles? We had found two principles, associated with these pyramids, although there must be many more. *The end of the economic art is personal profit;* this was one. *Tell the customer what he wants to hear;* this was the other. Let us review them in order.

In reflecting on the principle of profit, we are considering — it would seem, — the businessman. Socrates argued well for his principle: The end of any art is the good of its subject matter. And from this standpoint we were able to view society as a set of arts, satisfying needed functions. And the businessman fulfills at least two functions: He provides society with its instrumental goods, and supplies labor with its needed instrument of instruments — providing here, too, needed goods for human life. Now, consider! One must conclude from the *Republic* that *the end of the economic art is the good of its subject matter.* Its end, according to this principle, is a more stable and prosperous society, its members benefiting from the goods supplied, and from the side effects of investment and production. And labor is supplied with the requisites for self-development. This is not a trivial role within society. To put it more precisely: *The end of the economic art is the good of those involved in industry, and of society in general.* So far all is clear.

But look now at the avowed, and largely unquestioned principle of this art: The end of the economic art is personal profit. But this is impossible; no art *can* have such an end. The end of the economic art, like any other, must be the good of its subject matter. Hence, a conclusion follows. Any man who makes the end of economic life primarily, essentially, or unreservedly, his own personal profit is not a businessman but a man exploiting a business, as a tyrant exploits a commonwealth. Plato's luminous point would seem to be that the man with his private interest should never supersede the practitioner of the art. And just as there is little need for physicians who place considerations of payment above the welfare of their patients, or navigators placing private interest above the safety of their passengers, so (this application is, however, mine — not Plato's) there is little need for businessmen who place considerations of personal profit above the welfare of employees and of those whom their operations touch.

The principle would place businessmen where they truly belong — among the professions where the function performed has an importance far surpassing any private interest. The professions are the social arts in which, when practiced properly, the subject matter has priority. The painter is ruled by the best possibilities of his medium, the doctor by the best possibilities of his patients, and the true ruler by the well-being of his people. And no art can allow any extraneous purpose to override its basic principle.

Apparently, we need to see again, and clearly, what we saw (fitfully at best) some centuries ago. Any calling — recall the interest taken in one's calling — is one's profession; a difference of position makes no difference in this respect. Nothing is so menial that it falls below this rank; nothing so exalted that it flies above it. Every calling has its principles, the following of which will be one manner of reaching human excellence. The good of the subject matter will be its end; and notice how the filling of a needed function is, in fact, contributing to the common good. Together society, so conceived, becomes an interweaving of functions, made harmonious by the desire for excellence, and the presence of well-formed principles. And among these equals, the economic art is the equal of all the rest. To accept the view is to alter significantly, to refuse it is to embrace, the pyramid of status.

The oft-avowed principle of advertising substitutes for truth, it was our painful duty to record, the machinery of propaganda — a lathe, I think we found the machine to be. This substitution made of man an instrument, standing, thus, in conflict with the treatment proper to our sovereign man. The end of advertising, too, must be the good of its subject matter; it is not good for man to be turned into an instrument. If we are to be men of principle, advertising must revert to factual statements about its products, refreshingly informative about their possibilities, and candid about their limitations ("We'll try to do better another year, folks, but this year's model is a mess!"). I suppose this can never happen; but at least the obtrusive nature of this force upon our lives must somehow be diminished; and its harmful consequences must be somehow overcome. It has played the villain in the greater drama which has completely throttled the cultural possibilities of radio and television. And the same old false principle was at work: "Give the people what they want to hear — or see!" The principle of democratic functioning, which requires the striking of a balance between what is wanted, and what should be wanted — in order to provide the chance for growth — has been quite ignored. "Someone must pay for the programs!" Indeed; but the question is whether such programs are worth a single scraping bone by way of payment. The deepest error in all of this, among a baker's dozen, turns around a very improper use of propaganda. And in fact the only valid use of propaganda, it would seem to me, is the one use which renders propaganda ineffective. I mean, of course, the emotive appeal, not unmixed with reasons, serving to inspire our children — and why not ourselves as well? — into independent, self-disciplined, rational, and thoughtful human beings.

And now, having gone on at such a pace, providing my list of social principles, let me draw them together. I offer them as a sample of the kind of principles which may be emerging from your thinking; mine are not at all complete. But one's social principles at last would be a set of interconnected ideas, fit for guidance where one is facing issues having social and political importance.

The Principles of a Social Philosophy

I. The end of any art is the good of its subject matter; the end of government is, therefore, the well-being of its subjects.

II. The subjects are also sovereign; the sovereign power of the state resides, therefore, in the people.

III. There is a common good within society, requiring discovery or construction. The common good has two forms: that on which all men agree, and the total good achieved through the individual pursuit of different goods. The end of government is to be directed toward this common good.

IV. The function of law is to implement the end of government. It follows from (I) and (III) that laws are to be framed according to the common good; the statements of law must support the common elements in our individual striving, and preserve the "natural" boundaries between our lives.

V. It is the function of the parliament, or assembly, to discover through rational means the common elements which are the good of all. The parliament is a means of inducing or allowing social change through indirect action, transforming the brute conflicts of society into the elements of a problem, and as the means of resolution, substituting orderly procedure and debate for direct action and force.

VI. It follows from (II) and (IV) that men are to be equal before the law, and in their rights and opportunities. Equality of rights does not presuppose equality in abilities; it supposes only that, with differing abilities, we are yet equally human.

VII. It follows from (IV) and (VI) that the freedom of each man must be allowed to extend to the point where it would interfere with the freedom of another. This is the principle of liberty.

VIII. Behind all other rights stands the right of man to an authentic revolution, the guarantee of every other right. When the sovereign power within a state has been directed toward improper ends, man has the right, by whatever means are necessary, to redirect this power toward the increase of human rights and liberties.

IX. From the first seven principles it follows that it is not the end of democratic government to give the people what they want; democracy is a means of striking a balance between what we want and what we ought to want. Parliament is one means of striking this balance; education is another; in the modern world we must find still other means.

X. From the first eight principles it follows that society can be pictured as a plain in which each man stands his own height, as against other conceptions of society whose pictorial representation would be a pyramid.

XI. From the preceding ten principles it follows that it is part of the responsibility of government to provide a platform for its citizens, insuring their equal rights and opportunities, stimulating the increase of opportunities for their development.

XII. It follows from (VI) that it is not the role of government to arrange a factual equality among the circumstances and conditions of the lives of citizens. But since equality of rights is not possible where factual inequality is too extreme, it is the responsibility of government to show concern over increasing factual inequalities, and to act with circumspection from this concern.

XIII. It follows from (I) that the end of industry is the good of all who are involved in industry. Any man, involved in business, whose sole end is private profit is, hence, not a businessman, but a man exploiting a business.

XIV. It follows from (X) that the great pyramids of industry, so far as they force men into the role of instruments, and support the pyramids of status, are inconsistent with these principles.

XV. It follows from (IX) that the principle of advertising, "Tell the people what they want to hear"; the more recent principle, "Create in the people an artificial desire for what we want to sell"; and the principle (in part a result of advertising) of tabloid newspapers, radio, and television, "Give the people what they want to read, hear, and see," resulting in a loss of standards, and a cheapening of the value of these media, are gross violations of the principles of this social philosophy. It follows generally from the foregoing principles of our list that the only proper use of propaganda is the use which directs itself toward the end of making propaganda ineffective. Its proper use is in the procedures of education, bringing citizens to the point where, on the basis of their own thinking, they can make their decisions for themselves.

We have worked together in the lengthy exploration of our problem; and I, continuing on, have produced a set of social principles. Through these principles one might be able to find himself; one might discover the direction in which society should be moving. After reflection upon this rough-hewn work, you may be able to produce a "truer" set of principles, amending some of my statements, and adding others. But if your principles have greater strength, you must discover a more penetrating analysis, accompanied by stronger reasons. And if you can move from this point to a more cogent social outlook, I am willing to go with you. What I have produced seems to me, quite naturally and at the moment, one statement of the principles nerving our Western democratic culture for its slow ascent.

But is this, indeed, a statement of the principles which our whole age should be seeking to realize in human life? We had begun, after all, with nothing more definite than the knowledge that they are part of our history, and exercised a fascination over my nature. How does one move from this to the conclusion that these are our "true" principles?

Let me try an answer to the question. These principles, I shall claim, furnish the only clear way of understanding what we are. In history one seems to find a kind of development, which I shall call a logic of events. Sometimes what seems to have the slightest chance of making its way from thought to thing, or thought to fact, comes crashing into being as the events of history find their shape. And this was the case in America. Some are eager to point out how the principles of the plain were never supported by the whole people. This is true, but makes little difference. In the patterning of history a minority has always carried in itself the decisive viewpoint. Possibly in our case the minority discerned what many others felt. We were first of all a republic, one might argue, because of the people;

certainly, many not of the people would have had it otherwise. However we explain the origin of our social principles, the logic of events — aided by chance or fortune — wove itself around the view. It began with the affirmation of human rights, rights in which half the nation could not possibly have believed; it continued with the decision not to tolerate a ruling class — king and noble were not our style, and government must rest on the consent of the governed; it added the thesis that there could be no inferior class — a government of law is creed- and color-blind; it began to build a conviction in favor of the open society with equal opportunity; and last of all it assigned to government the duty of increasing the opportunities of citizens, of raising the platform of their lives. In this manner an intelligible pattern has developed. In terms of this pattern we can understand ourselves.

But I do not wish to gloss the facts; our history can be read in a very different way. Let me suppose you disbelieve my claim about this developing pattern. How would you make your case? You might argue in this manner:

The fathers of our country had an economic interest in their drive for liberty; land titles and taxes were involved; and notice the concern for "property" scattered through our Constitution; the war of Revolution did increase our fortunes. And remember how the Civil War opened a ruthless chapter in economic greed for northern industrialists. We welcomed the homeless of the world, and gained a needed labor force. We opened the west for settlers, and so enriched the east. Both world wars, entered — as we said — for freedom and democracy, in fact strengthened our economy. And our aid to other countries opened markets for our products. We have had, all along, a double set of principles. One set we have called the principles of the plain; in fact they are nothing more than surface principles; the other set, the principles of economic gain, constitute our feeding principles. We act before all the world as though the former guide us; in our hearts we know it is not so. The second set of principles is never sacrificed; it provides our underlying motive power.

How cynically you would read our history were you to read it so. The statement goes too far. And yet we, too, have discerned the mixture in our being. This mixture may date from early times. The missionary, I now remember, spent himself to convert some spot within a foreign land to the immense moral ideal of Christianity, and insensibly prepared the way for the trader whose interest was the other of our absolutes — profit and technology. Was this conjunction incomprehensible to our minds? We considered it the most natural happening in the world. Where else is one to find the calico, inducing a proper sense of Christian modesty? And this connection is, perhaps, the prototype of what your argument requires. And yet I would not for the world admit our most integral pattern to be the "principles" energizing economic man.

But part of the argument I must admit. In the last half of the nineteenth century, indeed, the cult of economic man was increasing geometrically in our land; never before had so many of us made this the reason of our lives. Do we not all now admit this to be our half-century of shame? Yet notice this! In its early years we freed our slaves — magnificently. What a triumph for our human sense; and how sadly mixed with profiteering. The west is to be homesteaded? Splendid! Land for all; but see the record of bribed legislators as our other absolute went to work; count the millions of acres granted speculators in rails and mines. The homeless imigrants are to be given haven in the land of the free? Nothing could be finer; but see the record of one of our first families netting millions by throwing up acres of tenements in which to house them.

And yet, explain it away who can, we did in fact disavow royalty; we did in fact free our slaves; we did in fact open the west to settlers from the east and overseas, allowing them a better life; we did in fact welcome the imigrant; we have in fact come to the aid of the Europe of our social principles, not once but twice. No end is served in cutting the garment smaller than its pattern. The argument shows no more than this: We have twin absolutes, and pursue them both. Possibly, we do push these twin absolutes with all our might, and keeping them together, while insensible of their conflict, we appear to others this object of mingled fear and hope.

How does this admission affect my claim about our developing pattern? It forces me to admit the presence of two interwoven patterns in our history. These themes will blend into a final pattern; what we are to be depends upon how the themes are to be related, which are to become subordinate, which dominant; which are to be carried to completion, which dropped along the way. And the answer to the question, "What is America, in fact?" may be simply this: "It is not yet decided."

In one sense I could ask for nothing more. We had wished a

task capable of requiring, and so releasing, all our energies. And here is a task: To make the principles of the plain dominant in our national life, even against the modern pyramids, by a growth of principle within our lives and throughout our institutions. And if the movement of our lives fits the ends defined by the developing pattern of our social thought, then have we not gained our needed purpose? Have we not found the relation between our lives and the movement of society?

But more than this is needed; and one further step is possible. We can say: There is an America which ought to be; an America which floats, as it were, above our heads. It has scarcely been mistaken. It has moved successively through all the affirmations of the plain; and its decisions have had their base in the deepest thought of our Western world. Indeed, the pattern of our history has moved this social thought beyond its furthest instancing in the life of any other nation — despite the mixture of our national being. And the only question remaining is this one: Do these insights belong not merely to the working of our history, but to us as a people? We ought to become the America which ought to be.

We will become the America above our heads, or remain mongrel, misshapen, ill-defined. How is this much stronger statement possible? Well, how is anything defined and understood? Not by naming every quality and accident of its being, but through discovering the pattern of its essential qualities. No one in fairness could understand America in terms of our economic drive alone. Can America be understood in terms of our double, and conflicting, pattern? But there are two patterns, and each aspect of one is able to negate the other. In this case we have no definition; we remain a question mark. But there is a possible pattern for us to complete; and we cannot call back history to shape for us a different pattern. We can understand ourselves in terms of the succession of decisions making up the planar pattern; and this alone provides the possibility of our definition. And so, I claim, we shall reach this definition, or remain ill-defined. We shall achieve our possible destiny, reflecting in ourselves the high promise of the Western world, or remain a question mark. We shall become this, or nothing. And if we deny our pattern, we have made our past meaningless and our future doubtful. Further, we have become the leader, so we say, of the free world. But in order to lead one must have a goal. A question mark is not a goal. If we are to be a question mark then, although cast into a position of leadership, we shall be unable to lead. Are we headed somewhere or are we not?

If the planar principles furnish the only means of understanding what we are, the America above our heads must be the real America. And the necessity in this statement records in part a fact, and for the rest an inner determination to become a fact. Earlier, we had mentioned how impossible was the task before us. And yet there is no nation whose power is called forth more completely by the "impossible" task. The impossible, as we say, takes a little longer. We have undertaken other impossible tasks. We must try this one, too.

"This people is the hope of the human race. It may become the model." So, Turgot once more. No one in the present writes about us in this manner. Nor do we feel ourselves to be the hope of the human race, the model. And yet, almost despite ourselves, I think we are the hope; at times one feels like adding, "the almost hopeless hope." But Turgot's words have come true of the America above our heads. This America is the bearer of the authentic revolution, and of man's hope for human rights and liberties. We must become the responsible bearers of this authentic revolution. No other people has both the necessary power and the needed heritage. In this sense we have a destiny; and the stakes are high.

Chapter Seven

The Question of Culture

I. The Problem of a Philosophy of History

What is the meaning of the larger whole of which our society and we ourselves are part? Why, in some sense of this querulous word, do we exist where and as we do within the larger pattern of man's total history? Has human history a direction, a purpose, and a goal? Something like this immensely large and unclear question is before us.

Imagine to yourself that we have encountered complete success in our journey through the problems we have faced; and surely we have worked to some effect on every problem; at least we worried with, while being worried by, these problems. The measure of our success is marked by an approximate knowledge of where we stand with respect to human freedom, value, truth, beauty, and ethical goodness; we have even broken through the isolation which surrounds our modern lives, finding a relation between ourselves, and some pattern, with which we can identify, within our corporate life. But should our success have been as considerable as I now pretend, our account is not complete. And if you had thought our task almost at its end, the thought was very

322

wrong. We still have a course to run, and the way seems even more difficult than before. Why are we not finished?

Any change or development within society, any progress or any regress, refers beyond itself. It had its origin in developing patterns prior to itself; it has its end in a future which lies beyond our time. Here are we marching bravely, or riding in air-conditioned comfort, through the maze of patterns marking out this fateful century. We occupy a certain space and a certain time. Americans occupy more spaces in succession than do most other peoples. We might journey to Rome, spending half an hour in its crumbling Coliseum, fitting ourselves with the solidity and dignity of a Ceasar into the approximate space once occupied by his august person. This we could do, but we could never fit into his span of time. We could fit into the space of Galileo, dropping objects from the ever more widely leaning Tower of Pisa, testing his law of falling bodies; but we should have done our testing at a later time. We have come upon the fact of temporal passage. Its complicated patterning has worked its way into precision, almost to the "period" which ends this sentence, lying just eight, now six, now four, now two words hence. The countdown is continuous in our world, leaving a perfectly definite past and, if the results of our first discussion are to be accepted, a somewhat indefinite future still to come. And we stand always between this "before" and "after."

Our society had its origin in other societies before its time; our society, it would appear, will help to provide a point of origin for societies which will be successor to our own. There would seem to be no ground for the moving claim, "There will always be an England" — or a France, or even an America, unless we learn to succeed where all the wisdom of the past has failed. It is no longer, then, the principles of a nation which are before us. Our reach leaps radically beyond such former bounds. Our attention has been confined to the human other-than-oneself, extending several thousand miles in space, and several hundred years in time. We were concerned with nothing but a segment of the awesome span which is before us, a segment in cross-section which we had lifted out, held up, and turned around for the resolving of our former problem. Well, we must extend our minds. And should one fear great heights and distances, it may be dizzying, standing where we are, trying to determine how we relate to all of this. How far must our interest now extend? The span to which we must attend calls to mind our most encompassing notion of society, the totality we had called by the name of "culture," its dimensions vast in space, extending millenia in time.

"And how does my life relate to all of this? It simply doesn't," either of us might say. We might intone with another American, "The past is a bucket of ashes." You may shrug your shoulders: "My concern is with the present; I draw the boundaries close in space and time; what lies beyond the boundary is beyond my interest and comprehension." The answer treats history as very alien to human life. Many persons in this part of the Western world discount what lies behind them in the past. And yet the whole history of Western culture has led precisely to the exemplary individual which is yourself. This achievement of the Western world should spark your interest in our total past. The lives of those kings, nobles, and admirals of our family trees, plus the ancestor who came over on the Mayflower, that largest ocean-going vessel of any time, traced two hundred generations back into the past, would extend to the origin of all that is most valuable in our Western culture. And as these forms of culture were in their process of development, the inmates of debtors' prisons, as I have said, the slaves, serfs, deckhands, plus the forebear who went through Ellis Island, making up our personal ancestries, were living with almost as much intensity as we live today. If our total Western history is spanned by the two hundred acts of personal generation leading to ourselves, history can not be alien to our natures. Two hundred people might crowd into one's living room, supposing the symphony orchestra of our faraway discussion had packed its stands and gone away. In scientific honesty, I must admit, four hundred people would seem to be required to constitute one's personal regress. Well, these ghostly generations could stand side by side in your back yard. Such visitation by one's relatives would be unnerving in more than a single sense. But my point is simply this: We know more families by name than are required to trace our ancestry back four thousand years to the first faint premonitions of the Western world. History alien to your life? It is your life. The limit of our interest should not be confined too closely to the present.

And man is as much an historical creature, as he is a social creature, an ethical creature, or whatever other groupings may be found to be appropriate.

Man, the Historical Creature

Earlier, we had spoken of man as a "symbolific creature." This description blends into our present topic. We had spoken of how the world for man is packed with signs, of his penchant for the kind of sign called "symbol." Symbols are, of course, used in the construction of any written history; and history, simply to blurt it out, is the story of man's adventures in the world from the earliest times. Symbols are used to communicate to other men the story of man's adventures. And in another sense symbols play a role in making history possible.

It is part of the miracle and mystery of language which has made possible among men both a developing history, and a sense of history, in contrast to other beings, living and nonliving, whose whole existence and shaping stand to this as nothing more than the play of natural law. Through language men share and preserve their experiences; through language men have been able to add a new dimension to experience; indeed, its fourth dimension. They have been able to live out "hypothetical" experiences in the curious theater of mental life, reproducing in their way the conditions which would obtain were contemplation to give way to action.

"Action" is a dramatic term, and man is first the actor, dramatizing and rehearsing the role he may or may not play. Through the hypothetical experience man is able to see somewhat before and after, avoiding the sheer compulsions of the natural world. Indeed, the word "experience" already tells us of man's role, in part within and partly somehow without, the world. The "world" of man's experience is not the total world. The materials of the total world become transformed into signs for our awareness; we live behind a screen, changing the world into a set of signs, and making possible the imaginative rehearsal of alternative proposals. And the screen allows a separation between our lives and those of other creatures, making us "historical," somehow different, and, without offense to any other species, "superior" to the rest.

This same capacity allows man, even while engaged in the fateful actions which cannot be recalled, to view his action as though it were the action of another. He is a spectator even as he acts. The capacity has often been remarked: Man is able to engage in the details of living, making definite what had been indefinite before, adding then to the pattern of history; and at the same time preserv-

ing his role as onlooker. He is aware of what he is doing, and aware
of this awareness. It is man's nature to be actor and spectator at
once. It is thus the same capacity in man which makes it possible
for him to act within the world, and to understand the history which
contains this action.

In the widest sense, then, part of our essential nature is to be
discovered in the histories of our humankind. History can seem alien
only when man's natural awareness has been somehow blunted.
It is natural and proper for man to greet history, not as something
alien to be grasped from without, but rather as an extension of his
life, to be understood as he understands himself; indeed, standing
to his life as source material for coming to discover where and
what he is. And history is nothing alien, because it is saturated with
the materials of human decision and, therefore, full of purpose.

Because a sense for history is part of the nature of the creature
who lives in a time-determining sequence of events, it is appropriate from the human point of view to ask about its purpose, its direction, and its goal. And this is the material of our present problem.

The problem, as you may have noticed, is only an extension of
the problem which concerned our social principles. In both it
was, and is, our task to understand how we relate to the human
other-than-oneself. The extended scope alone has required the
posing of a separate question. We attend now not to the patterns
of separate institutions, but to the pattern of our total history. But
has history, taken as such and in the large, a pattern? It is composed of many interweaving patterns, left by the success and failure
of human purposes. This all of us admit. Indeed, we tend to think
of history as a tracing of the necessary and sufficient conditions for
the events which lie behind us. We trace the events of history,
seeking their connections. We sometimes speculate on what would
change in history had one event been otherwise. "Had Cleopatra's
nose been one inch longer. . . ." Had Blücher's cannon not been
mired on the road to Waterloo. . . ." We have developed a sensitive appreciation for the logical dependence among events. We are
even interested in the use of history to instruct and illuminate our
time. The death struggle of Athens and Sparta suggests to us a
lesson of importance for Russia and America. Should you happen
to live in New England, or take the London Times, the relation
between Athens and Rome may seem to you to be the type of the
relation between England and America. In short, we find an inner,

causal meaning for the events of history. But this meaning does not quite touch what is suggested by our problem.

Do you also find a plot within the pattern, a direction, a purpose, and a goal? You well may answer, "I do not!" Once we found a plot within the patterning of history, but we have become objective. And our gain in clear-headedness has not been made without some loss. We have lost the sense of an overarching purpose around our separate lives, working within the events of history. The loss of this portion of our early thought may not matter in the least. And yet there is a question which joins the last discussion to the one before us now.

If the purpose of one's life required the discovery of valid purposes within the movement of society, will not the purpose and meaning of society require the presence of a purpose within the larger pattern of events making up our total history? If the whole has no external meaning, does this not cause the parts to lose their meaning? And if the parts lack meaning, what happens to the meanings of our lives? Possibly, it is the threat of engaging in a meaningless existence which has led me to arrange the asking of the immense and unclear question about the meaning, direction, purpose, and goal of the total pattern. And it would be very strange to make of history a meaningless flow of happenings, when history includes the development of every human meaning.

And yet, you must be warned, some would insist our question has no meaning. At least we have been learning in our day how frequently such questions have been posed. We can ask about the purpose of a single human being. We have just completed the posing of a question which concerned the "purpose" of society. And this usage imposed a kind of strain upon the word. But the "purpose" of our total human history? Is it even possible to put the question? You must decide on the basis of what we are able to accomplish.

What the question accomplishes, if it can be asked, is to direct our attention away from the particular events of history, and toward the tendency of these events. Discussion of this tendency is called the Philosophy of History. And many thinkers have given their attention to this problem. Now, the posing of our question supposes our role as a spectator of time and existence; and should we gain an answer to the question, our answer will have some relation to the way we are to act within our history. The subtlety and importance of the problem lie in this: Our decision about the nature of history will qualify the way we act in history, possibly bringing history out at a different point.

How, then, shall we proceed? Concerned, as we are, with history, a possible approach occurs to me. Let us turn first to the history of the philosophy of history. Reviewing the basic attitudes toward history will furnish material for our work; and their chronology will reveal a changing point of view within the west. And since we have gained our current problem by extension, we might also extend more widely the analysis of our last discussion. In all of this we may discover the valid elements from which to build our own philosophy of history. We turn then to the vast historical sweep, to the history of the philosophy of history within the Western world.

Fragmentary Sketches in the Philosophy of History

I. Fate and Recurrence

We cannot speak of a philosophy of history among the Greeks; but in the conjunction of two views we can find an attitude toward history which helped to shape their thought. The first theme derives from tragedy. It is the thought of fate, an inscrutable, face-less power, working in the world, binding the gods as well as men, standing behind the mask of comedy as well as tragedy, bringing events to an appropriate conclusion with a consistency of its own. Man must, hence, walk carefully on the scene of history; even good fortune can be pushed beyond its proper bounds; and who among us lacks the tragic flaw? "Nothing to excess" was the prime motto of the age. The second theme, lying beside the first — the two not woven into a doctrine — was the view of eternal recurrence, time moving in cycles through the great world year. And in these cycles societies had risen and declined repeatedly. The human tendency was to find one's own society in decline, and the golden age some-where in the past. This expectation about the past would continue until, appropriately enough, man's backward glance would find this golden age among the Greeks themselves. But the working of fate, and cycles of recurrence, have no discernible purpose. And pes-simism is an easy consequence of this and many other views.

But in that great change called the Christianizing of the West the nameless gained a name; the faceless power became the face of God; and the cycle of time became transformed into the line of his advance.

II. Universal Purpose

This did not happen all at once; but as it happened history was invested with a purpose beyond all human purposes. The force behind history became a person, beyond all human persons, as ethical properties were added to the dramatic properties of fate. History thus became a scene of promise, and of judgment. For the first time history had a goal. It was the blessed city, the good society, the kingdom. Somehow through appalling tragedies and amazing triumphs, through the wreck of human purposes and the overturn of kingdoms, a plan, a pattern, was developing, and the goal of history was fixed.

This is the philosophy of history traditional to the West. Nor is it implausible to see in history a working of purposes not our own; something certainly stands against our purposes; it is as though the purposes of history were not quite consonant with our own. It is not completely inappropriate to think of a more universal purpose acting within our total human history, an actor-spectator like ourselves but with purposes of its own. The view has been expressed with many variations; sometimes, as with the Greeks, perfection lay within the past; sometimes, though in the future, its coming could not be by man's, but only God's design, and not within the scope of history as we know it. In whatever version, its power upon our minds has been immense.

But certain difficulties were to become apparent in the view. If every event in history is within the providence of God, then the collapse of every nation, and every tragic happening, must be read as a consequence of his judgment. Very subtle adjustments would be required to keep the view in balance. The more evil nation, it had been admitted very early, was often allowed to serve as the instrument of judgment upon a nation less evil than itself. Why? Something inscrutable remains within this view; the purposes of God are often hidden. It was agreed that good could be brought from evil. And to keep evil from the ultimate purpose a complex doctrine had to be maintained, relating the freedom and urge toward evil of man's lesser purposes with the purposes of God. But truth is often complex!

Even so, the collapse of nations, and many tragic happenings, could often be explained more readily by reference to natural causes. The collapse of a nation could sometimes be more easily understood as the consequence of plague than of the will of God. The place of rats and lice, says Zinsser, should not be underestimated in explaining the rise and fall of nations, and the kaleidoscopic pattern of historic change.[1] Yet in the most sacred of traditions plagues have been held to be part of the judgment of God in history. The modern mind is shaping when plague seems to relate more exactly to conditions of sanitation and of disease. In addition to rats and lice the factors of climate, temperature, food supply, technology, and material resources can serve as explanation of the collapse or triumph of human purposes within the scene of history. Volcanic eruption, flood, eclipse, thunder and lightning — each related at some time to the divine working — were increasingly drawn within the boundaries of natural explanation.

The scientific temper increased in strength, featuring the "efficient cause" of Aristotle, the sense of physical conditions producing effects, and tending always more forcibly to restrict the sense of "final cause," or purpose, to the human realm alone. But it was exactly the purpose not our own from which was formed our traditional attitude toward history.

Natural explanations increased in power and God became remote from history. It is surely no coincidence that the age which produced the vigorous rise of this scientific temper was also the age in which the popular view of Deism arose. In this view God was recognized as the craftsman of the universe, setting its mighty frame, establishing its principles, and retiring behind the scenes to allow the machine to run its course.

And in that age more than one man of history, not yet a modern historian, could be found who would have given the answer of Laplace, had you asked of history the question Napoleon asked about astronomy. "Where does the idea of God fit into your explanation of history?" "Sire, I have no need of that hypothesis."

The power of knowledge had forced this remoteness of the divine from history. Suppose, then, one were simply to remove the idea of God from the traditional philosophy of history, leaving all the rest unchanged. History would have a similar direction, and a similar goal. But what power could now ensure progress toward

[1] Hans Zinsser, *Rats, Lice and History* (Boston: Little, Brown and Co., 1938).

that goal? Here is a surprise! The power of knowledge, which had forced the remoteness of God from history, replaced the universal purpose. Knowledge became the engine of our human progress.

III. Progress

Consider the source of our present-day encyclopedia, placing a premium upon the vast collection of human knowledge! This enterprise, offering culture by the page and a premium every month, had its origin in the eighteenth century, and from man's belief in knowledge as the instrument of progress, leading toward the good society. The philosophers who contributed to this effort were known as the Encyclopaedists; and to list those connected with the project, those sympathetic to it, or those allied with it in their views, would be to call the roll of the philosophers of the age. Of course, as in any roll call, some would not respond — among them David Hume. The Encyclopaedia was published in the middle of the eighteenth centry in the belief that knowledge would lead to goodness. Its publication did not immediately produce the good society. Among these men the philosophy of history is centered around our progress in the natural understanding of the world.

It is somewhat difficult to list the doctrines of a group, working in different countries and at somewhat different times, even if agreeing in the main. But their general agreement can be stated in four points. You will recognize each point as having had power in recent times, and possibly over our own minds.

(1) History is progressing toward a state of perfect happiness; and progress in history is a natural and necessary product of its working. (Some viewed progress not as inevitable, but only as desirable and probable.)

(2) But why, we may ask, is progress natural and necessary? Because the evils of human existence are due to ignorance. The increase of human knowledge is, therefore, our most pressing need.

(3) Further, there is an "indissoluble union" of liberty, justice, equality, and the advance of knowledge in all its forms. The spread of knowledge will provide a force for change, leading to the end of history. Because human nature is identical in its essence, and men are perfectible, the evils of inequality, so powerful in the past, will gradually be overcome. As reason gains power over instinct and superstition, we become more equal — equally good and equally

perfect. (There are, of course, differences in the degree of optimism on this, as on the other, points.)

(4) For more than one of these philosophers the end of history is described in detail as a universal society, including all of mankind, living in harmony and happiness, in liberty and equality, according to the dictates of reason, and with their human possibilities fully realized.

You will notice the optimism of the view, possibly finding traces of it in your own emotions and loyalties. The movement toward the good society was expected to occur gradually and progressively; in general, these men did not believe in revolution. The force of truth would work quietly within society, slowly leading humanity toward its natural and necessary (or probable) envisioned goal. And yet within the country most saturated with this view of a gradual and constructive progress, there occurred a revolution. The reasons for its coming were many; among them were precisely the ideas of progress and of the planned society; joined to these were the doctrines of our social philosophers, and principally, the doctrines of Rousseau including his idea of the right of revolution. In the mingling of these views the object of revolution became the free, the rational, the planned society, based on progress in human knowledge. In evidence I offer the statement in the preface to the French Declaration of 1791: " . . . ignorance, forgetfulness or contempt of the rights of man are the sole cause of the public miseries and of the corruption of governments. . . ."

Reason had its day and reason failed, leading to the invention of Dr. J. I. Guillotin, and numerous books, including one by Burke on the conservative society, and the excellence of the unplanned plan of social ordering. The inability of reasonable men to control the revolution may be explained in many ways. The pressures exerted on the country were extreme; every army in Europe, including that of the Roman church, was converging on the French. But explanations are not really to the point. Whatever the reasons, the point was the failure of this revolution to achieve the promised good society. What the revolution achieved, of course, was the Imperial Order of Napoleon, posing as the liberator of Europe, directing revolutionary power to his personal ends; and yet, along the way, destroying in Europe the remnants of the feudal system.

Knowledge, the good society, and revolution — the blending of these themes can be discerned in a passage from Cabanis. Even as the era of Napoleon dawned, he was still ecstatic over the human prospect:

> You philosophers whose studies are directed to the improvement and happiness of the race, you no longer embrace vain shadows. Having watched, in alternating moods of hope and sadness, the great spectacle of our Revolution, you now see with joy the termination of its last act; you will see with rapture this new era, so long promised to the French people, at last open, in which all the benefits of nature, all the creations of genius, all the fruits of time, labour, and experience will be utilised, an era of glory and prosperity in which the dreams of your philanthropic enthusiasm should end by being realised.[2]

This revolution would be tried again, and yet again. But its failure set one of the conditions leading to our modern world. It is important to register the shock which the coming of this revolution, and its failure, had upon our world. I think it caused a shift in the subtle balance of man's thoughts about himself, and of his prospects. I think it led to a downgrading of the power of reason in human life. For the eighteenth century, as we have seen, reason was held to be, by and large, the instrument of our possible advance. The confidence in reason was extremely high, following the unbroken succession of its triumphs within the fields of science.

The nineteenth-century reaction, taking everything to extremes, spawned at least three attitudes toward history. We will notice a view in which science, not man's common reason, becomes the agent of advance. A second view restored the working of the universal purpose, but within a more troubled course of history. A third view insisted that the revolution, leading to the end of history, must be more extreme.

IV. The Law of the Three Stages, Comte

After the debacle of the French one might place the blame for failure upon the fragmentary character of human knowledge. The good society will come, but only with a vast and systematic increase in our knowledge. This nineteenth-century view is most similar in spirit to the eighteenth-century view of progress; both viewed

---

[2] J. B. Bury, *The Idea of Progress* (New York: The Macmillan Company, 1932), p. 216. Reprinted by permission of Dover Publications, Inc., New York 10, New York.

history under the aspect of human knowledge. If the greatest obstacle lying between man's present state and the good society is the power of custom, reinforced by habit, superstition, ignorance, and inertia, the path into the future will require a more antiseptic agent, a Positive Philosophy.

(1) From the earliest times men have marked out "periods" in the course of history; any philosopher who believes in progress will find in history stages of development. And if the lines were often drawn too firmly, still such demarcations allowed an increase in our understanding. Comte found three stages through which history had to pass. His stages mark a natural progression in human understanding. It is the third stage which contains the power to advance the human race. The world is first explained by reference to actions of the gods; in this stage theology furnishes the explanations which men accept. The highest point this stage can reach is monotheism, the explanation of the world lying in a single being. In the second stage men advance to philosophy. In philosophizing men frame "personified abstractions." Men classify and then explain by referring an event to its abstract term; thus, language becomes a substitute for knowledge. The conception of Nature is the highest achievement of the second stage. Only in the third stage do we come to knowledge. The scientific stage yields genuine knowledge in the discovery of the laws which govern phenomena. The Positive Philosophy will rest upon scientific knowledge. Men have arrived at the third stage, and yet theological, metaphysical, and scientific explanations stand side by side within their minds, engendering confusion. To insure our possible advance the confusion must be removed; this can be done by recognizing the early stages as outworn, and by accepting only scientific answers to scientific questions.

(2) Science itself is in a process of development. Every science has passed through its three stages. And the scheme of the sciences, says Comte, writing in the early nineteenth century, is not complete. Science develops first the abstract disciplines, gradually encompassing more and more of the concrete world. The first science to be developed was Mathematics, the fully abstract discipline. Others followed in its train. The science still to be provided is Sociology. In gaining the laws of human behavior Sociology will include every other science. It is the developed whole of science which will provide the instrument of our advance.

(3) In advancing to the third stage of explanation, and in completing the development of the sciences, we shall come naturally to the needed reorganization of society. "Ideas govern the world, or throw it into chaos; . . . all social mechanism rests upon Opinions. The great political and moral crisis that societies are now undergoing is shown by a rigid analysis to arise out of intellectual anarchy." [3] Let scientific knowledge increase; induce in the members of society a scientific attitude; and men will "spontaneously" direct their course to the planned and rational society. "This is the way to put an end to the revolutionary crisis which is tormenting the civilized nations of the world." [4]

Here is the origin of positivism, its power still growing in the modern world. The doctrine is more severe than the eighteenth-century confidence in reason. By a kind of mental discipline we must eliminate from our minds theology and metaphysics, turning to scientific knowledge, and realizing the essentially meaningless nature of man's early attempts to understand his world.

The second response we are to note contains the point of view most typical of the nineteenth century. The figure of Napoleon rose in majesty. As if in response Carlyle writes and lectures his *Heroes and Hero Worship*, praising the genius, the great man able to show other men (we, who are the valets of the world) their place and duties, leading them to the destiny which the genius alone can sense. In this century Hegel could write of the state as the final object of our loyalty. Romanticism with its emphasis upon will and feeling replaced the age of reason. The new century, I claim, was marked by a lack of confidence in the power of reason; it was an age of imperialism, the age initiating bigness in industry. What attitude toward history would be appropriate for one who was part of this reaction?

V. *The Endless Dialectic, Hegel*

Fate, purpose, and progress mingle in this view; and progress comes through conflict. Hegel even stresses the place of reason in the world; but this is not the eighteenth-century reason; his is a "cunning" reason. The world is "reasonable," yet something devious is to be found within the world, and in the movement of its history;

[3] Harriet Martineau, *Comte's Positive Philosophy* (London: George Bell and Sons, 1896), Vol. I, p. 15.
[4] *Ibid.*, p. 17.

and Hegel must have been delighted with Napoleon, seeking nothing beyond his own prestige, and thus destroying feudalism. In Hegel's terms this would be part of the "cunning" of reason in history. Here are the essential themes, making up his attitude toward history:

(1) History has a direction and a goal. We progress toward this goal, and yet our advance is within a never terminating flow of time. What is our direction; what is our goal? ". . . the History of the World is nothing but the development of the Idea of Freedom." [5]

(2) We try to realize our purposes in the world in the presence of conflict and opposition. Indeed, the world with its particular purposes is "the bacchanalian revel where not a soul is sober." [6] And yet through the conflict and opposition of the world, as a result of and despite our particular purposes, a process of development is occurring.

(3) In addition, then, to our purposes, there is another factor. The history of the world is the march of "the realization of" Spirit; so, "what has happened, and is happening every day, is not only not 'without God,' but is essentially His Work." [7]

(4) The process of history has a pattern. Anything which takes place in history will be partial, one-sided, and incomplete. For example, think of the history of philosophy. An insight occurs; it is announced by a philosopher and, meeting the needs of his age, becomes established in the world. This point of view we shall call the *thesis*. But because this point of view is necessarily partial and incomplete, its very presence in the world calls forth the appearance of its opposite. The opposing view we shall call its *antithesis*. But the antithesis is also partial and incomplete, requiring the thesis to which it is opposed. Thesis and antithesis stand in the world, an opposition in our thought requiring resolution. A third point of view is now required which will remove their opposition, while saving what is valid in each view. This point of view is the *synthesis*. The synthesis becomes a new thesis in the world. And although not partial in the same way as the preceding thesis, it will be in its own way inadequate. The new thesis also calls for its antithesis; and the process, called a *dialectic*, will continue. And

[5] G. W. F. Hegel, *The Philosophy of History*, trans. J. Sibree (New York: Dover Publications, 1956), p. 456.

[6] G. W. F. Hegel, *The Phenomenology of Mind*, trans. J. B. Baillie (New York: The Macmillan Company, 1910), Vol. I, p. 44.

[7] Hegel, *op. cit.*, p. 457.

there is no stopping point. Each resolution is a step in human progress leading toward the goal of history; but the goal is never fully reached. Hegel found this movement through opposition everywhere, even in the history of nations. In their successive rise to power, conflict, and replacement by another, they are terms for the working of the dialectic. This movement through opposition provided Hegel the key, as he thought, for understanding history.

The easy optimism of the eighteenth century has disappeared; the view is more starkly realistic than any but the first Greek view of fate. The goal of history beckons, but is not to be attained. If this is to be our view of history we might fall into a thorough pessimism. In this view, no sooner is a thing established in the world than it at once is challenged, and at last will perish. And even if advance is possible, still the goal recedes as the dialectic and history continue on their way. Pessimism was not at all unknown in the century within which Hegel wrote.

The most direct response to the failure of the French revolt is to be found within the third of our nineteenth-century attitudes toward history. This view retains the eighteenth-century optimism, expressing its nineteenth-century severity in another manner. The failure of the French revolt left many questioning minds in Europe. Why had the revolution not succeeded? One acceptable answer seemed to be that the revolution of the French was no more than a partial revolution. A revolution with power to bring the good society must be more complete; the good society requires drastic measures of human reconstruction. Among the rest, something must be done about the property relations which divide men's loyalties. Babeuf had made this claim while the revolution was coursing to its imperial end. The claim became respectable.

What if, looking at history, one were to find exactly the kind of conflict and opposition discerned by Hegel? What if, at the same time, one should retain the vision of the eighteenth-century philosophers about the goal of history: A state of culture, yielding happiness, and shared by men living in liberty and equality? Then a different view would be required, one which might even use the dialectic of thesis and antithesis, letting it lead to this promised good society. And if men have worked their way through all of the basic oppositions, the dialectic might stop its working, once this state is reached.

VI. The Terminating Dialectic, Marx

We should then have a terminating dialectic. And something close to this was the attitude of Marx, reared in Hegelian philosophy, and yet with sympathies for the eighteenth-century philosophers. I find these elements in his point of view.

(1) The basic conflicts in society have been struggles among social classes. The dialectic of history centers around class struggle. (The discussion of historical change no longer features national states, as was the case for Hegel; and the "classes" of society cut across the boundaries of the nation.)

(2) This opposition in society has been the same in character throughout history; no matter how its forms have varied, it has always contained these elements: oppressor and oppressed. The opposition has "each time ended, either in a revolutionary reconstitution of society at large, or in the common ruin of the contending classes." [8] (The dialectic does not always, then, work successfully toward a synthesis.)

(3) The conflict in the modern world grows increasingly more obvious. It was to some extent concealed in earlier societies by their elaborate social ordering. "In ancient Rome we have patricians, knights, plebeians, slaves; in the Middle Ages, feudal lords, vassals, guild-masters, journeymen, apprentices, serfs; in almost all of these classes, again, subordinate gradations." [9] In the modern world the thesis and antithesis are: capitalist and worker, bourgeoisie and proletariat.

(4) Conflicts among classes have their natural instrument of resolution. It is revolution; and because the modern conflict is international, the revolution must be international. And, with the successful revolution, the opposition of oppressor and oppressed will have been overcome at last, and the dialectic will have reached its end.

(5) This end, and so the end of history, is the "classless society" where "the free development of each is the condition for the free development of all." [10] This end will inevitably come. (Apparently, it cannot be prevented, but it can be helped or hindered.)

[8] Karl Marx, *Communist Manifesto.* My source was Karl Marx and Frederick Engels, *Selected Works in Two Volumes* (Moscow: Foreign Languages Publishing House, 1955), Vol. I, pp. 34, 35.
[9] *Ibid.*
[10] *Ibid.*, p. 54.

One further point must be added; and some discussion must surround its statement. The note of a possible tyranny, which one discerns sometimes in the depths of human freedom, is not lacking to this view. Rousseau had mentioned briefly the occasional duty of forcing men to be free; Robespierre had justified "the despotism of freedom against tyranny." Marx took to heart the lesson.

(6) In moving toward the end of history, a stage of despotism must follow the successful revolution. The dictatorship of the worker, the dictatorship of the proletariat, must intervene.

Why must this stage intervene? It must, because our human reason is often specious in its working. Our conclusions are molded by the conditions under which we live. The whole machinery of our economic system now colors our beliefs. The excitement about human rights and human liberty, the social principles of the West, are nothing more than the mental side of capitalism. From this point of view our basic right is the right of property; and the freedom we wish is a freedom in economic matters. Because of the falseness of our reason, dictatorship is required until a new economy provides a different mental life. But why is not the view of Marx also a reflection of the same economy? He claims to have escaped by having made, which he has not, an analysis which is "scientific."

Well, notice once again this nineteenth-century substitution of a "scientific" for our "philosophic" reason. Indeed, the doctrine of the more severe revolution, calling forth the professional revolutionary, betrays its nineteenth-century origin. The scaling down of philosophic reason is evidenced by the forming of cadres, based on discipline, trained to unquestioning obedience, willing to discount the result of any private reasoning in favor of the official reasons of the cause. If decisions come down to the individual through a pyramid of command, supposedly interpreting the way to achieve the rational society in keeping with the movement of history, reason has given way once more to the pyramid of command. The goal of revolution has changed; it is no longer directed specifically toward the increase of human rights and liberties, although in this respect one finds some inconsistency in the doctrine. The conception of the good society has somehow changed. Its goal now seems to hover between a factual equality (in contrast to the "elusive" moral equality of our pattern) and the planned society in which each man, according to his capacities, is fitted or fits himself (depending upon the stage) into his proper place.

And yet, in its optimism and sense of purpose about man's place in the movement of history, this view contains a power most like the sense of a divine purpose working in events. History has a direction we can know, an end which men can reach, and a means for reaching this end. Have we a view of history the equal of this in power and meaning?

If we tend to reflect our century, we may find ourselves adhering to a different kind of view; one of two twentieth-century views may fit our beliefs. I present these views as philosophies of history, even though the author of the first considers his work an unphilosophical philosophy, the last act of philosophy in our time; and the second is a practicing historian.

VII. The Lesser Cycle, Spengler

Every view before us, except the first, has found history to be moving both upward and onward. For some the ascent was gradual and continuous; for others, it was marked by opposition, and a somewhat jagged rising line. The line of progress for Spengler is an arc which rises to its furthest point, fixed by the possibilities of its people, and then reverses its direction as decline sets in.

(1) We are to think not of world history; indeed, "the history of humanity has no meaning whatsoever"; instead, our understanding must center on the life courses of individual cultures. The plurality of cultures, and the arcs they describe, return us to our early attitude of recurrence in history.

(2) Each culture has its term; it can be compared to the cycle of the seasons — spring, summer, autumn, winter; the corresponding cycle in vegetation — the springing into life, the ripening of its fruit, and its decay; and to the cycle of organic life — birth, maturity, and the decline toward death. There have been many such cultures, their birth marked by the achievement of social unity, and their death signaled by symptoms of breakdown and dissolution.

(3) The cycle can be divided into stages: culture, strictly so called, the realization of inner possibilities; and civilization — an external expansion from the base of internal achievement. By the time a culture becomes notable it is moving toward decline.

(4) Our Western history from the Grecian age to the present includes two distinct cycles, and so two distinct cultures: Classical culture and Western culture. In the first, Greece matured the culture, and Rome the civilization. In the second, the culture was

produced in the Middle Ages and the Renaissance; and we now represent the late stages of its civilization.

(5) Because men's lives are shaped by the part of the cycle in which their lives are cast, similar happenings and attitudes are to be found at similar stages of different cultures; these are spelled out in amazing, if deceptive, detail. Generally, in the stage of culture, man's energy is directed inward; in the stage of civilization it is directed outward. The ascending movement is always marked by religion, aristocracy, and art; the descending movement is marked by "irreligion, democracy, socialism, and the great city."

(6) Modern Western man, living within the dead winter of Western civilization, has realized his inner possibilities; his art and philosophy have been achieved. Hence, his tendency can only be expansive, applying thinly the cultural stock which he has received. Man's life is now external and not internal, quantitative and not qualitative. He has become the instrument of the machine, or money (double-entry bookkeeping), and of modern propaganda, directed by the state and the great financial interests. Modern men are, hence, "rootless and futureless," lonely, and lacking in conviction. They are mass men, and spiritual nomads. All of these phenomena have occurred before; they signal the approach of dissolution. It is our destiny, then, to be Rome in the modern world, and we can have no other destiny; we must will to be this, or nothing. And, writing during the first world war, Spengler predicts the rise of Caesarism in the West.

(7) Whenever the note of recurrence is sounded, it is echoed by the thought that the best has already been. What, then, is the end of history? We can ask the question only of our own cycle of history; and the end is our death as a separate culture.[11]

Here is a possible, if unhappy, attitude toward history. In whatever sense pessimism marks our century, in that sense Spengler's view may be taken as an integral expression of our time. His attitude toward history poses a challenge no less real than that of Marx. For Spengler society in its productive period has the form of an aristocracy; common men, the "peasants" (even such as you and I), are no more than breeding stock for the production of exceptional people. And the phrase "pyramid of culture" is used with obvious

[11] Oswald Spengler, *The Decline of the West*, trans. C. F. Atkinson (New York: Alfred A. Knopf, 1926). Two volumes.

approval; finally, democracy, as we have seen, is one of the symptoms of the declining movement of a culture. Just where we have found excellence and progress, Spengler finds retrogression and the beginning of decay. Something is haunting in this prophecy (for such it is) about our time; and the danger of believing it is the risk of the self-fulfilling prophecy.

A much more careful ordering of these items is offered us by Toynbee in his amazing study of history. Because of its many similarities to the view of Spengler, let us approach our new alternative by way of comparison.

VIII. Challenge and Response, Toynbee

(1) The scene of history remains a scene of desolation. The units of the scheme are, once again, societies with their histories of genesis, development, and decline. Twenty-six societies have had their origin in the five thousand years of history known to us. Of these twenty-five have passed away, or show symptoms of decline. Only one, our Western society, remains in doubt.

(2) Once again, the distinction is drawn between the inner, qualitative growth of culture which energizes a people; and the "expansive tendency" where quantitative elements are stressed. The expansive character of society is, again, a symptom of decline.

(3) But Toynbee is very careful to point out the figurative nature of the language which attributes "life and death" to the societies comprising history. These cycles do not reflect a law of nature or of fate. The issues of life and death turn around the terms "challenge" and "response." A society must be able to meet each challenge. The challenge can issue from nature, or from other social groupings. It can arise from within or from without; and most societies have died by their own hand. The challenge is the set of obstacles, the problems, whose removal and solution is a condition for continued life and growth. The response is the adequate solution, or set of solutions, offered to this challenge. If the challenge is too great, a society will be unable to enter upon its process of development; if the challenge is too slight, it will not have to do so. The life of a society will continue to develop until it meets a challenge for which it has, and can find, no adequate response.

(4) The "response" of a society to its "challenge" has its origin not in the total group who merely transmit and imitate; but in the

society's "creative minority." Here, again, is the suggestion of a theme by Spengler.

(5) Development within society is, hence, a complex process, including successive maturation of adequate responses by the "creative minority"; acceptance of these responses by the noncreative members of society; and their successful application. Under the stress of the "challenge" the members of the creative minority retire from the pressures of the moment, and later return with a possible response. When a society cannot provide for its creative minority, or transmit its response through the social order, the society forfeits the possibility of future adequate response.

(6) When the harmonious functioning of challenge, withdrawal and return, and response, breaks down a society is in decline. Disaffection then spreads through the members of society; society becomes polarized into dissident groupings; the creative minority will rely on its past achievements, or seek to become the dominant power within society; the mass of society will become incapable of change, their institutions encased in the inertia of the past, a loyalty to past forms making impossible their acceptance of an adequate response should it be offered; in addition, significant numbers of the mass may cease to feel any identity with, or share in, their society; meanwhile, the unsolved problems will exert continuous pressure upon the social structure, and successful response will become less likely as the possible advance of society is delayed. The society is now in a condition of disintegration, and moves toward breakdown; the breakdown may be delayed by various measures, enforcing conformity upon its members; but the presence of the unsolved problems disallows force as an adequate solution.

(7) Religion is an important factor in shaping the unity of spirit, necessary to the formation of societies; it has sometimes been a factor in the revival of a society showing symptoms of decline; it has been a factor in the creation of new societies from the death of those in decline. But this working is somewhat mysterious and not subject to prediction.

(8) And if we are to trust the evidence, it would seem that we in the West are in decline. We fit the pattern Toynbee finds in all declining civilizations. There is some slight hope of spiritual rebirth by means of our ancestral religion. There is some slight hope of a new world religion, sharing in the creation of a world society —

but this would be a new society. And the odds, for Toynbee as for Spengler, favor the decline of Western society. We, too, move toward death.[12]

The view is subtle, and developed with care. We have not done justice, of course, to Toynbee's monumental work. But we have provided a sample pattern for our thinking. And it would be a very attractive complement to our view to think of society in depth, recognizing different functions among its parts, and the need for a complex functioning to effect any advance through time. But Spengler finds no goal for history; nor had Toynbee until recent years, when he began to find its goal in God. With this he returns to the traditional Western view.

Casting About for a Philosophy of History

We have sketched eight possible attitudes toward history. And many of these views are still at work among us.

The lives of ordinary men continue to be energized by the sense of a universal purpose, although for many this sense has become somewhat enfeebled by the events of our present century; among the more extreme, and no wonder, one begins to hear again the murmuring of a coming and final judgment upon mankind. The view of necessary progress swept along through the eighteenth century, was still maintained — although by a small portion of the philosophic world — in the nineteenth century; and has run into its roughest weather in our day. The attitude of Comte has intensified within our time, although the "indissoluble union" of liberty, justice, equality, and scientific knowledge has dissolved away. If the positivists of our day have an attitude toward history, it turns around the claim that only science can contribute to man's advance. Accepting only scientific answers, allowing only scientific questions, regarding the assertions of theology, metaphysics, and poetry as equally expressive and equally meaningless, this view has spread widely among

[12] Arnold J. Toynbee, A *Study of History* (London: Oxford University Press, 1933–1954). Ten volumes. In shortened form, see Arnold J. Toynbee, A *Study of History*, abridgment of Volumes I–VI by D. C. Somerwell (London: Oxford University Press, 1947).

philosophers. And it was essentially Hegel's philosophy of history, recognizing the supremacy of the state, which informed two European adventures in the leader-principle during the first half of our century; of course, other nineteenth- and early twentieth-century figures added to, and modified, the view (Carlyle, Gobineau, Nietzsche, Pareto). The Marxist philosophy of history has revealed its power, and seems to advance in at least half of the world. And the claim of Spengler, supported in fact by Toynbee, that we have come to the age of the masses, to the quantitative and expansive stage of culture, cannot be lightly dismissed. We do seem to find this analysis applying to our world; whether or not this fact marks decline is, of course, another question.

Of one thing I am certain: We cannot counter the Marxist philosophy of history with our widespread feeling of drifting through a meaningless sequence of events. At least we must be able to discern within our own strand of history something of its proper direction, and of its proper goal. Let me try, as a kind of substitute for you, to fix an attitude toward history by sifting through the eight views which are before us. The decisions we have made on other problems will serve as a kind of screen, excluding any elements which cannot belong to our authentic point of view.

Purpose. We can no longer identify each happening in the world with the will of God. And yet if history is not to be a meaningless sequence of events, the working out of broad purposes through great spans of time cannot be sheer illusion. This view, if possible in any sense, would be possible for us only in a carefully thought out form. The problem is difficult, and while this element is consistent with, it may not be necessary to, our point of view.

Progress. If the twentieth century has taught us anything at all, it has taught us that progress is not an inevitable consequence of history. The manner in which we tremble on the edge of barbarism is evidence enough. And yet, once again, part of our philosophy of history must be a conception of the good society with man involved in the construction of its plan. Movement toward this goal is what we mean by progress. And if we are not to place our sole confidence in revolution, we must believe in education — better education than we have ever known — to serve as one, at least, of the engines of our progress.

Dialectic. Neither the endless nor the terminating dialectic reflects the chief feature of our history. The pendulum, to be sure, swings back and forth. There is, indeed, a dialectic going on. But the important contributions come from those who do not swing with this pendulum, who contribute to a cumulative movement. And in the history of societies there are many more elements than the conflict noticed by Hegel and by Marx. There exists, for example, the long accumulation of gains which need not be sacrified, and which do not crush each other out. The presence of conflict in history relates more exactly to our social philosophy. And we have recognized opposition as a feature of our social functioning; it is our method to raise the conflict of forces to the level of deliberation, transforming each conflict into a mental contradiction to be handled by debate, substituting the interplay of thought for the interplay of force. This solution favors the entrenched and powerful forces of our social world? Indeed, but this is the risk of the game; and a principle is not invalid simply because it can be misused! More generally, the problem is to resolve conflicts into contrasts, preserving a basic unity within society. An essential element, I think, of our natural philosophy of history is an emphasis on the possibilities of cumulative advance through time.

Positivism.   If knowledge is an important goal among us, still I think it is not part of our wisdom to regard scientific knowledge as the whole of knowledge. Indeed, part of our modern crisis lies in the pursuit of scientific knowledge, as if it were self-sufficient and self-justifying. We have been following, insensibly, the program of Comte, "transcending" our theology and philosophy; and throwing away the ladder by which we have made our climb. The result has not been admirable in every way. The three stages are to be found in history. But how ideas, capable of carrying the development of the forms of culture toward scientific knowledge, can be considered to have no meaning is beyond my comprehension. This account among us has for long, I think, been overdrawn.

Revolution.   Part of our philosophy of history must allow for revolution; it is an essential part of our Western social thought. And we have drawn a distinction between the authentic and the spurious revolution. But to make this *the* instrument for achieving the good society, to make the revolution so severe that it cancels all rights and liberties, is to move beyond — or rather, to regress behind — our pattern. Revolution has great importance when it comes to hewing the top from some political pyramid; but to achieve the good society a more patient and nerveless kind of work is needed.

Necessity. A number of our views — the view of progress, of the terminating dialectic, and of Spengler's lesser cycle — all found the movement of history to its end a necessary movement. We cannot admit this concept to our view. If the end of our authentic revolution is the increase of human rights and liberties, that is, the sovereign individual, we cannot cancel out his sovereign nature in our philosophy of history. And if the sovereign individual is not a valid notion, then the first change to be made is within our list of social principles. So long as this remains an aspect of our social thought, our view of history must leave the future open. Failure is always possible. But if failure is possible so, likewise, is success. We must depart from the pessimism of Spengler without losing his concern for the peril which may face our modern world. Cultures do decay; and doubtless no society can live forever. And perhaps for a society, as for a man, it is better to live well than to live forever. But the failure within society is always a human failure; and need not have occurred when and as it did. Toynbee reflects us here; the collapse of a society is due to a failure in "response."

In all of this the elements of our attitude toward history are moving toward definitude. One can speak, properly, of a direction and a goal within our history. Progress is not inevitable, yet it must be possible. In history, rather than sheer opposition, it is our pattern to stress the possibility of cumulative advance. And since the movement of history is not inevitable we become the agents responsible for its advance. We should not be hostile to the notion of a planned society; but a plan discounting "philosophic" reason is a most suspicious plan. And of our eight views the one which best reflects our temper is the view of Toynbee. His total scheme of challenge and response, withdrawal and return, the creative minority and the transmissive majority, the possibility of breakdown and decline as a result of human failure, seems consistent with the decisions we have made thus far. Let us accept for a time the attitude toward history implicit in these themes; and see if in its terms we can spell out the more general features of our time and place in the western world. We turn, then, to an extension of the analysis of our last discussion.

Trough and Crest

Thinking back to the single opposition we had stressed as the center of our social problem, do you not notice in this opposition a strangely inverse movement? The individual emerged as sovereign just as the functional pyramids were appearing with their serried ranks of privilege and obligation — in aspect like, although more efficient than, the feudal structures from which man had gained his freedom. In this sense we have an intersecting trough and crest in these strands of Western history. As the political pyramids were being levelled into the form of a plain, the functional pyramids, making their entry as though on cue, began to stand within this plain: Giza reborn and in the modern world.

Now, how could this opposition have occurred? Well, let us see. The application of philosophy to the social conditions of our lives produced the plain. The application of science to the physical conditions of our lives (that is, technology) required, again, a pyramid. Now, science and philosophy, what are these? They are different aspects of what we may call the "cultural fund." Spengler called it the "thought-stock" of a people. Very well; in the most general sense, then, the conditions which brought the one also required the other. Our modern world — and the opposition we have noted — has emerged from an application of the cultural fund to the conditions of our lives. The problem of our last discussion was the presence of this inverse movement, giving us no rest. At least, we might have been at peace were we pyramidal through and through; but we were not, and we are not.

What, then, is the cultural fund? It is the pattern of developing thought which began in ancient times; it is the total deposit of our science, philosophy, fine arts, history, and the principles of our arts of living. And our modern world has come from the application of various portions of this fund to modern life. Who, then, has been responsible for that aspect of our world which by our modern estimate has contributed so much to our advance; namely, the raising of our human level? Since this advance has been a result of theory, applied to the physical conditions of our lives, the answer is simple and unequivocal.

It is the "intellectual." His intellect has been the instrument of our advance. And who is this "intellectual?" He is — let us see if we can still recall — the suspect "highbrow," for so long considered the expendable, the barely admissible, member of society; and whose position — for all the wrong reasons — is slowly altering for the better at the present time. Suspect highbrow? A second point now stands out in startling clarity: he is part of the "creative minority" of our society. And his achievement in our behalf is the most convincing possible justification of the reflective life.

Now, how does this man differ from the rest of us? He differs by relating himself not to any specialized institutional concern, but to the cultural fund itself. He is strongly drawn to words and thought, to languages and still more mysterious symbolism. Words and symbols are, of course, our means of retaining in the present the experiences of the past. Devotion to the cultural fund allows anyone to live not merely in the immediate moment, but more broadly in the thoughts and experiences of the total human race. The richness of every generation is available to his mind; and every generation has made its further contribution. Our intellectual enters, in a sense, the pattern of developing thought which had its origin in ancient times, and he extends the pattern; as various aspects of this pattern develop toward fruition, he is able to discern their possible relevance to our present world. Technology is, thus, only the most obvious application of this fund; the technicians of our present age have been highly honored, as we firmly grasped this obvious point. And yet theirs has been by far the lesser work. The bright conceptions which they apply to life derive from men much less practical than themselves, living among esoteric symbols, their minds fascinated by pure theory, discerning but caring not at all for any applications. And pure theory lies at the base of the technological world in all its aspects. The intellectual, then, by relating himself to, and extending, the cultural fund has made possible this immense advance in the conditions of our lives.

And now let us ask: Under what conditions has the intellectual been able — through enrichment of our cultural fund — to bring us to this moment? The answer is simplicity itself. Artists created, philosophers pondered, scientists experimented, standing on the platform of special privilege. And this has been the case, regardless of whether one is thinking of the great Greek talent in this respect, or of the Middle Ages, or the Renaissance. Those who have wrought so magnificently with the cultural fund have been either themselves of the privileged classes, or were released from the toil required of others, and raised to this high level. They were drawn hand over hand to the platform of special privilege by patrons, impressed with the possibilities of our fund, even though not themselves capable of the tasks which it imposed; or (to refer one last time to the astonishing heel-in-the-face theory of social ordering) they made their way to this platform by sheer intellectual strength and cunning. All past ages have added to the amazing and subtle artistic, scientific, and philosophic culture to which the twentieth century is heir. And the plain fact is that the cultural fund, and indeed our culture, is in danger because of the excellence and vigor of its working in recent times.

How are we to understand this claim? The final and most amazing result of modern technology, of the applications of science to the physical conditions of our world, has been the achievement of the ultimate weapon. Its immense power, as we know, makes possible for the first time in history the efficient liquidation of an entire people. One who possesses an ultimate weapon can issue an ultimate threat; and an ultimate threat is ultimately a command, and related to the level of command. The achievement of the ultimate weapon is an interesting translation of knowledge into power, following the line of Lord Bacon's familiar phrase. And when Bacon's maxim is joined (as Castell has joined this maxim) to the no less familiar saying of Lord Acton, "Power corrupts; and absolute power corrupts absolutely," the danger in this weapon, not only to the rest of the world but to its possessors, can be sensed. And the presence of this weapon in the arsenals of two nations makes quite possible for the first time in human history the liquidation of the human race. I suppose it is our hope that Lord Acton may be partly wrong; absolute power in the hands of two nations may not prove corrupting to its possessors. It may, indeed (this is the hope), "critically alter" the role of force as a social instrument. It may elevate the role of social principles in the building of relations among nations. But the presence of a hope does not remove the danger. In this paragraph I have been referring to a discussion offered by Castell. Here is his version of the matter:

> From time immemorial men have faced the possibility that the use of force is, humanly speaking, their last court of appeal. And here is a weapon which, if it got out of hand, could nullify the use of force by liquidating both those who use it and those against whom it is used. If that possibility is there, the human

predicament is altered. To be useable a force must remain subject to your control. Otherwise you need access to a second and greater force to enable you to control the first one. If, finally, you produced one which you could not control, the role of force, as a last court of appeal in human affairs, would thereby be critically altered. . . .

The knowledge that no one can stop you only sharpens the question whether what you are doing is right. . . . To discover that you are immune to everything but self-criticism is to stand more than ever in need of philosophy.[13]

Achievement of the ultimate weapon has brought the West, and all mankind, to a significant and critical juncture in the movement of our history. But this is no more than half of my argument. The applications of science, this single portion of our cultural fund, to human life, have resulted in the ultimate weapon. What has been the result of the application of philosophy to the conditions of our lives? This portion of the cultural fund has been applied with much less brilliance, and yet the consequences have been quite as critical in their impact upon our lives. The application of philosophy to the social and political conditions of our lives resulted in the conception of a planned society, a conception of what society ought to be. Indeed, part of the insight of the developing cultural fund was just this: The full life should be the privilege of every man. Here was the origin of our planar theory of society. It was to be a rational society, where knowledge would obliterate the superstitions of the past, removing this support for the pyramids of special privilege. It was to be a society of individual fulfillment, of individuality. The destruction of the pyramid with its serried levels was to be the prelude to the good society, where for the first time this development might be possible.

And yet it was, as I have said, the platform at the top of the human pyramid which provided the support on which the intellectual was able to develop the forms of human culture. It was the gifted intellectual who discovered how groundless was the society which treated the bulk of its members as inferiors. The gifted ones discerned the importance of equality, and their discovery now threatens culture in a second manner. How can this be? The premise of equality, and the principles of technology, have lifted great

---

[13] Alburey Castell, *Science as a Goad to Philosophy* (Stockton, Calif.: College of the Pacific, 1953), pp. 12, 13.

masses of the members of society from their position of inferiority, so that they now recognize no superior. They have assumed power as the people, but not yet as persons. This is part of the thesis of Ortega, the Spanish philosopher, in his *Revolt of the Masses;* so far, I think his contention must be granted, although the truth of his claim is only one aspect of the point. As a result the gifted one, who had until now developed the forms of culture, is at present lost among the masses — and we arrive at the point I have in mind. He was not lost before; the mass had furnished the platform for his free activity.

It is as though, during an entertainment, the star performer at the top of a fleshly human pyramid, enjoying the plaudits of the audience, were to feel the human structure beneath him giving way, so that no longer was there top or bottom, but merely heap. Now the star, the exemplary individual, has no platform, and does not know his place. Of course, in many ways the figure is misleading. The plaudits given the exceptional person came from others on the platform, or from the structure which furnished his support, not from any added audience. There is no added audience, unless it be God himself. The figure is, again, misleading, because the fall of the star performer was not an ordinary mishap. His shift in status must be understood as a rise in the "vital level" of the classes which had provided his support, although not a rise in their level of sophistication. And the consequence lies in the figure — a heap instead of a structure.

As men of insight saw, the star performer deserved to fall; the platform for his support was special privilege, and no class really deserved to have the group as its platform. There was no reason why the lower levels should have absorbed the dangers and difficulties, inherent in living, to make possible from the dawn of the Middle Ages a life of comfort for another class. There was no reason why most of the members of society should have been excluded from culture to make possible the sophistication, charm, intellect, wit, and art developing in a privileged class and in the lives of those sponsored by this class — in the salons, that is, of Europe. It was not that the star performer did not deserve his full life; but that the full life should be the privilege of every man.

The social pyramid gave way before the vigor of our planar principles; and in the giving way the intellectual, their architect, lost his place of privilege, and by his own intention. What he had in mind was a society of equal privilege. What he got was something else again. What, then, did he achieve? It is to his never-ending credit that he achieved the forms of a social philosophy, based on the authentic revolution.

But these forms turned out to be the political forms in which the masses, released by technology, could rise. He contributed to the striking fact of the mass in our modern scene: The mass man, the mass mind, mass media, mass communication, mass education, mass recreation, mass production, and even reproduction — or so a glance at the birth rate would suggest. Technology and the planar principles have released these energies. And the serious question is whether a mass mind can show much mentality, or whether mass communication can communicate much worth-while information, or whether mass education is still education; but mass production, no one doubts, is still production.

This accession of the mass to power poses many problems; in the minds of some, Ortega for example, it is an unrelieved disaster. Notice what he says:

There is one fact which, whether for good or ill, is of utmost importance in the public life of Europe at the present moment. This fact is the accession of the masses to complete social power. As the masses, by definition, neither should nor can direct their own personal existence, and still less rule society in general, this fact means that actually Europe is suffering from the greatest crisis that can afflict peoples, nations, and civilisation.

The multitude has suddenly become visible, installing itself in the preferential positions in society. Before, if it existed, it passed unnoticed, occupying the background of the social stage; now it has advanced to the footlights and is the principal character. There are no longer protagonists; there is only the chorus.

Strictly speaking, the mass, as a psychological fact, can be defined without waiting for individuals to appear in mass formation. In the presence of one individual we can decide whether he is "mass" or not. The mass is all that which sets no value on itself — good or ill — based on specific grounds, but which feels itself "just like everybody," and nevertheless is not concerned about it; is, in fact, quite happy to feel itself as one with everybody else.

The characteristic of the hour is that the commonplace mind,

knowing itself to be commonplace, has the assurance to proclaim
the rights of the commonplace and to impose them wherever it
will. As they say in the United States: "to be different is to be
indecent." The mass crushes beneath it everything that is different, everything that is excellent, individual, qualified and select.
Anybody who is not like everybody, who does not think like
everybody, runs the risk of being eliminated. And it is clear, of
course, that this "everybody" is not "everybody." "Everybody"
was normally the complex unity of the mass and the divergent,
specialised minorities. Nowadays, "everybody" is the mass alone.
Here we have the formidable fact of our times, described without
any concealment of the brutality of its features.[14]

Ortega sees but half the problem. The other half is this: There are
positive values in the shift which has occurred; and, further, we
could not return to his aristocratic notion of society, even if we
wished.

Now, the intellectual, we insist, had not bargained for the world
which was partly his achievement. Nor has the world of his achievement demonstrated its ability to sustain the production of the forms
of culture. As the intellectual became lost among the masses, the
new pyramids were rising within the political plain; the new princes
were making their way to the tops of these functional pyramids;
and the new unofficial royalty with its Gospel of Wealth had little
appreciation for the cultural fund and the forms of culture. Indeed,
it was the new royalty which helped to establish the myth of the
useless intellectual. And in this sense our present social structure
is less adequate than the political pyramids of an earlier day. Here
we may take Toynbee as a warning: The society which does not
provide the necessary conditions for its creative minority cannot
continue to meet the problems it will face.

What, then, is our hope? Everyone seems to think the world must
take one of two alternatives: One is the working of the unplanned
plan which, qualified by the less severe plan for revolution, has led
us to our modern world, and to the problems we have noted. The
other is the planned society, outlined in the social philosophy and
philosophy of history of Marx; and represented in the world by the
more severe revolution.

Does our hope lie in this revolution? Intellectuals, I assert, have

[14] José Ortega y Gasset, *The Revolt of the Masses* (New York: W. W. Norton
and Co., and London: George Allen & Unwin Ltd., 1932). The selections
in order are taken from pp. 7, 8, 9 and 10, 12 and 13.

been responsible for the conception of the planned society. And the revolutions of recent times have not been a blind thrusting forth of the human will. Men have had in their minds, and possibly in their pockets, a blueprint of the good society. Rousseau's *Social Contract,* Thomas Paine's *Common Sense,* Marx's *Communist Manifesto* — at least three books for three revolutions. The modern revolution has been a bookish and intellectual venture, directed toward the good society. The failure of the French revolt shook the intellectual world, as we have said, resulting in a loss of nerve and opening a less optimistic line of thought; indeed, changing the manner in which philosophy was able to proceed. But even so, when the more severe revolution broke out within our century, a strange phenomenon was to be encountered widely: The intellectual, who had set his face against revolution as an instrument for the achievement of the good society, who had perhaps renounced the thought of a planned and rational society, nonetheless was able to discover in himself — to his astonishment and often to his dismay — unexpected facets of loyalty and hope for the outcome of this revolution.

And as the revolution succeeded, it was the pyramid of command — developed in the cadres of the professional revolutionaries — which enveloped a whole country, and a country which enveloped a whole subcontinent. And though the goal was still the rational society, freed from superstition, this was not the pure reason of the eighteenth century; it bore the marks of the nineteenth-century rediscovery of the pyramid of command. And in the country of revolution the monolith, including every citizen and institution within its borders, rose from its base to a peak of command, ending in a single council, or in a single man. From this narrow peak the whole pyramidal mass was, and is, subject to control by means of the physical power of the country as concentrated in its agents, and the power of propaganda through mass media, with the commanding persuasiveness known to us in other ways. Never before in history has there been a pyramid of command so complete and so inclusive. It is more imposing in dimension, if less eternal, than the pyramid of Giza. The latter also required command over thousands for many weary decades. It is the summation of all the forces of the modern world; it is capitalism brought to its final consummation in a single, inclusive monopoly — absolute capitalism; it is the labor movement increased to its maximum size in a single organization; it is total government, manipulating human lives from its pyramidal peak; it is truth exchanged for propaganda, the doctrines of the intellectuals shaped by the single viewpoint of the monolithic state. The more successful revolution, this is to say, was a greater failure than the first. And this failure is partial evidence against the philosophy of history of Marx. To be sure, the political descendants of the original revolutionaries are still in command. The political reality has occurred. And perhaps there have been some successes. The capitalists have gone, or else they are going; it depends upon the edition of *Pravda* which you read. A new right has been established, the right to work — or else it is a duty; it depends, I suppose, on whether you are a member of the Propaganda Ministry, or a member of the classless laboring class. Status has been abolished — or given another form — or at least has been arranged according to capacity — or mingled capacity and power; it depends upon whether you read the lines or between the lines of *Krokodil*, or whatever your Soviet source materials may be.

The more literal-minded revolution wished the plain with a vengeance; it wished a society organized laterally instead of vertically; the phrase, "classless society," had been its hallmark; it made the most of man's instrumental status in our modern world of industry. And wishing the principles of the plain so intensely, this revolution achieved the most complete pyramid of command in all of history, a modern all-inclusive and all-powerful, functional, and functioning pyramid.

The point is that for intellectuals the nerve, which might inspire them to social action, has been almost severed. This curious nerve (situated somewhere near the pineal gland and), unknown — I suppose — to physiologists, connects the posing of a problem with mental decision, and mental decision with human action. It was badly damaged in the failure of the French revolt. The success of the Russian revolt, with its very considerable admixture of grossness and brutality, cut much more deeply; and so the intellectuals, who found themselves identifying with both revolutions, are a disappointed and a disappointing lot. I do not mean that they are not clever, urbane, often extremely knowledgeable, and capable of furnishing a most stimulating evening's entertainment. They are all of this; but their knowledge stops just short of the social order; or if it extends so far, still it stops just short of any norms or principles.

Today they are, by and large, no longer capable of mental decision, concerning what society ought to be. They can furnish no cultural directive for our lives. The intellectual, as much as any other kind of man, and more than some, is and feels himself to be, lost within the modern world he helped to shape. In truth we need our intellectual, and we need him working at the height of his powers. His inability to work with confidence and power is an indication of an inner failure in our grand experiment. Whatever our philosophy of history may be, it must restore this harmonious interweaving of the portions of society in confidence and trust. Now this unfortunate failure of the Western intellectual may be related to our unwillingness to implement our social principles, and to the meaningless flux we tend to find in history. In any case we have not yet achieved wide support for either a social philosophy or an attitude toward history, capable of directing the ultimate power which we possess.

My conclusion, then is this: We have indeed come to a critical point in our development. One gains on occasion the sense of a fullness of time, the sense of themes coming together in the present, as though a resolution of all history were in the making. Men have had this sense before; it is partly an illusion of perspective; but today there is more reason than ever to believe in this intuition as a reflection, largely, of our actual situation. The relationship between the intellectual and his society could be improved; a failure in responsibility can be discerned on either side. At the same time the Marxist version of the planned society has revealed its utter incapacity to lead to any solution worthy of our confidence.

And the larger opposition in the world lies in the tension between two powers (thus, Hegel instead of Marx), each carrying industrialization and the technical society. Each power was born in revolution. In each an original commitment to the plain has given way to pyramidal forms of order. What, then, is the struggle against Communism? At times, I am not sure. I think I know the lines on which the struggle should proceed. The work of Marx empowered, and not by accident, a spurious revolution; the Marxist philosophy of history, hence, bears this spurious revolution. This then should be a struggle between the bearer of an authentic and the bearer of a spurious revolution. Our pattern is the revolution directed toward the increase of human rights and liberties. In this sense we, and not the Russians, stand for the culmination and the depth of Western thought. I think this should be a struggle between two philosophies of history, both of them beginning in an analysis of society, and both finding the end of history in the achievement of the good society, both working to achieve a plan but each a different kind of plan. One understands by the good society an all-inclusive functional pyramid, controlling its members from above. (If someone says, "But this is only a stage in their advance," I respond with our student of ethics, "When you pick up one end of a stick, you get the other with it.") The other understands the good society to be the gently rolling plain where government provides support for the freedom of its citizens. This should be a struggle between a view of history which finds the end of history fixed and coming by necessity; and a view which finds the field of history open at its further end, and subject to our free determination; a struggle between a view of history finding conflict and opposition its most distinctive feature, and another which finds in history a lengthwise binding, its most distinctive element a possibility of cumulative advance. Nor is the idea of this advance in conflict with the notion of a universal purpose working its way through time; not a few still find this purpose the most important element in the natural Western attitude toward history. The notion of a universal purpose may or may not belong to our philosophy of history; in any case the prospects of this view will provide the material for our last discussion. I do not know if our natural view of history can have the power of its Marxist counterpart; but it is closer to the facts, and much superior to any view which finds no meaning in the pattern.

II. Toward a Philosophy of History

If our natural view of history turns around the themes we have suggested, there remains only the problem of providing a context for the support and elaboration of these themes. This context will be a view of culture. If we are to believe in our possible progress, in some sense history will have a direction and a goal. If failure is possible, and the future somewhat open, we become the agents, responsible for discovery of this direction and this goal. If it is our genius to stress the cumulative advance through time, we must have a notion of cultural solidarity. If history is to have meaning and purpose, we cannot be elated over the evidence for societal decline, leaving history a scene of desolation. If we are the agents of the advance of history, we cannot believe altogether in the "unplanned plan" of social ordering. If we are to be committed to some version of the planned society, we must be able to separate the acceptable from every false version of the social plan. If we are to believe in cultural solidarity, while finding our possible advance through development within the cultural fund, the distinction between "creative" and "transmissive" members of society must be understood in a manner not in conflict with our social principles. A philosophy of history is possible, turning on these themes. I think it is native to ourselves, and to our Western culture.

Cultural Solidarity

For one thing we must find a sense of unity within the long perspective of our past. And, indeed, there is a breadthwise, lengthwise, depthwise binding in the strands of Western history, contributing to this sense of unity.

The Breadthwise Binding

In the discussion of our social principles we have already come upon a breadthwise binding, providing a common basis for our purposeful development. And since the discussion of any particular society takes place through viewing a segment in cross-section, drawn from the larger meaning of "society," it is proper to refer the problem of this breadthwise unity to our social principles. And then we would have to say: Properly organized, society will have an inner unity, each man's work contributing to the common good. And this unity is more fundamental — in our contention — than any of the conflicts to be found within society. The breadthwise binding, then, has been spelled out in our list of social principles. And, indeed, we can add two further items to our list, drawn from the first half of our discussion.

XVI. The cultural product must be made available to the whole people in order to insure the transmission of its elements. Our instruments of mass media have an obligation, which they have never fully accepted, of insuring this transmission.

XVII. Society must furnish adequate conditions, and support, for its "creative minority" in whose work lies the promise of cultural advance.

The Lengthwise Binding

In one sense the lengthwise binding within society refers to the direction of history, and to its goal. The reference is to the future. But the goal of history for us cannot be a single and necessary goal. If the future is somewhat open, history can have more than a single outcome. And the open future deprives us of the power which necessity sometimes lends to a philosophy of history. Whitehead who, possibly more than any other man, reflects our natural philosophy of history, finds the movement of history to consist of a gradual achievement of man's "formulated aspirations." And in this sense our social principles, furnishing both direction and goal to our development, contribute both the direction and the goal to at least our strand of Western history. For us the goal of our social philosophy and the end of history will be the same. We move toward the good society. And "progress" is the name for our movement toward this goal.

But the evidence favors the decline and breakdown of any society at last? The fact of decline in any society, including our own, can be put into perspective. And this brings us to a second aspect of lengthwise binding through great spans of time. In Whitehead's view advance is not inevitable; progress and decadence are both possible, and often mingled. And the problems of human culture are posed by the opposition of "senseless agencies and formulated aspirations." The example with which he works in the first part of his *Adventures of Ideas* is the opposition between the conception of man, and his status in the world; in short, it is the opposition between Stoic and Christian doctrines of the worth of man, and the fact of slavery.

Such oppositions cannot be resolved at once. Our aspirations must be formulated, and then must work within society, producing a "gradual growth of the requisite communal customs."

We see here the first stage of the introduction of great ideas. They start as speculative suggestions in the minds of a small, gifted group. They acquire a limited application to human life at the hands of various sets of leaders with special functions in the social structure. A whole literature arises which explains how inspiring is the general idea, and how slight need be its effect in disturbing a comfortable society. Some transition has been produced by the agency of the new idea. But on the whole the social system has been inoculated against the full infection of the new principle. It takes its place among the interesting notions which have a restricted application.

But a general idea is always a danger to the existing order. The whole bundle of its conceivable special embodiments in various usages of society constitutes a program of reform. At any moment the smouldering unhappiness of mankind may seize on some such program and initiate a period of rapid change guided by the light of its doctrines.[15]

But if civilization rests upon a base of slavery, and requires it for the carrying out of necessary functions, rapid change cannot occur successfully. Not until the physical aspect of society has been prepared (not until Steam), can Democracy, adhering to a sense of human worth, free the slave. The senseless agency and the formulated aspiration must reinforce each other.

Two thousand years elapsed between the sensing of this problem and its resolution. In Spengler's terms this two thousand years extends across two cultural cycles. This means there is a possible solidarity to our cultural advance, even across the breakdown of particular societies.

Our concept of culture includes families of societies, existing at the same time or in succession. And, upon reflection, other problems come to mind, transcending any one society, yet finding their solutions. There is the problem of social organization. At first, the human material to be organized extended only to the tribe and clan, then to the city-state, and next the nation. Today, the problem of organization confronts the community of nations. While the problem is being faced, and solved, societies may decline and fall; but this is no proof of the lack of progress. The cultural problem is resolved, despite the dissolution of societies. In this sense any society is an agent, directing itself toward the solution of the cultural problem. Failure may mean dissolution; but the failure within society is only a slight arrest in the advance of culture. Through however many failures, we have achieved successful organization up to national boundaries.

15 A. N. Whitehead, *Adventures of Ideas* (New York: The Macmillan Company, 1933), p. 17. Used by permission of The Macmillan Company.

The problem of development in our knowledge goes beyond the boundaries of any society, and continues, although more slowly, through societal decline; the production of knowledge does not halt in the world with the breakdown of any one society; the same is true of development in the arts. If societies break down, this is not the end of cultural advance. The general fact provides a mental bridge, leading from the boundaries of society back into the sources of our Western culture. And the lengthwise binding extends from our human origins to the present.

The Depthwise Binding

Our discussion has returned to the concept of culture. And this concept recalls, again, the cultural fund, and the distinction between the "creative" and "transmissive" members of society. Does not a hierarchy of a different kind return upon us? There is, I suggest, a depthwise binding in society which largely cancels out this difference.

Let us regard so slight a matter as the difference of speech between the intellectual and his social "other." How thin is the speech of our intellectual. His ideas are precise, yet paper thin. He speaks abstractly; and for most this speech will be devoid of common interest. By contrast the speech of an ordinary man is refreshingly full of metaphor and figure. His speech is richer, more poetic. In this difference I find the germ of a conception which concerns our cultural unity, the birth of meaning, and along the way providing an answer to our positivist. Take any one of the thin abstractions used by the intellectual, any abstract noun with a meaning as literal as you please; students of language assure us that this noun began as a figure of speech, a metaphor, and gained its present status only through a long and arduous "cleansing" through use. In a sense our intellectual makes his way by means of the "dead metaphors," contributed, and long ago discarded, by our ordinary man. Has the fact any importance? Let us see.

Man was a poet before he learned to be a philosopher; and a philosopher before he learned to be a scientist. Man's intellectual life began in the rank and luxurious vegetation of stories, images, and pictures of every kind, their variations sprouting in all directions. Homer and Hesiod did their work (however many "they" were) before Plato; and there is reason why this had to be the case. Homer gave men stories — about men and gods, life and death; acts of courage and cowardice, of wisdom and ignorance. Plato speculated about the nature of man, the nature of god, the meaning of life and death, the nature of courage, cowardice, wisdom, and the good. Hesiod, uncomfortable before the abundance and confusion of the stories about the gods, sought an ordering principle, and discovered it in biological relationships. His whole *Theogony* then unfolds, systematized by means of fathers, mothers, daughters, sons, aunts and uncles, among these gods and goddesses, disporting themselves in the pages of his book and in the theatre of the human mind — sometimes scandalously. In fact, Hesiod is discussing the values of human life; each god and goddess stands for some such value; and Hesiod did not originate his own material. He is simply trying to understand what his society had provided. Given this kind of systematic presentation, and the lapse of time, a different kind of order will appear. Plato, making a further abstraction, will be able to discuss with exactness, and at great length, wisdom, justice, courage, temperance, love, and beauty — no longer representing gods and goddesses, but standing by themselves as concepts. My claim is this: The philosophic enterprise was possible only because of an earlier kind of ordering in story and in myth. We are referring once again to the cultural fund in one of its early forms; the Greeks required this fund on which to do their work. The manner in which Greek philosophers, in the course of four or five centuries, were able to elaborate most of the philosophic "systems" with which we are acquainted in the West, is often presented as an object of proper wonder. No less an object of wonder is their anticipating in germ much of the content of our Western science. This was a great achievement; but let me suggest a simple reason for their success: The cultural fund had reached the point of richness, depth, and sheer confusion, which allowed and required these abstractions and systems to be made. These systems of ideas were not derived from an utter void. The Greek philosophers developed a novel sense of system. With this they were able to draw contents from the cultural fund, conforming to this sense, and providing an altogether novel object for our human understanding.

The Greeks also made rich and valuable anticipations of what our Western science would become; theories of the solar system, evolution, and atomic theory, were presented in germ but clear enough, and approximately "true" as we consider truth today. Notice in addition how every science has had its origin in something not a science. In one sense every science had its origin in philosophy. But, in relation to society, one can also notice the origin of mathematics in numerology, and the development of practical techniques for plotting land; the origin of astronomy in astrology, of chemistry in alchemy, of biology in the dissection of animals in religious rites, of physiology in phrenology and art, of physics — reading out the laws of an intelligible reality — in theology. Here, too, I suggest, the achievement of the ordering proper to each science was possible because a different kind of ordering had first prepared its material. Anyone who has worked with words is aware of the importance of a first draft, even if this is merely the point from which one will wish to depart as rapidly as possible.

Let us return to the abstraction which began as a figure of speech. With this in mind, I ask myself: How could mankind have achieved its present vast store of meanings, ready for use in the operation of our vastly complex human life? The only mechanism I can imagine is this: Given an initial set of meanings, however small, any two can be fused into a kind of metaphor, directed toward some area of life not yet covered by a meaning; the sense of its metaphorical origin will die away through time; and from the "dead metaphor" a symbol is born. The supply of meanings can increase by geometrical progression, allowing always a lapse of time for the "cleansing" process to do its work. And this was the doctrine of meaning which held importance in our discussion of the beautiful. We are now claiming the presence of metaphorical fusion at the point of entry of any meaning. Recall, again, how the fusion of any two ideas created not simply a third idea, but a range of meanings, accounting for the richness of the poetic enterprise! And my claim turns into this: The early thinkers of mankind were poets by necessity; their genius lay in their ability to interfuse the contents of our early culture. And the philosophies by which we live could be drawn from their results, because each philosophy is one possible reading of this rich and poetic cultural matrix; the philosophies were already there, implicit in the fund. But guided by the new ideal of coherence — impelled by a developing sense of logic — it was the genius of the philosopher to draw out and shape only the precise sense of meaning needed to complete his work, to construct — that is — his formal scheme. By a similar drawing out, abstraction, from the philosophic schemes of the meanings proper to their work, and from their own histories, each science has found its ordering. Science works, then, with ideas of ideas? Perhaps. At least, one must grant the thinness of philosophic and scientific concepts, however precise, the result of the splitting away of what was needed from the rich profusion of the cultural fund. The gain in coherence and precision, as everyone has noted, is accompanied by a loss in affective power — the source of the complaint about the dullness of philosophy, and the speech of intellectuals in general.

This bring us to the question: Are we to shear away from philosophy and science, this earlier stage, viewing it as meaningless? Or are we to shear away from science both philosophy, and all earlier stages of our cultural life, viewing them as meaningless? It is incredible even to pose the question. The difficulty with the cultural fund, the reason it must be altered by philosophers and scientists, is not its meaningless nature (it has been the source of all our meanings), but the embarrassment of its abundant and conflicting meanings. It is too meaningful to be retained within our minds unchanged; it yields no particular conceptual direction, because it suggests many directions, and all at once. Our purposeful minds must rework this fund into a set of systems. To shear away the early stages of our cultural fund is to shear away the source of the added meanings which we shall require for our philosophies and sciences. You have, of course, noticed the little metaphors framed by the scientist in gaining his hypotheses. Possibly, he will say, the evidence can be explained by a wave theory of light. A wave theory — of light? What diverse notions have been combined! I am then to associate my experience of the successive movement of the waves, stirred by the tossing of a rock into the pond, with my experience of light. How poetic! The scientific hypothesis begins in metaphorical fusion, and ends — when the hypothesis is successful — with the status of a concept.

And every philosophy, I suppose, is a blend of literal meaning, and metaphor. The metaphorical element is thicker in philosophy than in science. A philosopher requires a culture rich in images and in figures. When Plato could no longer continue his analysis by means of clear and precise meanings, he did not stop philosophizing. He gave his meaning in a figure, a story, or a myth. One can notice the myth of the cave, the myth of judgment, the myth of creation, and many more. It is as though he sensed the source of meaning; and knew that if he could not find the precise meaning for his purpose, he could at least present the figure which would be likely to contain, among its possible meanings, the proper meaning which he had not himself been able to discern.

It is the function of reason to work over the "given" — what we have called the "cultural fund" — introducing order and perspective, refining, clarifying, and sometimes achieving novelty through reordering this given. But if this is the function of reason, there must be another function. It is absolutely necessary to have also the poetic, imaginative insight which works by the fusion of ideas, adding richness and the possible conceptions which may become part of the reason of our advance.

I have then two conclusions. First, the cultural product can be held in unity; all its stages, despite Auguste Comte, can properly coexist. This conclusion supports the sense of a breadthwise, lengthwise binding. Second, the difference between the poetry of life and its prose, between the metaphor and the concept, or the jumble of significance compared to the precision of the conceptual system, is not simply a temporal relation of earlier to later forms of culture, but a working relation within the present, a matter of cultural depth.

Both the sciences and philosophies, more clear than the jumble of ideas in common life, rise from and rest on the rich metaphorical stuff by which men live. Insofar as one is just a man (not a scholar or practitioner of any art) he will think in figures and pictures; he will express himself in a shrug, a gesture, a metaphor. He will make his own little poems about the greatest matters. And the important practical institutions of life avoid the abstract ways of thought, adhering closely to the metaphor. Politicians do this; so do ministers. And religious literature is very rich in pictures, stories, and figures of speech in all their variety. Not only did religion precede philosophy; it is likewise closer to common life. The notion of cultural depth is not merely a recognition of the rise of meaning from figure and story; it is a recognition of the dependence of our modern conceptual enterprise upon the practical concerns of living with their richness of metaphor. Now an individual man can climb a considerable height — as he thinks at least — and then kick away the ladder by which he made his climb. This, it seems to me, is the course taken by the most enlightened minds of our day. (Believing this, I also believe these most enlightened minds not fully enlightened.) Such people have commanding intellectual tasks to absorb their energies; they are protected from the world by the institutions within which they do their work. They do not notice how the stability of the institution which protects and frees them is insured by the lives of common people, the meanings of whose lives are informed by the rich stuff of metaphor, including its forms of faith. The point I intend is relatively simple. When such a man kicks away the ladder by which he has climbed, he has disposed of an imaginary ladder. The steps of his ascent are still there, providing stability within society. There is also a cultural unity in depth.

The products of our reason, as we have seen, have their origin in something prior to our reason. The origin lies in the general cultural fund; that is, in the thought-forms of an earlier group of men. But these thought-forms characterize not only earlier men; they are the normal and natural forms of thought for most of the members of society. And it is the function of our reason to crystallize, sharpen, refine, and in the process, to attenuate these forms. I assert, then, a natural cultural interdependence between the creative minority of any society, and those who belong to its majority. It is the function of the former to reorder the cultural product, adding to its fund. It is the function of the latter to maintain the order of society, transmitting the cultural product which has already been achieved. And yet even the terms "creative" and "transmissive" are not proper. Each is creative in its own way. But order and novelty are both essential for the advance of culture. Nor is this a matter of superior and inferior. We cannot, of course, deny the fact of differences in ability. But when optimal conditions are provided, the flowering into excellence of the human spirit from every rank of any social group can be amazing. One thinks of Pope Boniface VIII saying of the whole people of Florence by the year 1300 that these people must have in their natures a fifth element, something in addition to the ordinary earth, air, fire, and water of the rest of humanity. The superiority of the Florentine in so many fields of art and learning is to be explained by the presence of conditions which allowed the maximum development of quite ordinary people. This is the fact which Spengler and Ortega failed to see; because of this, the rising human level is full of promise; but the appropriate conditions must be provided — and we must learn an inner discipline. And, in addition to all of this, the greatest of our human achievements, language, developed in all of its complexity as a product of the total group.

Cultural Advance

If the development of human culture continues, even across the breakdown of societies, one can look to the state of culture for social direction. And if, within the cultural fund, one is able to discover an ideal which has been progressively developing within our history, finding successive specializations, he can be certain of the role of this idea in the movement of our history. It could not be part of the movement of history had it not entered into the appreciations and motives of men. But cultural advance is the mutual accommodation of ideas and physical conditions. And the basic type of opposition within history is not class conflict, but the conflict of a maturing ideal, and a context lacking the physical conditions capable of supporting this ideal. The oppositions we have noted in our last two discussions are precisely similar to the oppositions which, on Whitehead's view, lead to cultural advance through time: the developing ideal of democracy in opposition to the productive functional pyramids; the ideal of culture, and the rising "vital level" of the total population. Not only is this the kind of opposition noticed by Whitehead; further, we show evidence of having arrived at that stage of the opposition where a solution is possible. Just as the appearance of machine industry made possible the end of slavery, so the productivity of the functional pyramid can now make possible abundance in the instrumental basis of the lives of sovereign individuals. In this sense our present scene is a scene of hope; but the curtain has not yet risen on the fulfillment of its promise.

We need to do a bit of lifting by our bootstraps. For instance, we need to become sufficiently clear-headed that we shall not deny our role as children and defenders of the authentic revolution; we must see with clarity how close we have come to disaster in beginning to think of every revolution as a spurious hatred of order, and a thing to be avoided. We must also come to terms with our confusion over the unplanned plan and the planned society. We are very much aware of those versions of the planned society which give to man only the value of an instrument. But we have also seen how the working of the unplanned plan has cast most men into the role of instruments. Well, we must find a third, and more fortunate, alternative.

The Planned Society

As we avoid the spurious revolution, so must we avoid the spurious, planned society. The spurious plan of social ordering takes reason beyond its proper limits. We have just found what I take to be the function of our reason. But when reason is identified with scientific knowledge, the sources of reason — providing the "given" for its work — come to be regarded as elements of ignorance and superstition, or meaningless sounds to be swept from human minds. There are plans of social ordering, exceedingly impatient of the forms of faith, of the mystic unity of the family, and of provincial national sentiment. Reason must of course work upon these forms; they need to be enlightened, purified, and possibly by rational persuasion we may be led to rise above some of the elements of this "given." But the work of reason requires an interplay of freedom. And this is quite different from a program to eliminate by propaganda what someone thinks to be a superstition.

The reasons we offer to ourselves for the most intimate aspects of our lives can have no other form than that of poetry. And here is their type. Once upon a time man was very strong, having four arms and four legs, able to move across the world at a tremendous pace, rolling like a tumbleweed. In this condition the human strength was so very great that it threatened the power of the gods. And so by the power of Zeus the self-sufficient human being was split in twain. We no longer threaten the gods, having to spend so much of our energy in the finding of our other half.[16] Have you not felt within yourself this seeking across the world one's complement, wishing to realize the ideal of self-completeness? Taken literally, the story would be a superstition; and yet it strikes more deeply than twenty pages of scientific knowledge. Poetry, I mean to say, justifies much of our most intimate belief. If poetry is not to be allowed, this fact will alter, more than we know, the basis of human life. At least, our critical faculties must be at the same time quite self-critical when probing into the deepest foundations of our personal beliefs.

And the reason which can accept only scientific answers to

[16] My reference is, of course, to the *Symposium* of Plato. The suggestion is there made that if we continue to cause trouble for Zeus, he will split us again, and then we shall have to hop about on one leg.

scientific questions will be able to discern in society only the factual inequalities among men. The planned society which would result from such a view of reason would be the social and functional pyramid, distinguishing superior and inferior; here the individual is no longer sovereign; he has his own atomic self, and a single object for his loyalty, the pyramid itself. If this is the rational society, something has gone wrong within our reason. When we become nakedly objective in our reason, man becomes an object to be studied — and then, perhaps, to be manipulated in terms of the findings of the study. But note the danger here. Man is the subject who selected the criteria for the building of the scheme which makes of him an object. Because man constructs the scheme, and could have constructed it in a different way, he is more than the simple object of any given scheme.

We must disavow, then, the spurious, planned society; but as there is an authentic revolution, so there is an authentic type of social plan. Its object is still the increase of our human rights and liberties.

The Age of Transition

A society with little inner contrast, Whitehead tells us, is in decline. A society with too much conflict faces dissolution. But the right kind of opposition can empower us in our advance. Not only do we find an object of loyalty in culture with greater permanence than that of any given society. There is an impulsion as well which derives from culture. It may come from a demand in the nature of man, or in the nature of things, for coherence. But the kind of opposition we have found allows one to think of our age, however many generations it may take, as an age of transition.

If this age, like every other time of promise and of threat, is an age of transition, this fact by itself explains our uncertainty and confusion. Let us remember how the pyramid of status existed with official sanction, and indeed the highest possible sanction, for a thousand years in the shape of a nation, and for many thousands of years prior to that. Even our Scriptures employ the words "King" and "Lord" as the highest of terms. And much of our folklore has taken as its theme a kind of living in imagination with, or being transformed into, members of the privileged classes. (This, I admit, is not a great advance over — indeed, is not very different from — the folksy lore of advertising, as mental content for our children.) But how could we expect the plainsmen in less than two centuries to work into perfection their new principle for the ordering of our social life, and standing to us as the end of history? If this is an age of transition, the less admirable aspects of our social life take on a different aspect. Much falseness can be endured if it is a temporary falseness; and much inner contradiction if it is a temporary contradiction.

What does one do in a time of transition? One fumbles, of course, one hesitates. But if we know the nature of the transition, we need not drift. The danger of a period of transition is, of course, that tradition is no longer our guide; and if we cannot find the way through our period of transition, we may drift backwards into something far worse than what had been destroyed. A grim irony, thus, still smiles upon the present scene. The whole course of human life is in danger of drifting into a primitivism — one way or another — from which culture, working its way with difficulty through long centuries, had rescued that life. The signs are all about us; and yet the signs are present, because we have taken more than one decisive step toward a society which promises a better life than man has ever known. The problem is not only to preserve ourselves, but to rescue with ourselves our culture. And not only to rescue our culture, but to find our way through the period of transition and to complete it. In a sense we can speak in terms of the universal purpose. We do not work alone; the working of culture, related to our logic of events, adds its impetus to our working.

Retroactive Meaninglessness

The significance of our personal lives takes increase from those developments within society, containing the marks of a welcome identity with our natures. The developing planar principles, I have suggested, can serve as the route of escape from a meaningless existence. But our society, according to the evidence, will at last break down. At some time its condition of decline will be beyond our power to reverse. Even so, we have learned that the working of a cultural ideal goes beyond the pattern of any given society; it continues, regardless of societal decline.

And yet, when our society is swept away by whatever tides of historical movement, our lives, except for whatever we have contributed to human culture, will likewise by swept away in its collapse. When the reforming synod at last achieved a successful action, canceling out the doctrine of predestination to hell, the elder was not entirely beyond the bounds of sanity who moved that the action be made retroactive. At least in the present case, our lives can lose their meaning retroactively. And the question is: Is there any manner of preserving the meaning of our lives? The question leads us to our final consideration.

Chapter Eight

First and Last Things: The Problems of God and Immortality

I. The Place of Man in the Universe

The scope of our reflections has been steadily increasing, leading us to a final problem: What is man's place in the total universe? We become more cosmic by the page. Offhand, one might expect a widespread, murmuring response: "What an impossible question!" But it is surprising that the murmuring is so scattered. In one way or another most of us declare with the solemnity of Margaret Fuller, "I accept the universe." Carlyle's retort, on hearing of this declaration, was: "Egad! She'd better!" How can one not accept it, whatever it is? But it would be interesting to discover what Miss Fuller thought she was accepting when she declared her willingness to accept the universe. And it would be important to discover if the universe did, or could, accept Miss Fuller. Most of us seem to know what it is we are accepting.

At least two questions intersect within this problem. We may

ask: What is my fate? This is a question about one's immortality.
We may ask: Has the universe at its "heart" awareness of, and concern for, creatures; or anything like awareness and concern? This
is the problem of God.

One would expect our problem, finding what we are accepting
when we accept the universe, to be difficult in the extreme; and
yet on this question almost everyone has his mind made up, has
arrived ticket in hand at some solution, so that the question is no
longer live and vital. My mind is made up, we say, as though making up one's mind were like making up one's bed — a task to be
completed as quickly as possible, to be put behind one and forgotten. But is this not the best possible situation? Everyone knows
what he believes on this important double question; and if it is
the task of philosophy to settle beliefs which are in doubt, on this
final question there is no philosophic work to do.

I would accept the judgment, terminate our final essay after
twenty lines, and begin to prepare the index, had I not begun to
notice a most curious circumstance which requires some comment.
Any prudent hostess, when the conversation begins to veer un-
towardly (that is, away from the safe and easy topics of our social
interchange; that is, toward this important topic) will interpose
between the question, and any possible response, the rule: "We
never discuss politics or religion." Everyone has resolved the problem; the question is settled; and yet we are not allowed to enter
into its discussion. Is this not curious? It is exactly the settled
questions which provide the hostess her material for construction
of the lively and yet harmoniously unstimulating evening's conversation. If the question is, indeed, settled why the prohibition on this
topic? The prohibition, inspired by the hostesses of our matriarchal
social life, links together politics and religion. Apparently, our
present question is settled quite as definitely as is the political question, and possibly in a similar manner. Here, then, is a clue. The
question of our political alignment has, indeed, been settled, but
not in a rational manner; the political question is resolved very
seldom by a fair analysis. We have chosen sides, of course; we
have our minds made up; but often, as we have observed, the choice
was not our own; our situation had chosen for us. We chose, quite
as much as modern women have chosen to wear high heels, walking
all their lives upon their toes; we have chosen, quite as much as
men have chosen to wear the vestigial scarf about their necks, its

useless strip of cloth reducing circulation; or the vermiform buttons at their wrists for the attaching of nonexistent medieval gauntlets. That is, we have chosen not at all; we have inherited our political alignment from the past. And because in this instance we have not made a rational choice, it is beyond us to discuss the differences among us rationally. And what is true of our political beliefs is no less true of our settled beliefs concerning man's place in the total universe. The reason, then, for the social prohibition is the lack of reason in these portions of our lives.

We may come upon this lack of reason in another way. Beliefs which have been gained along some other route, and which are retained by some other means, than the operation of our reason, tend to be surrounded by emotion. When anyone has touched too closely, opposed, or criticized such beliefs, one can notice the flickering of an incipient anger. Have you not noticed the occasional moments in questions, say, of race, as well as those of politics and religion, when the response to a probing question will be a quick surge of uncontrollable, or scarcely controlled, anger accompanied, perhaps, by an obviously livid lip and trembling hand? We are in the presence of a firmly held belief which, yet, has not become for the person anything like a rational belief. Hence, he cannot reason; he can only respond.

When we are told that everyone has already settled our present question, has had his mind made up for years, with the statement we can agree. And yet most often the question has not been well settled; and so we cannot agree that there remains no philosophic work to do.

The Settlement of Belief

If everyone has settled the question, has everyone settled it in the same way? Not quite! And to take only the most general differences, we have settled the question in one of three ways. And your decision will fall, roughly speaking, into one of these divisions. We can distinguish the "devout believer"; the unbeliever, sometimes even more devout, and often less; and the man who neither believes nor disbelieves, having made up his mind not to make up his mind. Each of these, I claim, has his mind made up, holds his view by the method of tenacity, and feels no inner need to engage in any further questioning. We have before us, then, a set of problems as difficult as any other; and no one seems to wish a discussion of these problems.

The Believer

The devout believer does not find our question difficult in the least. He does not mind the raising of our question because he has its answer. He knows man's place in the universe. And probably he knew the answer, living by this answer, some years before he knew the question for which his mental ordering provides an answer. And yet, if I understand this type of man, he will find perplexing and distasteful any working with the question which might imply its answer were uncertain. He understands the question. But between the posing of the question, and the statement of its answer, he does not see the need for allotting any space to argument. And, in general, he will not see why our whole discussion should extend beyond the space required for setting down the shorter catechism.

The Unbeliever

Nor does the unbeliever mind the posing of our question; he too knows its answer, even though his answer is quite the opposite of the answer known to our devout believer. Unlike the believer, the unbeliever has had to work his way by personal struggle toward his answer. And he would be willing to cite a fund of evidence in support of the point of view now in possession of his mind. His evidence will consist of items from the vast stock of scientific information, of instances of man's (and nature's) inhumanity to man, of the lack of progress in our human history; these have compelled a turning of his mind from our traditional and time-honored point of view. In general, this man is somewhat more sophisticated than the devout believer. Because he has faced our question, the unbeliever does not object to the posing of this question; he is willing to discuss the evidence in terms of which it might be answered. But because he has traversed the ground before, he will not expect from our raising of the question any insight which would lead him to modify his present point of view. He has become experienced in the claims and counterclaims pertinent to this question; and against the believer he can always bring the argument out to his position. If the unbeliever is able to confuse and bewilder the believer, and if no one can present an argument which would lead him to change his mind, one might begin to think the unbeliever has the truth at his command. Certainly, he commands a strong position. And we might have agreed with this conclusion, were it not for a third type of man among us, one who neither believes nor disbelieves, but lives in a suspense of judgment.

The Agnostic

Naïveté is completely missing from this world-weary and somewhat disillusioned, man. There is no argument, he claims, capable of leading us to a conclusion on either hand. If a man, confident of the power of reason, is a "gnostic," this man who insists upon the lack of any knowledge sufficient to resolve the problem remains "agnostic." He lives in an attitude, permanently suspending the possibility of any final judgment about man's place in the total universe. Typically, he claims only to be awaiting further evidence. And at the start, in commendable honesty of spirit, he held all of the elements of our problem suspended in solution, because he found no proper catalyst to precipitate its resolution, around which the proper answer might begin to crystallize. He was, indeed, awaiting further evidence. But the years have passed, and this evidence has not appeared. Nor does he now expect any further evidence. His has become a permanent suspense of judgment. And he continues to defend this stand, or straddle, as the most reasonable posture in the world. Like our unbeliever, this man is willing to pose the problem; he is willing to argue any aspect of it we might wish, and some we may not wish. He is full of ideas, and he can demonstrate even to the unbeliever the sheer impossibility of arriving at any resolution of this problem. He has become professional in his orchestration of the elements which compose the problem. He will discuss and discuss, always bringing the argument out to his position; that is, to the impossibility of having a position. We might have accepted the unbeliever's claim to truth, but our agnostic shows his greater power against the position of the unbeliever. In fact, he is the most rational of the three. Has our agnostic, then, the truth? But must not the belief of our believer be either true or false; and the belief of our unbeliever either false or true? And what, then, of the belief of the agnostic? However fantastic this may seem, the agnostic, possessing a considerable edge in the power and subtlety of his argument, has not the slightest chance of standing for the truth. The believer and the unbeliever have a chance, at least, for truth; but our agnostic is not even in the game. How this comes about I do not know; but the agnostic seems to be mistaken in his understanding of the nature of our problem. He finds no difference between a question about first and last things, and a question about the weather. If one is puzzled about tomorrow's weather, it is reasonable to claim the absence of sufficient grounds for reaching a decision. One can suspend his judgment until tomorrow when the evidence will be at hand. But the question of first and last things is not at all like the question of the weather. The days pass, and we gain more and more evidence about the weather, while the evidence which would solve our larger problem is not supplied.

And each of these — the devout believer; the unbeliever, more or less devout; the agnostic — has his mind made up to believe, to disbelieve, or to remain in a suspense of judgment. No one of the three would expect our present raising of the question to force any alteration in his present state of mind. With whom, then, can I discuss this question?

The Reader

I must count upon your willingness to take a slight and voluntary step in the direction of our problem, not to attempt its resolution at the moment, but to confront yourself in an effort to discover the exact nature of this belief, which has been settled in your mind for so very long. The question is settled, and yet the nature of this settlement is often far from clear, when one begins to think about it. Certainly, it will not do to accept the first thought which pops into one's head as the statement of one's own position. It is not as though our three varieties of men were produced, each in a different area, so that we might say: The Eastern states produce agnostics; in the Far West unbelievers thrive, while the climate of the Middle West is favorable to devout believers. Instead, all is intermixture and confusion. One cannot estimate his real position, even by listing the institutions of which he is a member. Among the devout believers, and meeting with them at every opportunity, are to be found unbelievers and agnostics. And, surprisingly, this is the case even among those who lead the devout believers in their worship. The reason is clear enough. Such men, pressing their studies beyond the ordinary limits, have reduced their naïveté, adding to the level of their sophistication; and often the beliefs, which had started them on their inner quest, have undergone a radical transformation. And in terms of sophistication, as we have seen, our agnostic has a considerable edge over both the believer and the unbeliever. We cannot, then, allow any accident of our personal histories into the evidence, determining where we stand on this important problem. More than one person has shared the experience of Don Manuel, the priest in Unamuno's story. The events are narrated by his friend, Lazaro:

> And I shall never forget the day when I said to him: 'But, Don Manuel, the truth, the truth above all,' and he, trembling, whispered to me, in spite of the fact that we were alone, in the middle of the fields: 'The truth? The truth, Lazaro, is something so terrible, so unbearable, so deadly, that perhaps simple people could not live with it.' 'And why do you let me get a glimpse of it here, as though in the confessional?' I asked him. And he answered: 'Because if I didn't it would torment me so much, so much that I would finally shout it in the middle of the square, and that, never, never, never. I am here to make the souls of my faithful live, to make them happy, to make them dream they are immortal, and not to destroy them. What is needed here is for them to live in health, to live in unity of feeling, and with the truth; with my truth they would not live. Let them live. And that is what the Church does, make them live. True religion? All religions are true in so far as they make the people who profess them live spiritually, in so far as they console them for having had to be born to die, and the truest religion for every people is its own, the one that has made it. And mine? Mine is consoling myself by consoling others, even if the consolation I give them is not mine.' I shall never forget these words of his.[1]

Don Manuel is not alone in feeling the despair of utter unbelief, where belief might have been expected. Nor is he alone in his manner of resolving the professional problem involved in this despair. It is no wonder that men court the thoughtless attitude; if only we can remain incurious, if only we can manage to remain on the verbal surface of our beliefs, the abyss will have no chance to open within our lives! And, indeed, life is more comfortable when lived unquestioningly, and under the control of our traditional beliefs. One can toil all his life without distinction, deferring satisfaction to another world. Should the abyss open, life becomes

---

[1] Miguel de Unamuno, "Saint Manuel Bueno, Martyr," *Spanish Stories and Tales,* ed. Harriet de Onis (New York: Alfred A. Knopf, 1956), p. 67.

incredibly more difficult. One has, then, the exacting problem of making his present life significant, of finding its satisfactions through the ordinary materials of experience.

But what, then, of our intermixture and confusion, our not knowing where we stand or why? The problem is not merely the spectacle of unbelief among believers. One must likewise notice the presence of belief among the unbelievers; for among those who claim a sturdy unbelief are to be found believers who will not admit the sentiments of their hearts.

If we are to make any progress in our personal confrontation, we must learn to look somewhat dispassionately upon our lives. I suggest the application of a rule: "Let us not pretend to doubt in our philosophy what we do not doubt in our hearts." The rule was suggested by Charles Peirce. I make one slight addition: "Let us likewise not pretend to believe in our philosophy what we do not believe in our hearts." Neither "feigned doubt" nor "feigned belief" can serve our present purpose. If "feigned belief" is not entirely lacking in our world, neither is "feigned doubt" notable by its absence. And with the application of our double rule, I imagine a considerable reshuffling in the ranks of believers, unbelievers, and agnostics; and if the realignment is in anything like the same proportion, my imagination discerns a swelling in the ranks of unbelievers and agnostics, the number of avowed believers is so very great.

By every possible means you are attempting to determine, this is what I must suppose, the exact quality of your belief. You may fit exactly, snugly, and without remainder, into one of the three main types which have passed before us. And if you do not, the simple operation of combining these three types in different ways may produce a subdivision exactly fitted to the quality of your mental life. Consider the many possible shadings of belief and unbelief which now occur, similar to the subtle differences within our actual lives. There is the agnostic who inclines toward belief, thinking this more likely than not to be the solution to our problem, a solution which would be indicated were our state of knowledge more complete. There is the unbeliever who, while remaining in his unbelief, is moved by the poetry of the belief which his reason will not allow him to adopt; reported of Santayana, and of others before his time, the saying goes: "There is no God, and the Virgin Mary is his mother." There is the unbeliever, certain of the truth of his position, and yet unwilling to discuss the problem: "When Zarathustra was alone, however, he said to his heart: 'Could it be possible! This old saint in the forest hath not yet heard of it, that *God is dead!*'"[2] And quite a sizeable group would fit the position of the believer who comes to his decision, while admitting the agnostic's claim of the absence of rational grounds for making any judgment. His belief thus becomes a kind of wager:

> Let us then examine this point, and say, 'God is, or He is not.' But to which side shall we incline? Reason can decide nothing here. There is an infinite chaos which separates us. A game is being played at the extremity of this infinite distance where heads or tails will turn up. What will you wager? According to reason, you can do neither the one thing nor the other; according to reason, you can defend neither of the propositions.
>
> Do not, then, reprove for error those who have made a choice; for you know nothing about it. 'No, but I blame them for having made, not this choice, but a choice; for again both he who chooses heads and he who chooses tails are equally at fault, they are both in the wrong. The true course is not to wager at all.'
>
> Yes; but you must wager. It is not optional. You are embarked. Which will you choose then? Let us see. Since you must choose, let us see which interests you least. You have two things to lose, the true and the good; and two things to stake, your reason and your will, your knowledge and your happiness; and your nature has two things to shun, error and misery. Your reason is no more shocked in choosing one rather than the other, since you must of necessity choose. This is one point settled. But your happiness? Let us weigh the gain and the loss in wagering that God is. Let us estimate these two chances. If you gain, you gain all; if you lose, you lose nothing. Wager, then, without hesitation that He is. 'That is very fine. Yes, I must wager; but I may perhaps wager too much.' Let us see. Since there is an equal risk of gain and of loss, if you had only to gain two lives, instead of one, you might still wager. But if there were three lives to gain, you would have to play (since you are under the necessity of playing), and you would be imprudent, when you are forced to play, not to chance your life to gain three at a game where there is an equal risk of loss and gain. But there is an eternity of life and happiness. And this being so, if there were an infinity of

---

[2] Friedrich Nietzsche, "Thus Spake Zarathustra," *The Philosophy of Nietzsche* (New York: The Modern Library), p. 6. Reprinted by permission of George Allen & Unwin Ltd.

chances, of which one only would be for you, you would still be right in wagering one to win two, and you would act stupidly, being obliged to play, by refusing to stake one life against three at a game in which out of an infinity of chances there is one for you, if there were an infinity of an infinitely happy life to gain. But there is here an infinity of an infinitely happy life to gain, a chance of gain against a finite number of chances of loss, and what you stake is finite. . . .

Now, what harm will befall you in taking this side? You will be faithful, honest, humble, grateful, generous, a sincere friend, truthful. Certainly you will not have those poisonous pleasures, glory and luxury; but will you not have others? I will tell you that you will thereby gain in this life, and that, at each step you take on this road, you will see so great certainty of gain, so much nothingness in what you risk, that you will at last recognise that you have wagered for something certain and infinite, for which you have given nothing.[3]

The famous wager of Pascal may fit your mental life. Many other combinations could be arranged with ease. And doubtless we could find someone standing in, and being willing to defend, if not by reason then with teeth and nails, every one of these possible positions. Nothing could be more important than this exercise of trying to determine in all honesty the exact quality of your position with respect to belief, unbelief, or a permanent suspense of judgment.

Indeed, I have supposed an inner searching, whatever this may require, directed toward the discovery of your authentic point of view. The problem can require a lifetime? Of course, it can; and yet after a lapse of thirty minutes, I ask the question: Now do you know what you believe? Your situation is one of three: Either you have been able to determine your set of ultimate beliefs, or you have not been able to do so, or else you do not intend to try.

If you have succeeded, then you have found the truth of what you believe; that is, you have discovered no more than a tentative belief. When one marks out a position, the question of its further truth at once is relevant. Now how is this further truth determined? Truth, so far as it is available to man, is determined by the play of argument, by the presentation of reasons, and by the criticism of

[3] Blaise Pascal, *Pensées*, trans. W. F. Trotter, Everyman's Library (New York: E. P. Dutton and Co., Inc., and London: J. M. Dent & Sons, Ltd., 1931), pp. 66–68.

these reasons. But on this problem, many claim, our human reason fails. Then let us see it fail! Even failure can furnish guidance. If you have succeeded in determining what you believe, we must take a second step into the question of the truth of this belief. When the question of truth is raised, we shall be able to work with two alternatives instead of three, even if your position exceeds our plan in subtlety. Since the third alternative is not even in the game, we can direct our thought toward the believer and the unbeliever, holding agnosticism in reserve (as we have reserved one alternative before) as a view of last resort.

And if you have not been able to determine your beliefs, we must arrange our program to allow for the gradual revelation of your thought. What could be more helpful than a more extended discussion of the problem? If you have not been able to determine your belief, we must take the second step.

And if you do not intend to try, your thought is clinging to a set of patterned words behind which you will not venture. If this is the case with you — believer, unbeliever, or agnostic — you are a non-philosopher and a dogmatist. The dangers of dogmatism are perhaps not worth mentioning; I proceed to mention some of them. If you are a religious dogmatist, your attitude will lead to qualities quite the opposite of what might be expected from any high religion. Holding to a somewhat opaque set of words, it is not quite clear to you what it is you cherish with such zeal. It is possible that you demand altogether too little of yourself, accepting a personal mediocrity. Having taken God, immortality, and the expected side effects of these traditional views, as a crutch to hold your life upright, this crutch tends to gain an added function; it can be used, and in your circumstances tends to be used, as a club against the lives of others. Never having faced the problems of belief, you can afford to be intolerant of all who depart from your belief; and you do this without any understanding of the view from which they are departing, or the position to which they are arriving. You do all of this in a kind of blindness from which you might be saved by a confrontation with our problem. In another reading the point applies to the thoughtless unbeliever or agnostic — and his irreligion. Our second step may provide nothing our dogmatists would be willing to accept. And yet the tension and opposition they feel between belief and unbelief may have come from their belaboring each other so severely, and not from anything like the truth. Let

them stay with us just a little longer to see if the opposition between these views may not be reduced, if not removed. The priest
of Unamuno's story lived in agony because he held a truth which
he felt his people could not stand. For him the truth was written
large. Many believers have just this feeling, and live in an attitude
of righteous indignation toward those who do not share their
"truth." The feeling in both cases is inwardly much the same. But
should the truth be subtle, written in a very minuscule kind of script;
and should the problems of belief be more complex than we imagine, this agony and indignation may be beside the point.

In two cases out of three, it is necessary for us to take this second
step, which no one had desired, into the discussion of our problem.
And anyone who has taken our first step is now committed to the
second. I bow to the wishes of this logical majority, and proceed
with the discussion of our problem. And yet our discussion for
some time to come will have a double goal. We wish to find the
quality of our beliefs; and we wish to find the truth through assessing the positions of the believer and the unbeliever. Within our
Western world the position of the unbeliever is almost certainly the
scientific outlook. And the position of the believer is quite as certainly the luminous and compelling, if somewhat misty, point of
view of the Christian faith. Consequently, our discussion must
revolve (in an ellipse?) at least initially around these two perspectives on the world. But can we hope to determine how each of
these stands with respect to truth? In fact, these two views had
passed before us as we struggled with the problem which concerned
the nature of the truth. And at the time we could not say of
either that it possessed a final truth. If we cannot hope to determine
this, we shall reduce our expectations. Perhaps somewhat short of
"truth," we can estimate the strength of each position, and the consequences which result from the holding of each point of view.

And because the challenge to belief is found within our scientific
thought about the world, it is perhaps best to begin with the unbeliever. His point of view is nowhere better sketched than in an
essay by one of the great philosophers of the English-speaking
world. And this essay helped us turn an especially acute angle into
the exciting, if somewhat spiritually obtuse, twentieth century.
We shall quote only the beginning paragraphs of this brilliant
essay, which should if possible be read in full:

The Position of Unbelief

To Dr. Faustus in his study Mephistopheles told the history of the Creation, saying:

"The endless praises of the choirs of angels had begun to grow wearisome; for, after all, did he not deserve their praise? Had he not given them endless joy? Would it not be more amusing to obtain undeserved praise, to be worshipped by beings whom he tortured? He smiled inwardly, and resolved that the great drama should be performed.

"For countless ages the hot nebula whirled aimlessly through space. At length it began to take shape, the central mass threw off planets, the planets cooled, boiling seas and burning mountains heaved and tossed, from black masses of cloud hot sheets of rain deluged the barely solid crust. And now the first germ of life grew in the depths of the ocean, and developed rapidly in the fructifying warmth into vast forest trees, huge ferns springing from the damp mould, sea monsters breeding, fighting, devouring, and passing away. And from the monsters, as the play unfolded itself, Man was born, with the power of thought, the knowledge of good and evil, and the cruel thirst for worship. And Man saw that all is passing in this mad, monstrous world, that all is struggling to snatch, at any cost, a few brief moments of life before Death's inexorable decree. And Man said: 'There is a hidden purpose, could we but fathom it, and the purpose is good; for we must reverence something, and in the visible world there is nothing worthy of reverence.' And Man stood aside from the struggle, resolving that God intended harmony to come out of chaos by human efforts. And when he followed the instincts which God had transmitted to him from his ancestry of beasts of prey, he called it Sin, and asked God to forgive him. But he doubted whether he could be justly forgiven, until he invented a divine Plan by which God's wrath was to have been appeased. And seeing the present was bad, he made it yet worse, that thereby the future might be better. And he gave God thanks for the strength that enabled him to forego even the joys that were possible. And God smiled; and when he saw that Man had become perfect in renunciation and worship, he sent another sun through the sky, which crashed into Man's sun; and all returned again to nebula.

"'Yes,' he murmured, 'it was a good play; I will have it performed again.'"

Such, in outline, but even more purposeless, more void of meaning, is the world which Science presents for our belief. Amid such a world, if anywhere, our ideals henceforward must find a home. That Man is the product of causes which had no prevision of the end they were achieving; that his origin, his growth, his hopes and fears, his loves and his beliefs, are but the outcome of accidental collocations of atoms; that no fire, no heroism, no intensity of thought and feeling, can preserve an individual life beyond the grave; that all the labours of the ages, all the devotion, all the inspiration, all the noonday brightness of human genius, are destined to extinction in the vast death of the solar system, and that the whole temple of Man's achievement must inevitably be buried beneath the debris of a universe in ruins — all these things, if not quite beyond dispute, are yet so nearly certain, that no philosophy which rejects them can hope to stand. Only within the scaffolding of these truths, only on the firm foundation of unyielding despair, can the soul's habitation henceforth be safely built.

How, in such an alien and inhuman world, can so powerless a creature as Man preserve his aspirations untarnished? A strange mystery it is that Nature, omnipotent but blind, in the revolutions of her secular hurryings through the abysses of space, has brought forth at last a child, subject still to her power, but gifted with sight, with knowledge of good and evil, with the capacity of judging all the works of his unthinking Mother. In spite of Death, the mark and seal of the parental control, Man is yet free, during his brief years, to examine, to criticise, to know, and in imagination to create. To him alone, in the world with which he is acquainted, this freedom belongs; and in this lies his superiority to the resistless forces that control his outward life.

The savage, like ourselves, feels the oppression of his impotence before the powers of Nature; but having in himself nothing that he respects more than Power, he is willing to prostrate himself before his gods, without inquiring whether they are worthy of his worship. Pathetic and very terrible is the long history of cruelty and torture, of degradation and human sacrifice, endured in the hope of placating the jealous gods: surely, the trembling believer thinks, when what is most precious has been freely given, their lust for blood must be appeased, and more will not be required. The religion of Moloch — as such creeds may be generically called — is in essence the cringing submission of the slave, who dare not, even in his heart, allow the thought that his master deserves no adulation. Since the independence of ideals is not yet acknowledged, Power may be freely worshipped, and receive an unlimited respect, despite its wanton infliction of pain.

But gradually, as morality grows bolder, the claim of the ideal world begins to be felt; and worship, if it is not to cease, must be given to gods of another kind than those created by the savage. Some, though they feel the demands of the ideal, will still consciously reject them, still urging that naked Power is worthy of worship. Such is the attitude inculcated in God's answer to Job out of the whirlwind: the divine power and knowledge are paraded, but of the divine goodness there is no hint. Such also is the attitude of those who, in our own day, base their morality upon the struggle for survival, maintaining that the survivors are necessarily the fittest. But others, not content with an answer so repugnant to the moral sense, will adopt the position which we have become accustomed to regard as specially religious, maintaining that, in some hidden manner, the world of fact is really harmonious with the world of ideals. Thus Man creates God, all-powerful and all-good, the mystic unity of what is and what should be.[4]

Mr. Russell has presented the position of our unbeliever. And even these few paragraphs can provide a slender test of the extent to which we are believers, unbelievers, or something in between. Because our ultimate beliefs are so enmeshed in the substance of emotion, we can easily administer a brief reaction test. If you followed this description of the world with satisfaction, if you felt an inner glow, you may be an unbeliever. And if you exclaimed, "At last, we come to the point!" I become more certain of your unbelief. But if as you read, a slight feeling of irritation or revulsion began, growing with each paragraph, a feeling of pain rising toward the throat, you may be a believer. And if at this point you slammed the covers of the book, you are certainly (Tell him someone!) a hypersensitive and even intolerant believer. But how amazing! In these paragraphs you found no argument. What kind of philosophers are we, susceptible of flying off headlong in reaction without insisting first upon the presentation of a reason?

And how are we to test the claim when no argument appears on the surface of these words? We have become accustomed to the

[4] Bertrand Russell, "A Free Man's Worship," first published in the *Independent Review*, 1903. The essay has been many times reprinted. My source is Russell's *Mysticism and Logic and Other Essays* (London: Longmans, Green and Co., 1918), pp. 46–49. Reprinted by permission of George Allen & Unwin Ltd.

holding of our ultimate beliefs without reference to any set of reasons. But surely not among philosophers! We shall have no difficulty in finding reasons. But suppose we are devout believers. If we are believers, and if we find the reasons which support the attitude of unbelief, and if the reasons are strong and cogent, standing against our most pointed objections, are we to become unbelievers in half an hour, adhering henceforth only to this "scientific" point of view? The thought of such an impasse may keep some believers from entering into free discussion. And even if on these conditions we have an obligation to accept the point of view, could we bring ourselves to do so? Might we not agree verbally with the unbeliever, and yet remain believers in our hearts? But then our real position has not changed. We have only changed our verbal posture. And while it is our duty to assess the position of the unbeliever, I begin to wonder what the purpose of this assessment can be, if we cannot bring ourselves to share his unbelief, even on the assumption that we are not able to meet his arguments. In speaking of opposed beliefs we may have oversimplified our problem — grossly. I think we should be puzzled by the tremendous staying power of ultimate beliefs. And, before coming to our assessment of the point of view, we should find some explanation of the lack of power in argument to alter such beliefs.

A Considerable Digression

Turning somewhat to the side of the problem, there is a point of interest in these paragraphs deserving of attention. Did you notice the description of three types of men, existing in our day, each with a different point of view? They were: the savage who worships power; the believer who feels "the mystic unity of what is and what should be"; and the unbeliever who almost certainly has the truth, building on the "firm foundation" of despair. Here is an ironic circumstance. We had just succeeded in reducing our three types to two, when Russell provides us with another type. To our believer and unbeliever he adds the savage. Why? What is his intent? He intends, of course, an argument. He is presenting a deliberate scale. He thinks of the scientific point of view as something like the truth toward which all earlier stages of human thought have led. He wishes the view of the devout believer to be regarded, no less than the view of the savage, as outmoded and outworn. But why should one expect the most recent point of view to contain the truth? Were we assessing his position at the moment, we would pose this question. I am interested in a different point, concerning our beliefs and human culture. If his three types are now discernible within society, the fact is not devoid of interest. Each of these — the viewpoints of the savage, the believer, and the scientist — had their origin in different times. Each matured at a different time, and together they would seem to represent three levels in our cultural advance. And the opposition we have stressed begins to shade into the somewhat different question of cultural levels. If each of these points of view exists today, here is one evidence of the immense power within the past to help in the shaping of the present, and even by means of outworn points of view.

The fact is that our way of looking at the world has become as much a part of us as the clothes we wear. And just as we do not philosophize about our clothing, so our mental dress becomes an accessory not seeming to require discussion of any fact. And the savage, the devout believer, and the scientist, arrived in succession on the Western scene, each with his distinctive mental dress. When one thinks of it their physical costumes were distinctive, too. And if all three of these still exist, then the lives of men, however outwardly they may seem to be alike, remain inwardly at different levels of the cultural advance. Let us see if this view can be sustained. The deceptive conformity among men might easily be broken, simply by imagining each man clad in the outer garments appropriate to his inner point of view. How different the outer appearance of our world would be if we were to take this step, trying to estimate the relative strength of each level of our cultural ordering. Along the way we may come upon a more decisive kind of insight.

The Costume Ball

If we think back to the picture we had drawn of the members of our busy society rushing down Main Street, moving through our shopping centers, opening the numerous cans and bottles which provide the substance of a modern, home-cooked meal, vast numbers of our people would be clad in the first-century garb of that luminous time from which their ultimate beliefs have been derived. Many, at least, of the workers on the line in modern industry would be dressed in the red, blue, and brown robes — according to our imaginations — of a first-century Mediterranean people. The startling contrast between the whir of the machines, the functional design of the factory, and these garments is no less startling, really, than the actual contrast between our modern technical society and our inner costumes. However inappropriate these garments may be to the age of the machine, unfitting and, indeed, unsafe, they are by and large the garments of our mental life.

In this fitting of our outer garments to our inner life, the first-century robe, if the dominant costume, is not the only one. Russell speaks of the savage, respecting only power, and of his modern counterpart, the man who spends his life in a struggle for survival, believing in nothing beyond the survival of the fit. And Veblen, a philosopher in economics, argued that the value behind the drive to succeed in economic life is the value of the primitive, simply "prowess." This is the value, Veblen thought, behind the hunt and tribal warfare, goading primitive man to seek distinction. To be sure there used to be a kind of speech among many of those in economic life stressing the survival of the fit, talking of a "nature red in tooth and claw," as though the scene of industry were some natural scene, and thriving on the raw flesh of interpersonal conflict. And had a curious change not come over us, I would have imagined among the first-century figures standing on the line; among the men walking up and down this line — possibly in the role of management; among those sitting in their offices every day; and among those sitting once a week around long, oval conference tables, a goodly number dressed in the skins of the primitive — the age of the world in which their thought was shaped. Not long ago this was the speech of men engaged in business; today, I am informed, such rough talk has been replaced by a gentler kind of speech about "togetherness." Has the primitive, then, disappeared from the modern world? We continue to knock on wood, suspicious of the age of metals; we are nervous in the presence of certain numbers; and how quickly in most buildings the elevator takes us from the twelfth to the fourteenth floor; some vestiges of the primitive remain on the surface of our awareness, and possibly there is more of which we are not aware. Indeed, if the savage traits are no longer to be found in business, I can think of no modern instance, observable day by day, unless it is the spectacle of modern woman shopping. Of course, the instance would be vestigial, no more than a remaining trace of the primitives which

once we were. But if ours has become, as I have heard, a matriarchal society, then in some dimly conscious way modern women
may be turning to the fulfillment, as they feel, of their obligations
to the tribe and to themselves. And the resemblances to the tribal
hunt, or tribal warfare, are very striking. There is the forming of
the plan; to be sure, intelligence about the hunt is flashed about
the countryside by the Bell System and never, so far as I have
heard, by drums; and sometimes a preliminary meeting is called
for the heightening of enthusiasm. In both there is a ritual preparation. Pigments are applied with care to various portions of the
face. In both there is the wearing of a special costume, a ceremonial dress often including plumage; the body is encased in a kind
of metal sheath, apparently for purposes of defense, somewhat more
scant than medieval armor, as would be appropriate for a more
advanced society. They depart, early in the morning, full of confidence; and at times one detects a slight flaring of the nostrils as
their energy level rises sharply for this encounter. With heels
clicking smartly, veil drawn low to serve as visor, gauntlets in
place upon their arms, and "Charga-plates" in hand, they advance
into the maelstrom — to the hunt, or to give battle. Both of these
figures continue to apply, now one and then the other. The successful party consists of more than a single huntress. Typically,
some will be assigned to scouting duty to find the enemy, or flush
the game, aisle by aisle, while others advance to the attack. They
provide cover for each other and support. The special bargain
racks throughout the merchandising district are checked in sequence, as a hunter revisits his traps. An ability to make quick
decisions is essential here, leaving the less for the more promising
spoor. Finally, there is the decisive closing in upon the quarry,
the conversation with the clerk, the call to the purchaser, and the
achievement of the bargain. The tea room is their bivouac, a temporary shelter for any redrawing of the plan, a moment of respite
for recounting the heroic adventures in this chase or battle, and the
source of their supply of ritual salad. And in the evening they return, exhausted; gathering around the gleaming percolator, their
trophies are displayed; the details of their enterprise become a saga,
more than once recounted to the less adventurous members of the
clan. The special trophy of this hunt, chase, and unusual kind of
warfare, is the "bargain." The point is not alone to buy, but to
buy a bargain, and under conditions which amount — at least in the

imagination of the shopper — to outright theft, excelling the corporation at its game. The greater bargain carries with it the greater
distinction. This is where husbands cannot avoid confusion. However clearly they may demonstrate that this way of saving thirty
dollars has done nothing to improve the finances of the family, the
argument will not reduce the thrill of the purchase in any way.
The remonstrance may not even be heard. Inevitably, husbands
miss the point. Thirty dollars have not been saved; but thirty dollars worth of "prowess" has been gained; and it is this which is at
issue. The mental ordering of this enterprise might require, as its
outer expression, the skins of the primitive. Indeed, modern
woman seems to turn quite naturally to such a garment as her
outer covering, the manner in which she wishes to appear before
the world. I do not wish to make women more savage than they
really are. But what, apart from "prowess," could be the goal of
this important aspect of their lives?

The description, presented tongue in cheek, but only slightly —
uncertainly — so, has taken us beyond any point I may have
wished to make. However attractive the prospect, I do not really
intend for us to view all modern women, as though dressed in the
skins of the primitive. Our point was the vestigial presence of
primitive attitudes within our lives, their mere remaining trace.
The robes of the devout believer are quite as appropriate as the
skins of the primitive for modern women, for some of them at
least, equally, and interchangeably so. The suggestion of ordered
levels within our inner lives begins to emerge. Sometimes, and
under some conditions, the robes of the believer will be exchanged
for the skins of the primitive. The suggestion, if important, will
appear again; in fact, I think I can remember its having appeared
before — in other words, and in other of our discussions. For the
moment we shall imagine, wherever it may be appropriate, members of our society here and there — on the line, in offices, on Main
Street — wearing primitive dress when the dominant ordering of
their inner lives reflects the quality (or its lack) which Russell,
Veblen, and we ourselves have stressed.

Our gigantic costume ball nears completion. But we must turn
to a final costume, which appears with greater frequency year by
year. Russell mentions with undisguised approval the scientific
point of view, a third possibility for our mental ordering, offering
a third manner of explaining the details of our world. In the last

few centuries we have gained a new symbol. Its power in the world has increased dramatically in very recent years. Not long ago quite the most powerful symbol to place before men's eyes was the man of distinction. He was, I take it, a man of prowess, and his outer costume has already been arranged. To discover the new symbol it is only necessary to turn on one's television set — for instruction or entertainment — and the commercial begins at once (if we may refer to this area of our lives once more). The actor who is to give the "sell," as hardily as it can be softly done, is dressed in the authoritative garb. He is not a "man of distinction" in the older sense; he appears to be a man of science. His white, hip-length smock is spotless. In the background colored liquids bubble in gleaming beakers. The comforting flames of Bunsen burners flicker beneath these beakers, and the whole complex assembly is joined by a maze of glass and plastic tubing, leading in and out. It appears to be a still; at least the distillation of something is taking place, perhaps no more than the distillation of our credibility. And the symbol works upon us in this way: The white-smocked man, we feel, who dedicates his life to Bunsen burners, beakers, and gleaming liquids, must know and tell the truth. The symbol is effective only because the point of view has gained so tremendously in power. And throughout our society we may, hence, imagine a group of increasing size — and not only in the laboratories, the colleges, and research foundations; but in offices, modern kitchens, and standing on assembly lines — dressed appropriately in the white smocks, possibly belted in the back, which designate our new high priests of truth.

We can visualize the men and women of our society dressed in these three costumes. Most, as I imagine, wear the simple robes of a Mediterranean, agrarian people; but scattered through society, more numerously as we scan the status level upward, we shall find the skins of the primitive, and the white smocks of the scientist. And in this panorama we may discern our own appropriate garb.

This description, although in some ways grotesque, has not been offered with any trivial point in view. I have asked you to determine your "real" position, possibly an attitude different even from the "verbal" posture which may result from careful and extended discussion. But what is a "real" position? The costumes we have mentioned represent three great levels of cultural ordering. More than one level, the suggestion has arisen, can be present within a human life. And, to return to the theme of our previous discussion, when a man makes his way to the scientific level, and kicks away the ladder by which he made his climb, he has disposed of an imaginary ladder. How would this be possible? It is possible if the costumes of our imagination are, indeed, appropriate to the members of our society. The act of kicking away the ladder is even more an imaginary act, should these levels underly each other in our lives. Let us see if this further claim may not be upheld. Even if you are so "free" of dogma, "enlightened," and chary of unwarranted belief that you scarcely admit the existence of your room on the evenings when you are out, playing bridge down to the last trump, whist, or backgammon with your friends; nonetheless I ask if the views of the devout believer may not be found at another level of your being. As you discern the pattern of your life forming, according to or against your wish, do you not believe in some dimly conscious way in a kind of "accidental" providence, working out its themes? Your attitude of hopeful resignation seems to me no different than the attitude of the believer who says in his mind, "Thy will be done." And in moments of personal stress I greatly suspect the falling away of your keen-edged scientific reason, even if you guard your secret from every other person; and the appearance of a prayer, rising into awareness from some unknown depth, "Lord, help me." No matter how clearly you have thought your way to a position of agnosticism, or unbelief, I think you have spoken in your mind these words, and not in a light or cynical attitude of mind. And this inner, if only occasional, feeling must be taken into account in determining the quality of your belief. No matter what you say, are you really an unbeliever; are you in truth agnostic? To come to the details of our youthful and luxuriant belief, "the last trump," some may have to be reminded, did not have its origin in reference to a game of cards. And let me register this fantastic claim: Should you hear a trumpet sounding across this Western world one day, with a final, insistent, and judgmental sound, even you — enlightened unbeliever with a scientific turn of mind — would perhaps find yourself dropping to your knees. How do you know you would not? In a breakdown of communal order, statistics tell us (possibly lying, as statistics can) you would in all probability be among the looters of your community. Well, I assert, if you heard the sound of a final trump, you would in all probability be found upon your knees beside the devout believer. If neither of these contentions lends itself to proof, at least mine is the more complimentary of the two.

As a matter of fact, it may be necessary to support both of these apparently opposite claims. On some occasions, I assert, your sharply honed scientific objectivity and detachment will dissolve, and you will find yourself a devout believer. This language has the sound of the believer's familiar argument: There is no atheist; every man believes within his heart. In the main, I support the argument. While not altogether true, this is the case for most of us. But the argument carries a further step, even if some believers may not wish another step. It is not only bankers, businessmen, and the statisticians themselves, who will be found among the looters in any breakdown of established order. Beside them one may find the devout believer. And, of course, the phenomenon is not confined to looting; it extends to all of the instances of savagery which erupt from time to time within the social order. The reason is not difficult to find. Breakdown in the ordering, external to our lives, has removed the support from the settled inner ordering of our beliefs. And the presence of this possibility is the strongest possible reason for entering into the discussion of our problem. If a breakdown in society can alter our beliefs, these beliefs were never more than a kind of mental clothing, helpful to our other purposes, and conforming to the expectations of the world. All, or almost all, of the white-smocked figures in our society are devout believers in their hearts; and all, or almost all, of these devout believers are primitives at heart; and since this is the case, because so many of us hold our ultimate beliefs in the suggested manner, the question which concerns our social principles, and the nature of the society with which we surround our lives, becomes all the more important. But still more important is the problem of coming to terms with the details of our ultimate beliefs.

If there is some truth in our contention of the multiple cultural levels within our lives, the insight alters, somehow softening, the tense opposition among ultimate beliefs. Our insight blunts the edges of this opposition which tends to choke off the discussion of our problem. In addition, our fact explains the personal difficulty which comes to one who tries to find beyond the hackneyed words of any verbal posture his own position. Here again we come upon the intermixture of belief within our being. What should be done about this mixture? Should we try more strenuously to fit our lives into a single framework? This is the answer of Auguste Comte; and Russell would agree. His presentation of cultural levels contains the claim, as we have seen: The scientific attitude is the appropriate mental ordering for this stage of our advance and, therefore, true, or nearly so. But against this claim there is another fact to be registered in our account. Each level of culture has added something of importance to the world. We are speaking at the moment, let this be clear, of "importance" and not at all of truth. We are speaking of value and not of fact. And yet this fact about "importance" must enter our discussion.

The Three Levels and Their Value

The outlook of the primitive was world-wide, the first human attempt at mental ordering. At least, this is my claim. In no other manner can I understand the widespread traces of similar cultural practices in every part of the world. Men walked in a very dim light. They lived by fetish, totem, taboo, and sympathetic magic. Their ritual endeavors took the form of what I have called the "physical metaphor." They would enact figuratively what they expected of nature in actuality. In the hope of rain, and following the proper ritual, drops of water would be sprinkled on the ground, an imitation rain. Ritual love in the fields during the planting season was expected to induce fertility in the soil, producing an abundant harvest. (Let us not forget our ancestry, or indeed ourselves, in the rites of May.) Fertility rites seem to have formed the first powerful impulse behind our common worship. The goal of these ritual endeavours had every appearance of forcing the universe to conform to the pressing needs of man. They placed great confidence in the power of word, of image, and of ritual. And in this they were never disappointed. If the expected result did not occur, the ritual in use was not sufficient in its power; or a member of the tribe had destroyed its power through the breaking of some taboo. Adjustments were made; and in every case the validity of their ritual was justified at last. At last it would rain, — or at last the harvest would be abundant. I do not wonder at man, remaining for so many thousand years at the level of the savage; I wonder at his advance beyond this level. In seeking to explain their world, a poetry of myth and legend began to form. I have seized upon this matrix of myth and legend as the fulcrum of man's advance.

The mind of man had to be full of myth and legend, crammed with its variety and running over, before the necessary sense of system, and its consequent abstraction could begin to operate.

Russell insists upon the man-created God, and something of his claim is true; for out of magic, ritual, and a projection of man's feelings into his universe, the gods appeared. It is a fascinating story, this one of the development of the gods. One key, I take it, is the extension over ordinary objects of the quality of man's inner life — including his sense of purpose. The experience is known to all of us; we find it in the play of children; we find it in ourselves. Do you remember the brief spirit of revenge you felt against the chair which caused you to stumble in the dark? "I shall pay this insidious chair back in kind." At least, this would seem to have been the response of your nervous system, as you kicked the chair once more, adding to your pain. And if our savage finds the limb, which has fallen from the tree, striking his head "on purpose," will you then scoff at his construction? In the growth of the idea of God I find, as the other key, a working out of metaphorical interchange. In the extension of human meanings "predicates" are exchanged between man and nature; this interchange is essential to the growth of meaning. "John is a rock," we say today. "Og is a rock," the primitive may have said. And on occasion both of us would say: "The skies are angry." Further, we might say: How stormy was the face of my friend! The sea is raging! The man thundered against his enemies! Nature is placid after the storm. His explanation cleared the air. Nature is reliable. The result of this interchange and fusion is a humanized nature, and a man who sees his life as part of the scene of nature. The idea of God is a natural and necessary product of the growth of meaning, the final metaphor in which is fused every meaning of our human lives. But of course this view of God required thousands upon thousands of years to make its way into the minds of men.

The several thousand-year development, leading to the viewpoint of our devout believer, the dominant costume among our people, was an amazing vaulting movement upward from the gods of the primitives to a unitary principle of the divine. I wonder, too, at this advance. The single God and single universe arrived together, "God" and "Nature": the "Universe" — turning on a single center; and "God" — a center on which the universe could turn. The double conception has made possible more of our later achievement than we can easily imagine. The achievement of monotheism made possible an advance in the ethical appreciations of Western man, the unitary principle working on the conflicting sanctions of human conduct to produce a "higher" code, the ways of acting which can be held in a precise and clear unity of purpose. In such a unitary world it was possible to view each happening as a sign of the divine. The result was the strange and luminous world in which so many of our people live, where every happening, every object and experience, can be viewed both in terms of itself, and in terms of its spiritual, or value-carrying, equivalent. Thus viewed, every detail of our world bears the mark of a purpose beyond our own. And everywhere water is being turned into wine. Never has man's imagination produced a context for life with greater personal meaning. Our lives generally have been enlightened by this luminous time. It enters into the shaping of our natures. Let us make no mistake about it; this period of the world marked a great, original awakening. And my point is this: Within our century we have witnessed the eruption of tremendous savagery; whole peoples have more than once returned to the level of the primitive in their loyalties, attitudes, and appreciations, forgetting whatever might prevent their brutal destruction of human lives and values. When the higher level wears thin, the energies of the primitive rise once more.

Now when the third, great level came, it was its genius to stress fact instead of value, to seek out lawlike behavior, to reduce the world to a set of equations, and through the transformation of these symbols to transform the features of the world. Its power over fact is very clear. Its methods need not be described; we know these methods well enough, having lived our lives among them. The unbeliever claims we must rest all our hopes upon the third level of our cultural ordering. And I pose a value question. Has our modern attitude toward the world sufficient power to mold and keep our people beyond the level of the primitive? I examine with care every aspect of the world of science open to my view. I find not one single shred of evidence that from its functioning any compelling "ought to be" could ever form; here I find no bridge between the "is" and "ought to be." Further, I find these men of science generally at work within the narrow boundaries of a narrow field. Each knows his duty; each has a sense of the questions he can fairly ask; often great machines help to find the answers as our scientific workers stand by, notebooks in their hands, recording the dicta of the great machines. What they do and what they find have much importance. But they can do their work without knowledge of the sources of our culture. A precise and technical reason is the necessary mental instrument; and they require no other kind of knowledge. They can do their work, although they need not do so, while remaining barbarians in their inner lives. Even if it is the truth, the scientific attitude is lacking in a number of components which are essential to our lives.

On the other hand, the view of the devout believer may be a myth. Even if it is a myth, it has been our salvation, or so I claim. Introduction to the first-century world has largely shut us off from barbarism in our personal lives. This we must never forget, although the value of this achievement has nothing to do with the question of its truth. If the view in question has shut us off from barbarism, this is an indication of its power to stand within our lives as something more than an appropriate bit of mental clothing. For some this point of view has been not only an object of their affections, but also an object of their understanding, held in full awareness, and central to their being. The thought forms of the first-century world, then, have had sufficient power to keep many of those whom it has touched from slipping back beyond this century — into barbarism. If these forms present a myth, it is the most fortunate myth in Western history. The "scientific attitude" could not begin to do the work within our lives which this compelling myth has done.

And we have found the robes of the devout believer to be the dominant costume of our time. My only plaint is this: We have been enlightened generally by the luminous first-century world, and, generally, by no later Renaissance. But every Renaissance has added something. We too much lack whatever has been added in every other awakening. In particular, the devout believer may not have felt the new pulse of life which stirred centuries since in Athens, Greece; nor beheld the strange new light which began to shine from Florence, Italy; he may not have experienced the age of Reason, or of the Enlightenment; he may not have passed through his French Revolution, or even his American Revolution. The tragic fact is not our first-century character, but the general absence from our lives of the developments within our culture, extending across nineteen hundred other years. Consequently, we may have important elements missing from our being; nothing as obvious, perhaps, as an arm or a leg; but perhaps something as subtle as a lack of appreciation for another's right to be his own individual man. We need, of course, to define and to develop our own persons. And for this we need to gain the inner attitudes, the missing elements, from these other luminous periods of our world.

In answer to the question, "What is your ultimate belief?" one might find himself holding at once to points of view from all three of our cultural levels. In some sense, each of these is part or parcel of our natures. And yet these views, if not as strongly opposed as we at first had thought, contain more than a single type of opposition. We must rework their mixture. But "the truth, the truth above all!" Perhaps we can rework this mixture in terms of truth. Once again we are recalled from other questions to the unavoidable question which asks about the truth of our beliefs. We turn to the view of the unbeliever.

The Position of the Unbeliever, Seriously Treated

Description of a Possible Position

For the unbeliever, allowing Russell's essay to express the point of view, the world is purposeless and void of meaning, alien and inhuman, the product of senseless causes. And our individual and collective life is destined for extinction. The vision of desolation is more awesome here than in the most extreme utterances of a Spengler or a Toynbee. They foresaw each society at last in ruins. Russell, by extension of the "laws" of physics, sees the universe in ruins, unfit for human life, the victim of heat death, cold death, or some other catastrophic end.

In such a view what transformation must take place within the traditional patterns of our thought concerning "soul" and "God"? Consider, first, the arc of human life. One becomes established in the world. He is infant, youth, and man in quick succession; and as his powers increase, so they come to their decline, down through a second childhood, plummeting once again below the level of personality, as the arc completes itself. At first he was only a candidate for personality; unless death intervenes to halt the process, he will reach the point in his decline where he is again below the human level.

Our increasing knowledge of the brain and nervous system strongly suggests, if it does not require, the viewing of man's self or personality as the sheer result of bodily functioning, and coincident with its life. Certainly, this view is suitable to the functional age in which we live. And a serious question can be raised about the usefulness of the concept, "soul," based upon our recent knowledge of the intimate relationship between our various responses and the areas of the brain.

The idea of a soul, separable from the body, had been an anomaly long before the rapid increase in this aspect of our knowledge. This idea began in the mistaken identification of the air we breathe with the source of life. The term stood for the literal inspiration and expiration of our breath; this was a soul which could be felt. But consider what happened to the concept in its development. It became the idea of a something which was just the opposite of the body: a thing which occupied no space, and had no mass, a quality without quantity, a something which was yet a nothing. Thomas Hobbes thought the idea of soul to be a contradiction; the idea requires an "immaterial material." Is this not very like calling for a "round square"? It makes no sense to speak of a "round square." Very likely, it is equally nonsensical to speak of an "immaterial material."

And if the idea of "soul" began in a mistake, and developed into a meaningless contradiction, the case is hardly better with the concept, "God." Beginning in man's intuition of the living power around him, it became associated with various sacred objects, this tree, that mountain; among nomadic tribes the god became associated with the people as their guide and destiny. At last the concept grew into the universal being. Indeed, if one can read the future from the past, because the histories of these two ideas have been so much alike, their destinies are probably also tied together. Where is God? One could say "where," so long as this power was the god of a tree or of a mountain. One could still say "where" when heaven was just above the clouds. But where is he now? The answer, given by theologians for quite a long time, is: God is "everywhere and nowhere." But consider the formula: What is "everywhere" is everything; what is "nowhere" is nothing. Does this not make God into an "everything-nothing"? How much like the "immaterial-material"! How very like the "round square"! Once again, we move toward contradiction.

The power which at first explained the falling stick became the power "explaining" the existence of the universe. But how useful is this very general explanation? And what evidence can be cited in its support? No scientist requires the help of "God" in forming scientific explanations. The biological world would rock with laughter should some geneticist explain mutations, saying: "God has made the change." We can examine the parts of the nearby universe in some detail. No God is to be seen when the astronomer sweeps the skies by telescope. No God is evident when the biologist sweeps his microscope over the field of the minute. And no God enters into the calculations of the physicist.

Neither God nor soul is "seen" at any time; neither God nor soul performs a useful function in modern explanations. The ideas of both "soul" and "God" have developed into, or toward, meaningless contradictions; they share a most anomalous position in our day. And if all of this is so, our attitude must center in the present world, and on man's present life. We must build our philosophies on a different base; such is the contention.

By means of the idea of "God," man was able to feel a relation between his life and the total universe. The idea of "soul" allowed men to believe in their own immortality. What substitute can the unbeliever provide for these two concepts? We may allow Russell to begin the answer:

> Brief and powerless is Man's life; on him and all his race the slow, sure doom falls pitiless and dark. Blind to good and evil, reckless of destruction, omnipotent matter rolls on its relentless way; for Man, condemned to-day to lose his dearest, to-morrow himself to pass through the gate of darkness, it remains only to cherish, ere yet the blow falls, the lofty thoughts that ennoble his little day; disdaining the coward terrors of the slave of Fate, to worship at the shrine that his own hands have built; undismayed by the empire of chance, to preserve a mind free from the wanton tyranny that rules his outward life; proudly defiant of the irresistible forces that tolerate, for a moment, his knowledge and his condemnation, to sustain alone, a weary but unyielding Atlas, the world that his own ideals have fashioned despite the trampling march of unconscious power.[5]

In the universe of the unbeliever one does not revert to savagery; man sustains the world of his ideals alone. Is there in this view a

[5] *Ibid.*, p. 54.

substitute for the idea of God, associated for so long with our vision of perfection? I think there is. First, observe the title of Russell's essay: "The Religion of Free Men." In ordinary terms a demand issues from any religion. And the religious demand is, ordinarily, a demand for faith in God. In the ordinary view this demand is expected to retain its force even against the organized power of the state when necessary. The religious person is expected to adhere to his ideal even against organized power. Suppose, then, the power — indifferent or hostile to this ideal — is not the state, but the universe itself. You answer, "The fact sweeps away every vestige of this demand. How can one have faith in a nonexistent God?" If one were to have faith in a nonexistent person, say a friend who has passed away, one would have faith in that for which he stood. To have faith in a nonexistent God one would have faith in that for which this God had stood in the minds of men. The unbeliever extends the religious demand to its furthest limits; he has faith in a vision of perfection not instanced by the universe. He feels his ideal of perfection to be superior to the total drift of cosmic force, even though his surgent concept is a sheer ideal with no cosmic power at its command, save the bits of power in human purposes.

How else would you have it? Surely, it is possible that God does not exist. If he does not exist, then the universe is no more than a display of force. Will you grovel before mere force? If not in the state, why in the universe? One's faith may be a bit more comfortable if one has to stand only against the power of men, and not also against the universe. But is there a difference here in principle? "Unhappily, God is dead," one may imagine the unbeliever saying. "Henceforth, the burden of this ideal belongs to man alone." And if he is right in his facts, I think we must agree with his conclusion. The religious demand, stretched to its furthest point, is a demand to stand for the vision of perfection against the power of an indifferent, and indeed hostile (although unintentionally hostile) universe. The vision of perfection, along with the counsel to stand together against "the trampling march of unconscious power," replaces the concept of God in the philosophy of the unbelievers.

In place of "soul" with its consequence of personal immortality, one finds the idea of "self" with a finite conscious span. What happens to our personal immortality? In the first place our attention is recalled from the unknown future to the short span of life in which our opportunity lies. Is this not proper? Our concern is to be with life, not death. In a second sense a form of social immortality replaces the personal immortality of the older view. One lives on in his contributions to society, and in the memories of his friends. Russell, of course, cannot share this point; we shall come to the reason shortly.

Our description of the unbeliever's position is now complete. And should his view be true, one who had postponed the possible development of his life in a thoughtless bending to tradition would have gambled wrongly, living not for the day but for an eternity after, not bringing eternity into life, as Spinoza would say, but enduring life for an eternity added to the bargain. I think there is a quality in every man which is called out by the austerity of this view. Even if the truth should be unpleasant, it would be worth something, would it not, to have our eyes open at last? It would be worth something to be forced to throw away his mental crutches. And why not stand against the universe? Why should our desire for security be so intense as to require a view in which every misfortune has its counter, and every tragedy turns out at last to be a gay romance with never-ending curtain calls? And why should not death be real, lasting, and final?

A Consequence of Russell's View

Russell's extension of the universe of scientific discourse into a picture of the world — let us be clear about this — is no part of science. Nor does Russell make this claim. He does seem to believe his view to be a reflection of the "scientific attitude." In this he may be right; but the working attitude of a scientist, and the truth of the universe, may be two quite different matters. Much is persuasive in this view; but as I think about it, the argument begins to turn around in my hands. I remember Russell's vision of a universe in ruins, an event which is inevitable if one's attitude is formed merely by extension of the scientific outlook; and I begin to require a conversation with the unbeliever. Here is the question in my mind: "Since personal immortality is a sheer delusion, what provides the permanence for human life?" The unbeliever, although not Russell, will tend to answer, "It lies in man's social immortality."

Of course. But society remembers very little. Were you a property owner or did you rent? Did you have much property or none whatever? Who will know or care a century from now? Did you achieve first rank in your community in some particular line of work? Were you the president of the Rotary Club? Were you treasurer of the Elks? Were you a member of the country club? Probably, no one will know within a century, or will care should the knowledge be at hand. Do you realize that within a century no one will remember your birthplace, the place of the momentous event which for so long you had expected to somehow change the course of history? This little glimpse, which occurs to everyone occasionally, is really a slight view of the world under the aspect of eternity. More important, the vestiges of "you" which remain for a time in the world are no longer part of you, but sentences written somewhere, or traces of some kind, understood by all to be about "another" — and this makes a difference. The vital center has shifted. It is only his own birthplace which a man cannot forget. At length the sentences, the traces, will be forgotten. And if someone, much later, should come upon these traces of your life, it is almost impossible for us to realize how external and unimportant they will seem to be. If it is your name on a piece of paper, it will no longer leap out impressively, a luminous tracing around its edges, as does this name of yours when you read it in the New York Times (SARAH JONES ENGAGED IN SCHENECTADY, or JOHN SMITH ENGAGED IN ARSON). It will be just another name. And at last every trace and every sentence will be forgotten.

The unbeliever may answer thus: "What you say is true, and yet what I have done, what I have accomplished, the causes I have started up, will go on working within the fabric of society, even if my name is not attached to them. And my children; they allow even my name to be remembered."

I answer: To be sure, the causes you have started will continue for a time; and it is something to be an ancestor, if only of a causal chain. To be an ancestor in the proper sense is better still. Few parents will deny the sense of a continuance, a sense of lengthening the spans of their own lives, through the birth of an heir — or heiress. How we court this form of immortality! And should the expected completely fulfill all expectations, should an heir arrive, how immortal, how like a Greek god, is the appearance of the father. "The family name will continue," he says in satisfaction. But do you not recall the decision to which we had to come about the patterning of history? The framework in which your life is lived, and the lives of your posterity, the industry in which you labored, the society in which the country club exists, will pass away. And along with this will end all of the types of social immortality you have mentioned.

"Then culture will continue. Other societies form, we had agreed, to inherit whatever can be saved from the breakdown of any particular society."

If this is the only form of social immortality, it removes for most of us, as we well know, the possibility of permanence for our lives. What have you contributed to human culture? Forgive me! You may have done, or expect to do, a great deal for the advance of culture. In any event only a few will be remembered in this manner. And the memory is so external and impersonal, a chore for school children and a problem for scholars! These memories, a word, a sentence, a fragment, will concern us only if we should happen to be among the chief movers of our age. And beyond all of this there is the firm conviction of a Russell, which can be reached by anyone who extends the scientific outlook: The conditions of the universe, providing a shelter for human life, are slowly changing. Heat death, cold death, sheer loss of working energy, catastrophic end, one of these surely faces the human race if the time dimension is lengthened out enough; and it lengthens — moment by moment.

I can think of but one final reply to the meaninglessness which begins to invest our human life. "Very well," the unbeliever may reply, "What has been said may rob my constructive purposes of their meaning. But consider my sense of enjoyment. The pleasures I enjoy were intended to satisfy me only for the moment, and in this they have succeeded. Your argument is only forcing us to live within the present, seeking pleasure with Epicurus."

The argument must be forceful if it succeeds in reducing your position, and man's position in the world, to nothing beyond the pursuit of pleasure. If this is the situation only a very indifferent life could satisfy the truth of things. The position of our unbeliever has changed radically in the course of this short conversation. But I must ask even of his final view: "Of what moment were you speaking?" In our present understanding of the world, the moment in which your pleasures were satisfied will also be swept away; every trace of that moment will disappear. The state of the universe will be exactly as though the moment in question had never occurred. It will be as though there had been no moment, no pleasure, and no "you." In one of these many types of annihilation, the reason for a satisfying pleasure shall have likewise disappeared. The meaning, in short, of every aspect of your existence shall have been removed.

What is the argument? The heart of man's endeavor is the maturation of his purposes. Man acts upon his purposes, achieving something in the world. And if our lives are reduced to nothing the achievement is swept away and man's purpose with it. Reduction to nothing blanks out the reason for acting upon any purpose. For the unbeliever a retroactive meaninglessness destroys the purpose of his life.

And if our lives are to have meaning, there must be a permanence beyond that of people remembering (who don't remember), and people caring (who don't care). And if our discussion has not convinced you of the meaningless nature of your personal life, I think you simply do not believe in even a possible destruction of every trace of what you have accomplished, or will accomplish. You must have a sense of the permanence of things which goes beyond any form of social immortality. You may share with many others the intuition that whatever has happened has happened forever. Indeed, you may have the feeling that your total life will be remembered, as you remember and dwell upon your past. But the view which emerges from this feeling is suspiciously like a divine memory, retaining every detail of the past. And this is not a possible position for the philosophy of unbelief.

Either God exists or life is meaningless! Can this be the conclusion of our argument? Perhaps we have made a false step along the way; and yet I cannot find an error. Certainly in its initial description the philosophy of unbelief seemed perfectly tailored to our free and value-centered man. But see where it has led!

In any case this is not an argument for God. It is an argument for the meaningless character of human life, if the view of the unbeliever is the truth. The conclusion should encourage us to pore through even the musty volumes of theologians before settling definitely upon this view of human life. The view may be true, and human life quite meaningless. One must admire the modern existentialists who, in honesty, come to this conclusion of the meaningless character of existence. Beginning with Nietzsche's statement, "God is dead," and leaving out a number of intermediate steps, we might compress their view into the following: "God is dead . . . therefore, life is meaningless." The absence of God would not seem to make this much difference; and the possibility of a false step is still present to my mind.

Our argument started from the assumption of an isolated self within a barren universe. Should one begin from the idea of God, there is still a point to be mentioned against the philosophy of unbelief. I think man could live in struggle against a barren universe. Man has courage when it is needed; he knows how to stand against his fears; and he need not remain afraid of death, once its possibility has been squarely faced. The point about the barren universe is not man's inability to control his fears. He is simply not convinced. However useless the idea of God may be for scientific explanations, there is a strange quality in our thought about existence which the idea of a powerful God helps man to explain. Perhaps Schelling strikes upon this quality with his mysterious question: "Why is there not Nothing?" If someone urges that man is, after all, an expression of the universe, to be explained in natural terms, this does not remove our curious wonder: "Why then this kind of a universe which can have man as its natural expression?" Or if, on the contrary, the claim is made that man is an isolated and peculiar phenomenon, clinging to existence in a well-insulated but infinitesimal portion of a vast and barren space, the wonder takes this form: "Why should there have been this exception to the barren and the vast, which is our often warm and cheerful human life?" And if, in reply, it is urged that man occurred through evolutionary struggle, one is amazed at the occurrence of struggle in a barren universe. And when the struggle is explained as a chance affair in which through imagination-shattering lengths of time, compatible factors merged to yield a protoplasm capable of struggle, one may be surprised by his feeling that the universe cannot be so very unlike man, if life has emerged even through its most capricious chance effects. And one will even be amazed at the run of luck, which has allowed this chance universe to exist through such lengths of time. The question occurs on many levels. That the question can occur, and recur, a new question forming from each answer, is another reason why, or perhaps merely a recursive statement of the fact that, man remains unconvinced by the arguments of unbelief. Both of these lines of comment suggest further discussion of the philosophy of belief.

The Position of the Believer

It is not impossible to discern how one might arrive at the idea of God, even with our sophisticated attitudes on so many aspects of the world; and, indeed, partly because of just these attitudes. Of course, we would not be arriving at our goal by the same long and tortuous route taken by Western culture in its reflection through many centuries. And yet if one looks behind the metaphors of "Father," "King," and "Lord," searching for the common meaning of these terms, he will find something like a concept of perfection to be placed in contrast to our obviously imperfect world. How these very imperfect beings, the gods and goddesses of an earlier age, became the "perfect" being, is one of the less clear aspects of our topic. But if the unitary principle, once achieved, could enlighten the material of our conduct, still ethical insight must have helped in the shaping of the ideal being. And if our present reflection cannot duplicate the long evolution of the concept, still any believer will find his thought beginning in the imperfections of the world; he will find something incomplete, or not quite satisfying, about his world; and his thought will end in something other than the world, an object more satisfying and more "adequate."

Are we not aware of the many times we have fallen into error, the times we have been mistaken? To say we are mistaken is to say that the truth lies elsewhere. But where does it lie? Where is it? One feels the need of saying: There is a truth to correct my error. Now, even if I do not have this truth, must it not *be* somewhere, must it not be *somewhere?* What is a truth possessed by no one? When there is a truth still to be discovered, when we know we are in error, God becomes for the believer the fact that the truth lies somewhere and in some direction. The errors of experience suggest a truth somehow beyond experience.

And are we not aware, at times, of having taken the lesser course, of having chosen the second-best? When we come to this conviction, should it be a true conviction, then there must somehow be the first-best, the greater course, a real perfection, compared to which we have chosen poorly. But you will say: The point requires only the possibility of the first-best, the greater course, and the real perfection. Even so, this possibility must be real. And God becomes the fact that the first-best, and greater course, is really possible.

And should this happen in your experience — it will be more likely to happen if you are drawn rather more to value than to fact — in the most important sense you would have traced again the path of history. God, we had said, is the final metaphor in which is fused every meaning of human life — transfigured, ennobled, and refined, as we had later added. The result would be a rich and interesting concept; of course, it might appear to you to be no more than an esthetic object. And perhaps it is.

Even so, from this kind of movement in our thought one might arrive at a view of the universe which contrasted the error and imperfection of our lives, the changeable nature of the world with its marching time, its fragmentary split-apartness, with an eternal and real perfection, a total truth standing as our impossible goal. And we might understand the contrast not only as one between time and eternity, finite and infinite; but also as a contrast between human and divine, man and God. At least it would not be stubborn nonsense to read the world in such a manner.

If this were your manner of reading out the world, doubtless you could not avoid some problems. The very richness of your concept might lead to numerous contradictions, including the "everywhere-nowhere" manner of existence, cited by theologians. And yet some men, struggling with this "everywhere-nowhere" contradiction, have learned to be believers. St. Augustine reports how this contradiction had kept him from the Christian faith for many years; he had thought an infinite being would require an infinite body; and yet through the study of Plato he found, or so he thought, the key which made it possible for him to accept the concept. Now the movement of this rich idea toward contradiction can be seen in St. Augustine's description of this being:

What, then, art Thou, O my God — what, I ask, but the Lord God? For who is Lord but the Lord? or who is God save our God? Most high, most excellent, most potent, most omnipotent; most merciful and most just; most hidden and most near; most beauteous and most strong, stable, yet contained of none; unchangeable, yet changing all things; never new, never old; making all things new, yet bringing old age upon the proud and they know it not; always working, yet ever at rest; gathering, yet needing nothing; sustaining, pervading, and protecting; creating, nourishing, and developing; seeking, and yet possessing all things. Thou lovest, and burnest not; art jealous, yet free from care; repentest, and hast no sorrow; art angry, yet serene; changest Thy ways, leaving unchanged Thy plans; recoverest what Thou findest, having yet never lost; art never in want, whilst Thou rejoicest in gain; never covetous, though requiring usury. That Thou mayest owe, more than enough is given to Thee; yet who hath anything that is not Thine? Thou payest debts while owing nothing; and when Thou forgivest debts, losest nothing. Yet, O my God, my life, my holy joy, what is this that I have said? And what saith any man when he speaks of Thee? Yet woe to them that keep silence, seeing that even they who say most are as the dumb.[6]

Not all of the statements coupled in this passage are contradictions; but if you begin to have the feeling that Augustine would have wished them so, your feeling would be close, I think, to being true. Saint Augustine, this is obvious enough, has gone out of his way to place side by side a group of statements, not all of which can be literally held together in any system of philosophy. Some systems can express more of these ideas than others; and the effect of the passage on our minds is much, I think, like the effect of music. One feels a sense of power in the expression, a sense of importance; one is stirred, and possibly disturbed; but literal, prosaic meanings are not present in abundance. The richness of the resulting "concept" seemed to Saint Augustine to take his view beyond the realm of mere philosophy; thus, he rejoiced in the presence of paradox; and a paradox is just a contradiction for anyone who is not a theologian.

If you could come to terms with the everywhere-nowhere problem, if you could learn to say that God, like any of Plato's ideas, *is* where it is relevant, in a sense everywhere and in the same sense nowhere, there would be other problems. How can one understand the existence of something eternal over against the time of which we are aware? Whatever eternity might be, it would seem to be quite different from the time of our expeiience. The Augustinian way of expressing this is to regard eternity as the whole of time, concentrated at an instant. The conception is powerful, and has become a standard view for many varieties of the Western believer; it serves the purpose of granting to the eternal being knowledge

[6] St. Augustine, *Confessions*, Bk. I, Chap. IV, from *Basic Writings of Saint Augustine*, ed. Whitney J. Oates (New York: Random House, 1948), Vol. I, p. 5.

of every detail of our temporal world; it brings together eternity and truth. Whatever has been is now in God's eternity; at once, the meaningless world of the unbeliever disappears. And yet this view makes a shadow-play of time. Whatever is to be in the future now is, and has always been, a part of God's eternity. Unless I am mistaken, this conclusion interferes with the meaningful life which the view restores to man. If the total future is fixed by God's prevision, there can be no human freedom. We could not do other than what is even now contained in this already definite future time.

The problems present in this view are sufficient in their number to provide an active imagination with years of mental exercise. Such struggle might not be unrewarding for, basically, if the tangle about the future could be resolved, this view retains meaning within our human lives. And, possibly, something can be done to lessen the sense of paradox (or contradiction) which so delighted Augustine. The source of these problems can be traced, as we had found, to the concept's being a fusion of every human meaning, concentrated at a point. My evidence is the saying, used by philosophers until recent times: God is the sum of all positive predicates. No problem of consistency arises so long as our human meanings concerning beauty, truth, goodness, and the details of temporal passage, exist in fragments within our separate experiences. But concentrate these qualities at a point, add eternity to them, infinity, and a block existence; one is immediately in the middle of a thicket. Affirm less of the divine being, and one's problems diminish; at the same time the concept loses in its power over our imaginations.

The infinite being, standard object of our Western religious devotion, is a difficult conception, yet perhaps more subtle than an outright contradiction, and possibly rather too rich in meanings, instead of being completely meaningless. But if the idea of God is not simply absurd, we may ask about its possible defense. As for the idea of "soul," we can offer no more than a single comment. Imagine, if you will or can, David Hume among the Brahmans (the Indian, and not the Boston, branch of this proud, Aryan stock) who spend decades of their lives in an effort to understand, to "realize," their "souls" or "selves," concentrating with breathless interest on the unusual "awareness of awareness" in the human creature; and after many years, by their own admission, becoming aware of a self or soul within their lives. Imagine David Hume saying about one of these men what he has said for us: "He may, perhaps, perceive something simple and continued which he calls *himself;* though I am certain there is no such principle in me." How would the Brahman reply? "How long have you tried . . . and how hard?" If David Hume sits at his desk, and "looks" into the theatre of his mind for an hour or so, finding only change and succession, a dance of impressions, is this not to be expected? I am not arguing for the reality of the human "soul"; but I am arguing against a facile and "out-of-hand" rejection of the notion.

The Arguments of the Believer

We are virtually committed to turn to the literature of our past — dull, technical and prosaic though it may be — in order to re-examine the concepts of soul and God. Many arguments have been constructed with the conclusion: God exists. In sum, I doubt if any other kind of argument occupies more space in the libraries of the West — or gathers more dust. Men argue sometimes to satisfy their doubts. The presence of this literature suggests men may never have been quite certain about the existence of this God; or else men have been dissatisfied with the arguments they have found; or unhappy about the difficulties present in our affirmations concerning God, compared to the straight forward nature of our ordinary knowledge. How do these arguments proceed? They tend to pick up some important, notable, or pervasive element of the world — the presence of pattern, of causation, of imperfection, of contingency — and weave this element into an argument. God stands to the argument as the explanation of the pattern, its ultimate cause, perfection, and the necessity which sustains our finitude. Or, to put the same thought in a better manner, the arguments for God draw a contrast between the world as imperfect, finite, incomplete, not self-sufficient, derivative, and contingent; and God as the perfect, infinite, complete, self-sufficient, primal, and necessary being. And the argument finds the first side of this contrast requiring the second side for its completion. Phrasing my explanation in this way allows us to mention the most unusual argument which begins from the second side of our contrast, and from the conception of this being alone moves grandly to the conclusion of its actual existence. Much disagreement may be found concerning what these arguments prove — if anything. For each argument I shall try to provide two things: First, the argument itself; and then its standard criticism.

The chief critics of our traditional beliefs have been David Hume and Immanuel Kant. In every case but one we shall take our criticism from Hume's great classic, the *Dialogues on Natural Religion*. In every case but one we shall allow Thomas Aquinas to present the argument. And, ultimately, the final decision will be left to you.

The Argument from Design

The most familiar of these arguments, written even on billboards across America, begins from the presence of order, design, or apparent purpose in the world; this is the quality one would expect should the world have been the result of an intelligent plan. Certainly, to achieve order within our human experience intelligence is required. The functional watch requires a watchmaker. If intelligence is necessary in the achievement of order among men, how much more intelligence and purpose must have been required in establishing the various levels and types of order within the whole of nature. One should consider carefully the "how much more" feature of these arguments. Thomas Aquinas gives the argument in this form:

> We see that things which lack knowledge, such as natural bodies, act for an end, and this is evident from their acting always, or nearly always, in the same way, so as to obtain the best result. Hence it is plain that they achieve their end, not fortuitously, but designedly. Now whatever lacks knowledge cannot move towards an end, unless it be directed by some being endowed with knowledge and intelligence; as the arrow is directed by the archer. Therefore some intelligent being exists by whom all natural things are directed to their end; and this being we call God.[7]

What is the criticism of this argument? One can ask if this is not an instance of reasoning by analogy. Is it a strong analogy? One may ask, next, about the presence of disorder in nature. Can the "how much more" conclusion be drawn from such mixed evidence? Hume makes both of these points.

> A very small part of this great system, during a very short time, is very imperfectly discovered to us; and do we then pronounce decisively concerning the origin of the whole?

[7] Thomas Aquinas, *Summa Theologica*, Part I, Ques. 2, Art. 3, *Basic Writings of Saint Thomas Aquinas*, ed. Anton C. Pegis (New York: Random House, and London: Burns & Washbourne Ltd., 1945), Vol. I, p. 23.

Admirable conclusion! Stone, wood, brick, iron, brass, have not, at this time, in this minute globe of earth, an order or arrangement without human art and contrivance; therefore the universe could not originally attain its order and arrangement, without something similar to human art. But is a part of nature a rule for another part very wide of the former? Is it a rule for the whole? Is a very small part a rule for the universe? Is nature in one situation, a certain rule for nature in another situation vastly different from the former? . . . When two *species* of objects have always been observed to be conjoined together, I can *infer*, by custom, the existence of one wherever I *see* the existence of the other; and this I call an argument from experience. But how this argument can have place, where the objects, as in the present case, are single, individual, without parallel, or specific resemblance, may be difficult to explain. And will any man tell me with a serious countenance, that an orderly universe must arise from some thought and art like the human, because we have experience of it? To ascertain this reasoning, it were requisite that we had experience of the origin of worlds; and it is not sufficient, surely, that we have seen ships and cities arise from human art and contrivance.[8]

The conditions requiring intelligence in our human arts, and the conditions of the universe, are so unlike that no true argument can be made in reasoning from one to the other. In addition to this fact, Hume finds another; the evidence is too mixed to allow an inference from the order of the universe to a supreme being. Imagine a limited being, appearing in our world, one who does not share the prejudgments we take to the world. Would he make the inference to a wise and powerful deity?

Did I show you a house or palace, where there was not one apartment convenient or agreeable; where the windows, doors, fires, passages, stairs, and the whole economy of the building, were the source of noise, confusion, fatigue, darkness, and the extremes of heat and cold; you would certainly blame the contrivance, without any further examination. The architect would in vain display his subtilty, and prove to you, that if this door or that window were altered, greater ills would ensue. What he says may be strictly true: the alteration of one particular, while the other parts of the building remain, may only augment the

[8] David Hume, *Dialogues Concerning Natural Religion, The Philosophical Works of David Hume* (Boston: Little, Brown and Co., 1854), Vol. II, pp. 440–441.

inconveniences. But still you would assert in general, that, if the architect had had skill and good intentions, he might have formed such a plan of the whole, and might have adjusted the parts in such a manner, as would have remedied all or most of these inconveniences. His ignorance, or even your own ignorance of such a plan, will never convince you of the impossibility of it. If you find any inconveniences and deformities in the building, you will always, without entering into any detail, condemn the architect. . . . Is the world, considered in general, and as it appears to us in this life, different from what a man, or such a limited being, would, *beforehand,* expect from a very powerful, wise, and benevolent Deity? It must be strange prejudice to assert the contrary. And from thence I conclude, that however consistent the world may be, allowing certain suppositions and conjectures, with the idea of such a Deity, it can never afford us an inference concerning his existence.[9]

The objection begins to gain in weight. And to all of this we must add the fact of Darwin. For a long time men, impressed by the intricacies of the developed eye, ear, brain, and much else, produced countless books following the argument from design, and ending with the conclusion of God's existence as the architect of our world. Then came Darwin's *The Origin of Species,* and now the forms of order in biology are explained by chance mutations, the struggle for existence, and the survival of the fit. Even more, the claim seems to be made more frequently that the basic regularities of the world can be explained by chance. Some of the logical force of the argument is lost through such criticism. So little is known of chance and probability that it is simply not possible to know if, as many claim, given any state of chaos one may please, and sufficient time, order would emerge by chance.

The Argument from Cause

There is a second argument, beginning from our experience of cause and effect. One very important kind of explanation requires the discovery of a cause. And our argument, beginning with the causal sequence, concludes with an idea of God as First Cause of the universe. The argument has two forms. One of these is what everyone would mean by a First Cause of the universe: namely, a creator who initiated time and the universe together in 4,004 B.C. or in 4,000,004 B.C. The other form of the argument is the one used

9 *Ibid.,* pp. 509–510.

by philosophy instructors when explaining Thomas Aquinas' argument for a First Cause; the latter argument is not concerned with the origin of the temporal world. Its concern is with the origin of any causal series you may please. "Pick any effect," Aquinas would say in his own way, and in Latin. "I can demonstrate God to be at the origin of the causal chain leading to this effect." Ask for the cause of anything; knowing this cause will not complete the task of explanation. You must ask also for the cause of the cause, and then the cause of the cause of the cause. If you should have to keep on in this manner forever, you could never arrive at the whole series of causes, which together would explain the effect in which you were interested. And if there is no cause to begin the series, you could never have the effect in question. At some point you must come to a cause which is the First Cause. But this cause cannot be any of the things in the world, since the things of the world are themselves caused by something else in the world. In the explanation of anything whatever, reference to a First Cause, the initiator of every causal series, is required. Again, Aquinas' formulation of the argument! His phrase, "efficient cause," which we have met before, is what we ordinarily mean by cause.

> In the world of sensible things we find there is an order of efficient causes. There is no case known (neither is it, indeed, possible) in which a thing is found to be the efficient cause of itself; for so it would be prior to itself, which is impossible. Now in efficient causes it is not possible to go on to infinity, because in all efficient causes following in order, the first is the cause of the intermediate cause, and the intermediate is the cause of the ultimate cause, whether the intermediate cause be several, or one only. Now to take away the cause is to take away the effect. Therefore, if there be no first cause among efficient causes, there will be no ultimate, nor any intermediate, cause. But if in efficient causes it is possible to go on to infinity, there will be no first efficient cause, neither will there be an ultimate effect, nor any intermediate efficient causes; all of which is plainly false. Therefore it is necessary to admit a first efficient cause, to which everyone gives the name of God.[10]

Aquinas seems to be thinking of cause and effect within a unique and single series, keeping its own identity through time. In fact, causation would seem to be almost always multiple. To explain

[10] Thomas Aquinas, *op. cit.*, p. 22.

the cause of the chair on which you sit, one would have to consider the material and its sources, the weaving of the fabric, the metal of which the springs were made, the processes through which the ore was put, the craft of the artisans, the assembly line of the factory, the structure of corporations, and even the balance of nature. Much of the antecedent world would be required to explain this chair. If every cause is multiple, including much or all of the antecedent world, if the antecedent world funnels in to produce the effect, then in looking for the cause one will look for a state of the world. Thus far there is no need to go beyond the world. In seeking the cause of the antecedent world, one would be directed to a still earlier state of the world. And the causal sequence has turned into a sequence of states or phases of the world. And if the causes of things are constituted by each state of the world, we are not driven to look outside the world, that is, to the first cause of a single causal series, for the explanation of the effect which is before us.

But our comments on the second form of the causal argument seem to have led us to the first. Must there not, then, be a First Cause to initiate the series of states which is our world? Perhaps. Half of the philosophers of the world, including Plato, would agree. But notice the mystery concerning the first effect if this is so. To prevent the question being pushed still farther back (And what, then, is the cause of God?), this has to be a moment mingling eternity with time. If the eternal is timeless, how could the eternal act in time? How could it initiate time? And if reality originates, it must come out of nothing. How could a world be produced from nothing? Or how could a spiritual reality produce a material reality? The last mystery may have no dampening effect upon your spirits; this first effect, our world, we begin to find, is somewhat like nothing at all — space, and energy in space, creating fields of force.

Hume's objection, while it may be directed against both forms of our argument, appears to have its greater force against this common form. As though continuing from his earlier comment, Hume writes:

> Add to this, that in tracing an eternal succession of objects, it seems absurd to inquire for a general cause or first author. . . . In such a chain, too, or succession of objects, each part is caused by that which preceded it, and causes that which succeeds it. Where then is the difficulty? But the WHOLE, you say, wants a cause. I answer, that the uniting of these parts into a whole,

like the uniting of several distinct countries into one kingdom, or several distinct members into one body, is performed merely by an arbitrary act of the mind, and has no influence on the nature of things. Did I show you the particular causes of each individual in a collection of twenty particles of matter, I should think it very unreasonable, should you afterwards ask me, what was the cause of the whole twenty. This is sufficiently explained in explaining the cause of the parts.[11]

If Hume's criticism is appropriate, and if every effect is to be explained by a cause preceding this effect in time, the world cannot have had a beginning; reality must have always have been. If such backward references continue endlessly, the past is infinite in extent. With this judgment the other half of the philosophers of the world, including Aristotle, would agree.

Despite our criticism of the argument as given by Aquinas, we have been forced to admit either a first cause at the origin of the world, or an infinite past. We may escape the First Cause by denying a creation, but, alas, there is also an argument for God which begins from the supposition of an infinite past. It is the argument from contingency.

The Argument from a Contingent World

None of the objects within our experience is self-sufficient; each can be destroyed and one day is destroyed; each depends on other things, its existence "contingent" on favorable conditions. The things of our experience, then, are contingent in their being. If the things of the world are contingent, an argument from "contingency" is possible.

The argument requires two assumptions. One of these will certainly be allowed: One cannot derive something from nothing. We have become familiar with the second assumption: The world had no beginning. But you may not find this to be a reasonable assumption. If you deny the assumption, this argument will not follow. But if the world had no beginning, then the passage of time up until the present moment will form an infinite series. In an infinite series of numbers — of course, we could not set down such a series — would appear every number pertinent to that series, and possible for it. One property of an infinite series is the occurence of every possibility of the series somewhere within it.

Now let us suppose all the things of the universe to be contingent;

[11] David Hume, op. cit., pp. 491–492.

each thing can be destroyed. One possibility of the series, since it is composed of members which can be destroyed, is their simultaneous destruction. But this is most unlikely, you will say. It is unlikely, and yet with our assumptions it is possible. Normally, within a family, the parents produce their children, and pass away while the children continue to exist; unhappily, we do know of cases where an entire family has perished together. And if everything in the universe is contingent, it is at least possible that the whole universe would perish in a similar manner. And, in the strictest sense, if the universe had no beginning, and if everything is contingent, this unlikely possibility would have had to occur at some time in the infinite temporal series of the past, since every possibility must occur somewhere within such a series. Should this have happened, since one cannot get something from nothing, there would at present be nothing in existence. But there is existence now. Thus, not all things are contingent; there is some necessity in the world; and this necessity is the necessary being, called God.

> We find in nature things that are possible to be and not to be, since they are found to be generated, and to be corrupted, and consequently, it is possible for them to be and not to be. But it is impossible for these always to exist, for that which can not-be at some time is not. Therefore, if everything can not-be, then at one time there was nothing in existence. Now if this were true, even now there would be nothing in existence, because that which does not exist begins to exist only through something already existing. Therefore, if at one time nothing was in existence, it would have been impossible for anything to have begun to exist; and thus even now nothing would be in existence — which is absurd. Therefore, not all beings are merely possible, but there must exist something the existence of which is necessary. But every necessary thing either has its necessity caused by another, or not. Now it is impossible to go on to infinity in necessary things which have their necessity caused by another, as has been already proved in regard to efficient causes. Therefore we cannot but admit the existence of some being having of itself its own necessity, and not receiving it from another, but rather causing in others their necessity. This all men speak of as God.[12]

The standard reply to the argument questions going outside the world to find the "necessary" being. It claims the necessity of, or

[12] Thomas Aquinas, *op. cit.*, pp. 22–23.

finds necessity in, the world itself. Hume continues, as though it were from the last objection.

But further, why may not the material universe be the necessarily existent being, according to this pretended explication of necessity? We dare not affirm that we know all the qualities of matter; and for aught we can determine, it may contain some qualities, which, were they known, would make its non-existence appear as great a contradiction as that twice two is five. I find only one argument employed to prove, that the material world is not the necessarily existing Being: and this argument is derived from the contingency both of the matter and the form of the world. 'Any particle of matter,' it is said, 'may be *conceived* to be annihilated; and any form may be *conceived* to be altered. Such an annihilation or alteration, therefore, is not impossible.' But it seems a great partiality not to perceive, that the same argument extends equally to the Deity, so far as we have any conception of him; and that the mind can at least imagine him to be non-existent, or his attributes to be altered. It must be some unknown, inconceivable qualities, which can make his non-existence appear impossible, or his attributes unalterable: and no reason can be assigned, why these qualities may not belong to matter.[13]

The unbeliever may claim to find in the natural world all of the "necessity" which is required. And where in the scientific world is this necessity to be discovered? Speaking in modern terms, the unbeliever might say: "The first law of thermodynamics finds the area of this necessity: Energy can be neither created nor destroyed, its sum remaining constant." The believer, I imagine, would have to ponder for a time the substance of this claim. But then he might reply, "What of the second law? The universe is tending toward a state of entropy in which this energy can serve no further 'use,' having reached a uniform dispersion, no longer packaged, and having no structure." Indeed, this was part of the vision of desolation in Russell's mind; like Russell's vision, here too we have an extension of the universe of scientific discourse into a picture of the world. And even in these terms our argument is able to arrive at its conclusion. The state of final entropy with energy in a uniform dispersion is exactly the possibility of the series to which Aquinas was referring in his medieval way. Since this happening is possible

[13] David Hume, *op. cit.*, p. 491.

for the universe, when one looks at the universe in modern terms, and if the past is an infinite series, this final state would have been reached at some time in the past; and if it had occurred there would be no structured energy at the present moment, since even among scientists one cannot get something from nothing. Thus, one must posit a kind of necessity beyond anything required by the scientific point of view.

The Ontological Argument

Let us recall the difference between the contingent beings with which the preceding argument had begun, and the necessary being in its conclusion. Contingent beings come into and go out of existence. Their existence is possible under certain conditions, but not necessary. The necessary being of the conclusion, on the other hand, could not fail to exist. Its existence is unconditional. We come to the unusual argument, whose movement of thought has a direction the opposite of any other. Beginning with the idea of the necessary being, this argument concludes to its existence. As soon as we understand the idea of this necessary being, we understand that it must exist, and does exist.

Anselm, its twelfth-century author, will be our source; and we must break in upon his reflections, as he approaches his statement of our present argument:

And, indeed, we believe that thou art a being than which nothing greater can be conceived. Or is there no such nature, since the fool hath said in his heart, there is no God? But, at any rate, this very fool, when he hears of this being of which I speak — a being than which nothing greater can be conceived — understands what he hears, and what he understands is in his understanding; although he does not understand it to exist.

For it is one thing for an object to be in the understanding, and another to understand that the object exists. When a painter first conceives of what he will afterwards perform, he has it in his understanding, but he does not yet understand it to be, because he has not yet performed it. But after he has made the painting, he both has it in his understanding, and he understands that it exists, because he has made it.

Hence, even the fool is convinced that something exists in the understanding, at least, than which nothing greater can be conceived. For, when he hears of this, he understands it. And whatever is understood, exists in the understanding. And assuredly that, than which nothing greater can be conceived, cannot exist in the understanding alone. For, suppose it exists in the understanding alone: then it can be conceived to exist in reality; which is greater.

Therefore, if that, than which nothing greater can be conceived, exists in the understanding alone, the very being, than which nothing greater can be conceived, is one, than which a greater can be conceived. But obviously this is impossible. Hence, there is no doubt that there exists a being, than which nothing greater can be conceived, and it exists both in the understanding and in reality. . . .

And it assuredly exists so truly, that it cannot be conceived not to exist. For, it is possible to conceive of a being which cannot be conceived not to exist; and this is greater than one which can be conceived not to exist. Hence, if that, than which nothing greater can be conceived, can be conceived not to exist, it is not that, than which nothing greater can be conceived. But this is an irreconcilable contradiction. There is, then, so truly a being than which nothing greater can be conceived to exist, that it cannot even be conceived not to exist; and this being thou art, O Lord, our God.[14]

And the final position to which Anselm comes is this: Either God is not conceivable, or God exists. In modern terms we might say: Either the idea of God is meaningless, or God exists. But you cannot understand the idea of God, this is Anselm's claim, and understand the object of this idea to be lacking in existence.

The well-known critic of this view is Immanuel Kant. Kant replies to the ontological argument in this manner: When we say of anything that it "exists" we are not saying anything *about* the thing. Descriptive words and concepts tell us about things. Their existence or nonexistence is determined by perception and experience generally. For this reason the *fact* of existence cannot be contained in the idea of a perfect being.

Being is evidently not a real predicate, or a concept of something that can be added to the concept of a thing. It is merely the admission of a thing, and of certain determinations in it. Logically, it is merely the copula of a judgment. The proposition, *God is almighty*, contains two concepts, each having its object, namely, God and almightiness. The small word *is*, is not

14 St. Anselm, *Proslogium; Monologium*, trans. S. N. Deane (La Salle, Ill.: Open Court Publishing Co., 1945, pp. 7–11.

an additional predicate, but only serves to put the predicate *in relation* to the subject. If, then, I take the subject (God) with all its predicates (including that of almightiness), and say, *God is,* or there is a God, I do not put a new predicate to the concept of God, but I only put the subject by itself, with all its predicates, in relation to my concept, as its object. Both must contain exactly the same kind of thing, and nothing can have been added to the concept, which expresses possibility only, by my thinking its object as simply given and saying, it is. And thus the real does not contain more than the possible. A hundred real dollars do not contain a penny more than a hundred possible dollars. For as the latter signify the concept, the former the object and its position by itself, it is clear that, in case the former contained more than the latter, my concept would not express the whole object, and would not therefore be its adequate concept. In my financial position no doubt there exists more by one hundred real dollars, than by their concept only (that is their possibility) . . . but the conceived hundred dollars are not in the least increased through the existence which is outside my concept.[15]

The Argument from Imperfection

We have just discussed the argument from perfection; this argument can be reversed, turned inside out, and taken in another way. We shall present a final argument which begins with the obviously imperfect world of our experience, and purports to reason to the existence of a perfect being. The argument is an interesting reenactment of the experience of believers, moving from the imperfections of the world to a vision of perfection.

The imperfection of the world is a fact no one can avoid. The circles we construct, or find, are not quite circular; the triangles of our personal (or even of our social) life are never quite triangular; truth is available only in fragments mixed with falsehood; justice is only imperfectly established in the world. Plato, beginning with this fact and noting our ability to judge these imperfections, insisted on the reality of perfect norms within the universe, his renowned "ideas." And Thomas Aquinas takes a further step. Avoiding one version of Aquinas' argument, we shall take the suggestion of a second version which will have to be developed:

---

[15] Immanuel Kant, *Critique of Pure Reason,* trans. F. Max Müller (New York: The Macmillan Company, and London: Macmillan & Company, Ltd., 1927), pp. 480–481. Used by permission of the publishers.

Another argument may also be gathered from the words of Aristotle. In *Metaphysics II* he shows that what is most true is also most a being. But in *Metaphysics IV* he shows the existence of something supremely true from the observed fact that of two false things one is more false than the other, which means that one is more true than the other. This comparison is based on the nearness to that which is absolutely and supremely true. From these Aristotelian texts we may further infer that there is something that is supremely being. This we call God.[16]

Checking references across the centuries, we can easily supply the material needed for our argument. In the second book of his *Metaphysics* Aristotle writes:

> . . . the principles of eternal things must be always most true (for they are not merely sometimes true, nor is there any cause of their being, but they themselves are the cause of the being of other things), so that as each thing is in respect of being, so is it in respect of truth.[17]

And in the fourth book our other passage reads:

> . . . there is a more and a less in the nature of things; for we should not say that two and three are equally even, nor is he who thinks four things are five equally wrong with him who thinks they are a thousand. If then they are not equally wrong, obviously one is less wrong and therefore more right. If then that which has more of any quality is nearer the norm, there must be some truth to which the more true is nearer. And even if there is not, still there is already something better founded and liker the truth, and we shall have gotten rid of the unqualified doctrine which would prevent us from determining anything in our thought.[18]

Aquinas ignored the qualification of the last sentence and, comparing the two texts, the latent Platonism in Aristotle's thought sprang forth; the result was an argument for God as the standard and norm of the universe. Our version of the argument, cast in terms of

---

[16] Thomas Aquinas, *Summa Contra Gentiles*, Bk. I, Chap. 13, trans. Anton C. Pegis (New York: Doubleday and Co., Inc., 1955), pp. 95–96.

[17] Aristotle, *Metaphysics*, Bk. II, Chap. 1, 993b, *The Basic Works of Aristotle,* ed. Richard McKeon (New York: Random House, 1941), p. 713. Used by permission of the Oxford University Press.

[18] *Ibid.*, Bk. IV, Chap. 4, 1008b, p. 743.

truth and error, may be compared to Aquinas' other version where "goodness" and "nobility" are also mentioned.[19] The argument contains, I suggest, the following steps:

> He who thinks four things are five is less wrong than he who thinks them a thousand. If he who thinks them five is less wrong than the other, then he is more right. If he is more right, then he is nearer to the truth than is the other. If he is nearer to the truth, then there must be a truth to serve as his norm, or 'being nearer' would have no meaning. If there is a truth, this truth must be, have being. If it has being, it must be a being. If it is a being, able to serve properly as a norm, it must be a supreme being. And if it is a supreme being, it must be the supreme being.

The heart of this argument is the progression from error, injustice, or the mixture of good and evil, to the need for a norm (How could we recognize all of our circles to be ellipses, unless we had in mind the norm of perfect circularity?); and from the norm the argument proceeds to the reality of the perfect being, whose existence explains our ability to make these judgments by serving as their norm.

Is the argument convincing? There are two points where we might jump the track of the argument. In the first place, we may not believe in any norms or absolutes. How we could deny the absolute of truth I do not know, even if this absolute is not readily available to our minds. But this is an age in which we talk of the "relativity of values," and we may have been influenced by this talk. But one might allow the norms, and yet deny the perfect being. The weakest portion of the argument lies between the assertion of the norms and the conclusion which grants existence to the normative and perfect being.

Assessment of the Arguments

It would seem that we might be able to evaluate these arguments simply by means of an exacting scrutiny, paying close attention to each step. But as I try to review our arguments in this manner, many problems occur to my mind which cannot be settled merely by concentrating upon the argument. Think of the argument from

[19] Thomas Aquinas, *Summa Theologica, op. cit.,* p. 23.

design with its great persuasive power. The longer I reflect upon this argument, the less am I able either to affirm or deny its conclusion. I am able to see how the argument depends upon the idea of order. And to my surprise I discover within myself no exact idea of what constitutes an "order." I find my knowledge of the proper meanings of "chance" and "probability" extremely vague; and upon extending my reflection to other men, I discover a general uncertainty even among our most knowledgeable minds concerning the proper interpretation of these terms; and I am no longer certain if the argument from design carries to its conclusion, or falls considerably short of this conclusion. The same quality of uncertainty begins to infect the other arguments. One key term for both the causal argument and the argument from contingency is the notion of an "infinite series." "There can be no infinite series of causes." "The series of past times may be infinite in extent." But the properties of an infinite series are by no means clear to me. Mathematicians, aided by philosophers, are only beginning to understand the properties of such series. The meanings of "time" and "cause" are clear only until we begin to think about them; and these meanings are altering even at the present time. How, then, can I know if these two arguments arrive at their expected conclusions? Nor is the idea of perfection really clear within my mind. In earlier centuries this idea carried a weighty and important meaning. Today the concept is in a state of disuse, or is relegated to the task of describing admirable social functions, creatures of the opposite sex, and almost anything except the universe in which we live. If I am not certain of the proper meaning of the word, how can I evaluate the two arguments for whch this is the essential term? I begin to find, in short, a set of key terms — order, chance, probability, time, cause, infinity, necessity, and perfection; and the success of each argument depends upon the shade of meaning carried by these terms. Do these arguments carry to their conclusions? With a certain interpretation of each important term, all of our arguments are valid and convincing. Do the arguments fail? When other interpretations are given to their central terms, each argument fails completely. And when I recall the courtesy, granted to each person, of defining one's terms as he pleases, the realm of meaning suddenly appears to me more like a turbulent sea with its shifting currents of opinion, than a field with its parts definitely set forth by some patterning of man or nature.

And yet, along with this uncertainty, an interesting thought occurs to me. The argument to a First Cause from the finite past was not conclusive, since one has only to appeal beyond any set beginning, at last regarding the past as infinite in duration. And the argument from an infinite past would not be conclusive, if the past should be finite in extent. But surely it is one or the other! If it is finite in extent, no one would care to claim existence as an accidental happening out of nothing. The mystery of the first effect holds more promise as an object of our understanding than does this alternative. And if the past is infinite in duration, the argument from contingency at once applies. Taking these two arguments together, we would seem to have established a presumption in favor of God's existence — in favor, that is to say, of either a necessary being or a creator of the universe. The possibility suggests itself of a program of mutual aid among the arguments, and you may be able to elaborate this bare suggestion. The arguments, revolving around the idea of perfection, may increase this presumption slightly. Obviously, I am committed, if you are not, to the admission, or at least the hope, of norms somehow present in the universe. Does this admission require the normative being suggested by our final argument? Certainly, it is difficult to see how norms or standards could have any place in the vast and barren universe of Russell. If norms are necessary, and if they cannot be understood to exist within a barren universe, we can add to our presumption which favors the universe of the believer. Now, what of the argument which runs the other way, from the idea of a perfect being to the fact of his existence? Kant's criticism is often accepted as the final word to be said about this argument. And, admittedly, it is very strange to find one idea which stands as warrant for its own existence. But consider the step which Kant must take in order to invalidate the argument. The word, or idea of, "existence" is not a predicate. This is his claim. Yet, when I say, "God, the United Nations, and whatever you may wish to add, have existence," the word "existence" is in the predicate; it is the predicate. The word functions as a predicate in our language. To make an exception of one word, not allowing it to stand for any descriptive quality, is at least as strange as finding one idea to imply its own existence. What is the result? "Existence" is implicit in the idea of a truly perfect, infinite, complete, self-sufficient, primal, and necessary being. How could it be otherwise? Existence cannot be separated from this

idea, and it can be separated from the idea of any contingent
being. And yet, as soon as I have made the statement I feel mis-
givings about my argument. Granting the uniqueness of this idea,
and its claim to special treatment, how can any idea insure the
existence of its object? Have we not made a leap? It is only the
idea of God's existence which is implicit in the other ideas making
up this concept. Then we are still in the realm of concepts, and the
argument fails? We are, and not quite. In fact, the point brings
us to a step of considerable importance for the whole of our discussion. The step will not be obvious at once, because we intend to
insist, at the moment, on nothing more than Anselm's claim in
modern dress: Either the idea of God is meaningless, or God exists.
If the idea of God has meaning, then God exists. No panic, please!
The statement gives away less of the game than you imagine. Consider how contradictory our Western idea of God appeared in the
description of Saint Augustine. Only ideas which are consistent
can have meaning. And only consistent ideas hold any promise of
having their objects instanced by the world. If it is possible for
us to hold an idea consistently in our thought, then it is at least
not impossible to find the object of this idea in the universe. We
can phrase the assertion in a slightly different manner: "If 'God' is
possible, then God exists necessarily." How strange the language
of this paragraph! But stay with us for the sequel. How do we
know when an idea has meaning, is consistent, is a possible object
for our thought? We know this by our examination of the idea,
both internally and by tracing its relations to other ideas. We
discover this quality of an idea, in short, by exploring the system of
thought to which it belongs. And such a system of thought is a
system of philosophy. We can know of the meaningfulness, consistency, and possibility of this idea, only through a discovery of its
proper system. And should this system of thought be the adequate
philosophy for interpreting the world; if the idea of God and the
structure of this philosophy imply each other, without even looking
around the world we can conclude that God exists. And looking
about the world is very little help to this idea. We are claiming for
philosophy nothing beyond the role of interpretation with respect to
every other thing; but with respect to God the system of philosophy
must tell us of his existence, or his nonexistence, since the idea of
God implies the idea of his existence. In a different manner what
is true of this argument is true of every other. The meanings of

the key terms, which led to our uncertainty, are developed within the sciences to some extent — when scientists are being philosophical — but their major incidence and shaping occurs within the systems of philosophy. The strength of every argument for God depends upon whether the necessary shade of meaning, allowing this argument to succeed, would be imparted to its terms by the adequate system of philosophy. And if, within the adequate philosophy, the adequate interpretation of the past should find it to be neither finite nor infinite, but possessed of some other quality, possibly one which we have not imagined, our presumption of God's existence becomes more problematical. The presumption now depends upon whether or not this adequate interpretation allows an argument, leading to the conclusion that God exists.

The Believer and Unbeliever Compared

Now, what is the adequate philosophy? We had described the nature of this system in our struggle with the problem of truth. It was possible to give no more than an outline drawing, because in fact the adequate philosophy would be the final truth. And, short of this unattainable ideal, we cannot arrive at certainty with respect to the existence, or the nonexistence, of God. Our conclusion broadens the problem which is before us, requiring added knowledge about the positions of our believer and our unbeliever.

If we do not know this adequate philosophy which would stand as the final truth, still we know of many philosophies which are adequate, more or less. The presence of these philosophies is the embarrassment of riches, otherwise known as the breakdown, within philosophy. And if, with the thought of philosophic system in our minds, we turn back to Russell's essay, his extension of the universe of scientific discourse into a general, and encompassing, attitude toward the world becomes an extension of this universe of discourse into philosophy. His philosophic attitude is, quite naturally, capable of preserving much of the scientific attitude. His philosophy is like science at least in the direction of its attention — toward the facts, rather than toward the values, of the world. In general, the position of the unbeliever will lead to a philosophy, centering itself around fact instead of value, relying on the kinds of evidence which can be felt, tasted, sensed, observed directly or indirectly, gathered by man or machine — and by the machine as well as, and sometimes better than, by the man. It will be the kind of evidence which makes a palpable difference. One great division among the systems of philosophy is populated thickly with men who share this attitude and whose "isms" are named — in a partial reading — materialism, naturalism, and positivism. In such systems the meanings granted to the key terms of our list allow not one of the arguments for God to reach its hoped-for conclusion.

And if the position of the unbeliever leads to a general philosophy about the world, this is no less true of the position of the believer. If the position of the unbeliever leads to some variety of materialism, stressing fact instead of value, the position of the believer will be one which stresses the values of the world somewhat more strongly than its facts. The believer will be led, as he discovers the ideas related to his central beliefs, toward some one of the many varieties of idealism. Typical of idealism is a kind of value progression which begins in the actual world, and rises toward a vision of perfection. This progression is exactly suited to the inclinations of the devout believer. And in the systems of idealism, the meanings in our list of terms are such that every argument for God is able to reach its sure conclusion.

We have in the believer and the unbeliever, when they understand themselves, an opposition of the two most distinctive and durable philosophies of the Western mind. There are many other philosophies, but each of them tends to stand with one or the other of these two types. Whether we are believers or unbelievers, an excellent reason for the staying power of our ultimate beliefs has just been found. The fact is that either attitude toward the universe, reflecting the two achievements of our cultural ordering is, or at least within the boundaries of our present knowledge cannot be shown not to be, as reasonable as the other.

And now you would smile, were I to ask: "Which of these philosophies is true?" And I am afraid yours would be a very agnostic kind of smile. The possibility of this smile troubles me exceedingly. Here is the reason! For some little time I have been hearing in imagination the covers of copies of this volume being closed, gently or brusquely, one after another, and slipped into the shelves of bookcases of every variety. Our numbers have been gradually reduced by a process of careful and continual screening. Section by section our group has become more exclusive. By now only the particular reader is left. Certainly, we must have lost the intolerant believer in examining the arguments for unbelief. Surely, the intolerant unbeliever closed his copy of the book when we began to work with the immensely complicated arguments for belief. Left in our discussion are only those judicious and exceptional persons —"Thou and I" and perhaps one other — who are willing to consider carefully and at length both the argument and counterargument on any issue. And the possibility of your knowing smile is disturbing to me for the excellent reason that we who remain are exactly the segment of society from which the agnostics of the world are generally recruited.

I shall not ask which of these philosophies is true. But materialists of all varieties claim their philosophy to be consistent with the whole of scientific knowledge, as though this fact increased the likelihood of its being true. And, indeed, it is consistent, as they claim. The consistency of this philosophy with the whole of scientific knowledge is not surprising, since it has been shaped deliberately to accord with fact. But there is a second reason which keeps this consistency from being in the least surprising. Any more or less adequate philosophy is able to account for every detail of the world. And if the philosophy of the believer is some one of the many species of idealism, this philosophy as well will be consistent with the whole of scientific knowledge. Thus far we have a stand-off.

To remain consistent with the whole of knowledge would not seem to be a simple task. But because of the minimal nature of their commitments, those philosophies which have been shaped by fact retain this consistency with something approaching a natural ease. On the other hand, the position of the believer has often been stated in a manner inconsistent with later developments in our scientific knowledge. The view of the believer has suffered the disadvantage of continual reshaping not from within, but as a result of external pressures. Its doctrines have been modified more than once to bring them into line with the advance of science; and sometimes believers have strenuously resisted this advance. And, beyond the pressures of advancing knowledge, the unbeliever has often launched a powerful offensive against the doctrines of believers; and more than once this offense has forced modifications in these doctrines. The view of the believer has been waging for some centuries a defensive battle in the world. The performance of believers, as a natural result, has often presented the appearance of special pleading: "I shall skew the evidence, equivocate, stretch the language to its limits in order to preserve the doctrines I so deeply cherish." So has the intellectual activity of the believer often appeared to the unbeliever.

And the final defense of the unbeliever with his position of materialism would be cast, I think, in terms of relevance. These attitudes toward the world with the minimal nature of their demands are more appropriate to the age in which we live. The position of the unbeliever would seem to rest upon the view of history of Auguste Comte. Much is to be said for the appropriateness of this doctrine for our age.

And what is one to think of the believer in an age of science, always anxiously adjusting his manner of procedure, and his rational scheme, in order to accommodate our growing sum of knowledge to his privileged beliefs, carrying far beyond its evidential value any apparent evidence which can be interpreted in his favor? And yet, despite his anxious care, these beliefs become more attenuated by the century. Is there not some force in the unbeliever's question: "Why not drop the pretense?" The views of the unbeliever, certainly, have not required such anxious readjustment. It is more natural, it is more fitting — this is the claim — to hold a minimal point of view. And do you not find some cogency in all of this, at least when your health is sound, your spirits high, and the world is moving, in the main, according to your wishes?

But to hold a doctrine appropriate to one's age, a philosophy which does not require much readjustment — however convenient this may be — is no guarantee of truth. And to hold the opposite doctrine, despite its need for constant reinterpretation, is no sign of falsehood. The truth might be quite complex, and require just such complex formulations. No one has ever been able to show that the doctrine easiest to defend is therefore true. And by far the greater number of philosophers have required an idea of God in order to complete their systems. The basic schemes employed by Plato, Aristotle, Plotinus, Augustine, Aquinas, Descartes, Spinoza, Leibniz, Locke, Berkeley, Kant, Hegel, Schopenhauer, Peirce, Royce, James, Bergson, and Whitehead — to list some of the major philosophers of the West — all required in one form or another the idea of God.

In short, we cannot claim an absolute superiority for either view. Both are able to find support for their positions; and the support of each is very different in kind. The defense of the unbeliever rests upon the facts, construing these facts in a minimal and "natural" manner. The defense of the believer is much more complicated, turning around grand arguments from order, cause, contingency, and perfection. The "offense" of the unbeliever consists in demonstrating the meaningless nature of the believer's central concepts of "soul" and "God." The "offense" of the believer consists in showing the meaningless nature of human life under the conditions set forth by the unbeliever.

And short of our possessing a final perspective from which to judge, we have nothing to report beyond the judgment of our feelings. I have the surprising feeling that each side has acquitted itself very well. The defense and offense of each have power; yet the two positions are very much opposed. Are our experiences similar in these two ways? First, did you find yourself tending to agree with the argument of the unbeliever as his case was presented, and then with the believer? How could this occur? Subject as we are to psychological, as well as logical, considerations, the mere working of the "machinery" of proof on either side may have caused this inclination toward the attitudes of belief and unbelief, as we paid attention first to one and then the other. Second, during the exposition of the point of view of the unbeliever, did you find his argument most convincing, while later beginning to lose in force? So, too, with respect to the argument of the believer. How is this to be explained? In the theatre we accept whatever plausible assumptions are required for the development of the plot within the play. In a similar manner we may accept for the time the general and unstated framework of the argument as it is presented. And the conclusions retain their force until this context of assumptions disappears. In the present case the context of assumptions is the appropriate system of philosophy.

But if we are capable of responding so, the assumptions on either side must be "plausible" to our minds. And this is understandable only if the pendulum-like movement of our minds and inner attitudes relates to an earlier fact which has come into our notice. Possibly, all or almost all of us are both believers and unbelievers in our hearts. Possibly, we are committed to both of the two great levels of cultural ordering which have removed us from the primitive status, and from the primitive mentality, of our origin. In our complex persons there are attitudes which may prepare us to accept the conclusions of both of these alternatives, even if they are opposed. And we swing from one side to the other. Under some conditions we are prepared for belief, and the evidence of belief is almost completely convincing. Under other conditions the attitude of unbelief is most nearly relevant. What, then, are we to do when we are the ones who cannot tolerate, much less believe in, a contradiction?

Not having in our possession the adequate philosophy, or at least not knowing that we have it, must we say, speaking from the context of the more or less adequate varieties of materialism and idealism which surround us: It is reasonable to believe in God, and just as reasonable to hold the position of unbelief? If this is to be the nature of our conclusion, you must be thinking, it will be still more reasonable to remain in a suspense of judgment. And you reach for the card, entitling you to a life membership among those who pattern their lives in keeping with the posture of suspended judgment.

The Neglected Alternative of Faith

As a measure of desperation I call your attention to a neglected alternative, to Pascal and the terms of his exciting wager. But to wager is to act not entirely in company with one's reason. What is this act?

> The heart has its reasons, which reason does not know. We feel it in a thousand things. I say that the heart naturally loves the Universal Being, and also itself naturally, according as it gives itself to them; and it hardens itself against one or the other at its will. You have rejected the one and kept the other. Is it by reason that you love yourself?
>
> It is the heart which experiences God, and not the reason. This, then, is faith: God felt by the heart, not by the reason.[20]

The act of wagering is an act of faith. If we cannot achieve final certainty by means of reason, perhaps we shall be able to reach this certainty by means of faith. If this is possible, then faith is superior to reason as an instrument for the discovery of final truth.

Is faith the proper instrument for the settling of our ultimate beliefs? Many questions begin to arise. How is the heart to know

[20] Blaise Pascal, *op. cit.*, p. 222.

it is experiencing God and not the devil, or some personal illusion? There are truths, certainly, about ourselves, our world, God, and immortality, which are not now amenable to our reason. And these truths may be among the opinions held by someone or other, somewhere or other. But if reason is not allowed to help in sifting truth from error, how shall we be able to separate out the most final truth from the most blatant error? Reason is sometimes more, and sometimes less, productive. And in the context of our present problem, reason has proven itself to be rather somewhat less, than more, productive. But, in general, reason is self-corrective. If its methods are not to be employed, has faith, one wonders, a method for the detection and correction of its errors? I have searched for this method more than a little; I have found nothing, nothing of importance. And should you find within the forms of faith a self-corrective method, able to separate the reasons of the heart from its delusions, let me know how you have managed it. I shall, at once, acknowledge and accept your findings.

The Summing Up

What has been the nature of our discovery? The way of unbelief leads to existentialism, a recognition of the meaningless character of human life. The way of belief leads to concepts which verge upon sheer contradiction; and a contradiction is, likewise, meaningless in its way. And the philosophies underlying these attitudes of belief and unbelief, despite the best efforts of their adherents, remain to some extent problematical. At the same time we cannot abandon reason in favor of the alternative of faith, for faith is at last a form of authority; and we have already discovered how authority must give way to the work of reason. And yet, when applied to this problem, reason does not seem to work with its customary power. Clearly, we have failed to discover the key which might resolve our problem. Both of us require this key. In the last part of our discussion I shall try to find a possible key, based on the whole course of our common intellectual endeavor.

II. Toward a Partial Resolution of These Problems

What is to be done about this curious deficiency of reason in relation to the problems of ultimate belief? The question goes to the heart of our problem. And if reason is deficient, we cannot hope to escape by means of faith. Two terms are now before us, as we reconsider the ordering of our ultimate beliefs. Where one has two terms, at least four alternatives are possible. Our ultimate beliefs might be ordered by reason alone, by faith alone, or by one of two relations combining faith and reason. Pascal's claim for the supremacy of faith can be understood as a statement of our second alternative. Faith alone, "God felt by the heart, not by the reason," is to determine our ultimate beliefs. Or we might understand his claim as the suggestion of a third alternative. Faith and reason must function together in the ordering of our beliefs, although faith is superior to our human reason. There remains a fourth possibility, but let us consider the three alternatives which are now before us. Each of these has been advanced within our Western history as the proper means for ordering our ultimate beliefs.

The Ordering of Ultimate Beliefs

Reason Alone

If you have signed a card in celebration of your new status as a dues-paying member of the International Association of Agnostics (I beg you not to attend a meeting!), you will be able to remain in a state of suspended judgment with respect to our larger problem. But in order to achieve this admirable balance and lack of personal concern, you have made a judgment with respect to the proper manner of ordering your beliefs. You are now indifferent to the problems of God and immortality, because the grounds for reaching a decision were insufficient. And if I were to ask: "Under what conditions are you willing to hold a belief of any kind?" this might well be your answer: "I believe only what has been proven. The grounds for my belief must be completely certain." And I respond: "Then you can believe in virtually nothing whatever." Consider your position. You cannot believe in the doctrines of religion, or in the doctrines of science; you cannot believe in the existence of the world in which we live, and which all of us accept in fact. If you are to found your life on reason alone, you must become not only an agnostic but an utter skeptic. And your position will resemble that of David Hume; no one could have wished more fervently to conduct his life by the single guide of reason. But when Hume had pulled himself up onto the platform of reason, he could not be certain of his room's existence in his absence; he could learn nothing of an external world; he could not be certain of the presence of any qualities — the vividness so important in our experience — within this problematic world; he could not be certain the world was there at all; he could find no connection between cause and effect; and he could have no certainty concerning the gods. In practice, he had to admit a great deal more than he could prove.

This fact should be more widely known. The rule by which the agnostic avoids our questions of God and immortality reaches far beyond these two questions. And any man whose firm decision is to conduct his life on a basis of reason alone has committed himself to become an utter skeptic. I think you did not bargain for so much. Viewed in extension, the rule's ineptitude is all the more apparent. The alternative of ordering our ultimate beliefs by reason alone works no better now than at the start of our discussion. It holds not the slightest promise of success.

Faith Alone

But, you say, no one is willing to occupy this position. Faith, alone, can offer no solution to our problem; our sheer feelings of belief about the ultimate have the blindness of any feeling. And feeling, when not enlightened by our reason, is all too ready to descend into ignoble forms of superstition. Faith, unrelated to human reason, might return us to the level of the primitive; and the energies of faith would then constitute a danger. Yet among the proponents of a vital faith are some who find an essential conflict between faith and reason. Faith is true, because it is absurd, a stumbling block to the wise. Faith is the contradiction of our reason, and faith represents the final truth. Ultimately, in this view, reason is a false guide for human life. And if reason is false, faith alone is adequate to the task of ordering our beliefs.

But if all human distinctions are to be denied, then this claim of the primacy of faith must also be denied. And, far from being an adequate method of leading us toward the truth, the view cannot even be expressed, since its expression would require the distinctions of our reason.

The Supremacy of Faith to Reason

If neither faith nor reason, taken separately, can provide a structure of sufficient power for the ordering of our lives, we must turn to some combination of the two. And the most widely held doctrine of their union is one which grants a measure of adequacy to reason within its proper sphere, while pointing out its limitations. Further, in this view, when each is properly controlled the results of faith and reason are held to be consistent; and yet there are truths beyond the reach of reason which can be established only by the working of our faith. Faith, then, is the instrument for determining our ultimate beliefs, and quite superior to human reason. Reason should be followed, so far as it is able to guide our lives with profit. And the point where reason gives way to the operation of faith varies with each individual, and the strength of his intellect.

Imagine, then, a pyramid, letting reason form its base. Rising toward the apex, faith comes more and more into play — the area of the pyramid under the control of faith varying with each individual — until finally for all of us somewhere near the apex will be found those truths which must be accepted in an attitude of pure and unmixed faith.

Superior to the alternative of faith alone, the view is yet not adequate. At the apex of the pyramid, reason has given way to authority once again — and beyond the reach of any self-corrective method. If faith is superior to reason, and contains the final truth, then those who are capable of faith possess truths which cannot be checked by reason. If we make anything of this supposed fact, especially if we find the locus of this faith within an institution, then — having assumed so much — we should not be surprised if some consequences begin to follow. Even if one possessed of faith believes in the consistency of faith and reason, when the inevitable conflict begins to appear between the two, those endowed with faith will be inclined to find the error, leading to this conflict, within the sphere of reason. And anyone who believes himself to hold the final truth, while others struggle along in error, will find the temptation very great to help the erring ones; in this case leading them, gently or otherwise, to recant, retract, or alter their positions in order to restore the fine consistency between the works of reason and the articles of faith. When men of faith set themselves the task of binding other men, this is already an indication that the object of their faith is false. If the superiority of faith is allowed in theory, this is enough to justify the practice. And in practice this means blocking the road of inquiry, placing a control upon our reason from without the sphere of reason, a control which has not shown itself to be productive, as reason is generally productive. It is a control, in fact, which reason cannot allow. And this would seem to mean that the suggested relation between faith and reason is not reasonable after all. Too much had been assumed.

If faith is superior to human reason, and identified with an institution, the logical consequence is a society controlled by men of faith, a theocratic state. With our assumptions those who have the final truth will be allowed to shape the society in which they live, according to their special insight. All parties engaged in the religious dispute of the Reformation claimed the supremacy of faith to reason; and they claimed the authority of faith over the national state. This struggle illumines very brightly the only possible answer to the question: Has faith a method, as has reason, of establishing its claims to truth? The answer is, "It has not!" This answer comes out of those fearful times when the conflict of one faith with another revealed itself to be a power struggle within our Western societies. The point is: We have been through all of that, and we will not return to it. And while our philosophies are theories, still to hold in theory a view which we have had to reject in practice, and in our social philosophies, is to blink at the relevant data which should be of use in the shaping of our theories. The tradition which placed faith above reason was perhaps reflecting into theory the social structure of its day. The institutions representing the claims of faith were, indeed, more powerful than the enterprise of reason. But this is not the case today, even though the formula continues to be widely held. The structures of science in their vigor and transforming power exceed, and in this sense stand above, the structures of religious faith — and science stands for the unfettered reason. We cannot afford to solve our problem through the third alternative.

The Supremacy of Reason to Faith

One alternative remains. In assessing the claims of the believer and the unbeliever, we had found ourselves adhering in turn, depending upon the situation, to both points of view. And in considering the depth of human nature, we found man to be the creature capable of building sciences, and by their means transforming the face of nature; beneath this we discerned the child of faith; and underneath both of these we found man, the primitive, the untutored animal. But the animal is not man. Man is the reasoner, and the creature of mystic faith.

I propose, then, that we adopt a natural relationship of faith and reason, following the levels of cultural ordering, as they appeared within the world. The natural manner of their relation requires us to exchange the terms in the traditional pyramid of faith and reason, allowing reason the superior place, and designating faith as its support. The rest of the traditional description can be retained. With its terms reversed our pyramidal ordering of faith and reason provides an instrument of self-correction relating to the whole of life. Reason must be granted superiority, because reason is self-corrective; and yet it rests upon the materials of faith, because reason is not self-sufficient. Faith and reason require each other. Without the material of belief, reason would have no starting point. And without reason, belief would have no agent of enlightenment. Indeed, reason comes after belief, works with belief, enlightens, crystallizes, reworks, and transforms belief. If, then, reason requires the materials of faith, part of this material is constituted by the boundless and exuberant affirmations of religious faith.

But we have been using the single term, "faith," with two different meanings. Pascal understood by "faith," feeling God "by the heart, not by the reason." And each alternative, stressing faith, has used the term in a manner close to Pascal's meaning; faith was restricted to the material of our ultimate beliefs. Yet were one to discuss the question with any proponent of such a "faith," examples would be quickly offered of our faith in the sunrise tomorrow, of the faith we have in friends, and other instances of trust. The attitude in question applies now more narrowly, and then with a more inclusive meaning. Having reversed our terms within the pyramid, "faith" must be granted the wider and more inclusive meaning.

We have mentioned, more often than I care to count, the many elements present in the shaping of our lives before we were even capable of thinking about their grounds, reasons, or support. And why did we find ourselves holding to this amazing number and variety of opinions? We had no reason; or at least the reasons were historical, biographical, accidental, and contingent. And why do we hold to so many of these opinions at the present time? We believe, because we have believed, because we have not doubted. And what we do not doubt, even when no adequate grounds for belief have been presented, we hold in the most elemental sense on faith.

In this elemental sense we have faith in the most varied things. We have some beliefs which cannot be doubted practically; we believe in a world of objects and of people, of space and time; we cannot doubt this world even if its actual "proof" has never been constructed; and we require no proof, this is our feeling. At most, we find the objections to such a world rather forced and unreal. The example reveals how faith extends beyond what can be firmly established by our reason. And, indeed, this elemental faith in what is conveyed persistently by our senses furnishes the data for the functioning of our human reason. Now faith, so understood — as beliefs firmly held without adequate formal grounds — extends indefinitely, and widely, through the opinions firmly settled in human minds. Belief in God has been almost as pervasive in the Western world, and seemingly as undeniable, as belief in the world revealed by our senses. And here, too, we have discovered something less than adequate formal grounds for this belief; the certainty of our grounds is weaker far than the feeling of certainty in the mind of the believer. And, with this meaning, faith extends to everything we have found in the trusting child, taking parent and teacher as his authority. It includes, also, the trust of the scientist in the basic ordering of nature. Faith, so understood, has another side. What is accepted as a result of propaganda is an article of faith; and, in the same sense, even the vicious tenets of Aryan or white supremacy are articles of faith.

We must class all of these together because, however different in their value, they are exactly alike in status. It is simply not possible to separate out some items from the group — for example, the articles of religious faith — and treat them in a manner different from the rest. Surely, some articles of faith have been found to be erroneous. And all religious persons are willing to point to the tribal origins of their religion, approving of the way in which superior insight has transformed the crude tenets of this original belief. And only a very complacent man would care to claim the absence of any possible error in the faith presented to him by the purified religion of his birth, or choice.

But, then, faith is no different from opinion? Admittedly, the description of the two comes out to be the same. An opinion is a belief held with or without grounds; and faith is belief held without adequate formal grounds. I must admit they are the same, observing only that the belief to which we attach the phrase "religious faith" is one held with a tenacity far beyond the ordinary.

The realm of faith includes whatever has not been established by our reason. And obviously this realm extends in breadth beyond the narrow scope of reason. Reason has not begun to establish or refute anything like a majority of the judgments proposed for human belief. And it could not begin to do so. This realm extends almost as widely as the cultural fund itself. The materials of our faith are part of the contents of this fund. The myth, poetry, and legend of the cultural fund have made possible both our philosophy and our science. And the Western idea of God is one of its early culminating points, an inevitable development out of the growth of meaning — at least an esthetic and ethical object of great power, and perhaps much more; at least the ground of meaning, and perhaps the ground of being.

The Impasse

We are ready to confront, once more, the impasse of our last discussion; but from a different perspective. The view of the believer had led us to some one of the varieties of idealism; the view of the unbeliever led us to one of the varieties of materialism. Each of these possessed a type of adequacy in interpreting the details of the world; and yet they were opposed. To speak only of the believer's view, it led by an inner necessity to some variety of idealism; but in its original form this view was not philosophy in any sense. It had the form of faith. And the thinking philosopher inevitably attenuates the rich matrix of this faith, abstracting only what can be of use within a system. Indeed, when the "Father," "King," and "Lord" became the perfect being, the abstractive power of reason was at work. Thinning of the matrix cannot be avoided; it is the way of the world, and the way of the human mind. What of the opposition, leading to our impasse? Materialism and idealism stand in opposition because they are philosophies. It is difficult to see how this opposition could ever be resolved. But idealism is not in conflict with our traditional faith. It is this faith, attenuated into philosophy. Is materialism, then, in conflict with the forms of faith? One thinks of answering immediately, "Of course!" Certainly it is in conflict with idealism. But let us reflect more carefully. Beginning with our present understanding of the relation between faith and reason, it would be quite possible for a man to find the efforts of his reason moving always contrary to the tradition of his faith, and yet requiring beyond the conclusions of his reason, additional beliefs for the basis of his personal life. If Hume required beliefs beyond his reason, who is to draw the line and say the acceptable contents of faith extend only to the existence of one's rooms, or the existence of the world? But if these requisite beliefs beyond the scope of reason include some elements of religious faith, will not this fact introduce tension into the life of our materialist? It will. And is not tension reduction the end of life? It is not. But this possibility raises a question concerning the truth of these beliefs.

Religious Truth

If our tolerant attitude is accepted, what is to become of truth? Will we not find ourselves believing in contradictions? This danger is part of the tension which has been mentioned. But, now, consider: Philosophy has several tests for truth; oddly, they can be satisfied by more than one system of philosophy. An adequate philosophy must be capable of interpreting every detail of the universe. Its basic notions must be clear, or moderately so. The system must not have inner contradictions; its ideas must cohere, supporting each other; its ideas must "correspond" with the world of our experience. And science has some further tests for truth. True ideas must lead to some prediction about the universe; from true ideas we should be able to infer, through however many steps are needed, some fact about the world open to our observation.

But if I were to say, "Tell me in terms of truth about the Christian faith. Is it true or false?" how would you reply? You would say, and should say: "I am sorry, but the question cannot be answered in this form. The Christian religion contains some true ideas, and perhaps some false ideas. But religion is not the kind of enterprise for which the tests of truth have been designed." Of course, it is not. The tests for truth appeared much later than the forms of faith, developing within philosophy and science. How curious to apply these tests to myth, story, and poem! How curious, and how unfair! The question is the same as asking: "Is Shakespeare's *Hamlet* true or false?" You answer, "It is neither of these; and yet it is highly significant." And so one might answer with respect to the details of religious faith; they are neither true nor false, and yet highly meaningful. Indeed, religion has never had much interest in tests for truth; it has been much more interested in what is significant for man; and if its rich fund of pictures, figures, and stories provides the support needed in human life, the religious concern is satisfied without a test of truth.

How are we to understand these mental objects which are neither true nor false, and yet replete with meanings? They are "undetermined" with respect to truth. Any proposition is undetermined until we find some way of handling it, a system for its inclusion, some ground for its support. And if the rich funded meanings within the realm of faith are undetermined, you have every right to hold them, no matter what may be the nature of the beliefs you have managed to pull together into a system. No logic in the world can give a reason why you should not adhere to a belief which is undetermined. If you believe in the idea of God, and no one can show this idea to be false, there exists no reason why the idea should be given up. You have a philosophic right to hold the belief. You can say you believe it to be true. From our present standpoint you cannot say, and should not say, you *know* it to be the truth.

What are we to say of the Christian faith? The question "Is it true?" is not a proper question. "True" and "false" apply to philosophies in one sense and, more clearly, to sciences in another. Can truths be gained from it? To my knowledge no scientific truths have been gleaned from the details of this faith, although it has helped to set the framework for the establishment of our sciences. Philosophic truths have been gained from faith, but only by attenuation of its subject matter. Can judgments be drawn from the material of faith, the truth or falsity of which remain unknown? Indeed, so many of them! And yet, as we have seen, one does not violate his nature in possessing an overbelief. And his capacities for development are affected by under-belief.

In any case it is more reasonable to believe in God than to remain agnostic. It is more reasonable to have an over-belief than to remain in a suspense of judgment. Important truths may be implicit in the undetermined judgment; but no truth is possible for the undetermined person who cannot bring himself to make a judgment. But may not the attitude of unbelief happen to be the truth? Thus far we have held belief and unbelief to be equally reasonable. And it would not be impossible, or improper, for a materialist to believe in the esthetic and ethical object of the Christian faith, even while his reason constructs a system which cannot possibly contain this object. And now the opposition between belief and unbelief becomes more like the thrust and strain within a freely standing structure, adding to its stability, than to a collision of similar objects within an ordered system. The opposition between belief and unbelief becomes identical with the tension which has empowered our Western culture in its advance. It is not properly a tension between two different persons. It is not an interpersonal, but an individual, inner, and personal tension, a problem for each man within himself. Of course, if the attitude of unbelief happens to be the truth, we could at once resolve this inner tension. And it may be true. And yet the attitude of unbelief led us to a picture of the world in which man's life became completely meaningless. Truth, we must remember, is also a value, an ideal to be achieved, requiring purposeful and dedicated human action. In the universe of the unbeliever every truth is to be swept away in one or another of the many varieties of destruction, making up our personal and social mortality. For this reason William James, among others, excludes the attitude of unbelief from the possible views which might conceivably be true. The firmness of his exclusion is perhaps extreme. The truth may be simply the alien, massive, other, and meaningless universe — as the existentialists have said. But from the standpoint of a developing truth the attitude of belief can be held to be more promising, more fruitful, and more likely to contain within it the implicit judgments which can bring to their completion the partial truths about the universe, making up an important aspect of our cultural achievement.

What is the conclusion? Scientific hypotheses can stand in opposition to each other; philosophic systems do stand in opposition, although they possess much common content. But neither hypotheses nor systems can stand in essential opposition to the realm of faith. The relation here is that of the crystal to the solution from which it is derived, of the determinate to the undetermined, and, to some extent, determinable.

The Function of Reason

And yet these words are not intended to suggest an absence of control over the forms of faith. It has not been my goal to remove the tension from your personal life. It is the function of reason to assess the grounds of belief, whenever this is possible. It is not the end of reason to make belief impossible. Its job is to explain, and this does not always mean explaining away. It is one task of reason to attempt to make faith reasonable. It is another task of reason to determine if faith may not be nonsensical. Reason sets itself the task, quite properly, of shearing away every trace of superstition; in doing this, more often than one might expect or wish, some of the flesh is taken, too.

But as reason works with its material, patterns of meaning rise out of the jumble of significant expression in the many forms of faith. The jumble was never enough for man; from the start he felt the need of pattern. This is the need for philosophy, and reason generally, in our lives. Because this discovery of pattern has led man to his place, it must be our rule to adhere to pattern, allowing systems of thought to be our guide. But if the patterns of meaning no longer stand in a lateral opposition to the elements of faith, we can conceive of faith, extending beneath our pattern, ready to furnish support when human reason fails. And on occasion, when properly controlled, one has the philosophic right to drop beneath reason to the more primal level of his faith. Why has one this right? The ground for the claim has already been suggested: Thought attentuates the rich matrix of belief. It adds logical power, and loses in affective power. And the meaning of life, as we have seen, cannot be gained from a detached system of ideas, containing nothing more than inner consistency, or logical strength.

We have discovered the attitude of belief to be more promising than the attitude of unbelief. Belief holds this promise only if its central doctrines are something other than outright contradictions. We have noticed the paradoxical nature of the perfect being in the description of Saint Augustine. Can the idea of a perfect being, already bearing the marks of intellectual shaping, be drawn still more fully into philosophy? This can be done, but only by means of further thinning. To demonstrate the point, let me place the religious themes within a system of philosophy. The system most appropriate for the purpose might well be the construction of A. N. Whitehead. What will happen to the claims of faith in a philosophy much like that of Whitehead?

God and Immortality Within a System of Philosophy

We shall think of a universe in constant change, using a language of events. What we ordinarily call "things" and "objects" will be understood as very complicated groupings of events. Time will be important in our philosophy, and will be understood as an irreversible sequence of events. We shall approach the question of God and immortality through two widespread intuitions about the world.

Here is the first intuition: Anything done is done forever, as the weaving of a cloth leaves its own record of how the weaving went. The event which has ceased to be is not destroyed but remains a fixed part of the total past. A moment hence I walked across the room in a perfectly definite way; this will always be true, even though no one was present to observe the fact. You have just taken a sudden, deep inspiration of air; this will be forever true, even if you were unaware of having done so. The point is clear enough; it involves the notion of time as a becoming definite of what was merely possible. Time weaves from among the possibilities of existence a finished pattern which is forever set. The world moves from the merely possible, which may or may not be, into actual happenings and events. As these events become part of the total past, they are forever fixed.

The second intuition is related to the one already given. We have discovered how, in coming to decisions, we are confronted by numerous possibilities relevant to the actual state of things. From among the possibilities we decide; and part of what was possible becomes actual. Now these possibilities, what are they? They are nothing actual; but they are not simply nonentity. They have some being; they are alternate forms of definiteness, awaiting your decision. The possible, then, is as much a part of reality as is the actual; and relevant possibilities confront not only a person, but every event or happening in the universe.

The future relates to the present as the set of relevant possibilities which may become actual; the past is the reality of events which are no longer in the present. We relate to the future by anticipation, and to the past by memory. But the actual world is signaled to us by the quality of resistance. By the time a signal has been received, the actual moment in question has passed away. We know the actual world through the resistance of one thing to another. I observe the room because my vision is obstructed by the wall, the carpet, and all of its contents. The sweep of my gaze meets another person as a fact of resistance; I recognize you as actual by means of your obtrusive nature. Any actual thing will share the features of the actual; it will stand out against other things. If God were a feature of the actual world, he would be encountered as a fact. But we would not expect the primal, infinite, and complete being of the arguments to be in relations of resistance to other beings. And existence is always leaving its present state of finitude by means of temporal passage — in order to reach another state of finitude. It would be reasonable to expect the locus of God to include the total process, rather than standing as an obstrusive fact in the actual world.

The past has perished, and yet it must still have some reality; the possible is as yet nothing, yet it cannot be sheer nonentity. The role of God, in this view, is to sustain these more extended aspects of the world, providing the conditions for becoming, adding the eternity and completeness which finite entities lack. God is the primal fact, explaining why the universe is rich in possibilites. God is also the consequent fact, holding in his being, and so in being, the past — providing, then, its immortality. God is also the generic character of existence, providing whatever necessity there may be in temporal passage. Every type of order established in the world is derived from God's primal ordering of possibilities, and qualified by the power, or efficacy, of the past. The two functions interweave, and an aspect of logical necessity results; this thing having happened, only this other kind of happening is now relevant. In this sense our logic of events in history might be related to the idea of God.

Clearly, much religious value is retained in this philosophy. "God" has long meant to man that the universe is a universe of promise, life is not self-defeating, and one's being is somehow preserved. In this view the universe holds promise because, no matter what has been, something better always stands before us as possible. There is always a possibility relevant to one's actual self, which can lead one beyond himself. If there is in the universe an ordering of possibilities, such that any actual achievement leads on to further possibilities, this is a doctrine saturated with hope. In the language of theologians this aspect of the world might be regarded as God's continual grace in the universe. A second aspect of religious value in this view concerns the force, or efficacy, of the past. What has happened helps to determine what will happen. "What a man sows he shall also reap." And this relation of the past to the present might be viewed as the role of God in judgment. Grace and judgment operate together and continuously.

What of the other half of our question? We have found the

world moving from the merely possible, the may-be's and may-not-be's, into individual events, objects, human lives, societies, and cultures. People gain this excellence or that, their choices leading them to become this sort of person or another; and as these things, events, people, societies, and cultures become part of the total past, the profile of each is, so far as past, forever fixed. In this sense we have no opportunity to avoid immortality. The fabric of your life will forever be part of the total past, even if your friends have forgotten. The material of your life will be molded into new forms; but every excellence and failure, every quality and event, will remain part of the total past. The past is composed not of quantities, but of qualities achieved in the actual world. Every quality descriptive of your life will be forever true of you.

But you may claim, "I am not a mere description, however infinitely detailed, but a person." What you say is true, and yet we must consider how much this view allows of what makes up your person. How is anything made a *this* instead of a *that?* How does a block of stone become a Venus instead of a Hercules? By gaining a certain quality of form. And how does one becomes a valuable person, instead of remaining a mere reflection of the world, focussed at a point? Through seeking what we have called intrinsic values — the final qualities, if you will, of life. And what is there to "us" anyway, but the qualities we have achieved, for which we stand, and in terms of which we act? Other than the mass of our bodies, their sheer and weighty mass, what is there to us besides this total set of qualities? There is nothing else. Then all of the "you" or the "I" which has importance, which distinguishes us from each other, making us distinctively ourselves, is forever a part of reality. On this view no one should seek sheer quantities of things, rather than attending to the complex qualities which are possible for human life. It is one excellence of the view that the values which are first, as we say, in life, are also first in reality.

And yet we have thinned down the traditional view of immortality. In the traditional view there have been two elements. One of these is the belief that in eternity man will "lay his burdens down." This element centers on the eternal fixity of things; it finds expression in this philosophy. The other element provides for the retention of an active self-identity. And this part of the traditional view cannot be expressed within our system of philosophy (nor in any system of *philosophy,* to my knowledge).

What, when the slate is at last broken? Is it all over? From our present standpoint, so far as our remaining centers of continuing activity, it is all over for us in eternity. One might argue for the sensible and appealing nature of this answer, even if part of the meaning of immortality has been sacrificed. Life, not as a straight line to infinity, but as an arc which rises from its initial conditions, finds its direction and completes itself, becoming then a settled part of the conditions for other lives, is more appealing — at least on esthetic grounds. A curved line is more attractive than one continuously extending. At last one lays his burdens down; one need not carry the burden of his life forever. In our discussion of value we had found Spinoza counseling us to live under the aspect of eternity. He spoke of an ascent, level by level, until one reached the point where eternity began to merge with time. We found this to be a difficult saying. But we, too, have had occasion to urge upon ourselves an ascent from instrumental values and toward final values. And in our system it is only the qualities of existence which remain a part of reality forever. The saying of Spinoza becomes easier, if we try to understand him from our present point of view. One is working with the eternal aspect of existence, when he is concerned with the qualities of life rather than with its quantities. It is possible for us to agree with Spinoza. One can bring eternity into time, and enjoy it now, merely by concerning himself with the qualities of existence. One cannot have an eternity in addition to time, at least in the stronger sense of immortality. And the free man will be concerned with life, and not with death. Let every man, then, live under the aspect of eternity by the direction of his attention to eternal things. And through the length of the arc of his life he will feel the deeper aspect of time, which is its silent flow into eternity.

We have "discovered" within the divine being a dual nature, antecedent and consequent, relating to possibility and the immortality of the past. Has our suggestion of a dual nature power to soften, or remove, the apparent contradictions within the concept of a perfect being? The problem of a fixed future, depriving man of freedom, can be resolved through paying close attention to the meaning of omniscience. "Omniscience" means the possession of all knowledge. In the universe developed by our system the future is partly open; and God's omniscience no longer removes the possibility of human freedom. In knowing the past, the present, and

whatever is settled about the future, plus the possibilities of existence, God knows all there is to know. And we have seen how in
our present system the operation of divine justice and grace no
longer requires a paradox. In this view God is to be understood
as infinite in one aspect and finite in another, eternal in one and
temporal in another, cause in one sense and ultimate effect in
another. One who has worked most intensely and most convincingly from this point of view, achieving results which require the
consideration of anyone interested in our present topic, is Charles
Hartshorne.[21]

Much of the traditional meaning of the ideas of God and immortality can be retained within this system. But you would be quite
correct in charging me with having attenuated the richer and more
contradictory affirmations of tradition. We have also gained greater
clarity, and a considerably heightened sense of consistency. The
change within the material of tradition is, perhaps, not so very
alarming after all. This is one of the more or less adequate philosophies of our time. Probably, it is not completely adequate. It is a
comfortable philosophy, retaining too much of our tradition to suit
the taste of many factually minded philosophers. The danger
in a comfortable philosophy is that we may accept it as though it
were the final truth — which it is not. The debate within philosophy
must continue, even if no one is certain of the rules which should
govern this debate.

Our Fourth Alternative a Norm

Reason works itself into a group of philosophic systems because
our human inclinations, and not our reason, control the selection
of the building blocks — the meanings and judgments of "importance" weighting one aspect of the world more heavily than another — from which these systems are contrived. Given an initial
set of meanings, reason is able to complete the structure; but the
very quality of reason, accounting for its power — its requirement
of consistency — provides a tamper-proof guarantee that the character of the final structure will be determined in this initial, and "unreasonable" selection. These building blocks are quarried from the
realm of faith, understanding "faith" in our most elemental sense.

---

[21] See the "Introduction" and "Epilogue" to Charles Hartshorne and William L. Reese, *Philosophers Speak of God* (Chicago: University of Chicago
Press, 1953).

Returning to the less inclusive sense of "faith," the religious pattern is not subject to a final demonstration; nor are our systems of thought ever quite complete — always, a few more changes must be made within the system. If one can never make the religious pattern clear and demonstrable, still one can never arrange the philosophic system in its proper, final form. In a mood of great searching one can almost arrange the religious pattern; and in a mood of great inner confidence one can almost cast his philosophic system into a form which seems completely adequate. In both instances it is a case of "almost — but not quite." The truth is that the two require each other, and both have value. No one needs to be ashamed of reason, and no one needs to be ashamed of faith. But it is shameful for a man of faith to refuse the power of reason, which might be able to enlighten the rich product of his faith. And the man is deserving of shame whose life is so fully endowed with reason that his reason tells him nothing, gives him no tasks, and lays down no cultural directives.

Most of us in this day cannot afford to sacrifice one or the other. Philosophy and science, as we have seen, derive from the cultural fund. In hidden and subtle ways their vitality depends upon the forms of faith. For our common good we must encourage the continued growth of these forms within our culture. But the forms of faith consist of undetermined judgments which, progressively through time — one hopes — we may be able further to determine. Theologians often say it is their function simply to testify to the tenets of their faith. In this I think they are correct. We must insist upon their testimony; it provides the possible ultimate insights beyond the reach of reason. If faith presents the undetermined judgment which is a starting point for reason, the instrument of faith must be persuasion rather than coercion. And our discussion suggests a final social principle:

> XVIII. Religion must be granted an area of freedom, presenting its testimony to the members of society by means of persuasion, the instrument of freedom.

Religions cannot be manufactured, and high religions are relatively rare. If we are to have religious faith at all, the faith which is our common possession must be our faith; not completely subject to reason, it yet forms part of the base of human life. It is almost an idle question from this perspective to ask if the faith is worthy. It had better be. But if, or where, it is not we shall transform it further, not by reason alone but also through a sensitive human intuition, into its proper form of greater worth.

The natural relation which exists between the forms of faith and reason has been presented almost as though we were engaging in a task of sheer description. But the further we explored our problem, the more this sheer description gained the appearance of a norm: Life must be grounded in faith, and yet controlled by reason. This balance between faith and reason may be the final, and most fortunate, adjustment of which man is capable.

The most productive periods of human life are those in which man's reason has begun to enlighten, to give eyes to, his faith; while at the same time reason has not yet made faith impossible. In such periods man has been able to free himself from dogma, while his religious faith continues to energize within his life. At this moment he is free and yet secure. The world is open to him. The force of his religious heritage has been internalized. It has not yet worn thin. His vital force has been enlightened by reason. His reason has not yet become involuted. It has not turned in upon itself to lead to skepticism, and a denial of the value of life. Wherever reason has made faith impossible, we are in the presence of a skeptic, or in an age of skepticism. But the productive period is a time of renaissance, personal or cultural — and we badly need them both. A faith, made internal and subject to reason, is capable of translation into immense human tasks. This is the very power needed by philosophy and in our personal lives, especially important for this age and the tasks which lie before us. What, then, is our conclusion? For reason to be significant life must keep its mystic base — the base of a divine support, of romantic love, of childlike fidelity, of the genial trust which leads to social unity. What I urge is a mystic base for the sake of one's personal unity, and the personal relations of human life. What I urge is a fine rationalism of the superstructure — of the sciences, philosophy, and the general aspects of every portion of our lives. We must remember, and it cannot and should not be otherwise, that our little raft of reason floats upon a sea of myth.

Memorandum — for the Devout Believer

It is not true, of course, not true as such, your demonstrably adequate and helpful faith. It is not really true for a young man in his vigor, and perhaps should not be true for him, not for a while. Perhaps it is more true always for a young woman. It is not true for science. It is not true of the universe in its factual audacity. It is not true when used to support a lie, or slavery, or a comfortable middle-class life, careless of human values. But when stripped of this, it may be something better than true. It may be proper for the life of man — a parable for every problem, an authentic support for every genuine impulse, a hope for every moment of despair. How admirable and important, even if untrue! It is not true to fact but true to life. It is viciously untrue whenever used to hamper man; it is better than the truth when it provides support for man's development.

If its glorious scheme, always altering by the way, cannot be made reasonable; why then neither can reason be made glorious. One for whom reason can be the sole support of life cannot have the whole of your vision. Such a man had better take the less glorious, but no less commendable, path of philosophy. One for whom reason is not enough should first prove to himself that he is not going beyond philosophy merely to humor a petty whim, or to further a bankrupt liaison between economics and religion, or to escape what everyone should face, life and oneself — life in its unlovely aspects, the problems of existence in a difficult century; oneself by laying down burdens which should have been fairly assumed. But if you must go beyond philosophy, not for these reasons, but for the simple reason that philosophy does not ring true enough; whatever its net may have caught, it has not caught enough to let you be your best person, then go beyond philosophy and godspeed! What are any human schemes, but helps along the way?

Or if it is a question of tragedy — not the self-pitying softening before events, this comedy which we often mistake for tragedy, not the spurious tragedies which we fabricate to relieve our feelings of responsibility — when the world turns hurricane and tears great gaps in life, when everything is swept away but one's mettle (this happens), then is the voice of philosophy stilled. In this moment it is your task to stand something like twice your former height in utter defiance of the evil thing. You must exemplify, for yourself and others, the nobility of the human spirit. This nobility of the spirit is not precisely the theme of Western philosophy; it is not the theme of all Western religion. But it is closer to the theme of religion — what its theme might be when best — than ever to a theme of philosophy. And, again, you must go beyond philosophy, listening to whatever voice still sounds.

Yet in going beyond philosophy you can be no longer religiously naïve. You cannot shut and lock the door of your mind, or pretend that belief discharges every human responsibility. You must require your belief to lead you, as it can, to the end of human greatness. Responding to its subtleties, you must be ennobled by its transfigurations, and be transfigured within yourself. But every step you take — if it is a forward step — will lead you back to a more profound reason; and to the adventure, which is at last neither biblical nor canonical, but the development of your being.

The course is ended, but the adventure has scarcely begun.

Suggestions For Further Reading

Some works in philosophy, an obvious point, are more readable than others. Philosophical writers, as a rule, tend to pack their ideas rather tightly, occasioning an initial difficulty for the reader. But the prose of some philosophers is highly readable. In the following lists of possible source material, I have seen fit to star the books which seem to me characterized by an easy style. Possession of this quality makes them neither more nor less valuable than others on the list.

Chapter One. Freedom. If, beyond our four meanings, a wider range of expressions concerning the nature of freedom is desirable, the reader may turn to Ruth Nanda Anshen's *Freedom: Its Meaning,** where many scholars from various fields address themselves to this problem.

The case for our first meaning can be made out with reference to Voltaire, *The Ignorant Philosopher,** Chap. XIII; Thomas Hobbes, *The Leviathan,* and David Hume, *An Inquiry Concerning Human Understanding,* Chap. VIII, as well as *A Treatise of Human Nature,* Book II, Part III. Upon reflection one can discover the causal necessity, so readily accepted by these and other men, to have its source in the "scientific" postulate of complete predictability. In our century the postulate is not so easily made. The reader may convince himself of this by referring to any of the available material on Heisenberg's Principle of Indeterminacy. If the second meaning for freedom is defensible, probably the causal network cannot be all-encompassing; but the fact of some indeterminacy would not by itself lead to a strong meaning for freedom. A. H. Compton's *The Freedom of Man,* P. W. Bridgeman's *Logic of Modern Physics,* and *Reflections of a Physicist,* Chap. VII; and A. S. Eddington, *The Nature of the Physical World,* Chap. XIV, and *New Pathways of Science,* Chap. IV, will provide information on this involved issue. It is also possible to come to a thoroughgoing necessity from the concept of an all-powerful God. Jonathan Edwards, *Freedom of the Will,* is a relevant instance.

We have presented Locke's discussion of the problem in *An Essay Concerning Human Understanding,* Vol. I, Book II, Chap. XXI, as a reflection of our second meaning. In reading Locke's essay you will notice that only near the end of a long discussion is he able to move outside the boundaries of the first meaning, reaching the second. The whole of William James' "Dilemma of Determinism" (*The Will to Believe and other Essays*)* should be read in support of this meaning. Henri Bergson's *Creative Evolution* * and *Time and Free Will* * are appropriate to the present meaning. Unhappily, the important reference for the discussion of A. N. Whitehead is to his most difficult work, *Process and Reality;* and because the discussion is not concentrated I must refer you to the index; *Adventures of Ideas* contains a very limited expression of his position on our problem. Nicolas Berdyaev, in *The Destiny of Man* and in most of his publications, argues for our second meaning. Several of the essays in Alburey Castell, *Science as a Goad to Philosophy,** are relevant here; the monograph, a College of the Pacific publication, 1952, deserves wider notice.

The third meaning of freedom finds expression in the fourth part of Spinoza's *Ethics;* here the specific quality is reason. A more completely individualized version of this alternative is to be found in Hegel's *Phenomenology of Mind,* and Friedrich Nietzsche's *Ecce Homo.* Erich Fromm, *Escape From Freedom,* presents this meaning in a contemporary context. Our fourth meaning may be encountered in St. Augustine, *On the Free Will,* as well as in Thomas Aquinas, *Summa Theologica.* A general discussion of arguments both for and against freedom is present in H. H. Horne's *Free Will and Human Responsibility.**

Chapter Two. Value. In going beyond our discussion of value a first step might lead one to the value discussion of Aristotle in his *Nicomachean Ethics,* * especially the first book; the writings of Epicurus in whatever form they may be available, such as Whitney J. Oates' *The Stoic and Epicurean Philosophers.** The Stoic point of view is obviously present in the last mentioned volume; in this or in some other form Marcus Aurelius' *Meditations,** and Epictetus' *Enchiridion* * will not be without interest. The whole of Spinoza's *Essay On the Improvement of the Understanding* * is pertinent to the inquiry. Nietzsche's *Will to Power* and *Thus Spake Zarathustra* * will provide a contrasting point of view. J. L. Liebmann's *Peace of Mind* * may be of interest as furnishing another contrast concerning the chief value of human life. José Ortega y Gasset in *Revolt of the Masses* * presents what is essentially a discussion of values, distinguishing in a provocative manner the "mass" from the "elite." *The Lonely Crowd* by David Riesman analyzes three value types.

If a more formal discussion of the nature of value is desirable, the following books will provide a starting point: Ray Lepley, *Value: A Cooperative Inquiry,* R. B. Perry, *General Theory of Value,* C. I. Lewis, *An Analysis of Knowledge and Valuation.*

Chapter Three. Truth. One might turn to Plato's *Republic,** especially

Book VII, for a discussion of our first view of truth; his *Theaetetus* is also of importance here. William James' *The Meaning of Truth* * provides a discussion of the second meaning. Our third meaning for truth is to be found in the writings of Charles Sanders Peirce. His essays, "The Fixation of Belief" * and "How To Make Our Ideas Clear" * may be found in his collected works; and in various collections such as Justus Buchler's *The Philosophy of Peirce.*

Material dealing with this problem saturates the entire period of modern philosophizing; in a partial listing one would find John Locke's *Essay on Human Understanding,* René Descartes' *Discourse on Method,* * and *The Rules for the Direction of the Mind;* * George Berkeley's *Principles of Human Knowledge;* Hume's *Essay on Human Nature;* Immanuel Kant's *Critique of Pure Reason.* All of these are concerned with our problem, and the material increases in complexity as one continues. More recently one might list Hans Vaihinger's *The Philosophy Of 'As If'* * and Joachim's *The Nature of Truth,* as well as Henri Bergson's *Introduction to Metaphysics.* * Three books from the present period may complete our brief listing: A. J. Ayer's *Language, Truth, and Logic;* * Brand Blanshard's two-volume *Nature of Thought,* and A. D. Woozley's *Theory of Knowledge.* * The last two of these volumes provide a convenient source for entry into the correspondence and coherence theories of truth.

Chapter Four. Beauty. Irwin Edman's *Arts and the Man* * offers an interesting treatment of many aspects of our problem. Suzanne Langer's *Philosophy in a New Key,* and John Hospers' *Meaning and Truth in the Arts* * provide a somewhat different approach. Nor should T. M. Greene's *The Arts and the Art of Criticism* be neglected. The views of those making up our digest of theories are to be found in the following works. For Plato one would turn to his *Symposium,* * the *Phaedrus,* * and the Tenth Book of the *Republic.* * Aristotle's view is presented in the *Poetics;* * the view of Plotinus in his *Enneads.* The view of Thomas Aquinas on beauty is presented in the *Summa Theologica,* Part I, Ques. 5, Art. 4. An interesting interpretation of this view is present in James Joyce, *A Portrait of the Artist as a Young Man.* * For the view of Immanuel Kant one would turn to his *Critique of Judgement;* Hegel has written a three-volume *Philosophy of Fine Art.* Benedetto Croce's *Esthetics* may be particularly helpful; and Schopenhauer's view is discussed in the appropriate sections of his *The World As Will and Idea.* The approach of Tolstoy is presented in his interesting discussion, *What Is Art?* * For George Santayana's view the appropriate volume, from among his writings, is *The Sense of Beauty.* * And the Freudian, or psychoanalytic, interpretation may be gleaned either from passages here and there in Sigmund Freud's *Civilization and Its Discontents, New Introductory Lectures on Psychoanalysis,* and elsewhere in his *Collected Papers,* or from an interpreter, such as Herbert Read, *Art and Society.* * Clive Bell's

Art * completes our list. Selections from a number of these thinkers, and many others, are available in the anthology by Melvin Rader, *A Modern Book of Esthetics.* *

Chapter Five. Ethics. Our discussion of this problem has turned principally around Jeremy Bentham's *Introduction to the Principles of Morals and Legislation,* * John Stuart Mill's *Utilitarianism,* * and Immanuel Kant's *Foundations of the Metaphysics of Morals,* as well as his *Critique of Practical Reason.* Aristotle's view is to be found in his *Nicomachean Ethics,* * generally, but note especially Books Two and Three. The view which relies on conscience, detaining us for no longer than a paragraph, is argued at length by Bishop Butler in his *Fifteen Sermons upon Human Nature,* * especially sermons I, II, III, and XI. And the cultural relativity, against which we struggled, has been elaborated into an ethic by Edward Westermarck in *The Origin and Development of the Ethical Ideas,* and *Ethical Relativity.* Among partially neglected alternatives, at least these must be mentioned: T. H. Green, *Prolegomena to Ethics,* offers an ethic of self-realization in a context of idealism. Friedrich Nietzsche attempts to surmount the customary basis of morality in *Beyond Good and Evil.* Herbert Spencer develops an evolutionary ethic in *The Data of Ethics.* Henry Sidgwick in *The Methods of Ethics* blends the Utilitarian and Kantian approaches to our problem. Josiah Royce presents an ethic based on the property of loyalty in *The Philosophy of Loyalty.* * G. E. Moore in *Principia Ethica* insists upon a special kind of ethical intuition. W. D. Ross relies upon a concept of the fitting, or morally suitable, in both *The Right and the Good,* and *Foundations of Ethics.* A. J. Ayer's *Language, Truth, and Logic* * may again be mentioned, this time as defending an emotive theory of ethics. Discussions, treating all of these views within a single volume, are available in great abundance.

Chapter Six. Social Principles. Thomas Hobbes, *The Leviathan;* John Locke, *The Second Treatise on Civil Government;* Jean Jacques Rousseau, *The Social Contract,* * are the books to which we had referred in making out the planar principles. John Stuart Mill's essays *On Liberty* * and *Representative Government* * can help to complete the picture. Nor should the writings of Thomas Jefferson and Thomas Paine be overlooked. For a contrast one might refer to Sir Robert Filmer's *Patriarcha,* where the pyramidal principles of social ordering are defended. An extended discussion of our problem is to be found in the two volumes of Karl Popper's *The Open Society and Its Enemies.* For both the present discussion and the one to follow, the writings of Karl Marx, including his *Communist Manifesto,* * are appropriate. The most convenient body of material, filling out our paraphrase of Marx from Helmut Kuhn, is to be found in Bottomore and Rubel, *Karl Marx, Selected Writings in Sociology* *and Social Philosophy;* among the selections one should note especially the translated excerpts from the Economic and Philosophical Manuscripts of 1844. R. H. Tawney, *The Acquisitive Society,*° is likewise to the point. The analyses of Thorstein Veblen in his *The Theory of the Leisure Class,* and *The Theory of Business Enterprise,* are provocative and valuable in assessing the social and industrial pyramids of our times. In addition, much literature on this topic has appeared in recent years: C. Wright Mills, *White Collar;* James Burnham's *The Managerial Revolution;* William Whyte's *The Organization Man;* and many others. Finally, Walter Lippmann's *The Public Philosophy* ° must be mentioned as an important analysis of our problem by a distinguished public figure. And *The Authentic Revolution,* a slender monograph by Erwin D. Canham, may well have supplied more than just this phrase to our discussion.

Chapter Seven. Culture. R. G. Collingwood's *The Idea of History* is capable of encouraging thought about many aspects of our problem. W. H. Walsh, *An Introduction to Philosophy of History,*° and Maurice Mandelbaum, *The Problem of Historical Knowledge,* perform the same general function. One should not overlook Herbert Butterfield's discussion of our topic in *The Whig Interpretation of History.*° Much material is available concerning the Greek view of fate; but the most direct reference would be to the Greek tragedies themselves by Aeschylus, Sophocles, and Euripides; Aristotle's discussion of tragedy in the *Poetics* ° may be helpful. For the Christian view of history St. Augustine's *The City of God* may be consulted, along with the discussion by Herbert Butterfield in *Christianity and History.* J. B. Bury's *The Idea of Progress* ° presents an important analysis of the view so named. Auguste Comte, *Positive Philosophy,* spells out the law of the three stages. Following down our alternatives in order one would refer to: G. W. F. Hegel, *The Philosophy of History;* the writings of Karl Marx; Oswald Spengler's two volumes, entitled *The Decline of the West;* Arnold J. Toynbee, *A Study of History* in ten volumes. A one-volume abridgment bearing the same title has been arranged by D. C. Somervell. In addition we had made use of A. N. Whitehead's *Adventures of Ideas.*°

In a more literary vein, the philosophy of history elaborated by Tolstoy, especially in the latter portions of his novel, *War and Peace,*° must be mentioned. Isaiah Berlin's *The Hedgehog and the Fox* ° provides commentary upon this point of view. Thomas Carlyle, *Heroes and Hero Worship,* presents a striking contrast to Tolstoy. And Edmund Burke's *Reflections on the French Revolution* ° offers still another alternative. In the most general sense Ernst Cassirer's *An Essay On Man* ° with its interest in developing forms of culture is relevant to our theme.

Chapter Eight. First and Last Things. Many of the arguments for

God can be found in Thomas Aquinas, *Summa Theologica*, Part I, and in his *Summa Contra Gentiles*, the first fourteen chapters. The ontological argument is to be found in Anselm's *Proslogium* and *Monologium;* a separate form of the argument is present in Descartes' *Meditations.* Hume's *Dialogues on Natural Religion* provides a criticism of these arguments; for trenchant criticism Kant's *Critique of Pure Reason* should not be neglected; his criticism applies to arguments in addition to the ontological.

In general, for the theistic view the reader might refer to Plato's *Timaeus,* and the tenth book of the *Laws;* to St. Augustine's *Confessions,* the works of Thomas Aquinas which have been mentioned; Pascal's *Pensées,* generally; Descartes' *Meditations.* The material is so abundant that it will not be inappropriate to mention a source which attempts to deal with the Western tradition with respect to this problem: Charles Hartshorne and William L. Reese, *Philosophers Speak of God.*

The contrary tradition is more difficult; one finds what is virtually this position in the early expression by Lucretius, *On the Nature of Things.* One seems to be approaching the position in Hobbes' *Leviathan,* and Hume's *Treatise on Human Nature.* With Comte theistic formulations become meaningless; A. J. Ayer's *Language, Truth, and Logic* contains a modern expression of this positivistic view. Bertrand Russell's writings are always rewarding; one might begin with *Problems of Philosophy* and *Mysticism and Logic.*

As for the problem of contrasting philosophies the reader may be referred to Wilmon H. Sheldon's *Process and Polarity;* and a volume by N. P. Stallknecht and R. S. Brumbaugh, *The Compass of Philosophy.*

Index

The index has been arranged around twelve major topics — Freedom, Value, Opinion, Truth, Beauty, Ethics (Standards of conduct), Society, Philosophy of history, Culture, Belief, God, Immortality — following the major emphases of the text. In the use of this index the reader is advised to refer to any topic not only under its own name but under one of the appropriate major divisions listed above.